The Great Silent Army
of Abolitionism

The Great Silent Army of Abolitionism

Ordinary Women in the

Antislavery Movement

Julie Roy Jeffrey

The University of North Carolina Press

Chapel Hill and London

The paper in this book meets the guidelines for
permanence and durability of the Committee on
Production Guidelines for Book Longevity of the
Council on Library Resources.

Library of Congress
Cataloging-in-Publication Data

Jeffrey, Julie Roy.

The great silent army of abolitionism : ordinary
women in the antislavery movement / by Julie Roy
Jeffrey.

   p. cm.

Includes bibliographical references and index.

ISBN 0-8078-2436-4 (alk. paper). —
ISBN 0-8078-4741-0 (pbk. : alk. paper)

1. Antislavery movements—United States—
History—19th century.   2. Women abolitionists—
United States—History—19th century.   3.
Women—United States—Political activity—
History—19th century.   I. Title.

E449.J46   1998   98-13550
326′.8′0820973—dc21   CIP

02 01 00 99 98   5   4   3   2   1

For Chris, Michael, Meri, & Sophia

Contents

Illustrations

Acknowledgments

As I near the completion of this book, I often recall, with gratitude, the many people who generously helped me in all phases of this study. Eric Foner, who initially suggested the need for a book on ordinary abolitionist women and who thereafter supported my application for an N.E.H. fellowship, heads the list of those to whom I owe much. Nancy Hewitt and my Goucher colleague Jean Baker also wrote letters to the N.E.H. The result of their help, a year's sabbatical, allowed me to finish the book in a far more timely fashion than would otherwise have been possible. Generous with their time and criticism were Laurie Kaplan, Peter Bardaglio, Peter Frederick, and the late Elaine Hedges, all of whom read the manuscript in its entirety. Their suggestions, usually but not always followed, were enormously helpful as I did final revisions. Readers for the University of North Carolina Press also had many good suggestions that I took to heart. Colleagues who attended a Goucher faculty forum where I talked about antislavery fairs had wonderful responses to the manuscript, especially provocative because they saw my work from the standpoint of disciplines other than history. They raised some new questions for me to consider as I revised chapter four.

Many people were extraordinarily generous in sharing their own work with me. Special thanks goes to Deborah Van Broeckhoven and Ron Burtchart, who allowed me to see their research before it was published, and to John Brooke who sent copies of primary sources to me.

Still another group of friends provided comfort and good cheer to me during research trips. Mary Jaffe, Sally Ropes Hinkle, Kennie Lyman, Jim and Jan Roy, Dave and Lee Porter, Ed Tarlov, Michael Jeffrey, and my husband, Chris, who actually accompanied me on a research trip, all helped to make the exploration of the past also a pleasant experience in the present.

Helpful staffs at the many different archives, libraries, and historical societies I visited played an invaluable part in assisting me with the research. I would like to thank those who furthered my research at the following institutions: the American Antiquarian Society, the Boston Public Library Rare Books and Manuscript Division, the Massachusetts Historical Society, the Boston Athenæum, the Smith College Library, the Bowdoin College Library, the Schlesinger and Houghton Libraries at Harvard, the Butler Library at Columbia, the Bentley Library at the University of Michigan, the Library of Congress, the Bangor Public Library, Kent State Library, Western Reserve Historical Society, Lynn Historical Society, the

Essex-Peabody Institute, the New Hampshire Historical Society, the Maine Historical Society, Vermont Historical Society, the Historical Society of Pennsylvania, and the Connecticut State Historical Library. Librarians at the Julia Rogers Library at Goucher College and the Witherlee Library in Castine, Maine, were resourceful in locating and securing for me many important works through interlibrary loan. I especially want to thank them for their continued good humor when faced with countless and seemingly unending requests.

For significant financial support for this project I wish to acknowledge Goucher College, who named me Elizabeth Connolly Todd Professor of History. I also appreciate that, despite its many political travails, the National Endowment for the Humanities was able to award me a fellowship, It came at a critical moment in the progress of this book.

Family members tolerated my preoccupation with abolitionist women, intervened in computer crises, and sympathized with my ups and downs. My husband, Chris, my daughter, Sophia, my son, Michael, and my daughter-in-law, Meri, have earned my thanks and appreciation many times over.

The Great Silent Army
of Abolitionism

When the true history of the antislavery cause shall be written, women will occupy a large space in its pages; for the cause of the slave has been peculiarly woman's cause.
—Frederick Douglass

Introduction

Say not that it is man's business to

destroy slavery. I know man ought to do it

—he should have done it a long time ago,

but he has been recreant to his duty. Now

let woman speak, and it shall be done.

—Signal of Liberty, *August 11, 1845*[1]

In 1847, William Lloyd Garrison's abolitionist newspaper, the *Liberator*, declared that "the Anti-Slavery cause cannot stop to estimate where the greatest indebtedness lies, but whenever the account is made up, there can be no doubt that the efforts and sacrifices of the WOMEN, who helped it, will hold a most honorable and conspicuous position." Garrison's certainty that participants in the great crusade would ultimately recognize the contributions of women to abolitionism was not shared by his son. While acknowledging the importance of women to the movement to free the slave, William Lloyd Garrison Jr. seems to have accepted the fact of abolitionist women's historical invisibility when he referred to that "great army of silent workers, unknown to fame, and yet without whom the generals were powerless."[2]

Scholars studying the most important reform movement before the Civil War have also tended until quite recently to overlook the army of silent workers. Although historians have offered differing interpretations of the significance of abolitionism, the motives and achievements of its leaders, and the relationship of abolitionism to historical processes and events, they have traditionally focused on male leaders and male activities like third-party politics. While the birth of women's history helped to remedy the neglect of abolitionist women, attention tended to center on the small number of radical women who became feminists. The majority of women who shied away from feminism still remained in the shadows. In a sign that ordinary women abolitionists are finally becoming part of the historical debate over abolitionism, David Brion Davis recently challenged the effort to link the discipline of the marketplace to the development of abolitionism because it failed to account for women's involvement in abolitionist activities.[3]

Historians have begun to explore new aspects of the drive to eliminate slavery in the antebellum period. Several studies have delineated the social, economic, and religious characteristics of the abolitionist rank and file, while others have investigated the involvement of black women in abolitionism. Essays and books have been written on women's antislavery work in Boston, Rochester, Philadelphia, New York, and Rhode Island and the political culture within which abolitionist women operated.

This book builds upon and extends these treatments in order to provide a comprehensive picture of the involvement of ordinary women in abolitionism from the 1830s through the Civil War. In the spirit of the great abolitionist orator Theodore Weld, who counseled, "let the great cities *alone* . . . The springs to torch *lie in the country*," I have particularly tried to recover the efforts and experiences of abolitionist women living in small towns and rural communities, the very areas where abolitionism was strongest.[4]

Frederick Douglass, who had ample reason to acknowledge the important role black and white abolitionist women played in sustaining his own activities, tried to describe why women were important to abolitionism. He pointed to the "skill, industry, patience and perseverance" shown at "every trial hour," the willingness to "do the work which in large degree supplied the sinews of war," and the "deep moral convictions" that helped to give abolitionism its character. As Douglass knew, it was white middle-class and some black women who did much of the day-to-day work of reform. For more than three decades, they raised money, created and distributed propaganda, circulated and signed petitions, and lobbied legislators. During the 1840s and 1850s, they helped to keep the moral content of abolitionism alive when a diluted political form of antislavery emerged.[5]

Women formed the backbone of the movement, and without their involvement, as William Lloyd Garrison Jr. recognized, the leaders would have been powerless. Observers acknowledged at the time that individual women and women's groups often sustained abolitionism when men became dispirited. In 1850, a resident of Portland, Maine, admitted the "mortifying" fact that, in a period of darkness and discouragement, men had allowed the antislavery society to die, while the women of the Portland Anti-Slavery Sewing Society had "kept up their meetings" and work for the cause. The same year, when the English abolitionist lecturer George Thompson visited Salem, Massachusetts, he noted the advances abolitionism had made since his earlier visit in 1835: "A few faithful women," members of the Salem Female Anti-Slavery Society, had been "scattering anti-slavery seed," for fifteen difficult years and had changed "almost the entire sentiment" of the community. Women, Thompson knew, did not play a peripheral role in abolitionism but a central one.[6]

Abolitionism was never a popular cause before the Civil War. Although it is impossible to know how many people either supported or worked for immediate emancipation between 1830 and 1865, one historian has estimated that, out of a population of over 20 million in 1860, only around 20,000, or 1 percent of all American men and women, were abolitionists. Not only was the reform unpopular, but it also generated hostility and even violence, as George Thompson learned when mobs accosted him during his first American tour in the 1830s. Women abolitionists belonged to a minority movement that many Americans distrusted and even despised.[7]

Despite the "social ostracism, persecution, slander, [and] insult" that Rhode Island abolitionist Elizabeth Chace recalled abolitionist women encountering, evidence suggests that some, like Elizabeth herself and those women belonging to the Portland and Salem female societies, maintained their interest over long periods of time. Others, including members of Rochester's Female Anti-Slavery Society, took up and then abandoned abolitionism, and then sometimes became interested again years later. Although public hostility, lack of progress, and dissension among abolitionists caused attrition, more continuous interest in the cause may have existed than it is possible to document. At the end of the 1830s, disagreements within abolitionist ranks over the place of women in antislavery organizations, the relationship of abolitionism to other reforms, and the advisability of pursuing antislavery through politics rather than through moral suasion led to noisy and rancorous divisions that some scholars have suggested reduced women's involvement in antislavery. Most abolitionist women disagreed with Garrisonian radicalism, to be sure, but they did not necessarily reject the necessity of working for immediate emancipation. Dover, New Hampshire, women reorganized their antislavery society as a non-Garrisonian sewing society in 1840 and kept up associational records for decades, but more informal groupings like church sewing circles usually left no written evidence of their involvement at all. Letters written by abolitionist women of one faction often bemoaned the fact that they were almost alone in their support for the cause even as they acknowledged that other women in their communities were pursuing antislavery in secular or church societies. The emphasis on division, then, possibly obscures the extent of female commitment.[8]

The collapse of a unified national antislavery effort in 1840 actually created a variety of individual and collective opportunities to work for the slave and encouraged different styles of activism. As Nancy Hewitt has shown in her study of Rochester, middle-class women from different social, economic, and religious backgrounds did not approach reform in similar ways.[9]

While women differed in their expression of abolitionism over the decades, common convictions undergirded their activities. They agreed that slavery was a sin that, as women, they had a moral and religious duty to eradicate. Despite the scope of the change they were seeking, they were confident that, in the end, their cause would triumph, that moral activism would be efficacious. What might happen to former slaves once slavery had ended was not a question that troubled most of them. Yet they were not indifferent to racism that permeated American life in both the North and South. Although few women were interested in racial equality as understood in the late twentieth century, they did believe that abolitionists should work to improve the situation of free blacks in the North. The 1835 constitution for the first female antislavery organization in Dover, New Hampshire, like those of many other societies, proclaimed the importance of elevating the character and condition of blacks, correcting the "wicked prejudices" of the majority of northern whites, and striving for civil and religious equality.[10]

Some groups and individuals, however, stressed certain of these ideas more than others. Black abolitionists, aware of the serious problems in their communities, became far more interested in improving the status of free blacks than most white abolitionists, and they felt the demands of moral duty far less keenly than the demands of racial responsibility. The egalitarian tradition of the Society of Friends led Quaker women abolitionists to minimize the idea of women's particular responsibility for moral causes that evangelical women stressed so strongly. But substantial ideological agreements undergirded abolitionist women's activism.[11]

As this study shows, female activism changed over time as abolitionism responded to outside events and internal realities. In the 1830s, for example, most abolitionist women expected that the church would support and further their cause. They joined secular antislavery societies and used them as their base for work like petitioning. When the reluctance of church leaders to take a stand against slavery became clear in the 1840s, however, strategies to expose and pressure Protestant denominations became more central, and the locus for activity often changed. For the abolitionists who established individual abolitionist congregations, the church became the main institutional home for antislavery work.[12]

Past accounts have frequently described the 1830s as the heyday of the antislavery society, and then, neglecting associational life and the projects women supported, have placed abolitionist politics at the center of the anti-slavery narrative during the 1840s and 1850s. Such a focus has relegated women to the margins. This study, while acknowledging the importance of electoral politics, attempts to provide a more balanced and comprehensive picture. It suggests both the shifting locations and patterns of female involvement as well as the political activities that women pursued even though denied the ballot.[13]

Despite the changing rhythms of activism as time passed, women from different abolitionist camps relied on similar tactics to pursue their goals. Securing financial support for abolitionist work consumed countless hours and energy. Although women devised numerous ways to collect money, one of their most successful measures was the antislavery fair. When the black women of New York State who determined to raise money for the *Impartial Citizen*, a black Liberty Party newspaper, decided to hold a fair, they were in good company. Women from all camps of abolitionism mounted fairs and bazaars. While a major purpose of the fair was to generate income, fair managers also used the occasion as an opportunity to make powerful symbolic statements about the nature of their cause and to connect abolitionists to one another. They relied upon fairs as a means of energizing and linking local antislavery groups and individuals who produced the goods to be sold at the fair.[14]

Despite disagreements on issues like the relevance of political action to abolitionism, abolitionist women undertook similar projects, ranging from collecting signatures on petitions to sewing. Although the greatest petitioning effort of the antebellum period occurred in the 1830s, women mounted petition drives throughout the 1840s and 1850s, culminating in a spectacular campaign during the Civil War. The work of creating and circulating antislavery propaganda and sponsoring lectures, as the Salem Female Anti-Slavery Society did for so many years, was also ubiquitous.

Sewing for fairs, fugitives, poor northern blacks, or for freedpeople during the war united abolitionist women of all stripes. The modest and tangible character of such work helped keep women involved in abolitionism. One Georgetown, Massachusetts, woman explained that the humble sewing circle had the power to "augment our numbers and cause a more punctual attendance." The exposure that members had to abolitionist conversation and literature during meetings meant that antislavery's "influence may be diffused into all the families where our members reside and thus the whole community be *abolitionised*." While she may have overestimated the impact of the local sewing circle, the concrete tasks women undertook seem to have kept many of them attached to the cause for long periods of time. That women had something tangible in which to root their loyalty may be one reason that women, not men, constituted the great silent army of abolitionism. Continuing and often humble labors bound women together and provided milestones on the way to a distant goal.[15]

In this book, I not only sketch out the contributions women made to the movement over time, which have, by and large, been neglected or viewed as trivial, but I also try to convey the meaning of abolitionism in ordinary women's lives. Most of the women who wrote the letters and diaries I read and who left the few surviving organizational records were busy women with substantial family and domestic commitments. Many came from modest backgrounds and did most of their own housework. Unmarried white women and married black women often also worked outside of the home. Written sources reveal some of the difficulties women experienced as they tried to mesh their abolitionist convictions with day-to-day responsibilities and suggest both the emotional costs and rewards involved in supporting the cause. They give brief but revealing glimpses of lives that are otherwise lost to the historical record. As often as possible, I have allowed the women to speak for themselves. Their words are not meant to replace analysis but to convey the color and meaning of an unusual commitment in what, in other respects, seem to have been ordinary lives.

Beyond detailing the contours of women's activism and its meaning, I hope to show the ways in which female abolitionism contributes to our understanding of white middle-class women in the antebellum period and to the debate over the meaning of private and public in middle-class life. The tendency to classify some women abolitionists as radical and others as conservative, usually based upon their attitude toward feminism, misses an essential truth about abolitionism and the ways in which it led its adherents to transgress ideological norms. No matter what one's attitude might be toward women's rights, to embrace abolitionism was to embrace radicalism. The commitment to immediate emancipation challenged the political, economic, religious, and social status quo. It also became a challenge to gender arrangements. The latter challenge was ironic, for, with the exception of Quaker women, most women who adopted abolitionism did so because they accepted a gendered view of the world and women's unique religious and moral responsibilities. Their positive response to the call of duty, however, led them in unexpected directions. In the early 1830s, when the parameters of women's participation were unclear, the prevailing expectation was that white middle-class women would quietly pursue abolitionism in the privacy of their own homes. But it soon became apparent that the beleaguered movement needed more from women than home life would allow.

Abolitionist women, more directly than other women reformers who enjoyed greater community approval than did antislavery advocates, gradually and often in a piecemeal fashion, contested many of the norms that supposedly governed their behavior and woman's sphere. Moral commitments demanded public expressions. Abolitionists could neither be silent nor inconspicuous. The struggle against slavery led them to speak out in a variety of settings, ranging from their parlors to the public streets and meetinghouses. They confronted authority even when it claimed sacred prerogatives, and they broke the law when it was unjust. Even the women who formed church circles to sew for fugitive slaves and supply their settlements in Canada were acting out their repudiation of the law of the land. The crisis in gender relations that some scholars have explored in terms of early feminism and the Civil War began as ordinary abolitionist women followed the dictates of duty. It affected not only women's relations with men but also their self-perception and self-image.[16]

For women, whose sphere was supposedly private and domestic, in whom innate qualities of sympathy and intuition sufficed, abolitionism proved a demanding taskmaster. Home life proved to be an inadequate preparation for new responsibilities. To advocate immediate emancipation successfully, women had to learn to reason and to argue, to appeal to the mind as well as to the heart and emotions. Routine projects led them to transgress the usual norms for female behavior in public places and to participate alongside men in political events. While they did not vote, some assumed a more visible and meaningful political presence than the symbolic ceremonial role Mary Ryan describes in *Women In Public*. Indeed, some women went so far as to distribute third-party propaganda to voters. Their activities suggest that they understood that political activities encompassed far more than going to the polls. Far from being shielded from the vagaries of a market economy, their interest in raising money enmeshed them in the marketplace and the consumer economy. They acquired and used an array of managerial and financial skills. As time passed, they more frequently entered the public debate about slavery, and, when a second generation of abolitionists emerged, they felt an ease in their public identity as abolitionists that had been rare in the 1830s.[17]

This study joins others that, while acknowledging the power of the ideology of public and private and the construction of male and female domains, demonstrate the intersection of public and private, male and female. In the decades during which abolitionists were active, a middle class, different from both the middling sort of the eighteenth century and the new industrial working class, was taking shape. Middle-class American men increasingly held nonmanual, "white collar" jobs that provided their families with the means for a respectable and genteel way of life. Because the process of class formation was incomplete and its membership and identity not yet set, there was room to contest class definitions and boundaries. The activities of abolitionist women defied emerging middle-class norms and helped to broaden the arena of action for white middle-class women, even though it did not lead most of them to feminism. The powerful conviction that women's moral duty demanded an abolitionist commitment limited the challenge to gender arrangements. Only a few women were willing to abandon woman's moral voice for feminist egalitarianism.[18]

Who were the women who form the basis for this study and what sources revealed their work in the cause? In my effort to uncover the experiences of abolitionist women, I read hundreds of unpublished letters from ordinary white middle-class women, often found in collections of prominent abolitionists, correspondence published in the abolitionist press, a handful of diaries, and scattered organizational records of women's antislavery societies. Reminiscences provided another window into female abolitionism. For black women, the microfilm and published versions of the *Black Abolitionist Papers* provided basic information that other sources supplemented. In comparison to the material on white women, evidence for black women's participation in abolitionism is scanty, and, especially from the 1830s and 1840s, their voices are more muted in this book than I would have wished.

Most of the women leaving a record of their involvement in abolitionism were white evangelical Protestant or Quaker women living in rural and small-town communities. The materials were richest for New England, where abolitionism was centered, but Midwestern, New York, and Pennsylvania archives yielded enough to make this account reflect the areas of abolitionist strength. Although many individuals left only one or two traces of their involvement, making it impossible to flesh out their circumstances, most evidence points to modest middle-class backgrounds. In the narrative, when it has been possible to piece together more comprehensive pictures of women's situations, I have tried to do so.

A few of the women who will appear in the following pages kept diaries, wrote numerous letters to other abolitionists or to the newspapers, or even recorded their recollections of antislavery activities in the decades after the Civil War. Several profiles suggest the nature of these ordinary women's lives and hint at the meaning abolitionism had for them.

Mary White (1778–1860), daughter of a minister, wife of a farmer and shopkeeper, and mother of ten children, lived in an old homestead, a "good specimen of New England domestic comfort," in Boylston, Massachusetts. Like most farm wives, she had varied responsibilities and chores, and her life was a busy one. Despite all her domestic commitments, she became active in antislavery in the mid-1830s. Mary joined a female antislavery society, circulated petitions, attended many antislavery lectures, and sewed for the Boston fair and for fugitives. In addition to her abolitionist activities, she also supported temperance and taught Sunday school. Her diary records the way in which she integrated her reformism into her day-to-day routine and shows the antislavery involvement of other members of her family and her community.[19]

Lucy Colman was perhaps as much as forty years younger than Mary White and never enjoyed the settled life that Mary took for granted. One of her early memories was of her mother singing an antislavery song to her before her early death, when Lucy was only six. Lucy married twice and found herself a widow for the second time when she was not yet forty. Although her determination to work for emancipation predated the accidental death of her second husband, the work took on another meaning with her widowhood. Lucy became an antislavery lecturer during the 1850s, first earning her own expenses and salary as an agent of the Western Anti-Slavery Society of New York and then winning a paid position from the American Anti-Slavery Society. Primitive traveling conditions, frequently unsympathetic audiences, and constant self-denial made her tours through the Midwest taxing. "I never allowed myself the luxury of more than one meal a day, nor a fire in my room," she later recalled. Although eventually a young black woman shared speaking responsibilities, Lucy found life as an agent exhausting. When the war broke out, she left lecturing to become a teacher at a school for black children in Georgetown, New

York. There, as she struggled to teach her students middle-class values, she concluded that "generations of the most debasing, abject slavery, is not productive of a high order of morals."[20]

For decades, Frances Drake, probably the wife of Jonathan Drake, was a tireless worker for abolitionism in central Massachusetts. In the 1840s and 1850s, she organized local women to work for the great Boston fairs, gathered and sent greens to decorate the halls, and helped to plan and mount local fairs in Fitchburg and Worcester. She arranged for antislavery lectures and, in 1856, nursed Bernardo, a black boy, during his final illness. She regarded her nursing as a privilege, and, when Bernardo died, she acknowledged that it had been a "great . . . blessing . . . to me, to pillow his dying head on my bosom." An 1862 issue of the *Liberator* provides the last view of Frances in her role serving as secretary for an antislavery convention in Leominister, Massachusetts.[21]

In Salem, New Jersey, Abigail Goodwin had kept her antislavery convictions alive for decades with little support from her immediate community. A Quaker and a friend of Esther Moore, first president of the Philadelphia Female Anti-Slavery Society, Abigail joined the society in its petition work during the 1830s. Determined to collect signatures and not to become discouraged, she found New Jersey weak in "the abolitionist faith." Local women did not even have enough enthusiasm "to form a society just yet." Twenty years later, Abigail, now a poor widow, again entered the historical record. A friend explained her new focus: "Giving to the colored people was a perfect *passion* with her." Abigail's correspondence with the Philadelphia Vigilance Committee reveals some of the details of this passion to assist fugitive slaves. Without the ability to dip into her own pocket for funds, Abigail either earned or solicited money to support her interests. In the 1860s she was still active, collecting dollars and clothing for contrabands. She died in 1867.[22]

Like many abolitionists, Andrew and Sarah Ernst carried their commitments with them when they moved west in 1841. Originally from Boston, Sarah Otis Ernst was a strong Garrisonian. When she arrived in Cincinnati, she found that the city did not have one antislavery society, although African Americans had established the Educational Society for the Colored. Like many white abolitionists, Sarah was less interested in free blacks than in slaves and dismissed the Educational Society because it did "nothing at all for the slave." When political and Christian abolitionists became active in the city, she rejected their approaches as misguided. Yet, although she worked hard to generate a "new . . . spirit," she ultimately found it expedient to cooperate with other abolitionist groups. She made a major contribution to antislavery in the Midwest through her work for the Cincinnati fair and inclusive antislavery conventions. Her commitment had personal and familial costs. She found organizing the fair a "physical drudgery" and feared her work might be harmful to her newborn baby, whom she was nursing. "Sleepless nights and anxious distressed days are not calculated to give a healthy constitution to my baby," she worried. Moreover, the storage of fair items in her home disrupted domestic life and was contrary to her husband's "*wishes* — his pride." As Sarah discovered, stress was part and parcel of abolitionism.[23]

Mary Still (1808–89), an African American who left traces of her abolitionist activities, was the daughter of a former slave from Maryland and his fugitive wife. She grew up in New Jersey and, like four of her siblings, moved to Philadelphia. In the late 1840s, she kept a school for black children there and became involved in the life of Philadelphia's black community. As a member of the Female Union Publication Society of Philadelphia, an organization affiliated with the African Methodist Episcopal Church, she helped raise money for publications that contributed "to the improvement and elevation of our people." Her professional and organizational commitments, like her abolitionism, helped to establish her place in the city's black middle class. During the war, she volunteered to teach freed slaves. Heading south, she found her "heart . . . very sad" and realized that "I have desided hastily about going so far from home alone." Although the climate in South Carolina proved problematic for her health, the enthusiasm of her pupils lifted her spirits. She adapted so well to her important work that in 1869 she moved to another American Missionary Association school in Florida, where she remained until 1872.[24]

The contributions of these and countless other women to abolitionism reveal the varied and important part they played in the most significant reform before the Civil War. Herbert Aptheker points out that abolitionism was the first major social movement to involve women in all aspects of the work. What he does not emphasize enough, however, is what many of the leaders realized: without women, abolitionism would have been far more marginal a movement for change than it was.[25]

This book follows a thematic and roughly chronological approach. Chapter 1 focuses on the 1830s and the efforts abolitionist leaders made to recruit women to the cause. Although some women had already demonstrated their interest in antislavery by supporting free produce movements or by writing antislavery pieces for publication, William Lloyd Garrison did not initially expect women to play a great part in abolitionism. Gradually he became aware of the benefits of their assistance and began to urge them to educate themselves so that they could argue the case for immediate emancipation. As abolitionist societies began to spring up, women formed and joined female antislavery societies. Chapter 2 explores women's experience in abolitionist organizations in the 1830s and the ways in which they met the challenges of organizational life. Active membership in an antislavery society and involvement in its projects demanded skills and attitudes that moved women beyond the conventional boundaries of middle-class female life. Petitioning, the central work for many antislavery societies, exemplifies the ways in which women confronted social norms in the cause of duty.

The division of the national antislavery movement in 1840 created a new set of circumstances for abolitionist women. Chapter 3 focuses on the impact of dissension and disunion on women working for immediate emancipation in the 1840s and 1850s. Some societies disbanded, while others managed to struggle along, often with reduced numbers. Women often felt beleaguered and isolated, although they may have felt more isolated than they were in fact. During these decades, the communications network, initiated in the 1830s, played a crucial role in connecting women to one another and to abolitionism. This network also facilitated the antislavery fair, the great work of the 1840s and 1850s . Chapter 3 argues that women's fairs made an important contribution to the survival of antislavery and enmeshed women in the commercial world. The role of work, especially handwork, in sustaining enthusiasm is a significant theme in the discussion of fairs and women's assistance to fugitive slaves.

Chapters 4 and 5 explore different aspects of female activism in the 1840s and 1850s. Chapter 4 follows women's paths in Christian and political abolitionism and shows how they spoke out against "proslavery" religion and supported political antislavery initiatives. Commitment to moral duty allowed them to redefine what was required of them as abolitionists and as women. Chapter 5 describes the response of women to the crises of the 1850s. By the 1850s, female activism included working in the underground railroad and lecturing for the antislavery cause. Sources are abundant enough for this period to demonstrate the involvement of black women in all aspects of antislavery, including public lecturing. During a decade of continuing crises over the expansion of slavery, northerners proved more tolerant of women's public participation in the antislavery crusade than they had been during the 1830s.

Chapter 6 focuses on the Civil War and shows how women's efforts for abolitionism during the war represent an extension of the work of three decades and the fruition of efforts to enlarge the scope of female activism. Although female abolitionism contributed to the crisis in gender relations, the reality of emancipation and the petering out of abolitionism limited most women's implicit or explicit challenge to the status quo. When women had done their duty, most disappeared from the historical record.

It is time to make them part of the historical record once more.

Chapter 1
Recruiting Women into the Cause

To Freedom's cause, the cause of truth,

With joy we dedicate our youth.

To Freedom's holy altar bring

Fortune and life as offering.[1]

When readers of the *Liberator* opened their newspaper one day in mid-August 1831, they discovered a fiery poem composed by a woman who identified herself only as a "female." While the author did not explain what had prompted her to compose her verses and to submit them for publication, her outrage over slavery and her desire to compel others to acknowledge its evils hinted at the significant role women would play in the movement to eradicate American slavery.

> Wake up, wake up, and be alive,
> Let the subject of the day revive!
> How can you sleep, how can you be at rest,
> And never pity the oppressed?[2]

The woman's urgent tone also indicated how drastically and rapidly the debate over American slavery was changing in the early 1830s. William Lloyd Garrison's own interest in abolitionism dated back to an 1829 meeting with Benjamin Lundy, the Quaker editor of *The Genius of Universal Emancipation*. The Society of Friends had long opposed slavery and had pressed for gradual emancipation in the North. Now Lundy was advocating gradual emancipation and voluntary colonization as the twin strategies for ending American slavery in the South. When Garrison moved to Baltimore to work with Lundy on his newspaper, however, he discovered that the free black community in that city, as elsewhere, rejected colonization. Their influence transformed his thinking. By 1831, Garrison was espousing a platform of immediate uncompensated emancipation and publicizing the program in the pages of his Boston paper, the *Liberator*. Within a few years, Lundy would adopt Garrison's view that colonization was "totally inadequate to abolition."[3]

Garrison did not invent the idea of immediate emancipation, nor did he provide a clear definition of its meaning. The slogan "immediate emancipation" made the simple point that the work to end slavery must begin at once. Furthermore, the phrase suggested a dramatic break between modern Garrisonian abolitionism and previous efforts to abolish American slavery.[4] Half a century earlier, opponents of slavery had hopes of gradually eliminating the institution so contrary to republican and revolutionary ideals. For several decades there were signs of progress. Methodist, Presbyterian, and Baptist ministers denounced slavery as a sin, and northern states, one by one, made slavery illegal. Quakers, recently forbidden to hold slaves, manumitted hundreds in Maryland and North Carolina. Even southern planters, particularly in the Upper South, where tobacco had worn out the land, emancipated their slaves in the 1780s and early 1790s. By 1810, more than 100,000 free blacks lived in the South, evidence of the scope of manumission in that region. Finally, in 1807, the infamous international slave trade, at least legally, came to an end.[5]

Whatever enthusiasm existed for ridding the nation of slavery faded rapidly in the early decades of the nineteenth century. In the South, the development of the cotton gin opened lucrative new possibilities for the region's economy and encouraged the expansion of the plantation system. In the Upper South, breeding slaves for the internal slave trade cemented loyalty to the institution once seen as moribund. By the time of the debate over the Missouri Compromise, it was clear that southerners had a vigorous attachment to slavery and were prepared to defend it as a positive good. Bargains struck during the Constitutional Convention such as assigning to the federal government the responsibility for crushing slave insurrections offered powerful protections for the rejuvenated slave system.[6]

Still, antislavery sentiment did not disappear. In 1816, a Presbyterian minister from New Jersey established the American Colonization Society (ACS). As the organization's name suggests, one of its primary goals was to send American free blacks back to Africa as colonists. This proposal appealed to conservative southern slaveholders who believed free blacks threatened the slave system and attracted those who wanted to rid the United States of its black population. Evangelicals, hopeful that former American slaves might convert the "pagan" Africans to Christianity, also supported the Colonization Society. Most free blacks had little interest in the scheme, however, and very few agreed to emigrate. By 1830, the ACS had transported only 1,420 African Americans to Liberia.[7]

The American Colonization Society's second goal, gradual emancipation, was as far from realization as its first. The idea that slaveholders would, over time, voluntarily emancipate their slaves if they could all be sent off to Africa was flawed. But many northerners clung to the ACS because its program held out the possibility that eventually slavery might be ended without ruinous consequences for the country. During the 1820s, prominent evangelical laymen, well-known clergy, and well-known national politicians all endorsed the ACS and its agenda.[8]

Like black abolitionists who had rejected colonization out of hand in the mid-1820s, Garrison now condemned the ACS's approach. The organization, he pointed out, did not regard slaveholding as a sin, and its attempt to rid the country of blacks revealed its prejudice against people of color. Garrison's demand for immediate emancipation in the first issue of the *Liberator* in January 1831 represented the first salvo in his campaign against the ACS and its program. Ironically enough, Garrison had already hinted at his future position in an 1829 lecture delivered to the ACS in Boston's Park Street Church. Slavery, he had declared on that occasion, was barbarous, despotic, and difficult to dislodge. Efforts to do so would require "a struggle with the worst passions of human nature," but that struggle must begin at once. Antislavery demanded action. The "cause . . . would be dishonored and betrayed," he argued, "if I contented myself with appealing only to the understanding." Such an approach was "too cold and its processes are too slow for the occasion." Barbarous, despotic, difficult to dislodge—slavery was all of these. But most important, slavery was a sin, not just for the slaveowner but for all Americans. It was a "national sin," Garrison insisted, and one of which "we are all alike guilty."[9] The *Liberator*'s anonymous female poet had been less sweeping in assigning guilt, but she shared Garrison's understanding of the moral universe. To the slaveholder, she issued a warning:

"Repent, repent, for you must die!
O, be admonished—turn and live." [10]

While most evangelical Protestants ignored Garrison's program of immediate emancipation, his identification of slavery as a sin that implicated all Americans grew out of an evangelical cultural perspective that provided a powerful moral and emotional context for abolitionism. Slavery was not just a flawed economic and social system. It was a moral transgression that could no longer be tolerated. The call to action that Garrison issued echoed the summons to repentance and a new life of active Christian commitment that had been sounded repeatedly in the Northeast since the 1820s. During the revivals of the Second Great Awakening, Protestant clergy had skillfully used an array of emotional techniques to stir up members of their churches to acknowledge their sinfulness and to turn to Christ. But conversion was not the final destination so much as it was the beginning of a new life. God, the pious believed, demanded more than a cultivation of the individual soul; those who had accepted Christ must struggle against sin. The converted Christian, disciplined against unseemly passions and committed to benevolence, should commence a new life in the world. Garrison's definition of slavery as a heinous sin (caused by the slaveholder's lust and self-indulgence) was capable of motivating evangelical Christians to action and could appeal to those, like Unitarians, who believed in the importance of good works in the world.[11]

Some members of the Society of Friends, whose historical and religious experiences differed dramatically from those of evangelical Protestants, also found Garrison's analysis convincing. The Quakers had adopted a forceful stand against slavery during the eighteenth century, refusing slaveholders membership, taking the lead in early abolitionist organizations like the Pennsylvania Abolition Society, and fostering the education of free blacks. Friends were no longer in the forefront of antislavery by the time Garrison announced his program of immediate emancipation. The Pennsylvania Abolition Society, for example, supported gradual change through political channels and focused more on assisting free blacks than on freeing slaves in the South. But the Quaker belief in the Inner Light that revealed what had to be done in this life to gain salvation in the next could prompt a commitment to immediatism. Although the guidance of the Inner Light became clear only over time, the emphasis on doing one's duty in the world did not differ so much from the compulsion that the climactic event of an evangelical conversion might unleash.[12]

In the late 1820s, controversies over the Inner Light and antislavery contributed to a division in the Society of Friends. Hicksites (the followers of Elias Hicks) laid more emphasis on the importance of the Inner Light and antislavery measures like the avoidance of slave products than Orthodox Friends. Orthodox Friends did became Garrisonians, but Hicksites were most responsive to Garrison's program of immediate emancipation. One scholar has suggested that the division offered Hicksite women leadership opportunities that could promote social activism. In advocating the Hicksite position before members of the local and more distant meetings, women participated in debates crucial to the Society's future and gained a heightened sense of female importance and equality. This self-confidence allowed some of them eventually to move into reform causes, whether or not more conservative Friends approved.[13]

While Garrison's speech before the ACS did not represent any fully developed plan for ridding the nation of slavery, the definition of women as moral guardians of nineteenth-century society and culture implied some female role in antislavery activities. In his address, Garrison encouraged women to join with their congregations in pouring out "supplication[s] to heaven on behalf of the slaves." Acknowledging three decades of women's involvement in organized charitable and benevolent work, he also recommended that women work within the framework of "charitable associations to relieve the degraded of their sex."[14]

When Garrison formally launched his antislavery effort in January 1831, he had given little further thought as to how women might contribute to the cause. Female readers, as his paper pointed out, could and should "fall upon . . . [their] knees, and lift up . . . [their] voices to heaven for those who are in bondage." Early children's stories in the *Liberator* also depicted parents instructing their children about slavery's evils and indicated that, at this early point, Garrison and others visualized abolitionist women's commitment as primarily domestic and familial. The belief that mothers were uniquely placed to shape children's thinking was so central to the way middle-class northerners thought about motherhood that this emphasis never disappeared, even when other possibilities for female participation emerged. As one abolitionist paper explained at the end of the decade, the mother who read antislavery stories to her children began the process of making an abolitionist. "The child of two or three years will be more interested in the story of the poor slave, than with the whole Catalogue of Nursery tales."[15]

In January 1832, Garrison, impressed by the antislavery work of British women, established a Ladies' Department in his paper. This new feature,

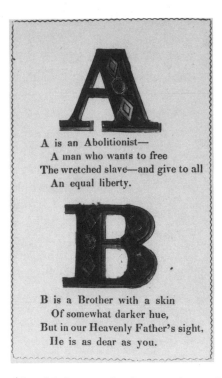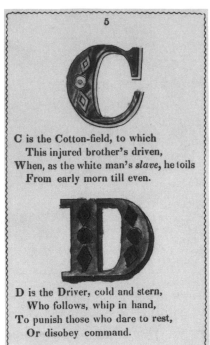

A is an Abolitionist—
A man who wants to free
The wretched slave—and give to all
An equal liberty.

B is a Brother with a skin
Of somewhat darker hue,
But in our Heavenly Father's sight,
He is as dear as you.

C is the Cotton-field, to which
This injured brother's driven,
When, as the white man's *slave*, he toils
From early morn till even.

D is the Driver, cold and stern,
Who follows, whip in hand,
To punish those who dare to rest,
Or disobey command.

*This alphabet, aimed at bringing the antislavery message to children, is an
example of the continuing interest in converting children to abolitionism within
the confines of the home. (Boston Athenæum)*

he hoped, would add to the interest women felt in the *Liberator* and "give a
new impetus to the cause of emancipation." Assuming that women needed
encouragement, even though some were already contributing to his paper,
he pointed out that a million enslaved women "ought to excite the sympathy and indignation of American women." Attracting female support was
hardly his most important priority, however. Because his ideas about the
scope of female activism were still vague, his paper continued to propose
the most obvious and least controversial possibilities. No doubt, the early
emphasis on using nonslave products stemmed partly from the fact that
"females who are interesting themselves in behalf of the poor slaves" could
and already were acting upon their commitments at home. The *Liberator*'s
anonymous poet had asked her readers:

"How can you eat, how can you drink,
How wear your finery, and ne'er think
Of those poor souls, in bondage held,
Whose painful labor is compelled?"

The implied response was that no true Christian, and certainly not a woman, could fail to understand the relationship between the articles of daily life and slavery. Domestic life could not continue as usual.[16]

A letter published in 1832, ostensibly from "a plain hardworking farmer," showed the internal ramifications of adopting free-labor principles. The farmer pictured his family in the midst of a domestic transformation in which women took the lead. "My wife and grown up daughters," he wrote, "have got a notion out of some tract they have been reading, that we ought not to eat rice, nor sugar, nor anything that is raised by the labor of slaves." Using the *Liberator* as her guide, his daughter had quizzed him about free and slave products. As she finished her list of questions, she announced triumphantly, " 'I am sure you will think just as we do.' "[17]

Boycotting goods not only drew upon impeccable historical precedents —in particular, the activities of women during the American Revolution— but it also accorded with the nineteenth-century view of women as unselfish, practiced in self-denial, and morally insightful. The practice was firmly rooted in the new realities of economic life. Although the plain and hardworking farmer still went to town for household supplies, in many middle-class households women were in the position to make or at least to influence consumption decisions.

The idea of boycotting products produced by slave labor also built upon Quaker principles and organizational efforts. Quaker leaders, including Elias Hicks, had urged Friends to use only "free" goods. In the late 1820s, associations pledged to the free produce principle were established in several cities with substantial Quaker communities. Black women belonging to Philadelphia's Bethel African Methodist Episcopal Church also established their own free produce association in 1829. Several of these women would later become active in the Philadelphia Female Anti-Slavery Society (PFAS).[18]

The fact that women who abhorred slavery formed the backbone of the early free produce movement doubtless prompted Garrison to urge female sympathizers to form free produce societies and patronize shopkeepers like Lydia White, an African American, who ran a dry goods store in Philadelphia that carried products of free labor. As the newspaper pointed out, women outside of Philadelphia could take advantage of her store: White took orders from states as distant as Vermont, Indiana, and Ohio.[19]

The hardworking farmer had raised the question of just how the efforts of one family might contribute to the demise of slavery. Theoretically, the boycott could undermine the market for slave products and goods made from them, thus undermining the viability of slavery itself. But there were other possible consequences especially appealing to women who took their moral role seriously. For example, a children's story that pictured mother and daughter explaining the merits of free produce to young Edward just home from boarding school resulted in a youthful convert to abolitionism. "If ever I am a man, and slavery is not abolished then," declared Edward, "you shall see that I have not forgotten what you have told me today." Women were also assured that their buying and consuming habits constituted valuable "testimony against this greatest of evils."[20]

The *Liberator* occasionally provided examples of women carrying their abolitionist commitment beyond the boundaries of family and household. They could, for instance, teach free blacks in a Sabbath school. While this activity challenged racial norms, the task and its location were familiar. One teacher quoted in the paper emphasized "the eagerness and intensity of interest with which . . . [her students] applied themselves to the study of God's work, and listened to instruction." The picture she provided of students thirsting for knowledge and her characterization of her work as God's minimized the radical nature of her efforts.[21]

Elizabeth Chandler's antislavery work suggested the ways in which a woman might actually express her commitment to the new cause without straying too far from her domestic setting. Elizabeth's quiet activism also serves as a reminder that some women's involvement in abolitionism preceded Garrison's own. First in Philadelphia and then in Michigan, the young Hicksite Quaker wrote antislavery pieces, observed free produce principles, and pricked the consciences of friends and family to take a stand against slavery. Her literary efforts began when her poem entitled the "Slave Ship" won a prize in a magazine poetry contest. Benjamin Lundy reprinted the piece in his paper, the *Genius of Universal Emancipation*. When Garrison joined Lundy in 1829, Elizabeth was writing for its Ladies' Department. Later, she also contributed to the *Liberator* and was perhaps responsible for the urgent verses beginning this chapter. Garrison, recognizing how skillfully Elizabeth used images of the anguished female slave to appeal to the emotions, described one of her early poems as a "thrilling effusion." Despite the problems she had in chaining her ideas "to one point sufficiently for serious writing," she managed to incorporate her antislavery commitments successfully into her domestic routine.[22]

Elizabeth supported the free produce movement, and her letters reveal the way her commitment affected her personal and domestic life. Avoiding slave products could be inconvenient, especially on the frontier, and inefficient. She could not always complete her chores promptly. As she explained to her aunt somewhat apologetically, "I should have sent thy patchwork by this opportunity, but have not yet got it finished, as sewing cotton runs low with us, and I felt unwilling, unless compelled by actual necessity to purchase any of the slave manufacture." Discovering the origins of even the most ordinary household necessities took time and effort. Was "Java coffee . . . the product of free labor," she asked her aunt? It was over a year before she learned "it comes from East India." [23]

Elizabeth not only observed free produce principles, she also tried to persuade friends and family to follow her example. To her brother, she explained that it was "his sister's earnest request that both he and his wife . . . promote the use of free produce as much as it is in their power." When she had visitors, she spoke so persuasively that "they seemed almost inclined to become supporters by renouncing the unnecessary use of slave products." Her advocacy of free produce in her poetry also encouraged women, like those in Clark County, Ohio, to organize free produce societies.[24]

While much of the early material in the *Liberator* directed at women fostered the idea that women might oppose slavery without violating their routines, as, in fact, Elizabeth Chandler did, there were also hints that Garrison was gradually seeing more ambitious possibilities. An "Appeal to Ladies," published in March 1832, called upon women to use all their powers, "whether moral, political, civil, or religious, or all combined," to further the antislavery cause. Yet, as the paper acknowledged, many women would be reluctant to adopt such a comprehensive approach. "Some of you may, perhaps plead the effeminacy of your sex, and some—mental inferiority; but oh! this is nothing else than vain mockery." [25]

Despite the designation of female reticence and reluctance as vain mockery, the reality was that women might well feel inferior and inadequate. Their domestic duties had not prepared most of them psychologically or intellectually to be advocates for emancipation. All too frequently, the paper pointed out, they "undervalue[d] their own power." Of course, "the voice of women should not be heard in public debates," but women could and should speak out forcefully in other settings. Thus, articles encouraged women to learn about the evils of slavery and then use this information effectively. Never should they neglect to enter conversations when slavery was being debated or fear to discuss their opinions. "The shield of wisdom will prove the best defence against the attacks of ridicule." [26]

Without any consideration of the long-term implications of such a course of action, Garrison and other abolitionist editors encouraged women to learn the skills of argumentation more familiar to those accustomed to public discourse than to those at home. As antislavery advocates, women had to learn to speak logically, to counter an opponent's position, to "reveal sophistry," and to muster evidence. "Use your powers of persuasion," the Maine antislavery paper, the *Advocate of Freedom*, counseled; "nine times out of ten you will succeed." While women's efforts should not involve them in any unbecoming behavior and should exhibit "long-suffering— and gentleness," they had to learn to appeal to the head. Presumably they already knew how to appeal to the heart.[27]

A series of pieces published in the *Liberator* in 1832 clearly intended to teach women some of the rudimentary information and skills they would need to become convincing speakers. Taking as subjects a variety of topics, including the importance of using free products, the part the North could play in abolishing slavery in the South, the relationship between the Constitution and slavery, and the need to be more active in the cause, the articles presented dialogues showing an abolitionist woman interacting with an uncommitted or unsympathetic speaker. The dialogue form was an effective literary device that not only introduced the reader to information but also showed her how to present it and how to counter anticipated objections. Presumably a woman could memorize parts of the dialogue if she chose and even practice responding to objections. While the exchanges depicted were between women, segments easily lent themselves to mixed company. Indeed, women were told not to turn a blind eye to the indifference of brothers and fathers (and presumably husbands), but to show them "the errors of their ways." And as the *Advocate of Freedom* suggested, if a husband was already an abolitionist, it was a woman's duty not to "allow him to fall asleep."[28]

What should be said to someone who regarded joining an antislavery society as quixotic or who felt she had no time to devote to such a cause? How could one respond to a person who had visited the South yet claimed that slavery was not so bad after all? What if someone should accuse women involved in antislavery activities of being immodest or of interfering in political business? Awkward silence or inarticulate stammerings were out of the question in such predictable situations. The answer: Tell the reluctant friend that if "without investigation [you] refuse to believe a tale of wrongs which you are called upon to help to redress, you are not acting as a Christian should." Counter the claim of having no time to act for the slave by acknowledging domestic obligation and appealing to class. Domestic duty, one might say, "cannot . . . completely occupy the time of any lady, or of any woman above the poorest class." Inquire of the southern traveler whether he or she had ever seen slaves working or being punished. Or had he or she, in fact, merely seen them in the great house? Point to evidence exposing the character of slavery that southerners revealed in their own political debates. As for the criticism of women's activities, how could it be immodest merely to read or lend books or to speak to female friends and neighbors?

The *Liberator*'s dialogues and other printed materials gave a clear message: have the right information, ask probing questions, parry responses. As the female-authored "Appeal to Females of [the] North" explained, women must dare "to exercise those powers of mind which the Almighty has bestowed upon us, or we shall be driven from the position by the objections and entreaties of those whose views are in opposition to ours."[29]

One of the dialogues published during 1832 described a situation in which the female reader asked her friend what was becoming an increasingly critical question: "'Are you a member of the LADIES' Anti-Slavery society in this neighborhood?'" As antislavery was taking institutional form, Garrison made more focused efforts to connect "female virtue and patriotism" with the movement. Indeed, soon after Garrison and other immediatists established the all-male New England Anti-Slavery Society in January 1832, the *Liberator* suggested that "something must be done . . . and it is in the power of American women to do much. . . . They can form societies; each member agreeing to do all in her power to abolish this horrible traffic—to spread the alarm by patronizing the *Liberator*—and to abstain from the fruits of inequity and oppression." The earliest female antislavery societies were formed within months.[30]

There was good evidence to encourage Garrison to support female antislavery associations. Three decades of female association for charitable and benevolent causes suggested the power of female activism. Since the 1790s, white upper- and middle-class women had formed organizations, adopted constitutions, communicated with similar societies elsewhere, raised money, and used it for a variety of causes, including relieving suffering, helping the worthy poor, especially widows and children, and spreading the faith to those in faraway lands and nearer to home, in impoverished neighborhoods or on the western frontier. Free black women also organized, but they directed their efforts at those with whom they shared bonds of friendship, kinship, and propinquity: the less fortunate members of their own fragile communities. Such benevolent and charitable activities had raised little criticism and gained much praise. In 1817, the Presbyterian General Assembly had announced that it was "among the distinguished glories of the nineteenth century that PIOUS FEMALES are more extensively associated, and the more actively useful, in promoting evangelical and benevolent objects than in any former period of the world." British female antislavery groups provided a stirring example of what organized women might accomplish with a more radical agenda than that of American benevolent and charitable associations and confirmed the idea that organizing American women could be an important step in the effort to end slavery. As the *Liberator* remarked, British women's antislavery societies were moving that whole nation forward on the question of abolitionism. British female antislavery societies, usually laboring independently of any male counterparts, raised substantial funds for the cause, created and disseminated propaganda, and were active in petition work.[31]

The effort to draw American women into similar antislavery associations obviously required from them a greater commitment than staying at home, avoiding the products of slave labor, and conversing, with quiet logic, with friends and family. But even Evelina Smith, of Hingham, Massachusetts, who admitted in 1836 that she needed "no arguments to prove that Slavery is wrong, & altogether in opposition to the Bible," did not yet feel herself "called upon, publicly to espouse abolitionism." As she explained, "I do not feel that such is my mission."[32]

To recruit women like Evelina Smith who already disapproved of slavery into organized antislavery activity and to reach women who did not yet realize the evils of the institution necessitated confronting those concerns and obligations that might prevent a woman from committing herself. One of the most contentious issues concerned female propriety. Was it seemly for women to join an antislavery society? The question was easier to answer initially than it would be later, when the impact of abolitionism on women became clearer than it was early in the decade. Garrison and others assured women that association did not involve any impropriety. One of the dialogues in the *Liberator*, for example, minimized any danger to reputation by emphasizing the familiarity of the work and stressing the local and female character of the proposed societies. "How can I possibly think that there would be any offence to modesty," remarked the *Liberator*'s female abolitionist ingenuously, "in meeting some of the ladies of your neighborhood to talk over your plans, and to endeavor to make your efforts more effectual by uniting in a society."[33]

Despite the ubiquity of female benevolent activity, antislavery was, in fact, a radical cause. Women interested in benevolent and charitable causes focused on those worthy individuals whom progress had left behind. While they promoted certain behaviors among their clients—industriousness, Christian piety, and sobriety, for example—they tended to accept society as it was. Often affiliated with a particular denomination, benevolent and charitable groups enjoyed not only clerical support but also the encouragement of prominent women who frequently served as officers. Like other moral reform groups emerging in the 1830s, especially those seeking to end prostitution, abolitionists sought to cleanse society, to change it. While most abolitionist women did not become feminists, their commitment would challenge racial, social, and political arrangements in both the North and the South. Their interpretation of moral duty would result in new understandings of gender and class norms. As one Unitarian minister who attempted to prevent the formation of an antislavery society in Taunton, Massachusetts, warned prophetically, "the successful prosecution of their measures would inevitably dissolve the Union, and cause civil war and bloodshed!!"[34]

The dialogues presented in the *Liberator* recognized a whole range of factors beyond the fear of transgressing the boundaries of acceptable female behavior that might prevent women from joining an antislavery society. The burden of women's domestic and family duties that, some women might argue, left not even ten minutes for the slave led the list that included bad health, a reluctance to read the "horrid accounts" about slavery, and the feeling that the institution was the government's responsibility. Particularly embarrassing to those insisting that slavery was a sin was the fact that "most religious people . . . decline taking any part in this business." Then there was always the underlying fear of impropriety, the accusation that women would be involving themselves with business "quite of out their province." Aware of these kinds of misgivings, antislavery editors and agents began several initiatives to overcome female reluctance and to secure women's loyalty to immediate emancipation. Newspapers, tracts, lectures, debates, and prayer meetings all reached out to a female audience that presumably needed outside stimulation to become involved. Although these sources reveal the efforts to recruit women, the existence of women's free produce societies, the early stream of antislavery literature, much of it written by black women, and letters women sent into the *Liberator* suggest that not all women needed as much encouragement as male organizers believed.[35]

Antislavery newspapers like the *Liberator, The Anti-Slavery Reporter*, and the *Advocate of Freedom*, though not women's newspapers, sought to address issues of consequence to women and to secure their loyalty. Elizur Wright, editor of *The Anti-Slavery Reporter*, worried that his paper might not be reaching women effectively. The style, he felt, was "not well adapted to move the mass; — to interest women and children — you know a great part of the mass are . . . such." In the *Liberator*, Garrison was careful to show that every one of the typical female objections to joining an antislavery society was of little consequence.[36]

Antislavery editors realized that many potential converts did not read abolitionist newspapers. Recognizing that the ties of family and friendship could provide an entry into households that they could not easily reach otherwise, editors continually exhorted female readers to persuade their friends to take a paper or even to send one to someone who might profit from it. Lucinda Storrs not only handed around her own newspaper but also bought one for a neighbor who was "warm in the cause" but "one of the Lords poor." The testimony of a widowed schoolmistress in Florence, Pennsylvania, attests to the success of such a strategy. "The paper you sent," she wrote her brother, "has indeed been [instrumental] in converting me to the abolitionist views so far as to desire the immediate emancipation of every negro in the world." [37]

Yet the increasingly radical reputation and cost of antislavery papers limited circulation. In North Marshfield, Louisa Phillips found few interested in subscribing to an abolitionist newspaper: "It is the last thing they think of, to increase their expences in that way." Amasa Walker apparently objected to content, not cost, declaring that he would not have an abolitionist newspaper in his house. For Grace Williams, abolitionist papers spelled domestic trouble, for they affected "most disastrously on Husband's tempers." And even though Sophia Davenport was committed to abolitionism when she moved to St. Louis, she felt that it would be foolish and "dangerous to myself and friends" to take the *Liberator* there.[38]

As Louisa Phillips explained when she reported that North Marshfield residents did not want to spend the money to subscribe to an antislavery paper, "Ours is not, generally speaking, a reading community." But she did not believe that all was lost: "A good lecture will do much to promote the cause." While the potential for violence might have kept away some of the more fearful members of the community, the public lecture became another essential strategy for stimulating interest, pricking the conscience, and converting both sexes to an active role in antislavery. The traveling lecturer or agent, already a familiar figure in American religious and benevolent circles, had proved his value in the British abolitionist campaign.[39]

The American Anti-Slavery Society (AAS), formed in 1833 by Garrison and others, recognized the value of lectures. Its recruiting effort started modestly with the appointment of four agents, Samuel May, Amos Phelps, Garrison, and Theodore Weld. Each was scheduled for a three-month tour. During this brief time, they were "to arouse the public mind by addresses and lectures—to enlighten and convert individuals by private interviews—especially to operate on ministers of the Gospel." Amos Phelps's 1834 commission also highlighted another important goal: the formation of "Auxiliary Societies, both male and female, in every place where it is practicable. Even if such societies are very small at the outset, they may do much good as centers of light, and means of future access to the people."[40]

The agency effort became a large and expensive part of the American Anti-Slavery Society's mission during the early part of the decade. In 1833–34, the AAS devoted 14 percent of its annual income to supporting agents. Two years later, the high point of expenditure for lecturers, over half of the association's annual income went for this purpose. By 1838, partly because of cost and the financial panic of the previous year, the AAS reduced its commitment to a system of national lecturers. But it did not abandon the strategy. To replace the corps of national lecturers, the society encouraged local agents, "men in settled life, who for their interest in the cause will take short lecturing excursions in their own vicinity and labor for the Society as a freewill offering." The rationale made economic sense, for the American Anti-Slavery Society reimbursed local agents only for expenses. The new policy also represented a realistic plan for transforming people's thinking, a task that demanded time and repeated effort. "Though the great work of changing public opinion may be successfully begun, it can by no means be finished by traveling agents. In every village and neighborhood of our wide country, slavery and its kindred and inseparable evil, the prejudice of caste, must be discussed and dwelt on till they are thoroughly understood in all their bearings."[41]

Some abolitionists believed that lectures represented a more powerful recruiting tactic than printed materials. Like revival meetings, antislavery lectures could reach large numbers of people in a collective setting that a skillful speaker could manipulate to arouse emotions and stimulate commitment. In addition to being powerful motivators, lectures could attract both those interested in the cause and those who were not. In quiet country villages and towns, the lecture was an event. For Fanny McDill in Franklin, Ohio, who was "not well enough acquainted with the subject to form a decided opinion," the upcoming antislavery lecture might provide the information to seal her loyalty to the new cause. In Dedham, Massachusetts, according to Sophia Davenport in 1835, the people were "in a deplorable state of ignorance concerning the subject . . . [and] very much prejudiced against abolition." Nevertheless, "they would all like to hear [the antislavery lecturer] Mr. Thompson."[42]

Because lecturers hoped that women would attend their presentations, they made efforts to respect female propriety. If lectures were tainted by scandal, the respectable and influential women as well as their timid sisters might stay away. In Kingston, Rhode Island, opponents of abolitionism claimed that the antislavery agent would advocate "amalgamation." As a result, "many ladies thought it would be very improper for them to attend." In Leicester, Massachusetts, no such threat existed. But when the town's minister informed his congregation that he supported the colonization society, his stance prevented "nearly all of the best portion of his congregation (the ladies) from attending" the antislavery lecture.[43]

The most desirable situation for encouraging the female presence was for one of the community's ministers to announce the lecture and lend his church for it. Obtaining sacred space legitimized the antislavery platform and reinforced the moral and religious imperative claimed by its advocates. Women felt at home in this space where they so often made up the majority of the congregation. The power of the building might occasionally serve as a counterweight to a denunciation from the pulpit; in Ware, Massachusetts, for example, agent Arnold Buffum discovered that the minister's antagonism had not prevented a crowd from gathering in the church (although ten minutes after he began, about a dozen ladies "simultaneously left the house.")[44]

Antislavery lectures had varied formats. Agents and local supporters hoped to attract a large turnout and to convert as many members of the audience to the antislavery position as they could. Whatever means might contribute to achieving their ends were used. A Plymouth, New Hampshire, lecture, for example, drew heavily upon religious associations to create a servicelike atmosphere. "The meeting-house was splendidly lighted; a choir of excellent singers performed several pieces appropriate to the occasion; a sweet sounding organ, made without instruction by a genuine abolitionist, was played by a young lady . . . who . . . was inspired with the true feeling of universal benevolence." Amos Phelps relied on props to fill his listeners with sympathy for the slave. He gripped the attention especially of the females in his audience when during his appeal for support he "brandished about in the sacred desk the slave driver's whip such as had 'lacerated the back of woman.' "[45]

Sometimes, in an effort to attract even fainthearted and conventional women, speakers had special lectures for women only. Samuel J. May designed his Fall River, Massachusetts, lecture "particularly for the ladies," and he spoke for over an hour in the Baptist meetinghouse. In Providence, again in a Baptist meetinghouse, not only did "many of . . . [the] most influential and worthy ladies, and some of the fairest of the fair" attend, but many also came forward to pledge themselves to the cause. Perhaps the female setting made the act of commitment more inviting than it would have been otherwise.[46]

During the 1830s, when agents were addressing mixed audiences, they reported that, in some places, women were in the majority. In a city like Boston, women tended to go to public lectures in greater numbers than men, and perhaps this was the reason for large female audiences in many places. During his August 1833 visit to Nantucket, for example, Arnold Buffum estimated that three-quarters of his listeners were women. In Albany, he found the same preponderance of women who "listened apparently with intense interest, for nearly two hours, to a delineation of slavery, and of our plan for its abolition." In the collection plate, Buffum discovered two gold rings, a pattern of female giving that was repeated in his other engagements in New York State. Accounts from agents about the women in their audiences and their respectability and interest appeared in the *Liberator*, thus reinforcing the moral credentials of antislavery and calming scruples that kept women away.[47]

When ministers refused to lend their churches, lecturers wishing to speak to audiences in country towns and villages might be hard-pressed to find a suitable substitute. The town hall, if available, could hold a good crowd, but with its public and political associations, it did not have as powerful symbolic legitimacy for women as did a church. Nonetheless, women were certainly willing to attend lectures in such space. In Boylston, Massachusetts, for instance, Mary White went to an antislavery lecture in the town hall in 1837, though she made the event sacred in her diary entry by inserting a short prayer of supplication for "the poor slaves." A month later, that hall was the site for the formation of the female antislavery society.[48]

Lectures proved an important venue for exposing women to abolition and for encouraging the formation of female antislavery societies. In Sangerville, Maine, the women, though interested in the cause, did not organize until they were visited by two agents. The visit acted as an incentive. As one of the officers of the society that emerged explained, "Our sympathies were enlisted . . . and most deeply did we feel, that the daughters of New England, surrounded by every comfort,—and conscious of their duty as females, should arise . . . [and] call for the freedom and protection of their sisters in bonds." In Dighton, Massachusetts, Abby Talbot reported a similar pattern that must have occurred in many country towns and villages. Few women, she wrote, "had thought much on the subject of slavery previous to Mr. Thompson,s lecturing [here]." But Thompson moved many of the women, and "from the impulse of the moment a society was foarmed & 23 gave in their names."[49]

Antislavery newspapers reported on these successful organizing efforts as a spur to other women. They often printed a society's constitution to serve as a useful example to other groups and the list of officers to encourage correspondence among them. Exhortations from British women also appeared. An 1832 letter from the London Female Anti-Slavery Society, for example, urged American women to unite. A later selection from an English tract vindicated female societies and argued that they were neither unbecoming nor unfeminine. Occasionally rebukes accompanied exhortations. An article reprinted from the *Genius of Universal Emancipation* sternly announced that "the females of this land are without excuse for their heartless indifference." Their duty to antislavery was obvious.[50]

While the agency system helped recruit women to antislavery, locally organized events also spread the abolitionist message. Because Garrison's attack on colonization had created a good deal of controversy, a town or village lyceum might devote an evening or more to the subject of colonization versus immediatism. In Augusta, Maine, speakers spent eight nights debating the topic. At the end of the series, members of the audience formed an antislavery society. Community prayer meetings, called "concerts," whether focused on the slave or not, could also be instrumental in garnering support. Young Deborah Weston found the concert she attended in 1835 "one of the most interesting meetings I ever attended." The flexible format of this service, which might include music, a choir, or a short address, afforded opportunities to move emotions, to shape perspectives, and to bear witness to the truth about slavery. Extemporaneous "prayers" combining prayer, exhortation, and instruction were standard features and allowed anyone present the chance to participate. Making supplications for the slave, as Lucinda Storrs realized, took "courage." But even females "seldom leaving the chimney corner" could summon up that courage and offer an appeal to the congregation's conscience on such an occasion.[51]

The fruits of these sorts of events might be modest or ambitious. After attending a concert in Boylston, Massachusetts, Mary White inserted in her diary a prayer that "God might bless efforts to abolish slavery." In Dover, New Hampshire, on the other hand, a concert of prayer held in 1835 fostered collective action. After the meeting, women gathered in the Methodist Parsonage to organize an antislavery society.[52]

Ministers could also help organize societies, announce meetings, and provide the church building for abolitionist events. They could pray for the slave during the regular Sabbath service and use other occasions to plead the cause. Two Dover ministers, for example, were instrumental in assisting in the formation of the ladies' antislavery society there. Later, when the group faltered, the Methodist minister helped to revive it. When Mary White attended a class meeting in Boylston in June 1836, she was not surprised when her minister, an active proponent of abolitionism, read "an interesting piece . . . entitled a voice from Scotland on the subject of American slavery." The AAS recognized the clergy's critical role in fostering women's loyalty and instructed agents to seek ministers out.[53]

In 1837, Mary White noted in her diary that the minister's wife, "Mrs. Sanford[,] called here this evening with a constitution to form an antislavery society." Her entry highlighted the role a minister's wife might play in organizing local women into a society and in lending her prestige as one of the community's influential women to the association. But organizing did not necessarily come only from the efforts of antislavery agents, local clergy, and their spouses. Ordinary women, moved by their reading, the solicitation of friends, or remarks from a visiting lecturer, also established local female antislavery societies on their own initiative. In 1836, for example, Deborah Weston reported from New Bedford, "Last saturday afternoon I went to Susan Taber's to help lay the foundation of a female society. There were very few there, but they were strong ones. There is to be another meeting next saturday afternoon." On the Michigan frontier, Elizabeth Chandler eventually encouraged some local women to form a society, even though "many have seldom heretofore thought much about the subject."[54]

Although printed sources highlight the organizing role of male abolitionists, as these examples suggest, women themselves turned into or, in some cases, already were able recruiters and publicists for abolitionist ideas. Letters provided one avenue for discussing the subject with friends and family. In Ohio, Mary Irwin wrote to her sister Eliza to probe her on the subject of abolitionism and to encourage her to make up her mind about such an important matter. "I think you will be an Abolitionist, soon if you are not already," Mary wrote. "I am conscientiously one." Like Eliza, Sarah Berrien was also undecided in her views, but, as she explained to her abolitionist cousin Betsy Cowles, "with regard to immediate emancipation I dont know that it would be best and on the other hand the colonization plan dont suit my views at all," thus offering Betsy an opening for debate in her reply.[55]

"What agent more powerful in correcting public sentiment as woman?" A. A. Guthrie asked Betsy Cowles rhetorically in 1835. While the task of correcting public sentiment regarding slavery was an ambitious one, women might weave the work into the familiar routines of everyday life. As Hannah Cranch observed, "It is pretty surprising to what a degree inquiry is awakened." And while Hannah suggested that the study and workshop were two locations where women might wield their influence, she anticipated most encounters would take place before "the *polished grate*, and the humble cook-stove, on the *sofa* and on the *settle*." In such settings, a woman might stimulate *"discussion . . . on . . . this all absorbing question."* In this spirit of mingling routine social occasions with recruiting, Elizabeth Chandler invited her frontier neighbors "to pass the . . . afternoon with me . . . for the purpose of looking over some papers on the subject of slavery."[56]

Among friends and acquaintances women did come face to face with the kinds of problems the *Liberator* had suggested they might experience. As women in Providence, Rhode Island, realized, they needed "strong minds and vigorous intellects" in order to be effective in the cause. To Louisa Phillips's dismay, she discovered she was dangerously ignorant about the subject of slavery. "I scarcely know the first half of the letter A about the subject," she confessed. "I find I shall have to study a long time to be thoroughly acquainted with their arguments." Other women found that their skills of argumentation were weak. Sybil Swetland in Rochester, New York, dismissed her arguments as "tame," at least in comparison to "those required to meet the aristocracy of sin, with which I combat." Sophia Davenport, who introduced the subject whenever she could, also felt that she was not as forceful as she would like to be, and certainly not so skillful as her friend Caroline Weston. She rather ruefully reflected, "I cannot talk and argue as she does." Sometimes it was not the arguments but the ability to get them out fast enough that was the problem. The Roote sisters concluded they were *"poor dunces"* when a supporter of slavery was able to outspeak them.[57]

Even bringing up the topic proved to be volatile and difficult. Abolitionists believed that northerners, including their friends and neighbors, shared responsibility for the sin of slavery. They proposed upsetting the political status quo to give freedom to a race that most white people considered inferior. They referred discretely but clearly to sexual relations between the southern white male elite and female slaves. No wonder Sophia Davenport described her conversations as "furious battle[s]" and discovered that some people were "unwilling to talk upon such a *delicate* subject." Lydia Maria Child, the author of influential abolitionist works including *An Appeal in Favor of That Class of Americans Called Africans* (1833), *The Oasis* (1834), and *The Evils of Slavery, and the Cure for Slavery* (1836), was an expert on slavery and felt more secure than many other women in talking about it. When she discussed abolitionism with the eminent Unitarian minister William Ellery Channing, who did not see the necessity of immediate emancipation, she countered him point by point. But genteel as their conversation undoubtedly was, she acknowledged its difficulties by classifying it as an argument.[58]

On some occasions the combat exhilarated Maria. During a stage journey in 1837, she countered the prejudiced racial views of a fellow passenger so effectively that the other travelers laughed and clapped. Pleased that she kept her temper, she thought that she had never been so brilliant and witty. "Oh, if I was a man, how I *would* lecture!" she concluded. "But I am a woman, and so I sit in the corner and knit socks."[59]

If a woman as well known and important in constructing the abolitionist attack on slavery as Maria Child saw herself as a knitter, or, as in her encounter with Channing, as a mouse, others not surprisingly found themselves silent when they should have spoken up. Octavia Gardner knew her duty and realized that she had "friends who would listen to me," but her parents' opposition kept her silent and troubled. Lucretia Cowings, who had the disadvantage of living among slaveholders in Annapolis, Maryland, was also mortified by her want of courage. She had not dared to admit that she was an abolitionist even when the conversation turned to the subject, and she concluded that she feared losing the "good opinion" of those with whom she lived and socialized. In a letter to a Boston friend, she vowed to reveal who she really was before she returned to the North. In Detroit, Mrs. Kingsbury was also silent. Only one other boarder in her boarding-house sympathized with abolitionism, and apparently Mrs. Kingsbury did not relish being in the minority. Had her husband supported her, perhaps she would have been more courageous. To her dismay, her "companion is not interested as formerly . . . which is a great trial to me. He does not oppose me at all, but still, you know . . . it would be pleasanter if he was interested with me in the good cause of Abolition."[60]

Because women often depended upon printed materials to furnish them with the ammunition they needed to discuss immediate emancipation and the evils of slavery effectively, many responded to editors' pleas to take and to circulate antislavery newspapers. For example, when Experience Billings made a trip from Foxborough, Massachusetts, to visit friends in Keene, New Hampshire, she discovered they were willing to read the papers she carried with her. Upon her return to Foxborough, she sent her Keene friends her *Liberator* every week.[61]

Many women thought that once they succeeded in getting an antislavery paper into people's hands, they would change their minds about the slavery issue. Betsy Newton identified the "great want of knowledge in this town on the subject" as the basic problem in Worcester, Massachusetts. Sarah Plummer concluded that the residents of Bangor, Maine, were prejudiced against the *Liberator*. But underlying the prejudice lurked the real obstacle, the "want of acquaintance" with the paper's character. She confessed that she understood this attitude since she had once shared it. Now she determined to change the situation by circulating the newspaper. Her success exceeded what she had "dared to hope." One gentleman had told her that he was "*decided*" to have nothing to do with any society connected with Garrison. When she discovered that he had never even seen the *Liberator*, she "prevailed" upon him to take a look at it. After reading two issues he was convinced of the rightness of the cause.

Modest economic circumstances and a want of ready cash limited the efforts of some women during the 1830s. Sarah Plummer was not able to afford enough copies of the paper to allow them to circulate freely. Instead, she had to lend her family's copy and then retrieve it to lend it again. Like Sarah, Betsy Newton's purse was "quite inadequate to the wants of this large town." [62] However, undeterred by her slender purse or the difficulties she faced in Worcester, she contemplated forming a society. After consulting with some friends, she suggested that having a lecture in Worcester would boost the cause. Louisa Phillips also wanted to establish a female society as an auxiliary to the Boston Female Anti-Slavery Society. She did not need a lecturer but advice about organizing the women of North Marshfield, which was "not thickly settled and [had] no village." [63]

Despite the obstacles abolitionists faced, however, Garrison was able to proudly announce in 1834 at the Second Annual Meeting of the New England Anti-Slavery Society: "We have a large number of male and female anti-slavery societies in various parts of the land which embrace the names of thousands who are pledged to the doctrine of immediate emancipation." In actuality, black women's organizations devoted to moral and educational uplift in the free black community as well as to abolitionism predated Garrison's interest in organizing women. In 1832, the African-American Female Intelligence Society in Boston had sponsored the public lectures of Maria W. Stewart, while black women in Salem, Massachusetts, had formed the first female abolitionist society in that city. Before long, female associations were established in major cities like Philadelphia, Boston, and New York; some were integrated, while others were all black or all white. Outside of the cities, associations sprang up in more remote places like Sudbury, Reading, or Groton, Massachusetts, and in mill communities like Lowell or Amesbury Mills. There were societies in Weybridge, Vermont; Dover, New Hampshire; Portland and Bangor, Maine; and Norwich and Brooklyn, Connecticut. In addition to societies for adult women, there were juvenile societies, perhaps modeled on juvenile missionary societies.

And in some places like Fall River, Massachusetts; Limington, Maine; and Jefferson, Ohio, men and women had already formed joint societies.[64]

Historians have made many efforts to explain why people supported abolitionism. Some analyses suggest the psychological factors motivating commitment. Others point to the large social, economic, and cultural forces that helped to create a climate for abolitionism. Scattered records of women abolitionists living in the towns, villages, and cities of the Northeast, the mid-Atlantic, and the Midwest do not reveal the deeper or structural reasons that may have led these mostly ordinary people to embrace an unpopular cause. Nor are there sufficient materials from any of the records to reveal the psychological basis for conviction. But it seems likely that the white woman who embraced this cause connected to her own individual need or "duty" the cultural definition of the female sex as a moral and religious force for good to define a *particular* work in the world. "All I ask," Sarah Baker explained, "is the right to suppress vice and promote virtue in the way and manner [my] conscience dictates." Abolitionism offered an opportunity, a choice, and a direction. For Maria Child, the commitment meant that "old dreams vanished, old associations departed, all things became new. . . . A new stimulus siezed me."[65]

Abolitionism gave a woman a personal emotional focus and allowed her to create a moral identity that was both rooted in and separate from her familial identity. As daughter, wife, and mother, a woman condemned slavery for its sins against her enslaved sisters. Yet her commitment also fulfilled a desire for both a real and imaginative distance from her own domestic situation. In Breemfield, New Jersey, Grace Williams explained that she entered another realm as she did her daily sewing. "Daily as I sit at my needle," she wrote, "I see the turbaned slaves pass casting their anxious glance towards me." When women met in their societies, often listening as one of their numbers read aloud from works about slavery, they also found the psychic space Grace Williams experienced in her own home.[66]

A black woman, on the other hand felt not distance but intimate involvement in her cause. Sarah Douglass quoted approvingly from an English writer who argued that, without "absorbing, heart-rendering compassion for ourselves," there could be no "deeper sympathy for others." Douglass need only look in the mirror to see the face that could belong to a slave. Slaves were, in a very real way, her own "brethren and sisters." The connections a black woman felt with southern slaves meshed with the responsibility she had for free blacks. While early black abolitionists used religious vocabulary as easily as their white counterparts, responsibility to the community, which included themselves, rather than moral duty, gave meaning to their activism.[67]

If the sources fail to reveal the deep and often unconscious roots of ordinary women's commitment to abolitionism, ample evidence discloses those conscious, "mighty and soul moving reasons," as the women of Canton, Ohio, put it, that "render it peculiarly incumbent on women to act in this cause." In 1834, a correspondent to the *Liberator* explained the relationship between the founding documents of the Portland Female Anti-Slavery Association and the motivations of those who joined it. The society's preamble and constitution expressed "a depth of feeling and a profound sense of duty, to the will of the Almighty God, which cannot fail to convince every one that the authors . . . were fully and devoutly impressed with the magnitude and importance of the cause." These carefully considered documents of female associations formed during the 1830s (or borrowed from another society because the ideas struck its members as true) convey what members and onlookers alike understood as the reasons for their association. Combined with letters from ordinary women devoted to the antislavery cause, these materials illuminate the conscious mental and moral world of the antislavery activists of the 1830s.[68]

The concept of moral duty was a critical one in stimulating an abolitionist commitment. Because many women took seriously the assignation of moral and religious power to women and accepted the idea of slavery as a sin, they felt it was their responsibility to act for the slave. Little realizing how duty might expand their notion of what activity was appropriate, women insisted antislavery work was not outside of their sphere but well within its perimeters. The Ohio women who formed the Ashtabula County Female Anti-Slavery Society expressed their understanding of what was demanded of them: "The undersigned ladies . . . under a solemn impression of the reality, extent, & unspeakable evils of the system of slavery" accepted "their obligation" to work for its elimination. In Brooklyn, Connecticut, women declared their willingness to confront the systematic nature of the problem when they decried the "atrocious and complicated system of iniquity." In Canton, Ohio, the preamble for the Ladies Anti-Slavery Society starkly stated, "We are persuaded that slavery is wrong and it ought to be immediately abolished."[69]

For some women, the duty to act was a clear extension of religious faith. Mrs. Kingsbury, for example, considered abolitionism "to be the *cause* of God" and grieved that she was not more "useful in the cause." Amy Rakestraw wrote her sister using the language of one recently converted and desirous to be "the instrument of doing some good." "Pray for me," she begged her sister, "that I may be qualified to be more useful than I ever have been." Doubtless the desire to be more engaged in life, the longing for focus and even excitement, also played a role. Sybil Swetland, for one, revealed to a friend, "I really long to be more active in the drama of life. I long to be actively engaged in something." [70]

While women who joined abolitionist societies believed in female influence, many were unsure how powerful it was. Some accepted the rhetoric, hoping its claim of female power was true. Betsey Lincott, writing from Amesbury Mills, where the members of the female society outnumbered the male, thought that "the great object at which we aim will, ere long, be accomplished," perhaps because she felt that women were carrying out God's purposes. Members of the Brooklyn (Connecticut) Female Anti-Slavery Society also were confident that "female influence is calculated to effect great good in such a cause, as has been abundantly shown" in Great Britain. Others, however, were doubtful, not about the need to act, but about the consequences of their actions. They displayed a modesty about female power or a skepticism about inflated cultural claims. The women who formed the Weybridge Anti-Slavery Society in Vermont expressed conservative views of what they might accomplish. In their constitution they explained, "We are encouraged to throw in our mite by the reflection, that our sphere of action may be more humble than that of our brethren, and an ability to do good proportionately circumscribed—yet historic records portray in lively colors the services of females for the Good of the state." [71]

Conservative (or realistic) though the Vermont women might have been about the limits of female influence, their constitution also expressed the widely shared belief that abolitionism was not only God's cause but also the cause of freedom. The emphasis on natural rights, liberty, and the principles of humanity revealed republican and revolutionary assumptions that were fundamental to the ways in which these women understood slavery. As Abby Cox explained, how could women be worthy of raising their sons for the Republic "if we cared nothing for its interests." References to the principles of humanity that for many women, like Martha Higginson, meant that blacks were "my fellow creatures" with natural rights contributed to the conviction that slavery was wrong. Slavery degraded the principles of American government. It was a disgrace, the Vermont women insisted, "in this land of Christian light and liberty!" [72]

The Weybridge constitution tellingly compared American slavery to the "horrible superstition" in pagan India that forced widows to burn on their husbands' funeral pyres. While the former did not arouse the sympathy of Americans, the latter did. The constitution suggested that Americans not only ignored evils in their midst but also overlooked the ways in which slavery blighted the country. Just as the custom of forcing Indian widows to end their lives with their husbands was a disgrace, so too was the practice of enslaving blacks. The women who joined antislavery societies felt the shame keenly because they accepted the idea of American exceptionalism. The United States was the country of light and liberty, the land of progress, peace, and prosperity. Slavery threatened this vision and therefore must be ended.[73]

Believing that the United States was a specially blessed place, abolitionist women saw their own sex as exceptionally privileged. Women who joined antislavery societies agreed with the 1836 *Anti-Slavery Almanac*'s description of women, those of New England at least, as "favored inhabitants" of their country. This status undergirded their willingness to "engage in the defence of a large class of . . . fellow immortals" and allowed them to act as the conscience of the nation. Demoralized by the "influence of the atrocious system," "voluntarily" engaged in "its barbarities," southern women had lost what was exceptional about American womanhood. While all Christians should pity southern females, women abolitionists appropriated any right southerners had to speak as women to the nation.[74]

Founding documents and letters frequently explained that women joined antislavery societies because they believed collective action was more efficient than individual exertion. This interest in efficiency may seem unimportant, especially when compared to the call of moral duty or patriotism, but it was not. The desire for efficiency showed how quickly women moved beyond the limited and ponderous domestic strategies that leaders had originally suggested as suitable for them. The emphasis on efficiency further revealed that women had accepted some of the values of the market economy, although they were supposedly shielded from it. The ideology of separate spheres drew distinctions between home and workplace that women were already ignoring in an understated and only dimly understood way.[75]

In their efforts to recruit women, abolitionist writers, antislavery editors, and lecturers had adopted a gender- and class-based strategy. When Amos Phelps had dramatically brandished the master's whip, he intended to encourage the women in his audience to feel a special imaginative and sympathetic connection with the female slave. The constitutions and private correspondence from the 1830s reveal that this approach struck a deep chord among women and motivated them to act. "We should be less women," one female society in Ohio explained, "if the nameless wrongs of . . . the slaves of our sex . . . did not fill us with horror" and awaken "a deep per-

Flogging American Women.   Page 100.

The illustration from George Bourne's Picture of Slavery in the United States of America *dramatically portrays the mistreatment of female slaves. Such depictions of the sufferings of slave women touched the hearts and imaginations of many northern abolitionist women. (Boston Athenæum)* sonal interest in this matter." Women undertook antislavery work not so much for slaves in general but for slave women, their *oppressed sisters.*[76]

Slavery robbed black women of the rights, privileges, and protections that white middle-class women believed belonged to women. Slave women were "groaning under the yoke of an insupportable and most degrading bondage." Their masters, without any vestige of "manly shame," covered them with "merciless stripes" and perpetrated "cruel outrage" on their bodies. As a group of Ohio women explained, "while man is scourged a woman is more than scourged she is insulted too." Northern women were horrified that "profligate" and "vile" men degraded "whatever there is of delicacy or dignity, in the name of woman, whatever of innocence or help-lessness in her nature, whatever of purity of loveliness in her character." If southern white women had abandoned their responsibilities, these women considered that "the dignity of our sex is spoil*d*, and we feel call*d* upon to assert that dignity fearlessly and earnestly."[77]

Although the black women who formed the first Salem Female Anti-Slavery Society in 1832 agreed with their white counterparts that union would make them more efficient and that it was important to promote the welfare of their race, they adopted a constitution that offered a different rationale for association. These women appeared most interested in com-bating the prejudice that adversely affected the lives of Salem's free blacks. Their organization supported self-improvement and assistance to "needy" members of Salem's black community. Like the Female Literary Associa-tion of Philadelphia, Salem women had a duty to elevate their race. Self-improvement would "break down the strong barrier of prejudice" and raise African Americans "to an equality with those of our fellow beings, who differ from us in complexion." Prejudice, the women believed, would dis-appear once blacks overcame poverty, lack of education, and bad habits.[78] But, concern with northern blacks did not mean indifference to slavery. In fact, as these women realized, northern racism and the southern slave sys-tem were linked by the belief that blacks were inferior. Destruction of the notion of intellectual inferiority would undermine both.[79]

As no white women could, black women abolitionists felt the cause to be their own. When Sarah Douglass attended a "Mental Feast" with a "number of respectable [black] females in Philadelphia," she explained how her connection to abolitionism occurred. Possibly because free blacks faced so many problems in the North, some, perhaps many, were more concerned with improving their own situation than they were in freeing southern slaves. Douglass confessed that she had not thought much about slaves until about a year before. The appearance of a kidnapper forced her to recognize the fragility of her own status as a free person and how easily she too could be enslaved as long as slavery existed: "I beheld the oppressor lurking on the border of my own peaceful home! I saw his iron hand stretched forth to seize me as his prey, and the cause of the slave became my own." The threat to her well-being and safety led her to abolitionism.[80]

In the spring of 1834, two years after the Salem Female Anti-Slavery Society was formed, "a few ladies, having carefully examined the subject of slavery" in order to determine "what duties—if any, devolve[d] upon the female portion of the community in reference to it," decided they were "obligated to lend their individual and united influences" to working for its elimination. After calling upon many other women in the town, they obtained enough support to form an association, which included women of both races and replaced the all-black association. The Salem black women did not leave any record of what they thought of the transition from an all-black to an integrated organization. Perhaps they agreed with what Sarah Douglass had written to Elizabeth Chandler in 1833. "Lade, we are a poor and ignorant people, but, believe me, we are not ungrateful. I wish it was in my power to give you an idea of the enthusiastic affection which we regard all those dear friends who are advocating immediate emancipation." White support for an unpopular cause won Douglass's appreciation.[81]

Salem women's depiction of themselves as "ladies" expressed their claim to middle-class respectability despite, or perhaps because of, the questionable nature of their cause and the mixed racial membership of their society. For similar reasons, the *Liberator* and other antislavery newspapers emphasized that *ladies* attended antislavery lectures and joined antislavery organizations. In a typical comment, the *Liberator* asserted that the Norwich, Connecticut, Female Anti-Slavery Society had "among its members some of the most respectable ladies in the place."[82] Yet although the women in the Salem Female Anti-Slavery Society considered themselves ladies, some must have had a tenuous grasp on middle-class status and economic security. As the society's president pointed out in 1839, "Nearly all the members of our board support themselves, by dressmaking or teaching school."[83]

Who, in fact, were the women who joined antislavery organizations during the 1830s? The description of the leaders of the Salem Female Anti-Slavery Society highlights the involvement of single women of modest means in that town. The term "ladies" reveals more about the self-conception of women in abolitionist societies than it does about their position in the community.

Studies of female antislavery societies in a few communities across the Northeast have provided a general overview of their membership. In cities like Boston, New York, and Rochester, New York, few of the white women abolitionists belonged to the established elite or made up the ranks of those who had worked in older benevolent causes. Rather, women from newly successful and often recently arrived families became advocates of antislavery. Though they belonged to the emerging middle class of their cities, their status was not yet secure. Joining them in their cause were women from artisan families. Their husbands worked in establishments like bakeries, printing shops, or tailor shops.[84]

The composition of the Boston Female Anti-Slavery Society (BFAS), organized in 1833, reveals the social and economic diversity that characterized the female societies that have been analyzed. Predictably, minister's wives and women from professional families were well represented in the association. The first president, Charlotte Phelps, was married to lecturer and Congregational minister Amos Phelps. A sizable percentage of members belonged to the emerging middle class, families whose livelihood came from manufacturing, sales, and business. Still others were artisans' wives. Some members were single women, like Martha and Lucy Ball, who taught school or who, like Mary Parker, ran boardinghouses in order to support themselves. From the vantage point of Caroline Weston, who belonged to one of the most prominent families connected with the society, most of the BFAS's members came from "narrow circumstances."[85]

Members of urban antislavery societies had varied religious affiliations. While almost all were Protestant and often evangelical, the denomination reflected in the membership of individual female associations mirrored the religious loyalties of their cities. Hicksite Quakers dominated the Philadelphia Female Anti-Slavery Society, for example. In Boston, members tended to belong to the Congregational, Baptist, and Unitarian Churches, while in New York City, many of the women were associated with Presbyterian or Dutch Reform congregations. In Rochester, New York, Presbyterian and Baptist women supported early antislavery. Some had been involved in the series of revivals led by Charles Grandison Finney, the great evangelist of the Second Great Awakening. It was not surprising, then, that the constitution of the Rochester Female Anti-Slavery Society proclaimed that God "made it the duty of all, of every sex, class, and condition in society to do what they can to remove this sin."[86]

Initially the BFAS, like the female antislavery societies in Fall River, New York City, and other northern centers with free black communities, was an all-white organization. Attempts to open the doors to black women met initial resistance. Writing to the BFAS in April 1834, Garrison expressed dismay that "in the minds of a majority of your numbers, [there was] an unwillingness to admit colored females." In Fall River, two Quaker sisters, Elizabeth and Lucy Buffum, invited the "respectable" young black women who had been attending the village's female antislavery society meetings to join and almost brought the society to a premature end. Although they did not mind having the black women at the meetings, some of the society's "leading members . . . did not think it was at all proper to invite them to join the society, thus putting them on an equality with ourselves." In the end, both Boston and Fall River accepted "respectable" black women as members, as did most other female antislavery societies during the 1830s.[87]

In Philadelphia, Hicksite Quaker women forming the female antislavery society welcomed black members from the beginning. Of the original forty-five members, nine were African American women from elite black families. The emphasis of the society's constitution on the sin of northern prejudice reflected its biracial composition. Members pledged themselves to work for emancipation and for "the restoration of the people of color to their inalienable rights." The Philadelphia society was among the most successful of the integrated societies. Although none of the black women ever became president, several served on the board of managers and held minor offices.[88]

Black members of the PFAS came from Philadelphia's most substantial black families and subscribed to conventional gender norms in so far as it was possible. For example, only three of them worked. While membership in the black middle class was typical of early black abolitionists, the Philadelphia women's secure economic situation that allowed them to honor genteel conventions was unusual. Members of racially mixed associations tended to come from more modest and more fragile backgrounds than the Philadelphia women and many of their white associates, and they thus found it difficult to observe the conventions that implied middle-class respectability.

Susan Paul, as the daughter of one of Boston's Baptist ministers, belonged to the city's black elite and was the Boston Female Anti-Slavery Society's most prominent black member. (Other black middle-class members were married to tailors, boardinghouse owners, waiters, and blacksmiths; several were teachers.) Perhaps Paul's status was the reason that a white member of the BFAS described her as "a favorable specimen of the colored race," although apparently others in the black community did not regard her as "one of themselves." Despite her position, Paul experienced a swift reversal of fortune when her father died in 1831. Without his income, her family was in perilous economic circumstances. Forced to move out of their house to cheaper quarters, Paul's mother and her orphaned nieces all

depended on Paul for their livelihood. For ten years Paul supported abolitionism while she worked as a seamstress and as a teacher in a desperate
struggle to meet the family's needs. When, at thirty-four, Paul died from
consumption, the family was "broken up & the children taken by sundry
friends." [89]

Although most black women did not participate in organized abolition
in these early days, most of those who did lived as close or even closer to
the margin than Susan Paul. The vast majority of working black women
labored as washerwomen, domestics, or seamstresses and had little in the
way of financial resources, economic security, or leisure time. Any associational involvement testified to their determination to work for the abolition
of slavery and the improvement of the fortunes of the free black community.
In Hartford County, Connecticut, for instance, Hannah Austin did washing in her own home, provided for an invalid husband and four children,
and still found time to support her church and local antislavery society.[90]

Some black women, like those in New York City; Nantucket; Middleton, Connecticut; and Rochester, New York, chose not to join integrated
societies but preferred to form their own organizations. The racism of
white abolitionists doubtlessly prompted this decision. Even Garrison in
his letter admonishing the BFAS for its exclusionist policy assured the
society to "remember that you are not called upon to decide, that you will
make bosom friends of colored females, or invite them into your parlor,
or eat or drink with them, or walk with them in the streets, (although if
they are truly virtuous and intelligent, you ought not to shrink from these
juxtapositions." Black members attended meetings but sat in a special section reserved for them. When on one occasion a black woman took a seat
in the white section, a member informed her that "colored people were
very well in their place" but apparently not out of it. In Salem, Massachusetts, the racially mixed association formed in 1834 included black women
among its officers, but its constitution held out the hand of friendship and
equality only to those blacks whose "characters and attainments" justified
them. Then, too, black women saw the abolitionist struggle in somewhat
different terms than white women. Although they shared the goal of ending slavery, they found the objective of working for equal rights for free
blacks far more central to abolitionism than most whites. The constitution
of all-black female antislavery societies emphasized the goal of improving
the lives of free blacks.[91]

Women in the female antislavery associations scholars have studied
often came from families active in the abolitionist cause. As wives, sisters,
daughters, and cousins they naturally sympathized with and supported

antislavery. Some grew up in abolitionism. Eliza Earle, for example, dated her commitment "from the hour, when, in earliest childhood, I learned from Father to lisp 'Forced from home and all its pleasures.'" Her cousin, Elizabeth Buffum Chace, felt she too had been "born and baptized into the Anti-Slavery spirit." Lucia Weston, a member of one of Boston's leading abolitionist families, joined a juvenile antislavery society and announced in the unformed handwriting of a young schoolgirl, "We expect to do great things." Susan Paul's uncles were abolitionists, and her brother not only became Garrison's apprentice but was also the first African American to receive a degree from Dartmouth College.[92]

One historian has suggested that single women played a more important role in antislavery societies than they did in benevolent organizations. Certainly, unmarried women were leading figures in the Salem antislavery association as well as in the BFAS, although their prominent presence in the latter group may have partly been a reflection of Boston's large population of single women. It is also true that many of the women joining societies in the 1830s were relatively young. In Boston, a sixth of the women who became members of the BFAS were under the age of twenty. In 1834, the average age of all members was only thirty-two, reflecting perhaps the city's youthful composition; the majority of women in Boston were between the ages of twenty and forty.[93]

Scholars have not intensively studied the patterns of female membership in small towns and rural villages. While impressionistic evidence illuminates similarities between the city and country abolitionists, it also suggests that there may have been greater variety in terms of age and marital status in the composition of nonurban societies than urban organizations. In Reading, Massachusetts, for example, the men and women formed separate antislavery associations in 1833. The combined influence of family and religion was evident in the composition of the two governing bodies. The Reverend Jared Reid headed the male antislavery society, while his wife, Sarah, became the president of the female association. No doubt, many members of the society came from his congregation. The vice presidents and treasurers of each organization were husband-wife teams. In fact, three families, the Parkers, the Peabodys, and the Kingmans, accounted for half of the officers of the two societies. Similarly, in Blissfield, Michigan, family ties linked together the members of the society. Only four of the eighteen women were not obviously related to either one another or to men in the organization formed in 1838. In Danvers, Massachussetts, the pattern was similar, with two Quaker families providing the nucleus for organizing.[94]

Family ties might have helped bring women into association, but they did not necessarily keep women involved for long. Hannah Smith, writing in 1839 from Glastonbury, Connecticut, reported that the previous year there had been an effort to form a society in Hartford. The women, Hannah thought, had joined because their husbands were abolitionists, and they hardly appeared to understand abolitionist principles. "Indeed," she concluded, "I do not know of one Antislavery woman of the right stamp in Connecticut, of sufficient information & energy to organize a society or manage its concerns." This failure supported Garrison's insistence that women must be knowledgeable about their cause.[95]

The relationship between leadership, membership, and marital status appears to have varied so much that patterns are difficult to articulate. In Salem as well as in Boston, single women played important roles in leading their societies. In Reading, however, married women dominated the leadership, while in Amesbury Mills both married and single women shared leadership responsibilities. In terms of general membership, Elizabeth Wright reported from Newburyport, Massachusetts, that the society there "consists chiefly of aged and middle aged persons, who have families"; Pauline Garry, writing from Stoneham, Massachusetts, described "a number" of the society as "misses," although others were "laboring women who discharge the cares & duty of a family."[96]

While some rural associations may have included a few of the community's prominent women, members often described themselves in humble terms. In Concord, New Hampshire, Mary Clark explained that "we are few and a feeble band compared with what we might be in this town. Most of our wealthiest women are either neutral or auxiliary to the American Union, alias Colonization, alias Liberian cause." This disinterest in abolitionism on the part of powerful and affluent women was also the case in Stoneham, Maine, where none of the society was a volunteer "from the circles of wealth and fashion." Reinforcing this view of the disinterest of the leading women were the references abolitionist women made to their own resources, their lack of domestic help, and sometimes their inferior education. Experience Billings, from Foxborough, Massachusetts, confessed both her "ignorance & want of ability to write correctly" and her limited means. In many cases, limited means must have indicated modest economic circumstances and the shortage of ready cash rather than poverty. As Louisa Phillips pointed out, the people of North Marshfield were poor but comfortable. And a member of the Lynn Female Anti-Slavery Society revealed that, "although most of us may think ourselves poor," it was only in comparison to "those who abound in the wealth and luxuries of the world."[97]

Coming after the efforts of the 1830s to draw women into the abolitionist cause, her appeal suggested some of the consequences for involvement. Those women who read and shared antislavery newspapers, talked with friends and neighbors, attended antislavery lectures, and took the step of forming an association sometimes found that their decisions brought "insult and derision" as well as "ill report" and "persecution." In 1840, when Ellen Sands wrote an appeal to the Young Ladies of Maine, asking for their help with the cause, she remembered "many a familiar face whose look expresses surprise, and on whose lips rests a something like contempt; and from voices which are music to my heart, I hear reproachful, and unbelieving enquiry—Are you an *Abolitionist*? To such I would promptly reply that—I am."[98] In the village of Florence, Pennsylvania, one woman who attended a debate on the relative merits of colonization and immediate emancipation rose to show her support for emancipation even after being labeled a vile abolitionist. "For my part," she explained, "if I once espouse a cause upon conviction of its truth, I am not ashamed to adhere to it, if it should cost me some reproach and ridicule."[99]

Not all the consequences were quite so traumatic, of course. As the poet and antislavery writer Elizabeth Chandler found, boycotting goods produced by slave labor was mainly an expensive inconvenience. Unfamiliar free products were often inferior, incurring time-consuming and often expensive trial-and-error. They demanded cooking experiments and produced culinary disasters, as Hannah Robie discovered during her "one or two attempts to make candy with our white sugar." Occasionally, principles demanded some small sacrifice. Deborah Weston's commitment to free products prevented her from eating "almost everything good" when she was entertained in New Bedford, but she had hopes that she was embarrassing her hostesses into switching to free labor goods. She was also resigned to having no new calico gowns and asked her aunt if they might trade dresses so that she would have something different to wear.[100]

Even something so seemingly innocent as acting upon free labor principles could occasionally involve a woman in an unpleasant social situation. Deborah Weston's comments about her visits in New Bedford hinted at the possibilities of creating a confrontation and of appearing rude. In a time when women's observance of social norms was considered a sign of her membership in the respectable middle class, deviance might bear a price. Deborah Weston, with a prominent family behind her, apparently could afford to be more casual about social approval than a young woman, Mary Ann, who visited Deborah's sister in Groton. "As soon as we were alone," Anne Weston explained, "she burst forth; it appears, that the day before, at Dr. Cutter's[,] on her declining slave labour, some how or other, the mine exploded." The situation had been so upsetting that Mary Ann could not even describe it in detail. " 'Dont ask me to tell you any more' said she 'for if I talk I shall get to crying.' " Anne responded by quieting and comforting the young woman, plying her with free labor blancmange and cake and assuring her "the storm would blow over." [101]

The more public step of forming an association might go off without incident and represented an important collective affirmation of commitment. This was the experience of the group of Dover, New Hampshire, women who met in the Methodist parsonage in February 1835. Inspired by concerts of prayer for the slave, the women decided to work collectively. At their organizing meeting, they established a committee to secure signatures for the constitution and were soon in operation. A similar process resulted in the creation of the Brooklyn Female Anti-Slavery Society. In 1834, a group of women gathered in a local hotel to consider what they might do for the slave. They heard several "interesting" articles read aloud, then "a very thrilling 'Appeal to American ladies' by a colored female." Conversation led to a unanimous vote in favor of forming an association. Then, as in Dover, New Hampshire, the women observed the rituals connected with beginning a voluntary organization. They formed a committee charged with preparing the constitution, drawing up a slate of officers, and starting a correspondence with other female associations.[102]

But women's involvement in abolitionism often provoked heated responses. When a woman from Uxbridge, Massachusetts, remarked in 1835 that there was much to discourage the women, she was not exaggerating. Like their counterparts in many communities, both large and small, the Uxbridge women faced "ridicule, persecution and danger." As lecturer Amos Phelps well knew, no matter what he expected ahead of time, "furious opposition" to his lectures and efforts to organize antislavery societies could arise.[103]

Throughout the 1830s, antislavery men and women in both rural and urban places faced behavior ranging from insulting and rude remarks to physical assault. When Garrison had first established the *Liberator* and issued his challenge to the American Colonization Society, most people disregarded or dismissed his variety of abolitionism. But as the antislavery movement gained adherents and the number of antislavery societies proliferated, opposition gathered strength. From 1834 to 1837, the *Liberator* and two other abolitionist papers, the *Philanthropist* and the *Emancipator*, took note of 157 antiabolitionist mob actions in the North. Some of the mobs were organized with specific and limited goals. In 1835, in Utica, New

York, for example, an unruly crowd forced an antislavery convention to end its meeting and wreaked destruction on the offices of the local newspaper that had written in favor of the convention. Other crowd actions were unplanned, however, and degenerated into orgies of violence, destruction, and death. These mobs included men of substance, manufacturers and merchants, and working-class artisans, farmers, and unskilled laborers. Fears of amalgamation, the desire to maintain the political and economic status quo, and deep-seated concerns about the unraveling of communal and family ties already threatened by economic change all played a part in motivating mob activity.[104]

Violence was especially likely to occur around organizing activities. From Portland, Maine, Merriam Hussey reported that the "fury of our opposers" had made people fearful of hearing antislavery lectures. Maine, however, was not as volatile as other New England states. Connecticut, where Phelps experienced "furious opposition" that stiffened his resolve to "stay and see the battle through," was the New England state most prone to violence when antislavery sympathizers began to organize, followed by New Hampshire and Rhode Island.[105]

Phelps's account of his troubles in Concord, New Hampshire, sheds light on what could face women who ventured forth to bear witness to their hatred of slavery. He wrote his wife that he had had a "grand meeting of the ladies and formed a ladies Anti-Slavery Society." But the occasion provoked "almost a mob. However no heads broken and no harm done farther than the throwing of one or two small stones through the windows and crying once or twice 'out with the ladies' etc." Undaunted, the women refused to leave the meeting. "We kept on talking until we had done and then took the names of such ladies (some 55 in all) who were willing to be organised into a society. The meeting was a grand one of the cause."[106]

An insight into the reaction of one of the women present comes from a letter written to her friend. The way this Concord woman describes the incident does not mean that she had not been fearful as the glass shattered and the male cries grew louder, but she distanced herself from the dangers of the situation by adopting a mocking tone. She told her friend of the "ridiculous scene" that had occurred, provoked by "poor cowards" who had "wracked their ingenuity" to come up with some method of scaring the women. She pricked male pride and prowess with her reference to the "war cry of these heroic leaders" ("out with the ladies") and the glorious battle that featured flying "pieces of glass." In a more serious vein, she soberly reflected, "Was it not appalling?"[107]

Caroline Weston, who was in Boston during the height of anti-abolition violence in 1835, expressed her fears in her diary. During the meetings of the New England Anti-Slavery Society, news came of mob action in Abington. Caroline spent a tense day, expecting trouble at any moment. In the morning, she "staid at home in great tribulation—thinking every noise I heard was the coming mob." Later, "as soon as school was over I ran down the street to learn how the battle went—I met a thorough abolitionist coming up looking comfortable so turned back." In the evening, Caroline went to a concert of prayer for the slave. Even as the prayer meeting went forward, she worried. "We supposed that the mob would turn out of course but we have a quiet & orderly meeting." [108]

If many women were frightened at the prospect of violence, others bravely confronted it and tried to use social norms to protect antislavery lecturers. They reasoned that men would—or should—think twice before hurting a lady. This was obviously the strategy in Camfield, Ohio. The speaker there was pelted with eggs, and although the speaker's sons raised their umbrellas to protect their father, the situation was lurching out of control. At this point, "the ladies closed around the lecturer, and the men formed a circle around *them*, and thus escorted, he proceeded to his carriage." [109]

Ohio lecturer Marius Robinson described several incidents in which women attempted to assist him. In Hartford, faced by "the veriest savages I ever saw," Marius met with "a fearless, noble band of women." When the meeting was delayed, the women tried to shame the opposition by praying aloud "that the Lord would make the wrath of men to praise him" rather than venting this wrath on their speaker. At another unruly lecture, one of the women "climbed into the meetinghouse at the window when I was hemmed in by the mob in the pulpit, determined to see what was going on and if possible to aid in my rescue." The bravery of this woman demonstrated that it was possible not only to manipulate gender norms but to also upset them. Rather than men lending their protection to weak women, strong women were rescuing besieged men. [110]

While such mob scenes must have deterred many men and women from responding to the abolitionist message, it may have cemented the loyalty of others. Persecution made the cause more, not less, important, and support more necessary. Living in a culture familiar with the Bible, it was not difficult to find parallels between the experience of abolitionists and early Christians or the prophets. Deborah Weston admitted that she found the trouble in Boston to be one of "the most distressing & exciting" times she had ever experienced. Indeed, the Boston Female Anti-Slavery Society regarded the events of 1835 as "exciting and thrilling," subjects of "great &

intense interest." So involving and stimulating were these events that the women had to be "careful that they do not become the topic of all absorbing interest. . . . that we do not forget the Slave himself." [111]

During the 1830s, abolitionist newspapers, lecturers, and already converted friends, neighbors, and kin urged women to remember the slave. The surviving sources do not reveal whether women initially played a significant role in Garrison's campaign for immediate emancipation, although the support of some for the free produce movement and the literary antislavery publications of others warn against assuming that they were altogether absent. In any case, the unpopularity of the cause made leaders feel that the support of women was at least symbolically desirable. What responsibilities women might assume only revealed themselves slowly, and few abolitionists, male or female, perceived the consequences of encouraging women to use their moral influence in the cause. While many people made soothing statements about the congruence of abolitionism with the usual female concerns, the efforts to teach women how to argue the abolitionist case and to encourage women to circulate antislavery materials and to recruit others suggested that the work of abolitionism might indeed take women far from the kitchen and parlor.

As leaders were groping toward an understanding of women's part in antislavery, women themselves were also finding their way in the new reform. Women articulated the powerful reasons that drew them to the new cause and emphasized the importance of listening to the call of moral duty. They began to learn new skills and ran the risks that went along with advocating an unpopular position. As they joined antislavery societies, they confronted organizational issues common to associational life and particular challenges related to the nature of their reform. As Mary Clark, from Concord, New Hampshire, explained in a letter to the Philadelphia Female Anti-Slavery Society, she, who relished the work, and other members of the antislavery society were more and more convinced that women especially were called to the work of abolitionism. In that work, there was a special part suitable for females and not adapted "to the sterner nature of man." [112]

Chapter 2
Antislavery Societies
The 1830s

Oh, turn ye not displeased away though I

should sometimes seem

Too much to press upon your ear, an oft

repeated theme;

The story of the negro's wrongs is heavy at my

heart,

And can I choose but wish from you a

sympathizing part?[1]

Although abolitionists continued to form antislavery societies until the Civil War, the 1830s were the heyday of antislavery organizational efforts. Antislavery advocates established associations on the local, county, state, and national levels. While membership figures may not be entirely trustworthy, by 1837 there were reportedly more than 1,000 state and local antislavery societies with at least 100,000 members.[2]

Many of those joining antislavery societies lived in rural communities, villages, and small towns clustered in New England, western New York, along the Pennsylvania-Ohio border, and in parts of the Midwest where New Englanders and Quakers from the South and the mid-Atlantic had settled. While abolitionist organizers could hardly afford to ignore the cities, they had followed the spirit of advice given to Lewis Tappan in 1836 by the energetic and compelling antislavery agent Theodore Weld. "Let the great cities *alone*: they must be burned down by *back fires*. The springs to touch in order to move them *lie in the country*. . . . Let every thing in the shape of agents, papers, etc. be poured upon the *country*—in the *country*—the villages—and the smaller cities in the interior."[3]

Common assumptions during the 1830s that associated women with virtue and characterized abolitionism as a moral reform made female support for the cause almost a legitimizing device. If the presence of women reinforced the moral character of abolitionism, women's moral character should make them naturally interested in the plight of the slave. As Rev. Ludlow reminded the annual meeting of the New York State Anti-Slavery Society in 1836, women were the "most important and powerful coadjutors in the glorious cause." Indeed, "every woman who is worthy of the name of woman," needed "only to be informed upon the subject, to find all the noble sympathies of her heart enlisted in the cause of emancipation." Although this heavily gendered appeal did not mesh with the Hicksite Quaker women's more egalitarian understanding of their gender, many evangelical women found it persuasive. Exhortations to American women to enter the ranks of abolitionism bore fruit as women established local and county female antislavery societies and held three national conventions in the last three years of the decade. Even before the controversy over the participation of women in the antislavery movement began to divide abolitionists at the end of the decade, some women and men were meeting together in joint associations.[4]

How many women joined antislavery societies is not known. Some figures are suggestive, however. Of 183 local antislavery organizations in Massachusetts in 1838, for example, 41 of these were women's associations. In addition, 13 juvenile societies, most likely supervised by women and primarily composed of "young misses," flourished.[5] Writing from Newburyport, Massachusetts, the president of the female antislavery society there noted that the men's society had disintegrated and observed "what is done [here] is chiefly by females." Yet no records for the Newburyport society exist. Even though the work of female antislavery societies was considerable and vital to the survival of the reform, the remaining records of women's organizations are few. Combined with other primary sources, however, these records suggest women's contributions to abolitionism and the ways in which they created and attempted to maintain an institutional identity. Sources also illuminate the difficulties, some common to male and female voluntarism, others specific to female societies, women abolitionists faced in organized antislavery.[6]

An examination of female institutional life reveals the fundamental importance of a gendered view of the world. Although seemingly conservative in its definition of woman's sphere as domestic and private, it was capable of demanding behavior that took women beyond the boundaries of what the culture at large defined as womanly. Abolitionism was not the only reform to highlight the tensions in and the elasticity of woman's sphere. Temperance and some moral reform activities also pressed against gender boundaries. But abolitionism raised these issues in a particularly vivid way. While most ministers did not denounce temperance or argue that prostitution should be left alone, many authoritative voices condemned abolitionist activities and women's participation in them. Women involved in abolitionism could not avoid confronting the ambiguities implicit in the view of women as society's moral voice.

As Chapter 1 pointed out, the formation of female antislavery societies might result from the efforts of a visiting lecturer or local clergy, or the exertions of individual women persuaded of the necessity of immediate emancipation. Some, like Louisa Phillips of North Marshfield, Massachusetts, were already working for the cause in their own communities before deciding the time had come to organize collectively. These women approached friends, neighbors and relatives in person to win support for the proposed society. Others, like Eliza Chace in Rhode Island and Betsy Cowles in Ohio, undertook letter writing campaigns to encourage women outside their own neighborhoods to start up female societies.[7]

The initiation of a female society could turn into a public ceremony demonstrating women's collective support for abolitionism. In the fall of 1835, after Theodore Weld's lecture in Austinburg, Ohio, 150 women were so solemnly impressed by "the reality, extent, & unspeakable evils of the system of Slavery" that they formed the Ashtabula County (Ohio) Female Anti-Slavery Society and formally signed their names under the society's constitution. Less impressive in terms of numbers but similar in terms of dynamics was the experience of women in Dighton, Massachusetts. Although "their was not more than three or four who had thought much on the subject of slavery," the eloquence of English lecturer George Thompson was so moving that twenty-three women formed an antislavery society.[8]

Such public rites had overtones of an evangelical revival meeting. Given the background of antislavery lecturers, many of whom were ministers or had contemplated entering the church, the evangelical atmosphere was predictable. Like sinners poised on the anxious seat, exhorted to come forward and be saved, those listening to antislavery lectures were urged to come forward and commit themselves to the holy cause of abolitionism.[9]

Though a spellbinding outside lecturer could act as the catalyst for the ceremony of commitment, local women might orchestrate the event. In Mellville, Massachusetts, some ladies of the village, recognizing they had "too long [been] slumbering over their duty," invited the antislavery lecturer Charles Burleigh to address them. At the end of his address, a constitution was circulated, and twenty-nine of those present signed it.[10]

Often the formation of an association must have been both less dramatic and public. A woman, alone or with a group of like-minded associates, called her friends and relatives together to consider the possibility of establishing a female antislavery society. Such a gathering could lead to immediate action, as it did when women in Brooklyn, Connecticut, met in Davison's Hotel during the summer of 1834. Fired up by the reading of several articles, the women voted to form an association and appointed a committee to prepare a constitution and a list of nominations for officers. But such congeniality and decisiveness was not always the case. The absence of a charismatic lecturer and the social character of the occasion also provided abolitionist opponents an opportunity to disrupt organizing efforts. In Dorcester, Massachusetts, a woman dubbed "Mrs. Pro-slavery" outmaneuvered a core of women who described themselves as modest and retiring. Her zeal against the idea of an antislavery society was such that the "large and respectable meeting, composed of ladies from all parts of the town, was dissolved." Her antagonism, however, merely delayed the formation of the society.[11]

Even after women decided to form an association, they faced a good deal of work before the organization could function. As Lucy Wright commented, "It takes us some time to get into operation." While lecturer James Thome persuaded fifteen or twenty women to join the newly formed Ladies Society after his lecture in Geneva, Ohio, Mrs. Cowles and a few others had to hunt down thirty additional women they thought they could get as supporters.[12]

Beyond recruiting for the association, the organizers had to make important initial decisions. The Dover, New Hampshire, women who agreed to begin an antislavery society in 1835, for example, were quickly involved in the weighty business of selecting a preamble and constitution. This was no formulaic task. As one member of another female antislavery society explained, a preamble constituted a society's "creed." And like any creed it would serve not only as an expression of collective identity but also as a statement of belief to be used with outsiders. In their preamble and constitution, Dover women stressed the themes of sin and duty and used temperance as an example of the individual and collective transformation that a radical reform might achieve. They carefully outlined their goals: immediate emancipation, the elevation of the character and condition of colored people, the circulation of literature, and fund-raising. With one of their major recruiting tools completed, they then selected a committee of four women (three single and one married) to canvass the other women in the community and secure their signatures to the document. Eventually 388 were listed as members of the new society.[13]

The use to which the Dover women put their new constitution makes it apparent why some abolitionist women decided to confront the question of propriety in their founding document. If women were to persuade their more timid neighbors to join in antislavery work, it was just as well to address their misgivings at once. Groton, Massachusetts, women adopted a constitution that not only called slavery a flagrant violation of God's principles but also emphasized that women had a duty as women to do what they could because slave women suffered "in more than equal proportion." In Winthrop, Maine, the female association's preamble stated that "women have intellects, sentiments, feelings and souls, . . . [and therefore] they have something to do, when intellects are wasted, sentiments perverted, feelings outraged, and souls lost." Similarly, women in Canton, Ohio, stated in their preamble, "We consider that we are *not moving out of our proper sphere* as females when we assume a *public* stand in favor of our *oppressed sisters.*" They went on to document the "mighty and soul moving reasons which render it peculiarly incumbent on women to act in this cause." [14]

No doubt women who were securing signatures for the constitution and members for the new society first sought out those sympathetic to their goals. In the summer of 1837 in Boylston, Massachusetts, Mrs. Sanford, the minister's wife, made calls to gain support for the proposed female abolitionist society. Sixty-year-old Mary White, daughter of a minister, wife of a farmer and storekeeper, Aaron White, and mother of ten children was an obvious choice for the proposed society. She had amply indicated her interest in religious and reform causes. Mary taught Sabbath school, attended temperance meetings, and accompanied her daughter Eliza to maternal meetings. For over a year she had joined in prayer meetings for the slaves and attended general meetings on the subject of slavery. Though Mrs. Sanford could only have sensed the cumulative impact of these activities, Mary's diary shows a deepening commitment to emancipation. After recording that she had heard an antislavery lecture, Mary routinely composed short prayers of supplication. On the day that she heard two sermons as well as an antislavery lecture at the town hall, for example, Mary ended her diary entry hoping that "the Lord . . . grant deliverance to the poor slaves." When Mrs. Sanford carried the constitution for the proposed society to the White farm one June evening, Mary responded positively. The next day, Mary came to the town hall to help in the formation of the society and to attend the prayer meeting afterward. Mary White and her daughters would continue to be active in the antislavery cause for years.[15]

Mary Frizell Manter, a resident of Walpole, Massachusetts, a member of the Baptist Church, and the mother of a little boy whom she persuaded to "put . . . all his money into the Anti-slavery cause" was also the kind of woman whom those soliciting signatures would target. Though Mary Manter was "poor and not much likely to be of much use in the world," her willingness "to be a poor despised one" and follow the demands of duty must have been apparent to friends and neighbors.[16]

The number of signatures that some women were able to secure suggests, though it does not prove, that, in some communities, female organizers moved beyond the obvious sympathizers to talk to those who had slight interest in their proposal. Such personal encounters, whether planned or unexpected, demanded more than the physical presentation of the constitution. Women found themselves explaining and trying to convince others about the nature of the cause.

In their efforts to win adherents to the cause of immediate emancipation, women drew upon published materials and information about slavery they had read or heard and resorted to a range of persuasive techniques. Sophia Davenport left a record of the techniques she used to bring acquaintances to "a right state of mind." Sophia and a friend cooperated in their venture; one evening the friend stayed up until after midnight presenting the case for immediate emancipation to Mr. Ford; the next night it was Sophia's turn. She read aloud "Mrs. Child's chapter upon prejudices." The treasurer of the Dorchester (Massachusetts) Female Anti-Slavery Society gave an account revealing similar tactics and her willingness to exploit social situations. During her stay in West Chester, Pennsylvania, the Dorchester woman received a visit from two ladies who were slaveholders. They challenged her, saying, "You certainly do not pretend that slavery is a sin, for we can prove by Scripture that it is not." Undaunted, the Dorchester officer replied that she could easily prove their error. "We then had a long conversation upon the subject, after which they took home, at my request, a copy of Miss Smith's Appeal to Christian Women of America."[17]

In Canton, Ohio, lecturer James Thome managed to secure the commitment of two young Baltimore women, daughters of a Maryland slaveholder. After they "proclaimed their conversion," they, in turn, "began to visit amongst their acquaintances and to labor with the first Ladies of the place to *convert them*. A ladies Society was formed and they both joined it." Two days after her conversion, one of the young women attended a "gay party, where there was not a single abolitionist, but where *ridiculing abolitionism* was the *order of the evening*." She passed through this occasion "boldly," proclaiming her newly found faith and producing "a great sensation."[18]

It was not uncommon for those engaged in organizing activities to use the term conversion to describe the fruits of their labors. Women who felt deeply about spiritual matters and the sacred nature of their cause naturally turned to religious terminology to describe their recruiting efforts. But their word choice also revealed the magnitude of the change that they sought and the sacred process in which they felt engaged. Like a religious conversion, acceptance of the antislavery cause signified a profound transformation. The moment of commitment, marked formally with the signing of the constitution, represented the beginning of a new life.

Benevolent and religious associations were a familiar part of the nineteenth-century rural and urban landscape for many northern middle-class women, including Mary White of Boylston, Massachusetts. Some historians have suggested that abolitionist societies attracted women whose social and class position precluded membership in traditional benevolent organizations. Evelina Smith's comment that "we see so much pride, ambition & desire of distinction, intermingled with benevolent purpose" suggests not only her critical perspective of benevolent activities but perhaps also her social location.[19] While organizational records and letters do not yield definitive evidence on the connection of women in antislavery associations to traditional benevolence, many recognized that they stood outside of the elite circle of women who directed established benevolent societies. Most antislavery women probably had participated in less formal groups like prayer meetings, but many confessed to meager organizational experience. As M. P. Rogers in Concord, New Hampshire, explained, "we are altogether new hands, and entirely unacquainted with the management of societies." Ann Buckman from Newton, Pennsylvania, echoed Rogers's sense of not knowing "how to proceed in our business."[20]

Whether experienced or not, especially in the first days of organizing and in small country places, women who were trying to establish female antislavery societies felt the heavy weight of responsibility. Abolitionism was not just another cause, it was *the* cause. The path was new and unfamiliar. For advice and moral support, they turned to other female antislavery societies and sympathizers and, in the process, created a grassroots network which, in the long term, was perhaps more critical to survival of the cause than the formation of societies themselves.[21]

When the women in Brooklyn, Connecticut, formed their association, they wrote to societies in Boston, Philadelphia, and New York to discover "what specific departments of labor" each was planning to undertake. In her reply, D. W. Bell, the corresponding secretary of the New York society, confessed her group's inexperience: "*This* we feel, *we* have *yet* to learn, as *we* like yourselves, are still in our infant state, not being quite four months old." She included, as requested, a copy of their constitution, although she thought "probably you have before *this*, arranged *such* as you think best suited to your necessities."[22]

Societies not only exchanged copies of constitutions but also offered advice and shared information ranging from the format of meetings to their plans for the future. As Boston corresponding secretary Mary Grew explained in her letter to the Reading (Massachusetts) Female Anti-Slavery Society, "We apprehend that much benefit may be derived from a mutual acquaintance with each other's plans, regulations, methods of appropriating funds, etc."[23]

So important was the creation of this female network to the early life of female antislavery societies that when women of Fitchburg, Massachusetts, formed their antislavery society in 1837, they made one of their objectives "epistolary social intercourse." Like Mary Grew, Fitchburg women realized that "intercommunication" could "stir up our minds, strengthen faith, confirm hope, and increase the ardor of love, and the fervor of prayer."[24]

The publication of the Fitchburg Female Anti-Slavery Society's founding documents in the *Liberator* made the society's goals and methods of procedure available to all who read the newspaper. In their efforts to exploit channels of communication, abolitionist women became part of the "new informational environment" created by the communications revolution of the early decades of the century.[25] Relying upon both the postal service and newspapers, female abolitionists were engaged in creating a new kind of "imagined community" that was able, as Mary Clark explained, to overcome hundreds of miles and lack of personal acquaintance. Unlike the imagined male community that derived its identity from reading political news, the antislavery community drew its strength from shared feelings and a sense of personal intimacy between women. Insistent though they were in claiming the status of "lady" in their dealings with the public, women felt comfortable in forgetting the rules of propriety that usually governed their social relations. As Melanie Ammidon explained in her letter to the Philadelphia Female Anti-Slavery Society (PFAS), "We shall forget all those little forms of etiquette, which under other circumstances we might adhere to." While the absence of familiar conventions might lend an air of abruptness to communications, the "community of interests" and the "bonds" between women compensated for any awkwardness.[26]

Abolitionist women freely adopted the conventions of friendship with those who were technically strangers. "We are yet made friends and sisters," explained Anne Weston, a theme repeated by other women over and over. In a letter to Betsy Cowles, Lucy Wright of Talmadge, Ohio, wrote that, "although an entire stranger," she saw Betsy as a "sister." As she explained, she had "confidence in addressing you" because of the "unanimity of sentiment in the sacred cause of *Liberty*."[27]

During the early stages of institutional life, abolitionist women made key decisions that helped shape their organizations' identities, the roles their societies would play in members' lives, and the ways in which they would view themselves within their organizations. The organizational structure of female antislavery societies was fairly uniform and typical of antebellum voluntary associations. The set of officers included a president, vice president, treasurer, corresponding secretary, and/or recording secretary. In some associations, the emphasis on reading and disseminating antislavery literature resulted in the addition of a librarian to the group. Every society also had a group of women managers. Sometimes they were referred to as counselors or collectors, suggesting somewhat different conceptions of what function those holding this position were to serve.

The decision, often expressed in the constitution, about the frequency of meetings was a critical one. It helped to determine the roles and commitment of both officers and the membership at large. Infrequent meetings, especially when combined with a large membership, meant that either the officers or a core of activists bore the responsibility for maintaining the vitality and carrying on the work of the organization. In Boston, a small group of women, most of whom did not hold office, ran that society on a day-to-day basis. Although they might well be involved in major projects like petition drives, many members (who numbered almost 300 by 1836) participated in the society mainly by attending quarterly and annual meetings. In Philadelphia, too, the board of managers made the decisions and then presented them to the society at large.[28]

When associations met more frequently, once or twice a month, or even weekly, a much greater chance existed that members would share the work and that the distinction between officers and members would be blurred. The report the secretary of the Brooklyn Female Anti-Slavery Society gave at the third annual meeting in 1837 suggested the organization's informal mode of operation and the collective nature of its efforts. Although none of the officers had kept minutes, the society was in a healthy state. Numbers had increased to fifty-six and "notwithstanding the silence of these records for the past year, our meetings had for the most part been continued as formerly once in two weeks, many of them well attended, and rendered profitable to our cause." Dover, New Hampshire, women apparently found that quarterly meetings to transact business were too infrequent and, in December 1836, their minutes reported that a number of ladies had also organized a sewing circle to meet one afternoon a week to make clothes for poor black students at Oneida Institute.[29]

The variety of arrangements suggests not only institutional vitality but also the varied meanings of participation. In some abolitionist societies, especially those that met infrequently, membership normally represented an insignificant involvement in terms of time and effort. Periodically members might work on a special project, but the abolitionist commitment functioned on the margins of life. In contrast, officers and the small circle of activists in such associations would find that antislavery could become almost a full-time job. Certainly, for the corresponding secretary, writing letters and copies of letters took a substantial amount of time. As Mary Clark of Concord wryly observed. "We Anti-Slavery secretaries must learn to write fast."[30]

For women who belonged to organizations that met regularly and often, membership represented a continuing thread in a busy life that was crowded with other interests and responsibilities. Mary White's diary entries, while lacking in details and certainly reticent about her emotional responses to her antislavery work, do give some idea of the part antislavery played in her life. In June 1837 she helped to form the Boylston Female Anti-Slavery Society. During that month, she attended several antislavery meetings, talked over a petition her minister brought to her house, and perhaps signed the document. A letter she wrote to Maria Chapman of the Boston Female Anti-Slavery Society at the end of the month indicated that antislavery was obviously a topic of family conversation: she reported that her daughter, Mary, was carrying two petitions around the neighborhood for signatures. As summer progressed into fall, along with her notations about church, daily chores, the weather, family activities, and deaths in the neighborhood, she recorded attending several more antislavery meetings, including one "very interesting lecture" given by the Grimké sisters. The commitment was clear and ongoing, but it was obviously sandwiched among other responsibilities to her church and her family. The next year, Mary added some afternoons of "work for the antislavery Society," probably sewing, and in October she did some calling to get signatures for antislavery petitions. Interspersed with these activities must have been numerous discussions about antislavery matters. For example, Mary recorded in June 1840 that she had visitors one afternoon and enjoyed "a very pleasant interview[. T]he subjects conversed upon the subject of Slavery on the influence of peace Societies & on the precidence of revivals of religion."

The rhythms of commitment revealed in Mary White's diary may well capture the part that abolitionism played in the day-to-day life of most women participating in the cause. As her diary shows, Mary was well known in her neighborhood as an abolitionist. In November 1841, she recorded that she had received a visit from Abby Kelley in January 1841 and that she also accompanied her minister when he called on the famous Grimké sisters. But Mary spent only a small part of her time and energy on abolitionist work. She faithfully attended meetings, but her domestic chores must have meant she was tired when she went to some of them. Surely she was fatigued in November 1841 when she went to a meeting after making several barrels of applesauce.[31]

Another important decision that affected the collective identity of an antislavery society concerned membership. Founding documents often included a statement of eligibility. The female antislavery society organized at the Chatham Street Chapel in New York in 1834, for example, opened membership to any woman "(not a slaveholder) approving of the principles of this Society, and contributing annually one dollar." In the village of Loudon, New Hampshire, membership dues of the sewing circle were in keeping with country ways and set at less than twenty-five cents annually. While abolitionism was a moral duty, constitutions revealed their social and economic assumptions about who might become a member. Abolitionist women might not have much money nor belong to the social elite, but they considered themselves ladies who could spare a mite for society dues or, like Mary Manter, could afford to give up some of the middle-class niceties of life. As Mary explained, "I have worn no ornament for some time and I wore no gloves in the summer and some things I do without so I can do a little in the cause of humanity." [32]

Perhaps because some abolitionists were less than secure in their own class position, they did not welcome the involvement of women whom they did not consider "ladies" or at least marginally middle class. In Lynn, Massachusetts, where many of the antislavery society's members were the wives and daughters of shoemakers, members were reminded at the second annual meeting that their individual duty toward abolitionism had not ended when they joined the society. Each woman had an individual duty to perform in the shop, school, kitchen, and, revealingly, "the parlor." The society did make some accommodations to hard times in 1837 with a resolution to waive the fee for women if they could furnish an article for the antislavery fair in Boston. Still, that resolution was followed by one that suggested fair articles should be "particular and handsome."[33]

While the Lynn society made some concessions on membership, a coterie of members in New Bedford demonstrated their wish to exclude certain undesirables. "Last sat," reported one New Bedford resident, "there was a kind of meeting not a regular one however. . . . There it was decided by two or three members that the clause in the constitution which said that any one can join by paying 50 cents &c—should be altered—that no one should join till the society has approved. . . . The reason they give is that . . . [a certain lady] has joined, & they want no such person among them."[34]

Racial assumptions about membership also operated. Although race was not mentioned directly in clauses dealing with membership qualifications, the term "lady" had race- as well as class-based overtones. In the North, most blacks lived in urban centers. Thus, in rural and small-town communities that lacked an African American population, women may have been unconscious of any racial prejudice. But in cities like Fall River or New Bedford, where. by 1838, blacks made up 8 percent of the population, the presence of women of color at meetings forced a clarification of values about race. Some of the Fall River white women who "did not think it was at all proper to invite them to join the society" were opposed to putting African American women "on an equality with ourselves." Other members disagreed, "maintained . . . [their] ground," and brought the "respectable young colored women" into the society. In New Bedford the attendance of a Mrs. Johnson did not raise the issue so dramatically because, in the opinion of one of the society's members, she was "rich & respectable & pretty white." The "finish of the game" was to come at the next meeting when eleven African American women intended to join the society.[35]

The resolution of such episodes usually involved incorporating African American women into white female antislavery societies. But the women were an addition and an afterthought, if not second-class members. At the first Anti-Slavery Convention of American Women, held in New York in 1837, Mary S. Parker, who presided over the gathering, acknowledged the resistance to racial inclusiveness when she told the gathering, "The abandonment of prejudice is required . . . as a proof of our sincerity and consistency." Few were able to live up to such exhortations, however. Even in the Philadelphia Female Anti-Slavery Society, where black and white women shared leadership responsibilities, the top officers were always white. Sarah Douglass, one of the black members, may or may not have been thinking about her colleagues when she commented that "even our professed friends have not yet rid themselves of prejudice." In the end, most black women preferred their own organizations with goals that combined assistance to the black free community with self-improvement and abolition.[36]

Forced consideration of the race issue in terms of membership did not encourage most white women to explore a significant paradox in female antislavery thought that was painfully apparent to free blacks. White women often justified their antislavery activism by explaining that they had not only special responsibilities to free black women from slavery but also a special sensitivity, based on gender, to their plight. As the Canton, Ohio, women explained in their constitution, they could not be "deaf to the cry of the sable mother" to whom they had the closest ties, that of sisterhood. That antislavery women could believe they were so intimately linked to and attuned to some black women (i.e., slaves) and not to others was a significant if largely unexplored contradiction.[37]

A few women, as the records of the PFAS show, did recognize the contradiction and attacked northern prejudice as a prop of the slave system. Black women in that organization gave ample evidence to their colleagues of the impact of racism. Sarah Douglass's mother, for example, was not allowed to sit with whites or to become a member when she attended the Arch Street Quaker meeting. The PFAS's constitution, drawn up by women of both races, reflected black women's experience and the Quaker women's sensitivity to racial issues. It denounced prejudice in the strongest terms and stated that African Americans possessed "inalienable rights." Some of the white members, like the Grimké sisters and Lucretia Mott, also made a point of associating with black women outside of the meetings.[38]

"I feel deeply for thee in thy suffering on account of the cruel and unchristian practice which thou has suffered so much from," wrote Sarah Grimké to Sarah Douglass. That sympathy was genuine, as were the efforts she and her sister, Angelina, made to free themselves from racial norms. Yet even though both women recognized the role white racism played in constricting the opportunities and experiences of free blacks, they still expected that blacks should do much of the work of reducing racism. As Angelina explained to Sarah Douglass, "You my dear Sister have a work to do in sorting out this wicked feeling as well as we. You *must* be *willing* to come among us though it *may be* your feelings *may* be wounded." Black women should help "paler sisters . . . to encounter . . . our sinful feelings."[39]

Religious assumptions also shaped the rationales and goals of antislavery societies. Founding documents did not explicitly refer to denominational matters, but a diffuse Protestantism permeated statements of purpose and expectations of membership. The definition of slavery as a sin violating divine law and demanding repentance suggested the experience of conversion; the references to duty and the necessity of forming "Holy & correct public opinion" pointed to the activism expected after conversion. Quotations from the King James version of the Bible reinforced the Protestant character of the organization and gave clues about who would feel comfortable in joining an antislavery society and who would not. Evangelical churchgoers, Unitarians, Quakers, and even Protestants and dissenters who did not attend church but who nonetheless felt at home in the culture at large all might feel called to join the abolitionist crusade. But Catholics, Jews, and others at the margin of Protestant society, recognizing the Protestant character of antislavery organizations, would not join antislavery associations in any numbers and were not expected as converts.[40]

Probably not apparent to abolitionist organizers in the first flush of enthusiasm, when many women pushed forward to sign a constitution, was the relationship between size and organizational vitality. What quickly became obvious was that many women signed an organization's constitution because of a momentary interest or as a general expression of support. Like signing a petition, subscribing to the female association's constitution could signify sympathy, perhaps a donation, and even attendance at a few meetings. But as Lucretia Mott said of Mira Townsend, she "is not among our active members."[41]

Maria Child saw the difference between the "active" members and those who were not as one between "the *nominal* abolitionists" and "*real* ones," those who "really sympathize with the slave." To recognize this difference was to raise fundamental questions. On the one hand, the whole point of abolitionism was to change public opinion and to gain adherents. Large numbers told the world that abolitionism was succeeding and carried a propaganda value. But the desire for large numbers conflicted with the reality of apathy and partial commitment, as well as the desire for efficiency. When Anne Weston wrote to Eliza Mason, a member of the Bangor Female Anti-Slavery Society, she conveyed not only the perspective of the Boston clique about the role of the general membership but also the problems caused by numbers. In her opinion, the Bangor society was wise not to try to augment its size. "The women who will prove in truth an addition will seek you, and the good that a large and inefficient Society will bring about cannot for a moment enter into competition with that produced by a board, however small, who have counted the cost, who are aware of the difficulties that they must encounter."[42]

If size might affect efficiency, a central value for many of the women's organizations, numbers also might influence the abolitionist women's own sense of themselves as a special band. While they did not discuss and perhaps did not think about the relationship between size and collective identity, committed abolitionist women felt part of a community distinct from the world at large. This sense of community was nourished by correspondence and communication in the pages of antislavery newspapers. It was symbolically conveyed in the initiation rites of joining an antislavery society and the use of the term conversion to signify that step.

Perhaps it was this sense of distinctiveness, this sense of being in the minority, that led to a curious episode in the life of the Canton Ladies Anti-Slavery Society. In March 1836, the society held a special meeting to consider the status of one of its members, Mrs. Betsy Reynolds. The records do not reveal what Betsy had said or done, only that the group determined that the society's president should call on Betsy to "ascertain whether it is her desire to have her name erased." A week later, the president reported the results of her visit: Betsy Reynolds wished to withdraw from the society. Members felt it was important to mark her leave-taking as a significant termination of fellowship. Betsy Reynolds would not just slip away. In a ceremonial way, the crossing of boundaries was given form as "the Secretary waited upon Mrs Reynolds, who erased her name and ceased to be a member." [43]

While organizational arrangements varied among antislavery organizations, there was substantial agreement upon the traits that should characterize the committed member of a female antislavery society. As they communicated with one another, ordinary women helped to construct an identity for themselves, collectively and individually. Not surprisingly, they drew upon familiar stereotypes. When Ashtabula County women called for a "mild & Christian spirit" and more prayer at their first annual meeting in 1836, for example, they were on safe ground. But the call for more energetic and muscular qualities, generated by a realistic assessment of the challenges of activism, suggested some departures from genteel and pious ideals.

By the third decade of the nineteenth century, certain character traits had taken on a gendered meaning. The idea that a woman had duties and obligations that superseded any of her own interests was commonplace. Organized antislavery women made female duty fundamental to their concept of themselves and gave it an important place in their constitutions. As a dialogue sent by a woman who identified herself as "C. W." to the *Liberator* in 1838 made clear, women should listen to the demands of duty even when the work offended their sensibilities. Purported to be true, the little drama presented a discussion between a lady and a gentleman about the lady's failure to do anything for the cause. Miss M. assured Mr. W. that, while she was opposed to slavery, she did not "approve your mode of action. The abolitionists are *so disagreeable* and violent, that I can't bear them," she declared. Mr. W. responded that, since she believed slavery was wrong, was it not "your duty to use all your power in opposing it?" [44]

As the vignette suggested, female duty justified commitment at the deepest level. Furthermore, in real life the sense that women were doing their duty helped to build up the confidence needed to carry on in what both Miss. M. and Mr. W. agreed was an unfashionable cause. And although Mr. W. did not succeed in persuading Miss M. to lend her influence to the cause, the appeal to duty did prick the female conscience. In the small drama, the reader could sense the power of that appeal and its potential to transform. The dialogue ended with Mr. W. casting "a look of pity after Miss. M.," who had fled the encounter "trying to smile." [45]

The Christian virtues of faith, perseverance, and self-sacrifice were also central to the ways abolitionist women constructed their identity. While male abolitionists may have ascribed to these virtues, they were more closely associated with cultural definitions of middle-class femininity. Like the appeal to duty, the emphasis on these qualities must have helped women to persist in and justify their support for the movement.

Other characteristics of the committed abolitionist departed from the familiar contours of middle-class female identity. One of the essential qualities for individual women and female antislavery societies was efficiency, a value drawn from the male world of the marketplace and production. The repeated refrain in letters was the need for the society and its members to operate efficiently and systematically in their meetings, in the way they handled their business, and in their efforts to raise money.

Linked to the idea of efficiency was the emphasis on industry, exertion, and, in the words of the women of Lynn, "energy of action." Women could not be passive. Although for some women, praying would be the primary means by which they expressed their antislavery beliefs, the ideal that was emerging prompted involvement and anticipated discord. Writing from Ohio, Lucy Wright talked about taking courage and going "*forward* for a desperate struggle." In the heat of what Lynn women agreed was a "moral conflict," female abolitionists must be bold. "We will *not fear* the *frown* of the *scornful*, nor the reproaches of the *prejudiced*," Canton women asserted. "We will[,] with the assistance of God, *persevere* in our work of mercy, until it shall be accomplishd." [46]

As the communication between women's societies made clear, there was consensus that an abolitionist should also be well informed about the facts of slavery and skillful at presenting them intelligently. But in the words of Lynn women, "*willing minds*" had to be matched by "*warm hearts*." A true female abolitionist must be able to feel the burdens and sufferings of the slaves, to make imaginative connections. Without the ability to use intellect and imagination, women would be unwilling to make the sacrifices demanded of them and would be ineffective advocates for immediate emancipation. At the fifth annual meeting of the Portland Female Anti-Slavery Society, for example, members were encouraged to visualize the slave mother nursing her babe "with the dread of the driver's whip before her eyes." Such a vision would "render us more prompt to utter the feelings with which it inspired us, and less fearful of exciting the disappointment of others, and by the zeal and sincerity which we should plead for our suffering fellow creatures many would be convinced and led to join us."[47]

In some respects, women were constructing an ideal that moved beyond the usual gender polarities. Abolitionist women should be skilled at processing information and using it just as men were. But they should also be able to use intuition and imagination to gain and give a visceral understanding of the evils of slavery. It was not enough to know about slavery or sympathize with the slaves. One had to be able to do both. As Mary Grew explained in her letter to the Brooklyn Female Anti-Slavery Society, the challenge was to "place *facts* before their minds, so vividly delineated" that they could not be forgotten.[48]

In one sense, conservative men and women were right when they argued years before the woman issue became a heated topic of debate within antislavery associations that abolitionist women ignored what many accepted as natural boundaries for female activity. But many abolitionist women sensed that definitions were elastic and capable of expansion, that there was more room for moral activism than conservatives would ever acknowledge. The number of references to propriety and woman's place in association constitutions shows that many women were conscious of both conservative norms and the way definitions could be stretched. They were adept at both acknowledging and transgressing gender expectations in almost the same breath. "We will never overstep the boundaries of propriety," the PFAS's Third Annual Report declared, "but when our brothers and sisters, lie crushed and bleeding . . . we must do with our might, what our hands find to do . . . pausing only to inquire, 'What is right?' "[49]

When attacked, some women were quite capable of lashing back at their detractors. Lucy Wright, writing for the Portage Female Anti-Slavery Society in Ohio, reported the society's growth from 37 to 390 members in a mere seven months and their efforts at petitioning. She also reported that the sight of so many active women had produced the predictable response, the insistence that women were out of their sphere. Lucy labeled that antagonistic force as "Satan" at work in the world. In Lynn, faced with the same kind of criticism, the women suggested that "a corrupt public sentiment" had "prescribed" the boundaries they were ignoring.[50]

The newcomers to antislavery societies soon came face-to-face with some of the fundamental challenges of organizational life. The emphasis on energy, perseverance, and work signified the recognition that enthusiasm was not sufficient to sustain female activism. There were many reasons that a female society might never amount to much, but the inability to attract the right kind of women to leadership positions especially damaged its chances of survival. In 1837, Deborah Weston wrote, "The Female Society here is struggling on & will I hope come to some thing." In New Bedford, there was "considerable trouble about a vice-president, if no New Bedford person who is suitable can be got, would you take the office if you were me?" Deborah asked. In Glastonbury, Connecticut, Hannah H. Smith understood that outside organizers could only initiate; she did "not know of one Antislavery woman of the right stamp in Connecticut, of sufficient information & energy to organize a society or manage its concerns."[51]

Associational records and letters show the consequences of poor leadership. In Providence, Rhode Island, the choice of a Mrs. Fairbanks as the president of the antislavery society alarmed some members about the society's future. With the reputation of being "notoriously inefficient," Mrs. Fairbanks had a history of destructive management. She had quarreled with the Juvenile Anti-Slavery Society some years earlier, and even more damaging, she had undermined the Ladies Society. By her reassurances that the women did not need to work, and that she was going to "do all," nothing was accomplished by either society members or Mrs. Fairbanks. As a Stoneham, Massachusetts, woman explained, leadership demanded "exertion on the part of the managers [or others in the society] & some self-sacrifice of each individual." Mrs. Fairbanks encouraged neither.[52]

As the selection of Mrs. Fairbanks suggests, it was not always easy to find those who were willing and able to organize and manage a society's concerns. When Dover women tried to put together an organizing committee of four, one of the single women refused to serve on the committee. And sometimes a society's officers held their position in tandem with their husbands' leadership in male associations. The disappearance of these women's names from the leadership rosters suggests that these wives did not have the interest, time, or perhaps talent to do what was necessary for the organization.[53]

The records of the Salem Female Anti-Slavery Society illuminate the difficulties encountered in the process of building up effective leadership. In

December 1837, the society voted that one of its members, Mary Spencer, prepare an address on slavery that the society would issue to the women of Essex County. The published address would not only serve as an important piece of propaganda for the cause but also help to establish the society's prominence locally. Mary was reluctant to agree and requested two weeks to think over the charge. At the end of this time, she turned down the assignment. While the minutes were silent about her reasons, the fear of publicity, possibly feelings of inadequacy, and the press of other obligations all could have played a part in her refusal. Within a month, the society faced another problem: the woman elected as president declined the office. The association then voted that the two Dodge sisters "prevail upon her to accept." Only a few years later, the pattern was repeated when Lucy Ives also refused the presidency. Once again, a committee was formed to try to reason with the candidate, this time with success. Lucy agreed to serve "until some other individual should be obtained." [54]

Salem was fortunate, for Lucy grew into her new position and became the association's long-term president. But she never became comfortable with all of her duties. When the Salem Female Anti-Slavery Society sponsored successful public lectures during the 1840s and 1850s, members agreed that a woman should chair the meetings. But Lucy would not, explaining that she had "not . . . sufficient confidence." Even with the passage of years, Lucy still "had not [acquired] sufficient confidence or experience in conducting public meetings" to act as the visible head of the organization.[55] But while she was not sufficiently relaxed to appear before audiences as the organization's spokesperson, Lucy did preside over one of the most long-lived and successful of all female antislavery societies.

In an unpopular cause without widespread community support, the role of elected officers or a few committed women was critical to institutional vitality and even survival. The Brooklyn Female Anti-Slavery Society's failure to hold its annual meeting, for example, signified fatal weakness in the organization. The society's minutes for August 1, 1840, reveal that the lapse was due to "the removal of some, and the absence and illness of others of the most active and efficient portion of our society." While the remaining members decided to "go on as a band of volunteers without even *officers* from the present," no more entries were ever made in the society's records.[56]

Society records do give examples of the way some women became leaders and suggest the impact of their leadership on associational life. The part Lydia Dodge played in the early years of the Salem Female Anti-Slavery Society, for example, contributed to its ability to survive the difficulties it encountered. Lydia and her sister Lucie were among the society's "most efficient women." Lydia never became president, most likely because she had a speech impediment that she felt prohibited her "from all conversational communication with my friends." Perhaps her speech was difficult to understand, but association minutes show her ability to mobilize members. Lydia suggested the address for the women of Essex County, and it was she who moved to have a committee investigate the situation of Salem blacks, suggested using funds to help fugitive slaves, and proposed to have a class so that the society could learn how to run better meetings. She was a member of numerous committees and hosted a small gathering of women who formed a sewing circle to make clothes for the teacher in the black school. The sewing circle, with its specific and realizable projects, remained a core of activism for the society. Lydia's energy and her ideas for projects contributed to the vitality and the interest of Salem meetings.[57]

As scattered letters show, Mrs. Sarah Rugg, president of the Groton Female Anti-Slavery Society, also learned how to provide forceful leadership. In her first surviving letter written in 1836, Sarah gave few signs of being able to take command. Even though she had the "heart to labor for the slave," her hand was "weak" and "trembling" (perhaps from a recent bout with lung fever). She needed advice. Within a year, she had developed the political skills necessary to influence her society. Before the March 1837 monthly meeting, Sarah met with a member of the Boston Female Anti-Slavery Society to discuss how she could ensure Groton's aid for the Boston group. Bad weather kept all but ten members at home, but those who came to the meeting enjoyed a carefully orchestrated afternoon. Sarah began by reading from the Bible "the most denouncing chapter she could find, & stopped to apply it to southern clergy." With the membership reminded of the horrid realities of the slave system, Sarah's resolution to assist the Boston society easily passed, as did her resolution supporting the first national women's antislavery convention scheduled for May. That summer, she was ready to move her society's members onto more radical ground. The Grimké sisters, who had scandalized conservatives by speaking to mixed audiences, were to visit Groton. Their proposed appearance was causing a " 'strife' of tongues" and failing hearts in the village. After some instruction to the Groton society about how to deal with passages from St. Paul, which conservatives had used to censure the Grimké sisters, Sarah tackled the volatile subject of women speaking in public. "I longed to have the matter over," Anne Weston wrote of the meeting, but Sarah acted "very boldly, and, indeed, I think very well of her courage, for probably no one in the female society dared to take the ground of defending women preaching save herself." [58]

The goal of creating energetic leaders and hard-working, committed members faced the constraints of social, economic, and gender realities. In Salem, Lucie Dodge, one of the antislavery society's "most efficient women," married and moved with her new husband to the West. While marriage preparations were under way, she and her sisters could not be counted upon to assist projects of the Salem Society. Transiency often appears in records and correspondence as an important reason for a society's weakness or failure to accomplish work. [59]

Circumstances that today would be considered irrelevant to institutional success loomed large in female antislavery circles. Despite the fact that antislavery societies communicated with one another through the mails, officers could not always convey to members the simple but necessary news of time, place, and date of meetings. While societies that had frequent regular meetings could rely on a schedule and word of mouth, associations meeting less often or changing the meeting time had no easy way of reaching all the members. Mrs. Eliza Gill testified to these difficulties in Fitchburg. She explained that she had hoped to give a definite reply on a task with which she had been charged, but the day of her society's regular meeting was rainy, and she couldn't go. Since then, she had set a meeting, "but a mistake in the day rendered this also a failure." [60]

The Salem Female Anti-Slavery Society decided in 1839 to publish notices of its meetings in the newspapers. For most of the 1830s, however, procedures for notifying members seem to have been more haphazard. Some antislavery societies relied upon local clergy to inform their congregations during the Sunday service of the time and place of the next meeting. Church was the one public place where one could count on reaching a large female audience, but the good will and willingness of clergy was uncertain. Especially as the decade progressed and abolitionism became more notorious, notices of meetings might not be read at all. As young Lucia Weston wrote to her sister, "*We intend* that is the Ladies intend to hold a meeting in the afternoon, and have two or three speeches. . . . Notices have been sent round to every church in the city. . . . Emma went to Mr. Pierpont's meeting[;] it was not read there." [61]

The weather also played an important role in assisting or weakening institutional vitality. In Dover, New Hampshire, for example, attendance dwindled in January because of "a storm and bad walking." It was also small in July, "the day being very warm and the distance so great." Weather was a particular obstacle in country places where members might live far from one another and have to walk to meetings. This simple reality frustrated Eliza Pope in 1840. In her Massachusetts town, ten miles in circumference, only two or three abolitionists lived in the same vicinity, "and most of them too poor to admit them to ride, (for you know 'not *many* rich not many mighty or noble' are called to this work)." As a result, Eliza felt it was "impracticable to get a sufficient number together" to work for the Boston society's annual fair. She confessed that indifference to abolitionism sometimes made her despair, but some of what she called indifference may have been caused by the physical circumstances over which she had no control.[62]

Constitutions stated and faithful abolitionists agreed that women's duty demanded their adherence to immediate emancipation. The implication was that duty to the cause of Christ came before all other duties. Mary Grew, in her letter to the Reading Female Anti-Slavery Society, reminded its members that an "*unhesitating* sacrifice of time" would be necessary. While most committed women might agree upon the goal, in reality, women's duties as wives, mothers, and daughters, responsibilities that were unquestioned for the most part, shaped what they could do and could not do. Particularly because many women working for abolitionism lived in modest circumstances, they could not pay others to do the family and domestic tasks that ate into their time and drained their energies.[63]

Surviving sources provide insights into the lives of many women who labored, unrecognized, to free the slaves. Written records demonstrate the impact of family duties on women's time, and since time and commitment are often related, they reflect the quality of their commitment. Although the fervor of Sarah Plummer's belief was evident in her correspondence and in her efforts to circulate copies of the *Liberator*, she admitted, "I find my time quite limited . . . being surrounded by a little family, without the help of any domestic." Indeed, when women spoke of their family responsibilities (S. W. Thomas's "helpless paralitic" mother who demanded most of her time, Mary Manter's youngest child "partially deranged and . . . a great deal of trouble," and the Ipswich Female Anti-Slavery Society president's consumptive daughter) and their domestic tasks (ranging from getting a family ready for the cold weather to baking pies for Thanksgiving), one wonders how they ever did any work for abolitionism.[64]

When Pauline Garry wrote to discuss her society's small contribution to the annual Boston fair, she regretted the limited means of her group. "We have only 27 members a number of them Misses & some of the adults are so situated they deem it impossible to assist much none are volunteers from the circles of wealth and fashion but labouring women who discharge the cares & duties of a family or provide for their own personal comfort & necessities." Her reference to single women, many of whom were self-supporting, suggests the limits on these women's contributions to antislavery. For both married and unmarried women, then, primary duties were time consuming and often tiring. The First Annual Report of the Sangerville (Maine) Female Anti-Slavery Society acknowledged this reality, although the writer claimed that the women's powers of imaginative sympathy for the slave helped them to overcome exhaustion. "Week after week as we have assembled from our homes, wearied with the fatigues of the day and the cares of labor, how has that weariness vanished and . . . cares . . . lightened, as the wail of the poor mother, and the cry of her famishing babe, has come to us." Reflecting on women's antislavery work in Dighton, Massachusetts, Abby Talbot explained that the society was a small one. "Many among us," she noted, "are weak & sickly." Uncertain health and the problems of age, while obviously not confined to members of female antislavery societies, also hindered associational life.[65]

Whatever the ideal composition for an active society was, many female associations did not have it. In Newburyport, Garrison's birthplace, Elizabeth Wright reported that members of the society did little besides praying and contributing money. The society was made up "chiefly of aged and middle aged persons, who have families and will not or cannot attend to the thing." Young women, she observed, found the cause too unpopular. In other societies, the presence of "poor common peple" who could do "only plain needlework" limited the sewing projects the society could take on.[66]

Active antislavery women often stressed the indifference and apathy they encountered. While they were correct that many of their friends and acquaintances just did not care about slavery, the conditions of women's everyday life obviously affected involvement. Some women did not participate in organized activities because they were too tired and overworked to do so.

At some level, many women sensed the interaction of the social, economic, and gender variables that shaped individual and collective possibilities for female antislavery activism. Annual meetings celebrated organizational survival. In its First Annual Report, the managers of the Ladies' New-York City Anti-Slavery Society found it "peculiarly appropriate" to express their "thanksgiving to the God of the oppressed, through whose favor they are permitted to record . . . [the society's] formation and undisturbed prosperity for even one year."[67]

The ceremonial occasion of the annual meeting also reminded members of the righteousness of their cause, detailed accomplishments, and tried to spur them on to ever greater efforts. In Austinburg, Ohio, for example, the members of the Ashtabula County Female Anti-Slavery Society listened to an address on the condition of the slave, then witnessed the addition of 150 new members, which tripled their size. Resolutions were offered stressing the sin of slavery and the need for prompt, efficient, and decided effort. At the conclusion of the meeting, the secretary recorded that "a fresh impulse was given to the cause." In Weymouth, Massachusetts, the secretary tried to cement active loyalty through "a pathetic appeal to . . . feelings to do more in the coming year." "Let every member of this society act in all respects as she would be induced to do, if her father, her mother, her child, her sister, or her brother was in slavery," she declared. "*Then* & only *then* she would be doing what was required of her."[68]

The First Annual Report of the Dorchester Female Anti-Slavery Society opened with an elaborate statement of the women's "insufficiency and inability to do that justice to the subject before us which its importance demands." After this bow to convention, the report continued, "Not being able to do as well as we could wish, is no reasonable excuse for not doing the best we can; therefore, without any more remarks by way of apology, we submit to every friend of God and the poor slave, this humble report." Despite their humility, the Dorchester women ensured that their report would reach the hands of some, if not every, friend of God and the slave, for they had their report published. The more prosperous societies were not the only ones to publish their annual reports. The women of South Reading, as did women in other societies, had the *Liberator* publish their report (a practice that Garrison observed until the end of the decade).[69]

The publicizing of annual reports points to the sense of achievement at survival. It also provided another link in the chain of communication with other women and other societies and a means of exposing to all who would read the report "the most horrid portrait of human depravity ever exhibited."[70]

The effort to use the annual report as one means of instructing members and nonmembers alike was part of a larger educational program undertaken by female societies. Even those who joined female societies might be ignorant about the facts of slavery and lack the proper feelings about the institution. Ruth Evans's observation about members in her Michigan antislavery society highlighted both their good will and their ignorance. She expected twelve women to join the society at its next monthly meeting. While "they heartily meet with it," she said, "many have seldom heretofore, thought much on the subject." In the bustling mill town of Amesbury Mills, Betsey Lincott echoed Ruth Evans's comment: "By many of our members, the subject has received but little of their attention, until about the time of our formation, therefore we have much to learn." The dangers of a commitment based on enthusiasm were obvious. As one woman in Attleborough pointed out, "It does not take much to discourage those who are not well established." [71]

Indeed, the instruction of members about the evils of slavery was as much a goal for some societies as was changing the minds and hearts of the outside world. Teaching women about their cause was perhaps as important for institutional vitality and longevity as the conversion of outsiders. Instructional needs played a significant role in shaping institutional life and helped to structure meetings. Reading antislavery materials aloud during meetings constituted an important part of group life and helped to produce the "animating conversation upon the subject of Slavery" that deepened commitment. The minutes of the Brooklyn Female Anti-Slavery Society show the range of materials to which members of this society listened: accounts of slavery, articles from antislavery papers, pamphlets (some apparently read in installments, as the notation "finished reading Right and Wrong" suggests), fiction, like the "beautiful story from the Oasis," and letters from other societies. In the society's library were also published lectures and poetry that could have been lent out but also may have been read aloud in a group setting.[72]

The format of associational meetings varied. Some had elaborate and formal procedures. The bylaws of the Lynn Female Anti-Slavery Society called for meetings to be opened with an appropriate Scripture reading, followed by the minutes and the transaction of business, then a reading from antislavery works "with remarks or conversation relating to the object of the society." Closing with a hymn and/or prayer was standard for many groups. Other societies, especially small ones that met frequently, must have had much more informal modes of operating. Surely during the Brooklyn society meetings in the winter of 1836, when the secretary noted "numbers small," the meetings must have been less structured. That society's failure to keep minutes for much of 1837 suggests a freedom from rules that probably was more typical than the structured approach of the Lynn women.[73]

When Groton's Sarah Rugg wrote that her society had been spending meeting time at prayer, her comment showed not only the belief in the sacred nature of the antislavery cause but how easily women might fall into the familiar patterns of the prayer meeting. Yet there were often special monthly concerts of prayer established for that purpose. The women of the Ashtabula County Female Anti-Slavery Society reminded one another during their first annual meeting of the importance of the concert and rec-ommended meeting "in different neighborhoods or even smaller circles; & where this is not practicable, we will observe it in our own closets." In Dover, New Hampshire, women supported a monthly concert that sur-vived for almost thirty years.[74]

As the establishment of monthly concerts made clear, an antislavery meeting was not a prayer meeting. Although reading aloud was common, unless the society was composed of black women, it was not a literary or self-improvement society. Each society had to work out a format that would serve the needs of its own members, secure the commitment of visitors who might attend meetings, and, of course, further the cause of emancipation.

A full account of an October 1836 meeting of the Weymouth Female Anti-Slavery Society shows the society in the midst of finding its own meet-ing style and collective identity. About twenty-eight women, including one or two visitors, gathered for the meeting, which began on an uncertain note. The appointed hour of three arrived and passed without the appear-ance of the president. Finally, members present agreed to begin, and one of them opened the meeting with a reading from the Book of Esther. When the president finally arrived, she was with the minister, who "walked in as if it had been a meeting of his own, & proceeded to read a chapt from James." The role of clergy in the women's society was unclear, and at least one member was annoyed at the minister's presumption that he should open the meeting. As he was leaving after the hymn, she thanked him, say-ing that his appearance was an unexpected pleasure. "This," she wrote, "I said to let Miss Mary know he was not invited, otherwise she would have thought he was in a manner compelled to come." The remainder of the meeting moved along more smoothly until the annual report's author re-fused to allow it to be sent into the *Liberator* for publication. Discussion over whether to have a lecture in the afternoon or evening also proved to be desultory. Members were perhaps not yet entirely socialized to the conver-sational norms that were in the process of being established. One member spoke to the question of the lecture "& tryed to make a discussion any-thing to get them to speak."[75]

"Shall we keep the steam up till the work is done?" wondered Maria Child, alluding to the challenge of maintaining members' initial enthu-siasm for the cause. As Mary Matthews discovered in Rochester, it was difficult to render the society's "meetings sufficiently interesting to induce ladies to attend." Praying, singing abolitionist hymns, listening to ad-dresses, readings, and letters, discussing slavery and what could be done to end it, making resolutions, and working on projects all helped keep women coming to meetings. The Pennsylvania Female Anti-Slavery Society's policy of forming small committees to carry out all assignments was a successful way of involving members in associational business. Although rarely discussed, the rituals of sociability also must often have played a part in attaching members to the group and cause.[76]

The role of sociability as well as the conflict some felt between sociability and antislavery goals appear in the records of the Dover Anti-Slavery Sewing Circle. The circle's object was to promote immediate emancipation through "discussion, collecting and dissemination of information on the subject of Slavery and raising funds in aid of the Anti-Slavery cause." It was early decided that the society should "adhere strictly to the rules of plainness in the refreshments furnished." Though perhaps unrelated to the refreshments policy, meetings were neglected the following year. At the next annual meeting, members decided to "retain the *good old custom* of having a *social cup* of tea." The society could not reach consensus on the appropriateness of social conventions. Some saw refreshment and conversation as critical, others as indulgence. In April 1844, members voted again on the tea question and decided to fine any member who provided more than "*one kind of cake*." Only a little over three months later, they voted "to *resign* the old practice of taking Tea." By the end of the year, they voted "to resume to practice of furnishing refreshments at our meetings." After over four years of going back and forth on the issue, they seemed to have reached agreement that sociability served a useful function for the society.[77]

While keeping up interest was a generic problem for voluntary associations, records reveal other challenges specifically related to gender. If in the world it was a sin to be silent on the question of slavery, it could also be a problem in female meetings. Women were not as used to public speech as men, and although they were being called upon to learn how to act as the slave's advocates, they had difficulty at times participating in group discussions. The corresponding secretary of the Boston Female Anti-Slavery Society described how many women at a recent meeting had been "unwilling to express their opinion." Abby Kelley hoped to deal with female reticence by offering the following resolution during the Lynn Female Anti-Slavery Society's annual meeting in 1837: "That as a free interchange of opinions and sentiments gives life and interest to our meetings, we feel called upon to forget ourselves, as much as in us lies, in the absorbing interest of the objects of our association, thereby overcoming any diffidence that may withhold us from coming forward and communicating our thoughts unreservedly." Perhaps Abby had something to learn, too. Soon after her resolution, another member made a motion inviting those with resolutions to face the audience, presumably so they could be heard.[78]

If some Lynn women did not speak loudly enough or often enough, others did not observe norms of organizational behavior. Some chatted when business was being transacted. The problem was such that in July 1837, the society added a bylaw to its constitution specifying that "all talking and moving must be suspended" until all the society's business had been finished. The same bylaw emphasized the hour at which the meetings were to begin. Lynn, like other societies, also had trouble getting women to come at the appointed hour so that the meeting could begin on time. The Salem society passed a resolution that its meeting was to start "precisely at the hour appointed," while Dover, New Hampshire, women voted to make special efforts to be punctual. Like workers in the mills, abolitionist women were moving, or being urged to move, away from fluid domestic time to the more regular schedules of the commercial and industrial world.[79]

The abolitionist woman was encouraged to take an active and constructive part in associational life. Female behaviors that did not promote interesting or productive meetings were discouraged, while other behaviors were promoted. Even contentiousness could be welcome, because it could "keep up animated discussion, and develop female eloquence." The ability to make forceful resolutions was prized, for resolutions sparked discussion, clarification of values, and decision making. While these resolutions often appear lifeless to the twentieth-century reader, they helped to create the sense that something important was happening during the meeting.[80]

Antislavery societies offered women more than the opportunity to support emancipation. They created opportunities for friendship, conviviality, and emotional support and a worthwhile pastime outside of the home. Efforts to foster an organizational culture encouraged the acquisition of skills and attitudes valued in the larger world. Educational activities informed women about public events and encouraged them to think about and discuss them. Although not all women would follow the logic of organized abolitionism to its conclusion, associational life provided women with the information, skills, and confidence needed for active citizenship and participation in public life.

In 1836, urging more emphasis on helping free blacks in the North, Theodore Weld suggested the importance of work for organizational vitality. Work gave abolitionists something to do and thus kept them "from *shrivelling*." Devising and carrying out projects animated association life, and the individual projects, while often modest in character, collectively lent important assistance to abolitionism. During the 1830s, women circulated abolitionist literature, secured subscriptions to newspapers, collected money, hired lecturers, sewed for and otherwise assisted needy African Americans, mounted fairs that brought in substantial sums, and were active in petition campaigns. Many of these projects demanded verbal skills and techniques that proved to be useful to women recruiting for their own societies, and they encouraged women to use these talents in a variety of settings, far from the privacy of their homes. As they worked for abolitionism, members of female antislavery societies moved closer to the conception of the woman abolitionist they had created.[81]

Some examples of projects undertaken by members of antislavery associations give an idea of the range of work in which women participated and their personal responses to doing it. Many of the activities female societies sponsored fall under the general category of propaganda. As one correspondent to the *Liberator* pointed out, an important part of publicizing the cause involved "the circulation of anti-slavery tracts, papers, documents, &c. among those, who if not opposed, are not known to be friendly to our views." Not all societies aggressively sought out those unsympathetic to the cause, however. Some, like the Brooklyn Female Anti-Slavery Society, collected materials to lend "to all who have a desire to read." At least one society, in Plymouth, Massachusetts, had a reading room that they considered "invaluable in spreading information where it would not otherwise reach." The society allowed the curious to take the initiative.[82]

But other societies were willing to venture out into their communities to solicit readers. As Grace Williams pointed out, this involved "much effort." In Nantucket, the women's society to which she belonged visited every family on the island with the *Anti-Slavery Almanac*. When the women of the Amesbury and Salisbury (Massachusetts) Female Anti-Slavery Society declared that their most important work was the support for and circulation of Garrison's "pioneer paper," they may well have visualized this sort of commitment. In order to circulate another antislavery paper *The Cradle of Liberty*, members of antislavery societies were instructed to spend two or three days scouring their communities, stopping at every household. In Maine, recognizing the effectiveness of women in this kind of work, the editor of the *Advocate of Freedom* commended the efforts of two women who had obtained seventy-four subscribers to that paper and encouraged others to imitate their success.[83]

None of this work was easy. People had all kinds of excuses not to read. "So many [publications] come. . . . they cannot read nor hear of such cruelties," Experience Billings explained, while "others are engaged for the heathen and have nothing for the slave." Sarah Plummer, who received the

1838.] APRIL—FOURTH MONTH. [30 days.

The slave Paul had suffered so much in slavery, that he chose to encounter h hard hips and perils of a runaway. He expo ed him-elf, in gloomy forests, to cold and starvat.on, and finally hung him elf, that he might not again fall into th. hands of his tormentor. [See Ball's Narrative, 2d Edit. p. 325.]

D M	Positions of the Sun, Moon and Stars....Tides, Weather, &c.
1	Alphard S. 8 37 a.
2	Low tides. *Rainy,*
3	Regulus S. 9 9 a. *with*
4	Alkes S. 9 58 a. *perhaps*
5	☿ ☊. *a snow squall*
6	☽ apogee. ♃ ☌ ☽. *or*
7	Mirach on mer. 9 47 a.
8	Dubhe on mer. 9 45 a.
9	☽ eclipsed, visible. *two.*
10	♀ at greatest brilliancy.
11	♎ ☌ ☿. Pretty high tides.
12	♀ rises 3 32 m. *Some snow*
13	♄ ☍ ☽. ♀ ☌ ♅. *from*
14	♃ S. 9 16 a. *eastward.*
15	♄ S. 2 11 m. *Rather un-*
16	Mirach on mer. 9 14 a.
17	Dubhe on mer. 9 11 a.
18	Low tides. *settled.*
19	Alkes S. 9 2 a. *An occa-*
20	♅ ☌ ☽. ♀ ☌ ☽. *sional*
21	Denebola S. 9 54 a. *shower.*
22	☽ perigee. *Now expect*
23	♂ ☌ ☽. *several days of*
24	High tides. *fine pleasant*
25	☿ greatest elon. E. ☿ ☌ ☽
26	Zavijava S. 9 26 a. *April*
27	Algorab S. 10 6 a.
28	♃ sets 3 1 m. *weather.*
29	♄ S. 1 17 a. *Rather*
30	♀ ☋. *cool.*

it would rather war against His attributes, than deny His being.

How then should Christians regard this *daring libeller* of the God they love? There can be but one answer to this question,—they must *abhor* it. Yes; let this truth be written upon the four walls of every church in these United States,—CHRISTIANS MUST ABHOR SLAVERY, OR RENOUNCE GOD.

Reader, you may now excuse yourself from acting, because the slaves are black. Will that excuse avail you when YOUR JUDGE shall own them as HIS BRETHREN?—when he shall say, 'Inasmuch as ye did it not *to one of the least of these*, ye did it not to me.' Will it not be insulting your Creator to his face to urge such a plea? If so, how DARE you use it now?

Francis Durret, in the Huntsville (Ala.) Democrat of March 8, 1837, advertises a mulatto slave who had escaped from him, who "had on when he left, a pair of hand-cuffs, a pair of drawing chains," &c.

What would you do to redeem yourself from slavery? '*Thou shalt love thy neighbor AS thyself.*'

Distributing abolitionist literature, like this Anti-Slavery Almanac, *was one of the activities undertaken by female antislavery societies and women working on their own. (Boston Athenæum)*

Liberator as a gift from the Boston Female Anti-Slavery Society (knowing that the cost of the paper limited its usefulness, the Boston Female Anti-Slavery Society had voted to have the *Liberator* delivered free throughout the state), spoke of her "unwearied effort" to circulate the paper. She had to "prevail" upon people, as she did with one Bangor gentleman who was determined not to patronize Garrison. Unwilling to let the matter politely drop, Sarah badgered him until he finally agreed to try the paper. Her letter hinted at the psychic costs of her work. When she met with indifference, she confessed, "My spirit is stirred within me, and my soul is in agony, as a burning fire shut up in my bones—then it is, that I flee to my closet, and I find if the ear of *man* is closed, that of the great Jehovah is ever open."[84]

Women also created their own propaganda. While the contributions of women like Maria Child and the Grimké sisters are well known, associations and members of associations also voiced their opinions in print. Only a few months after the formation of their female antislavery society, women in Uxbridge, Massachusetts, drafted a letter to "Professing Christian Women of Kentucky" and had it published in the *Philanthropist*. Appealing to the southern women as mothers, sisters, and daughters, the letter "affectionately" urged them to overthrow slavery and warned them of the consequences of inaction. Annual reports were another means to bolster membership and to make the abolitionist case before the indifferent public. While much of this sort of propaganda has not survived or appeared in antislavery newspapers without attribution, there are enough references to women's contributions to suggest how important they were. Certainly lecturer Marius Robinson, who described the efforts of the president of the Cadiz (Ohio) Female Anti-Slavery Society, recognized their impact. This woman, unwilling to let the local Presbyterian clergyman's defense of colonization go unchallenged, wrote an article for publication that, in Robinson's opinion, "annihilated" the cleric's speech.[85]

Female societies also paid for the publication of effective antislavery materials. On several occasions, the PFAS thought that an invited lecturer had made such a powerful case for abolitionism that his or her remarks should be published. On other occasions, societies picked up the bill for tracts and pamphlets.[86]

When the Lynn women reviewed their work at their second annual meeting, they concluded that publications and individual exertion had all been important for winning adherents to the cause (and to the association). But "more than from any other cause," they stated, "through the influence of the lecture we have received a considerable accession of members within the last few months." Antislavery societies not only sponsored lectures in their own communities but also hired agents to take the message elsewhere. In Salem in 1839, the association engaged Mrs. Abigail Ordway to serve as their agent in Essex County. She found her progress slow, reporting to the board that "the disagreeables far exceed the agreeables on such a route; and there is nothing which can sustain or console the sinking spirits, but the idea of the good eventually to be accomplished."[87]

For many, if not most, white women's organizations, the goal of improving the situation of freed blacks was of secondary importance to abolition, partly because there were so few free blacks in their communities. In cities like Boston, Philadelphia, and New York, however, the substantial black presence shaped organizations' responses to the freedperson's plight. In these places and in others like Salem, Massachusetts, white women followed Theodore Weld's advice and undertook a variety of projects aimed at assisting the black community. Guided by the same sorts of assumptions that initially limited association membership to white women, women's associations, like men's, were certainly not free of prejudice, paternalism, or middle-class values. The decision of a group of women in the Portland Female Anti-Slavery Society to meet twice a week to instruct "the female colored population in knitting, mending, and various kinds of needle work" in order to elevate "the character of an unjustly degraded race," and their later expenditures for clothing and books for children in the "colored school" exhibit all the limitations of the abolitionist approach. Blacks needed to live up to white standards if they were to overcome negative stereotypes and discriminatory treatment. Yet it is important to remember that in the context of the racism of the North, such efforts were risky to one's reputation and that women abolitionists were unusually free of the prejudices of the day. Projects aimed to provide African Americans with the middle-class skills and values that whites believed they lacked often proved useful and even profitable for those who were involved. Furthermore, black women's organizations during the 1830s also endorsed many of the same improvement strategies as the means of overcoming prejudice.[88]

Both all-black organizations and some integrated organizations undertook projects aimed at improving education for blacks. The most ambitious effort that surviving records reveal was undertaken by the PFAS in its early years. Quakers had been pioneers in black education in Pennsylvania, and given the prominence of Hicksites in the PFAS and that black women members were from the city's most elite families, an interest in education was predictable. Both groups believed that if blacks were properly educated, they would be more successful in life. In turn, their success would undermine white prejudice. Visits to black schools to evaluate the quality of education there, gifts of educational materials, and financial support for Sarah Douglass's school for girls demonstrated this organization's commitment during the 1830s. Other educational projects included a series of scientific lectures for blacks and sewing classes for women unacquainted with this "important branch of domestic industry." Despite the importance of the work, however, the efforts petered out. Perhaps because the "field of labor [proved] too extensive" for the size of the organization, it was difficult to get women to complete their assignments. Too many were "negligent," and eventually the society turned most of its energy toward fund-raising activities.[89]

The major fund-raising device for the PFAS and other female antislavery associations was the fair, but associations took on many other, more modest efforts. The American Anti-Slavery Society, as well as abolitionist newspaper editors, lecturers, and agents were often in financial straits. Garrison himself was often short of cash and the recipient of gifts from female societies. And Garrison was not the only impecunious abolitionist leader. The Boston Female Anti-Slavery Society paid part of Samuel J. May's salary and raised money to ensure that Maria Child had access to the Boston Athenæum library. Maria Child herself wrote letters begging for money, selecting persons who were not abolitionists, because abolitionists "have very limited means [and] . . . what they give to collateral objects [in this case, to help out the black Bostonian Susan Paul] must generally be deducted from their annual donation to the Anti-Slavery cause."[90]

Societies tried a variety of schemes to raise money. In 1838, the *Liberator* was pressing women to establish cent-a-week societies, which the paper claimed were having astonishing success. "Many little bands of female collectors are thus raising from $50 to $100 a year, in places where little would be done by any other plan." Black women's groups undertook similar work to support black papers, which were more economically vulnerable than mainstream papers like the *Liberator*.[91]

Women did not need to be reminded about the importance of money, nor did they need suggestions about how to raise it. Even the Bangor Juvenile Anti-Slavery Society, composed of about twenty-five "misses," concluded "that *money* is of great importance" and "resolved to do our utmost to cast in our mite for this purpose." Dover, New Hampshire, women, in order to work more "efficiently," came up with the idea of appointing eight women who belonged to the town's various religious societies to canvass for donations. At the time of their reorganization in 1840, they also decided to invite men as honorary—but dues-paying—members. As the Dedham

Female Anti-Slavery Society made clear, it was determined to "raise all we could to send in with our cent a week money."[92]

While the sums any one society was able to raise may have been small, collectively abolitionist organizations provided important assistance to a reform movement that often was short of cash. Samuel J. May acknowledged the financial debt the antislavery movement owed to women, even as he minimized the tedious nature of the task of fund-raising. "Often were they our self-appointed committees of ways and means, and by fairs and other pleasant devices raised much money to sustain our lecturers and periodicals," he recalled. Given the fact that most women did not have their own sources of income, the financial commitments they undertook assume an importance greater than the money itself.[93]

A few examples illustrate the frustrations women faced in fund-raising Frances Drake, after a day and a half of soliciting in response to a circular from the Massachusetts Anti-Slavery Society, had only collected $2.25, despite the fact that "every person I called on was an avowed abolitionist, and what is more, were all persons of standing, and *much* property." In Fitchburg, Eliza Gill's efforts to get male and female abolitionists to agree on a contribution plan proved abortive. Despite holding "meeting after meeting," nothing was resolved. Finally, "seeing clearly that if anything was done for the contribution plan it must be done by the women— we concluded to hold six meetings of our Soc. in districts and when we have met, I have made a point of getting as many boxes as we could. As yet I cannot speak of success but think it the best plan for us at present."[94]

Fund-raising, even when the sums collected were tiny, demanded that women carry the abolitionist message and the financial requirements of the movement to others. Sometimes, as was the case in Fitchburg, the audience and the place were familiar and friendly, even if contributions were not forthcoming. But in other cases, solicitations were made in more public and less sympathetic environments. Women's experience with indifference and hostility in the work of fund-raising was good preparation for petitioning.

The massive petition drives undertaken by female abolitionist societies after 1835 constituted women's most extensive grassroots work during that decade. In 1837, from Concord, New Hampshire, Mary Clark reported to the Boston Female Anti-Slavery Society that, with "great unanimity and earnestness," her society had voted to have a petition and circular prepared. That same year, at its annual meeting, the Lynn Society agreed that petitioning was "one of the most efficient [means] that we can employ." Unlike other petition efforts, like the one Hicksite Quakers put forth during the

1835 Genesee Yearly Meeting in New York, this work brought women like Mary Clark into "direct . . . [contact] with the classes of the community — with the pro-slavery, with the indifferent, with those who are as much as ourselves opposed to slavery, *but*" were reluctant to sign a petition. The personal interactions that collecting signatures required, Rochester women suggested, caused "many who would not otherwise think about it . . . to give it a little place in their minds."[95]

The experience of collecting signatures and the controversy this effort generated forced many women to confront the tensions between their newly constructed identity as female abolitionists and more conservative definitions of woman. The ambitious scope of women's petitioning activities represented their entry into the world of mass democratic politics and implicitly signified their rejection of quiet influence at the hearth for a voice in the civic sphere. While some women would back away once they understood the implications of an identity that was now stretched to include political activism, others would become more radical in their assault on convention, and still others would be comfortable in living with contradiction. But whatever the individual responses to the controversies petition work sparked, the effort did pull many women into political action, most probably for the first time in their lives, and expanded ideas about the meaning of women's citizenship.[96]

In 1832, when Garrison was feeling his way to defining a role for women in abolitionism, he sensed that women might play a modest role in petitioning work: "I cannot see the slightest force in the argument, that because women can have no part in the final decision, they ought not to take any part in helping the subject towards that decision." For Garrison, it was clear that "they do not . . . petition, they only try to call the attention of the men of the acquaintance or neighborhood to facts that may induce them to take the step of petitioning."[97]

This limited conception of the female role in petitioning disappeared as abolitionists made this activity one of their main strategies. In 1835, hoping to force the discussion of slavery in the halls of Congress and in the parlors of American citizens, the American Anti-Slavery Society initiated a petition drive. When Congress passed the Gag Law in 1836, which tabled abolitionist petitions, the issue broadened beyond slavery to include the highly charged and very political question of free speech. If legislators hoped to stem the flow of petitions by their actions, they must have been disappointed, for abolitionist petitioning persisted. In 1838, the American Anti-Slavery Society forwarded to Washington petitions bearing 400,000 signatures. Two years later, an astonishing number of Americans, more than two million, had signed abolitionist petitions.[98]

Encouraged by male antislavery organizations to participate in the drive, female societies responded enthusiastically. A member of the Boston Female Anti-Slavery Society described petitioning as "a magnificent plan." In 1836, the Boston, Philadelphia, and New York female societies coordinated campaigns that reached into country towns and villages as well as into their own communities. The free black women of Connecticut undertook a petition drive aimed especially at other free women. Women proved to be enormously successful at collecting signatures, especially those of other women. Various studies suggest that women were, in fact, far more successful than men at this work. One scholar points out that women's involvement "immediately tripled the number of petition names secured previously by paid male agents."[99]

While women's petitions adopted a humble posture initially, the modest pose did not prevent accusations that women were meddling in politics. During the Second Anti-Slavery Convention of American Women in 1838, Angelina Grimké took on the critics and folded the new activity into an expanded definition of female duty. "Men may settle these and other questions at the ballot box," she declared, "but you have no such right. It is only through our petitions that you can reach the Legislature. It is, therefore peculiarly your duty to petition."[100]

Petition campaigns touched individuals and antislavery organizations in multiple ways. For societies like Boston, Philadelphia, and New York, which coordinated the work of local groups, the project demanded time, energy, skill, and the ability to direct and supervise effectively. When Caroline Weston was a member of the Boston society's petition committee, she admitted to an acquaintance in Franklin County, "I hardly know what steps to take." Although she was to organize Franklin County, she had no idea to whom she should send requests for assistance and names of people "to whom it would be proper or politic to correspond." While organizers could count on the assistance of female antislavery societies where they existed (although each would have to be contacted), as Caroline's letter suggested, they had to extend the antislavery network and engage newcomers in the work. Antislavery newspapers urged participation, while circulars sent through the mail gave the call. The *Advocate of Freedom* instructed its readers in 1838 to "circulate your petitions! Give every individual an opportunity to *sign* them, or to *refuse*. Don't wait for others—*go yourself—you*, reader—*man* or *woman*. Delay is dangerous." Societies undertook a considerable amount of correspondence. Julianna Tappan, corresponding secretary of the Ladies' New-York City Anti-Slavery Society, apologizing for her hastily written letter, explained that she was so busy writing societies about petitioning that she had no time to write decently.[101]

Those who were directing the drives provided general instructions and advice for the less knowledgeable. Although Mary Clark and her Concord society had decided to participate in the work, Mary did not know how to draw up a petition about Texas. She requested either a form or written suggestions about how to proceed. Once the petitions had been completed, local societies sometimes forwarded them on so that they could be prepared to be sent to Congress. Mary Weston described working with 248 petitions from Weymouth and 130 from Braintree: "I labored like a dog to get them [ready]." In some cases, women copied their petitions over, which perhaps explains the comment of one woman who remarked, "Having to send both to House & Senate makes the work no little job." [102]

In addition to directing the petition work of local groups, city antislavery organizations also canvassed in their own communities. They established committees to divide up the city into manageable sections and to recruit volunteers to do the petitioning. As a member of the Lynn Female Anti-Slavery Society explained, because the "highly important" work was "one of much labor, requiring prompt attention and perseverance," it needed workers "who have *warm hearts* and *willing minds*." Suggesting what qualities were needed to be effective, Mary Grew mused, "Is it not strange, that an *argument*, nay, a *train of reasoning*, should even be necessary to convince a human mind." [103]

When Mary Clark wrote on behalf of the Concord Female Anti-Slavery Society, she sought concrete advice, but she also wished to convey her association's willingness to bear the expenses of having the petition sent to every town in New Hampshire. A committee had been formed to oversee the printing and mailing of the materials. Her association's project shows that, while individual female societies might not have the same duties as a Boston or Philadelphia organization, they still were responsible for coordinating local effort and sometimes even more than local efforts.[104]

Canvassing with petitions was done door to door, in the same way that women sometimes circulated papers, almanacs, and other antislavery material. One woman might be responsible for several streets and would have to call at every house and repeat her calls if no one was at home. In one week in 1840, Deborah Weston estimated that she had walked twenty-one miles in her pursuit of signatures. No wonder some women remarked after a stint of work, "I wore myself out." As Deborah herself had commented in 1836, "I shall be thankful when it is over with, for it is hard work & takes up more time than I can spare." [105]

Deborah occasionally referred to her efforts as amusing. Others found "a victory" when their "arguments find a lodgement in the mind or our expostulations arouse the sympathies of the heart." Few were so positive. Most found canvassing difficult, tiring, and frustrating. Presenting an unpopular cause was embarrassing for some and humiliating for others. Sarah Rugg, after commenting that the work was "humbling," remarked that nothing but duty would induce her to take it on. Maria Child summed up the feelings of most women: Petitioning was "the most odious of all tasks." [106]

What made it so odious? Both the demanding character of the work and the response it evoked made women uncomfortable. The *Advocate of Freedom* urged women to plead the cause with their friends of both sexes. The paper assured women who took its advice that "from deference to your sex you will be heard when your companion would be hushed into silence. You will not be accused of partyism, of aspiring for office, or of being a spoke in the wheel of political machinery." The assurances were comforting but false.[107]

Canvassing every household in a neighborhood brought women, as the Lynn society had pointed out, into contact with all classes and types of people. Women in Fall River, Massachusetts, for example, called on factory workers, some of them Irish. One woman described "finding our way through crooked and dark entries, up steep and winding stair-cases" of tenement buildings. Although women did not often reveal their feelings about entering into households quite different from their own, there are hints that the experience of encountering unfamiliar class settings might not be congenial. Julianna Tappan's assignment, visiting elite women, seems at first glance as if it should have proved less awkward than canvassing in working-class areas. Julianna did not find it so. Her letter exudes the embarrassment she felt in elegant surroundings, "the splendidly furnished drawing-rooms of wealthy citizens in Hudson Square." Although she tried to cover her embarrassment with scorn for the ill-educated women with whom she spoke, her fervent statement that she was willing "to be *any thing, do any thing* . . . to honor Him" suggests that she had done just that.[108]

In some cases, as records show, women collected signatures of other women only. Since their strategy was to visit households during the day, men must often have been out at work. But women also ended up soliciting signatures from men. In Nantucket, Charlotte Austin reported leaving petitions in shops frequented by men for their signatures. This technique was perhaps more acceptable than what Miss Smith did. In her visits to almost every house in Glastonbury, Connecticut, the young woman presented her case to and argued with men. It was "the men, generally who needed 'free discussion,' " she discovered, for "the women would not act contrary to the ideas of the male part of their families."[109]

After a January afternoon spent on the "petition business," Lucy Chase reported feeling dispirited by a task that was "disagreeable because so few are willing to sign." Other women spoke of almost being thrown out of people's houses, of uncivil treatment, and of accusations of behaving in an unwomanly fashion and of meddling in male matters. Louisa Phillips, for one, was told to go home and mind her own business. But there were even graver insults. Some people suggested that petitioners were trollops, linking their behavior with sexual and racial deviance. And one woman told Deborah Weston, "She hoped all the young ladies who interest themselves in the matter would get what she supposed they were after[,] namely nigger husbands." Such comments were uttered in person and sometimes repeated in the newspapers.[110]

Anna Cook, who was circulating two petitions in Hadley, Massachusetts, described her reception: kindness from some, "by some cold neglect & by others open abuse, without any regard to my feelings personally, or for the slave." The rudeness that women encountered questioned their claim to middle-class respectability. Incivility made it clear that some parts of the community had determined that if abolitionists did not adhere to norms, if they did not act like "ladies" in public (inconspicuously), they would not be treated like ladies. There was little question about how many Americans interpreted the meaning of women's work in petition drives.[111]

Beyond the possibility of an uncertain reception, fatigue came from the repetition of the task. Wrote Sarah Rugg, "I have just circulated two petitions, & sent them on, I thought I had got through this unpleasant part of the business for a while; but lo & behold another is forthcoming; so we must make up our minds to keep at the work. . . . You know my sister what humbling work it is, to circulate petitions, & repeat them so often." Each petition representing one aspect of the antislavery campaign needed its own rationale, even when a woman was carrying two or three at the same time. Lists of petitions sent from the same town show different numbers signing each, revealing that a signature on one did not automatically lead to a signature on another.[112]

Women's petitioning activities continued right up to and through the Civil War. An 1842 circular, for instance, rallied women to take up the arduous work once again despite the sense that results were not "proportionate" to their efforts. Petitioning, they were reminded, represented the "only means of direct political action . . . which we can exert upon our Legislatures." Women repeatedly sent petitions to Congress and to their state legislatures. Women in Massachusetts, for example, mounted a campaign to overturn laws forbidding interracial marriage. The massive drive finally put enough pressure on state legislators that they repealed the offensive legislation. In 1847, Illinois women were less successful in using the petition as an instrument to eliminate that state's black code.[113]

Petitioning was the one task that demanded that women be at their most articulate. Petitions had different objectives, all of which had to be explained as persuasively as possible. Why should Texas be barred from the Union? Why did Congress have the ability to abolish slavery in the District of Columbia? Why should racial intermarriage be allowed in Massachusetts? What was the problem with the resolution adopted by the House of Representatives on December 21, 1837, in relation to slavery? No wonder that Louisa Phillips found that she had to study "a long time to become thoroughly acquainted with . . . [the] arguments."[114]

The actual situations that women encountered demonstrated their need for a wide range of information about slavery and "the affairs of our country." They had to mount arguments as well as counter what the Lynn society called "misapprehensions" and "fears." (Was it fear that led at least one woman to sign a petition and then to scratch off her name?) They had to be flexible and able to decide what approach might work best in each encounter. Sometimes it was not facts, figures, and arguments that were needed but a basic appeal to "feelings of compassion." Women collecting signatures found themselves explaining the need for immediate emancipation, the evils of slavery, the pertinence of political action, the character of the Union, and the character of female duty and appealing to the heart.[115]

A few of the comments women reported hearing while petitioning give some idea of the kinds of responses that were called for. "One woman said 'no I dont want 'em free, I dont want to have nothing to do with 'em, for niggers will be niggers let 'em be where they will' "; " 'I'm willing to put my name down' t'wont do any good or any harm' "; "Said she would not sign for the world, she wished she had slaves etc."; " 'This going about Petitions is doing more harm than anything she knew of, it will dissolve the Union' "; from an Irishman, " 'No . . . we wish to be liberated ourselves first; wait till you treat us as you ought, before you ask us to help you about the negroes' "; " 'thought the men perfectly capable of managing the government without their help.' " Anna Clark, who, like other petitioners, took along antislavery almanacs when she went to collect signatures, found that some of her purchasers' husbands reviled her, threatening to burn the almanacs and thundering that she was helping to dissolve the Union.[116]

Rachel Stearns's description of canvassing in Springfield, Massachusetts, in 1842 captures the experience. "As you very well know," she began, petitioning "is a task requiring more than ordinary patience." With "one person after another," she had to "begin at the Anti-slavery Alphabet, and go through the first principles with every one; to answer the question '*who is* Latimer'? 50 times over. But there is one comfort, that 50 people know who Latimer is, that last week did not know. In one house, where they did not know . . . we got *10 names*, in another that and occasional assistance from others has swelled our list considerably. Mother and I have spent all the time we could command possibly." She estimated that she spent about half an hour at each household debating questions.[117]

As women carried out their various responsibilities as members of female antislavery societies and confronted the varying responses to their activism, they experienced a range of emotions from despair to elation, at the money raised, the signatures secured, the sense of duty well done. Despite the complex feelings they expressed during the 1830s, many women expected their cause to triumph. When it did, they would know how much they had done to bring about the sweet moment of victory. Some women even went so far as to suggest that women's societies were more central to the cause of emancipation than men's groups. What would happen if all female societies were dissolved, Dorchester women were asked during their first annual meeting. Sin and infidelity would triumph, they were told, "in spite of all our brethren could do." [118]

In seeking to understand their place in the world, some women moved beyond religious rationales to place their activities within a historical context. Abolitionist women were the daughters of pilgrims, or even more saliently, the descendants of the Revolutionary generation. As one woman in a long letter to the *Liberator* reminded readers, during the Revolution women had not confined themselves to their domestic duties. "Facts innumerable show the ardor and zeal with which they were inspired. Look back and see the societies that were formed to supply the destitute with clothing!" Her conclusion sweepingly rejected criticism. "Let not the fear of man's ridicule, or his pretended anxiety for the supposed welfare of our sex, deter you from using all proper influence which you possess against sin." [119]

The boldness and pride this woman exhibited were widespread and were reflected in the proceedings of the three Anti-Slavery Conventions of American Women that took place at the end of the decade. These events highlighted women's importance to the movement and marked their coming of age in abolitionism. The first, held in 1837 in New York during the week that other benevolent and moral reform groups were also meeting, drew about 200 women, both white and black, from nine states. One delegate from New England pointed out the unprecedented nature of this public gathering. "To attend a Female Convention!" she exclaimed. "Once I should have blushed at the thought." At the end of the three-day affair, which, as the *Liberator* pointed out, had been "conducted with dignity and talent," the women had condemned racial prejudice, decried the indifference of American churches to the sin of slavery, exhorted females to accept petitioning as a yearly duty, and insisted that it was "the province of woman . . . to do all that she can by her voice, and her pen, and her purse . . . to overthrow the horrible system of American Slavery." Angelina Grimké also urged American women to reject "the circumscribed limits with which corrupt custom and a perverted application of Scripture have encircled her." And although not all of those attending were willing to go so far as Angelina Grimké in ignoring convention, the debate caused by her resolution was "animated and interesting."[120]

The following year, many more women (about 300) were in attendance at the second convention, this time in Philadelphia. The success of grass-roots female organizing was apparent in the financial aid promised by antislavery societies located in small communities in Maine, Rhode Island, Massachusetts, Pennsylvania, and New Hampshire. Meeting in the luxurious new Pennsylvania Hall, which also housed a free produce store and the offices of the abolitionist newspaper, the *Pennsylvania Freeman*, the women debated whether to invite men to their evening session. The Grimkés had already aroused clerical anger by addressing mixed audiences in their speaking tour in Massachusetts, and some delegates were unwilling to overstep the boundaries of propriety at their national convention. As a result, men were urged to attend a public but not officially sponsored session. Meanwhile, a mob in Philadelphia, perhaps 10,000 strong, made its disapproval clear in its efforts to disrupt the evening gathering. The next day, the mob destroyed Pennsylvania Hall. The women persevered, though, finishing their convention business elsewhere. As one abolitionist made clear, despite the violence and destruction, "The women have done nobly today. They have held their convention to finish their business in the midst of the fearful agitation. Their moral daring and heroism are beyond all praise. They are worthy to plead the cause of peace and universal liberty."[121]

The shocking events in Philadelphia illuminated the women's moral courage, the mob's intolerance, and problems beginning to divide abolitionists from one another. Organizers of the following year's meeting in

Philadelphia had difficulty finding any space for the convention. In the end, the convention was held not in a luxurious hall, spacious meetinghouse, or church, but in a riding school. And it was the last meeting of the Anti-Slavery Convention of American Women.[122]

By the late 1830s, the controversies over women's participation in the work of antislavery societies, the difficulties inherent in efforts to abolish slavery, and conflict within the ranks of abolitionists all challenged individual and collective commitment to the cause. Some women dropped out altogether; others formed new societies or took up new forms of work. Still others labored along, feeling isolated and often discouraged. Aroline Chase, a member of the Lynn Female Anti-Slavery Society, wrote her friend Abby Kelley in 1843, "I feel that I can not contend much longer unless renewed. . . . Every professed friend of the poor slave, turn on another track—our society I *suppose* has a name to live, but it is dead." Although she was proud of the part she had played in the petition drive that eventually persuaded Massachusetts legislators to repeal laws against interracial marriage, she wondered about the future. "You say I must not give up until 50," she reminded her friend. "I am 30 now [and] I feel as though I stand alone." The next decade would sorely test the ties of loyalty and commitment of women like Aroline who had labored so hard for the cause in the 1830s.[123]

Chapter 3
Persisting in the Cause
The 1840s and 1850s

Sow the seed, be never weary,

Let not fear thy mind employ;

Though the prospect be most dreary,

Thou may'st reap the fruits of joy;

Lo! the scene of verdure bright'ning,

See the rising grain appear;

Look again! the fields are whit'ning,

Harvest-time is surely near.[1]

In November 1841, as J. W. Thomas reviewed her involvement in anti-slavery in Kingston, Rhode Island, she confessed that many times during the year and a half that had just passed she had "felt that as a society, our work was almost done—that we sh'd have in the future to depend upon our individual effort—what was formerly all harmony, seem'd to bring forth many discordant sounds." One of many women who despaired about the future of organized antislavery work, Thomas wondered about the ultimate triumph of immediate emancipation during the troubling decade of the 1840s. Sarah Stearns, who interpreted the disunity in the abolitionist ranks as the sign of decline, remarked, "It is hard working up and interesting those whose Anti-Slavery sympathies are locked fast in the sleep of the New Organization."[2]

The division, formalized in 1840 when thirty-one prominent abolitionists, including eight blacks, withdrew from the American Anti-Slavery Society to form the American and Foreign Anti-Slavery Society (the "New

Organization"), had roots in disagreements that had simmered for years. An early expression of discord surfaced during Sarah and Angelina Grimké's speaking tour of New England in 1837. Although not originally intending to transgress gender norms, the women found themselves lecturing to audiences containing both men and woman. Attacked for their breach of conduct, the sisters defended their right to speak in public before mixed groups. Abolitionists disagreed about the validity of their argument and the wisdom of their public appearances.

Garrison came out strongly in support of both the conduct and the rationale the two sisters developed to justify it. Eventually he concluded that women had the right to participate equally with men in all facets of organized antislavery. In 1839, members of the Massachusetts Anti-Slavery Society, who agreed with Garrison, implemented his position by endorsing women as full members of the organization. The following year, the American Anti-Slavery Society followed suit at its annual meeting when a majority, including a large number of delegates from Massachusetts, approved Abby Kelley's appointment to the business committee. Abolitionists holding more conservative ideas about women's involvement in the cause or believing that debate over the woman question drew attention away from the evil of slavery were dismayed at the turn of events.

As Garrison embraced women's rights he also enlarged the reform agenda. He came to see abolitionism as only one of changes needed to re-structure American society. He promoted pacifism and argued that, since both the church and the state were corrupt, abolitionists should abandon them. To the many abolitionists hungering to carry the struggle against slavery into the center of political and religious life, Garrison's advice was unwelcome and counterproductive. Even though all abolitionists supported immediate emancipation as a goal, they bitterly disagreed about how to reach that goal. The American Anti-Slavery Society remained the strong-hold of Garrisonians who clung to moral suasion. Those hesitant about women's rights, or eager to enter politics and to cleanse the churches, aligned themselves with the American and Foreign Anti-Slavery Society.[3]

Both national organizations attempted to line up local and state associations to buttress its positions. While local groups did align with one or the other of the two national societies, sometimes dividing in the process, many grassroots organizations did not find the disputes at the top comprehensible or even important. As Maria Child noted, Northampton abolitionists "have a very dim idea of what all this quarreling is about. They have a vague notion that is a squabble between Presbyterians and Quakers." In Ohio, a center of abolitionist fervor in the 1830s, antislavery advocates tried to sidestep the necessity of choosing sides and worked to compromise on issues that proved divisive in Boston and New York. To some black abolitionists, the disagreements diverted attention from the real struggle: the growth of slavery and the deteriorating condition of free blacks. White leaders, embroiled in controversies, were neglecting true abolitionism that ranged "from the mere act of riding in public conveyances to the liberation of every slave."[4]

As women examined the condition of abolitionism, not surprisingly they often noted strife and division. When one-time supporters abandoned antislavery altogether or gave their allegiance to rival organizations, committed women talked of apathy and slumber. Such comments suggest not only that these women accurately perceived that the days of rapid and unified growth had ended but also that they feared falling asleep or becoming apathetic themselves. And although many of them maintained their commitment (and, indeed, in a state like Rhode Island kept the cause of organized antislavery alive), they often judged their efforts insignificant in light of internal division and general indifference to the sacred cause of emancipation. "We are very feeble," wrote one Uxbridge, Massachusetts, woman, and her cry of distress was echoed throughout the decade.[5]

The experiences of working for the abolition of slavery during the 1840s were varied. Of the societies established during the 1830s, probably the majority divided into factions or died altogether, leaving those who had been members feeling frustrated and isolated. But new associations devoted exclusively to agitating for immediate emancipation continued to spring up. Because neither the old nor the new national body had the power or prestige of one unified organization or much influence over local and state associational affairs, and because there were no more meetings of the National Convention of Anti-Slavery Women to direct local energies, new societies faced the challenge of charting their own paths. In Michigan, the state antislavery society informed new female antislavery groups that they were on their own "as to the plans and manner of perfecting your organizations."[6]

Despite some women's feeling that the cause was declining or that they were laboring in isolation, and despite some scholars' suggestion that women who disagreed with Garrisonians retreated to safer causes than antislavery, the 1840s actually created new ways for women to express antislavery convictions. Working for emancipation through the program of moral suasion favored by the antislavery associations of the 1830s was only one among several alternatives. Political and religious initiatives attracted many who believed direct action could change institutions. Informal working groups like sewing circles adopted projects ranging from making items for antislavery fairs to raising money for slaves who had fled to Canada. Many women, by choice or necessity, worked alone, perhaps establishing a Sabbath school for freed blacks or concealing a fugitive slave and giving him or her a small sum to help the flight to freedom. Although historians have called some of these groups and activities conservative and others radical, in the context of the time, all these choices were radical, and often unpopular. Certainly, those espousing any form of abolitionist sentiment were firmly in the minority.[7]

The proliferation of opportunities to work for immediate emancipation had far more positive consequences than many realized at the time. On the one hand, people who disagreed with Garrison's stance on women and his insistence on linking the goal of ending slavery to other reforms could continue to pursue antislavery in ways that did not so obviously threaten gender norms or their claim to middle-class respectability. On the other hand, some men and women who had not been involved in abolitionism in the 1830s, like Rochester's Hicksite Quakers, were drawn into Garrisonian abolitionism by his emphasis on egalitarianism and his enthusiasm for reform. Others obsessed with a particular issue could concentrate their energies on that cause. Esther Moore, the first president of the Philadelphia Female Anti-Slavery Society (PFAS), withdrew because she was "more interested in the Vig[ilance] Com[mittee]" that aided escaping fugitives. Different strategies also offered different possibilities for leadership. Vigilance work engaged African Americans more than white abolitionists. The committee with which Esther Moore hoped to cooperate thus provided black women with leadership opportunities that were new.[8]

Ironically, the proliferation of approaches and choices made many abolitionists keenly conscious of their minority status. In 1845, Rhoda De Garma bemoaned "the deviations and betrayals of those that once stood faithful" in Rochester. Working alone or with just a few friends, counting the defectors and those who joined competing groups, contributed to a sense of isolation perhaps sharper than that felt in the 1830s when the angry hostility at least suggested that abolitionists were modern martyrs. For some, indifference was worse than hostility. In this situation, the antislavery network created by women in the 1830s and expanded in the following decade performed a vital role in sustaining community.[9]

Although accounts of abolitionism in the 1840s have concentrated on male activism in politics, women continued to make significant contributions to antislavery. Collecting signatures for petitions, circulating tracts and newspapers, and fund-raising were all tasks women undertook successfully. Increasingly, they played an important role in creating propaganda for the elimination of slavery, in mounting rituals to celebrate abolitionism, and in helping to devise a heroic history for antislavery.

In many communities, women helped to keep the spark of abolitionism alive, although that spark might appear to be a feeble one. Women who accepted Garrison's program of moral suasion rather than political action were not at the margins of antislavery but at its center. As Louisa Beal pointed out in 1845, "Most of the people here [in Hingham, Massachusetts] cannot perceive the intimate connexion they have with this diabolical institution." It was women like Louisa who kept insisting to neighbors and friends that the slavery question involved them personally.[10]

While the controversies that seemed so vital to abolitionist leaders contributed to division or disbandment of some antislavery societies, there were other reasons that associations formed in the 1830s faltered. The cause of emancipation seemed remote to many members of local antislavery societies who had never seen a slave; many of them most likely had never even seen a free African American. Certainly, most had not observed the institution of slavery firsthand. Furthermore, few could see much progress toward immediate emancipation. While the petition drives, the great grassroots effort of the 1830s, eventually resulted in some victories at the state level, there were none on the national level. The vocabulary used by female abolitionists—apathy, indifference, slumber—revealed not only their own fears about themselves but also their fatigue. "Our besetting temptation is to weary of the work," women in Weymouth and Braintree observed. Many did yield to that temptation. Eliza Boyd, a member of the Lynn Female Anti-Slavery Society, reported in 1839 that most of the "members of our society have fallen" into "a long and deep slumber." Aroline Chase felt the brunt of the apathy. Agreeing that other members of the society had given up and were going to "*dancing parties*," she feared she could "not contend much longer unless renewed." "I feel as though I stand alone," she lamented. Although a few Lynn women managed to keep an antislavery sewing circle going at least until 1846, they were, in their own view, "unorganized."[11]

Other factors, evidence of which is hard to recover 150 years later, doubtless played a part in weakening associational antislavery. One woman identified "the New Organization, pro Slavery opposition and the Harrison mania" as forces paralyzing antislavery. Religious enthusiasms, like political enthusiasms, also drew people away from associations. One woman noted the impact of the Millerite movement that convinced its thousands of adherents in New England and upstate New York that the second coming of Christ was imminent. As the 1840s advanced, she remarked, "many who

THE OLD GRANITE STATE,

Judson.   Abby.   John.   Asa.

A Song,

COMPOSED, ARRANGED AND SUNG, BY

THE HUTCHINSON FAMILY.

BOSTON,

Published by OLIVER DITSON Washington St.

Price 30 cts. nett

Cover from the sheet music of a song written and sung by the Hutchinson family, whose spirited singing enlivened abolitionist meetings in the 1840s. (Boston Athenæum)

have been heretofore good abolitionists, believe now that the world will be . . . [ended]," and all the slaves liberated, rendering it "unnecessary for them to do anything for the cause."[12]

Some associations did remain active during the 1840s. What differentiated these antislavery societies from those that quietly died was less the composition of the organization than the leadership, attention to organizational details, and type of work the society adopted. The history of three local antislavery societies highlights both the differences and commonalities between antislavery associations that survived divisions, disputes, and apathy. Certain characteristics and patterns of each individual society also suggest the ways in which these local groups resembled more prominent antislavery organizations in larger places.

Like its better-known big-city counterpart the Philadelphia Female Anti-Slavery Society, the Salem Female Anti-Slavery Society continued to operate as a female society through the Civil War. It remained loyal to Garrison and supported his stance on women, although members made no move to merge with a male society or to admit men. Garrison's condemnation of American churches, however, did strike a deep chord. The 1842 Annual Report emphatically rejected "the spirit of the American church, and its benevolent and religious societies, which cries union and peace before purity—we reject as antichristian the spirit which attempts to christianize far distant heathen, at the expense of heathen at home." [13]

While the Dover (New Hampshire) Anti-Slavery Sewing Circle also continued on until the Civil War, like the Ladies' New-York City Anti-Slavery Society of the previous decade, it had no quarrel with the American churches. The Dover circle enjoyed close connections with local clergy and helped to keep alive a monthly concert of prayer for the slave that rotated between the different Protestant churches. Its support of the American and Foreign Anti-Slavery Society (AFAS) rather than the American Anti-Slavery Society (AAS), expressed the group's evangelical sympathies. While its ideological commitments differed somewhat from those of the Salem women, the character of its work was not radically dissimilar. Despite close ties with clerical abolitionists, the Dover women were quite capable of exercising independence of judgment.

Like the better-known Western New York Anti-Slavery Society, the Portland (Maine) Anti-Slavery Society was on the cutting edge of abolitionism with both male and female members and officers. Like the Salem society, it tended to be critical of the religious establishment. The decision to hold meetings on Sunday symbolized the members' dissatisfaction with the religious status quo. Yet, the society's success probably owed more to the kind of work undertaken in Portland than its membership and meeting policies.[14]

Commonalities between the Dover, Salem, and Portland groups were more important than ideological disagreements. Each of the organizations was committed to immediate emancipation as a general goal. All three enjoyed effective leadership or had at least one person willing to shoulder the responsibility for seeing that associational life continued. Each society initiated substantial projects that involved the membership and, in two cases, reached out into the community. Surviving records make it clear that two of the groups paid careful attention to organizational issues. And all three generated enough funds to make decisions about spending them significant and engaging for the membership. Collectively, the societies made tangible for members a cause that all too easily could appear remote and abstract.

The Salem Female Anti-Slavery Society, formed in 1834 and reorganized in 1836, generally sided with Garrison in the disputes at the end of the decade. Its independence of spirit, however, was clear in its ability to retain its ties with Garrison while disagreeing with some of his positions. As one member of the society explained in 1839, members did not concur in all of Garrison's "doctrines—we are not decidedly non-resistent."[15] However, the society (like the PFAS) did support Garrison's position on women. In its 1840 annual report, the women declared that the work of antislavery was so important that they could not stop to discuss with their critics "the disputed question of woman's rights or even to disprove the oft-asserted fact, that in this laboring, we have advanced beyond the limits of our 'appropriate sphere.'" The society showed no interest in playing out their views of the women question in the company of men. It continued as a female society for more than thirty years.[16]

Perhaps the Salem women had no interest in including men into their society because over the years they had built up a strong, efficient, and businesslike organization. From the beginning, the women had taken organizational matters seriously. Early on, they dealt with the issue of promptness and voted to have a class to inform themselves "on the manner of properly conducting society meetings." In 1839, they further tightened procedures by voting to have regular quarterly business meetings, with "*no business be transacted at any other time* except it be a *special meeting* called for this purpose." At the same time they established a fine for absent board members and determined that no money could be paid from treasury "without a written order from the President." When the controversies beset the movement, the Salem association had its organizational house in order and was able to withstand the divisiveness it deplored.[17]

The projects the Salem society adopted also contributed to vitality and longevity. Women selected initiatives that were tangible and put them into continuous and fruitful contact with different segments of Salem's population. The presence of black members encouraged special initiatives. As Clarissa Lawrence, the society's African American vice president in 1839, insisted, "We meet the monster prejudice *everywhere*. We have not power to contend with it, we are so down-trodden. We cannot elevate ourselves. You must aid us." The society was responsive, and over the years, it undertook many efforts in Salem's African American community. A few examples show the range of their involvement. In 1836, the women provided supplies for the assistant teacher in the "Colored School"; in 1838, a committee studied the situation of Salem's black residents, and members decided to use some funds to help fugitive slaves. The same year, they established a sewing school for young black females. Later in the decade, they voted for funds to help in "redeeming the chapel of the colored people." In the 1840s, the society continued their commitment to African Americans, overseeing a sewing school for young girls, assisting fugitive slaves, and donating money to the Sabbath School for black children. The women also supported efforts to integrate Salem's public schools.[18]

The Salem society undertook major propaganda efforts. On several occasions, they hired traveling agents to lecture on abolitionism. Their most extensive propaganda work, however, consisted of the lecture series that they sponsored successfully for many years in Salem. Mounting the lectures involved a host of decisions, from selecting speakers, hiring halls and sometimes protection, to pricing and printing tickets, advertising the lectures, and spending the proceeds. The lecture series provided members with a sense of satisfaction, for it gave the society visibility and, when audiences were large, suggested that progress was being made toward the ultimate goal of emancipation. Members must have enjoyed hosting major figures of the antislavery movement and highlighting their society's role in connecting Salem to the larger world of abolitionism.

The Salem society funded its array of initiatives partly through the lecture series and partly through local fund-raising efforts. While Salem women contributed to fairs held in other communities, they also held several antislavery fairs in their own town. In keeping with their interest in the freed black community, the society made a point of featuring black involvement. Fairs offered goods made by black children and young people. In 1839, African American women were responsible for the refreshment room, and they furnished a dinner during the fair. On at least one occasion, some of the leftover items were given as presents to the African American children in the society's sewing school.[19]

In Salem, women who worked with the antislavery society found many rewarding projects that helped provide their organization with a strong sense of purpose and identity. Eventually, the women came to recognize that they had a history, one worth knowing and preserving. In 1852, the society decided to have one of its officers read aloud all the records of the organization, and eight years later, it voted that the corresponding secretary "be empowered to find if possible the old Record Book." The search succeeded, and, unlike most association documents, that record book has survived until the present.[20]

Another rare set of records reveals the women of Dover, New Hampshire, charting a somewhat different course than the Salem women. In 1835, a group of Dover abolitionists formed the Ladies Anti-Slavery Society. During the 1830s, they voted for funds to support the American Anti-Slavery Society, but in the ensuing controversy many of the members abandoned the AAS and Garrisonians. In October 1839, the minutes recorded that the society admitted several men as members, an action that probably precipitated the division. The following February, several women, including many of the officers, of the Ladies Anti-Slavery Society reorganized as the Dover Anti-Slavery Sewing Circle. The circle's goal of emancipation "by discussion, collecting, and disseminating information on the subject of Slavery and raising funds in aid of the Anti-Slavery cause" suggested that the inclusion of men rather than disagreement about ends had caused the reorganization.[21]

The circle's support for Lewis Tappan and the American Missionary Association further indicated its sympathy for the evangelical wing of abolitionism. But just as the Salem women believed they had the right to pick and choose among Garrison's positions, the Dover women felt a similar freedom. Despite the rejection of an organization in which men and women participated as equals, the women invited men to join as honorary and as dues-paying members. Some of the men were making motions as early as the July meeting of 1840, and minutes listed them as members by 1849. Obviously, the men were not sewing or working members, but to a limited extent, the circle united men and women in its organizational life. Perhaps the women's reluctance to include men in their original society had something to do with wanting to retain control of their own affairs. If so, we must modify the view of evangelical women's groups as being less autonomous than Garrisonian antislavery societies.[22]

While there were some lapses in organizational regularity, the circle took its purpose seriously. At the beginning of its new life, the women decided to undertake "some kind of useful or ornamental work" during meetings under the direction of the board of managers. Just as in Salem, where the women had put its organizational house in order, so too did the Dover circle attend to the relationship between organizational structure and work. During the 1840s, a "Purchasing and Appraising Committee" was established, and there were specially appointed managers for sewing and managers for knitting. Punctuality was held up as a goal, and members were expected to be present and to work. Their desire for active membership was apparent in the circle's decision to list in the record book "only the names of those who have paid for the last year," as well as in the election of two women to visit absent members and collect fines for nonattendance.[23]

Dover women did not sponsor public lecture series, but they did keep an antislavery concert of prayer alive in their community for nearly thirty years and used the collection money for the circle's projects. While there is no evidence of their involvement with New Hampshire's free blacks, the Dover women created strong connections with black people, particularly fugitive slaves. On one occasion, a member who knew "by experience the evils of Slavery gave some account of her escape." African American "gentlemen," "Mr. Clark a fugitive slave" and "Capt Jonathan Walker with the *branded hand*," were some of those who also attended meetings and helped make real the plight of slaves and fugitive slaves. On at least one occasion, the circle decided to use its funds to circulate scriptures among slaves and, on another, to support the dissemination of abolitionist propaganda in New Mexico. But the circle concentrated mainly on projects for fugitive slaves in Canada, corresponding with, among others, Fidelia Coburn, a teacher in Canada, to discover what aid Dover women might provide.[24] Women took keen interest in those projects for which they either worked directly or to which they made financial contributions. Lively discussion preceded their decisions, and they saw new information as a reason for reviewing and sometimes changing collective agreements.[25] And, despite its ties with a wing of abolitionism often labeled conservative (especially in terms of its views on women), Dover women did not confine themselves to sewing in one another's houses. They undertook several petition drives, paid to have tracts circulated, and, by the 1850s, summoned the citizens of Dover to a meeting on behalf of Kansas.[26]

Bringing men and women into the same association was no easy task, as the defection of Tappan and other evangelical abolitionists from the AAS dramatically indicated. A tart letter to Amos Phelps from a woman who identified herself only as Phebe appeared in the *Liberator* in 1838. If men and women were together in a social setting, she asked, would it be wrong for a women to "converse freely, on any question of religion or morals that might be introduced, giving their opinions, &cc.&cc?" What if the men and women adopted certain rules for the purpose of convenience? "Would it be sinful for women to open their lips?" Could women meet alone, adopt rules, and "use prayer, exhortation, discussion" without sin? And if a man should come into the meeting, "must every woman forthwith close her lips?"[27]

These queries were not academic, although Phebe had obviously already worked out her answers. In a similar vein, writing from Northborough, Massachusetts, in 1840, Maria Rice related the problems that had cropped up during her society's annual meeting a month before. "By my simply rising and shewing that I was in favor of a certain resolve," Maria wrote, "I became so obnoxious, that a certain gentleman said he wished the Ladies would form a society by themselves as they would do no good." Such disagreements, Maria felt, would certainly end in the division of her society. Alvan Ward told a similar story of opposition to a mixed society in Ashburton, where women were advised to act alone or to talk to their husbands at home: "Now it happens that many who join a society have no husbands[,] and there are others who have husbands who do not meet with the same society[,] and still another class who have husbands, if they should as[k] them 'at home' would answer them in such a snappish way if they answered at all that they would know little or nothing the better for it."[28]

In Maine, however, the Portland Anti-Slavery Society was open to both sexes. The society's constitution, which in part was modeled on the Declaration of Independence, used both political and religious language to condemn slavery but omitted gender-specific appeals. It made no special mention of the plight of female slaves and directed its call to duty to "every individual." A majority of those present at the organizing meeting in January 1844, were women, and the slate of officers selected made a modest gesture to gender equality. The president and treasurer were male, the directors female, while a man and a woman served as vice presidents. The efforts to work toward a more inclusive antislavery organization were in the same spirit as those made in the Western New York Antislavery Society.[29]

During the first years of its existence, the meetings of the society were lively. Men and women debated the most volatile issues of the day, including the relationship between the churches and abolitionism, compensated emancipation, political action, and the propriety of adding Garrisonian to the association's title. Discussion, carried on with "the most perfect friendliness," was often stimulated by a resolution or by the presence of nonmembers, like "our liberty party friends." The most troublesome issue was clearly the relationship between the church and abolitionism, "some members . . . thinking the church much less guilty than others charge it with being."[30]

In 1850, the society was reorganized, with many of the same people playing leadership roles in getting the society going again. It seems as if conversation alone, no matter how controversial the subject, could not ensure organizational longevity. This time the board of managers, particularly Elizabeth Montfort, took responsibility for continuity. The board made a critical decision about the function of the society. "We have proceeded immediately to action, not desiring or intending to profess merely a nominal existence," Elizabeth explained. The action consisted of lecture series, offered initially on Sundays, "that being the day when the ear of the people can be most readily gained." During the first year, the Portland Anti-Slavery Sewing Circle helped to defray the expenses and get the series off the ground. Even more than the Salem Female Anti-Slavery Society, which undertook a variety of projects, the Portland Anti-Slavery Society drew its energy from connecting the local community to some of the great figures of abolitionism, including Samuel May, Charles Remond, and Wendell Phillips.[31]

Like their big-city counterparts, small antislavery societies like Salem's embarked on a project that drew members together to labor on a common task and often linked societies with one another. The petition drives represented women's most visible and perhaps most important grassroots work for abolitionism during the 1830s. In 1834, the Boston Female Anti-Slavery Society began another sort of initiative with its small-scale antislavery fair. From this modest beginning, the practice of holding antislavery fairs spread. Increasingly in the 1840s and 1850s, antislavery fairs replaced petition drives as a central activity for abolitionist women of different ideological persuasions and races. Garrisonian and non-Garrisonian women, Liberty Party women, African American women, and women who worked to help fugitive slaves all held fairs. Although undertaken primarily to raise money, women's fairs made other contributions that were less tangible than cash but no less important. Above all, the fairs fostered communication and sympathy between women that helped keep them involved in the abolitionist cause.[32]

The most elaborate fairs were mounted in cities like Boston, Philadelphia, Rochester, and Utica. The big fairs, which might last more than a week, featured goods from Europe as well as items made by scores of individual women in country towns and villages. Some fairs were extremely lucrative. Over the years, the Boston Female Anti-Slavery Society raised $65,000, some of which helped to pay the debts of the *National Anti-Slavery Standard*, an abolitionist newspaper based in New York. Between 1840 and 1861, Philadelphia fairs realized $32,000, most of which went to keep the state abolitionist society afloat. Fairs held in Ohio to assist the Western Anti-Slavery Society were less profitable than ones in Boston and

Philadelphia, but, as the executive committee pointed out, the proceeds were essential: "Funds can thus be obtained to aid our cause, which could not so readily be acquired by any other means."[33]

Smaller fairs, like those held in Salem, Massachusetts, and Salem, Ohio, raised less money and lasted fewer days than the major city fairs. Although unsold goods were circulated from one fair to another, smaller fairs usually had less elaborate articles more suited for their buying public than for the more sophisticated urban consumers of Boston and Philadelphia. But while there were important differences between small fairs and large fairs, rural fairs and city fairs, and perhaps even between "new organization" and "old organization" fairs, all provided a focus for women's involvement in abolitionism and raised money for which they had to make distribution decisions. Fairs provided an important and immediate purpose and gave visibility and life to the cause of emancipation.[34]

Many of the goods sold at the fairs were sewed or crafted by women. Sewing was, of course, a traditional female activity. Before the introduction of manufactured cloth, women had focused on making clothes for their families. With ready-made cloth, however, that task had become less onerous. Women now had time to do more than plain sewing. Indeed, schools and magazines like *Godey's Lady Book* encouraged women to engage in fancy sewing and other forms of handwork. The middle-class woman's productions ornamented her person and her house. Her parlor was the showcase for her most successful efforts and a testimony to her skill and genteel taste.

But the creation of items to be sold at antislavery fairs was at once well within the parameters of genteel behavior and at odds with it. Items produced at home assumed a political and public purpose and meaning when they were sold for profit in settings designed to encourage consumption and the exchange of money. Like petitioning, fair work raised all sorts of questions about propriety. Should middle-class women be engaged in what was clearly a commercial activity? Should they make and sell frivolous goods that encouraged people to waste their money? When black and white women cooperated in producing goods for a fair, as they did in the New York Anti-Slavery Society sewing circle in 1842, other questions about interracial cooperation in both home settings and public spaces came to the fore. In the name of duty, abolitionist women again demonstrated a propensity to stake out areas for action that confounded notions of public, private, male, female, white and black.[35]

Even among the women who worked for fairs there were moments of tension between the values of a consumer culture and those of a producer culture, between standards of gentility, ostentation, and Christian plainness, and between rural usefulness and urban fashion. Yet, no matter where individual women stood on any one of these issues, their very participation in fair work enmeshed them in the modern marketplace. All of them wished to make a tidy profit.

Mounting a successful fair demanded considerable business and organizational acumen, entrepreneurial energy, and even courage. In Concord, New Hampshire, Mary Rogers reported that her society had voted to hold a fair yet were somewhat fearful about the new venture. "We felt as if we were stepping into the dark, and are still haunted by presages of failure and disappointment, but have pretty much decided to do the best we can." The experience must have been successful, for Concord women persisted in fair work. In Mary's mind, the utility of the effort surpassed profits; it was "necessary to have a common object of interest to concentrate our efforts and prevent them being diverted into other channels." [36]

Whether the fair was to be small or large, fair managers needed to start working months in advance of the event. First, they needed to choose a date that would ensure a large crowd of buyers (i.e., the Christmas holidays, the Worcester cattle show, the Brown University commencement). Then they had to compose and send out letters and flyers carrying the date of the fair, advertising its purpose, and soliciting aid. Women were urged to organize "speedily" into sewing circles to create "gifts of beauty and fancy articles." In order to have a plethora of tempting goods, well made and tantalizing for the prospective buyer, fair organizers might specify items that were appropriate for the anticipated market. It was often necessary to follow up with more detailed assistance. Elisabeth Nile and her sisters were more than willing to work for the Boston fair, but they were "totally ignorant of the manner of cutting or making" the right sorts of garments. To ensure they did not waste their labor they asked for a line with some directions. Fair managers often found themselves not only furnishing advice but also patterns and sometimes materials, for, in some communities like Kingston, Rhode Island, "there are some whose means are small, but whose hearts and hands are willing." In order to ensure the fair's profitability, they also solicited merchants for donations of goods or money. [37]

As the time of the fair grew near, managers secured a place for the fair and arranged for advertising, refreshments, and decorations. They engaged speakers and, occasionally, entertainment. They recruited workers to unpack and arrange the goods and to take responsibility for manning the tables. In Spring Garden, Ohio, the latter tasks were fraught with anxiety. Sarah Ernst reported that all of her table tenders were "uncertain, until the very week of the sale and of course only here to take charge of tables, which I had to spread and provide for." [38]

After the fair, organizers faced bookkeeping chores and the task of publicizing fair results so that workers who lived too far away to attend the fair would know their work was not in vain. Decisions had to be made about unsold goods. As fairs became common, a network of exchange developed, allowing unsold items to be sent on to another fair. But there were other options for the remainders. After the 1839 fair in New Bedford, for example, Deborah Weston, who had intended to "raise as much money as I can on the articles I have," ended up selling the remaining articles by hawking them door to door. After Deborah had sold the last item, she was thankful that "the last fair or sale of any kind that I am to have any thing to do with for the present is over, & I feel as if the weight of mountains had been taken off." [39] Altogether, having a fair was a formidable undertaking.

The Boston and Philadelphia fairs reached far into the hinterlands as well as to the British Isles for goods to sell. Products from Birmingham and Glasgow joined objects sent from Hudson, Ohio; Minnesota territory; and Staten Island. The offerings of the British women signified their solidarity with the American antislavery movement now that their own struggle for the emancipation of slaves in the West Indies had succeeded. For many American abolitionist women during the 1840s and 1850s, the articles they made for one of the big fairs represented a vital connection, perhaps their only connection, with the larger world of antislavery. As Sarah Stearns explained, "since our socy in Greenfield has but a nominal existence and scarcely that, I rejoice in being connected with one so zealous, self-denying and efficient as the Boston Female Anti-Slavery Socy." Fair work created the connections that could keep alive energy, commitment, and faith in the cause. [40]

In Georgetown, Massachusetts, Deborah Palmer anticipated that the fair work would recruit women and provide a focus for their efforts. "I think something to interest the attention of sewing circles would be very beneficial to the cause," she wrote. "I think it would augment our numbers and cause a more punctual attendance." In addition, Deborah felt that this work would have a transforming effect on the women who did it and would be the means by which "the families where our members reside . . . [might] be *abolitionised.*" Evelina Smith agreed that fair work could "waken up dormant zeal, that is slumbering in the hearts of our Hingham Abolitionists." But fair work not only provided a meaningful purpose, it also connected women to the distant goal of emancipation, a point made explicit in the 1843 Boston fair notice. "The steady continuance of such

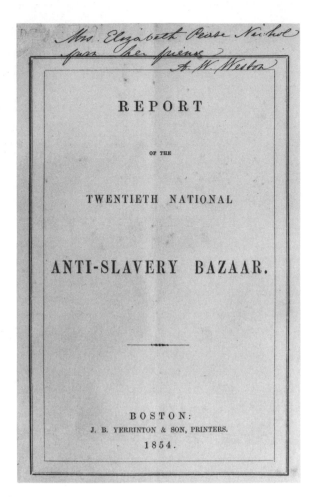

REPORT

OF THE

TWENTIETH NATIONAL

ANTI-SLAVERY BAZAAR.

BOSTON:
J. B. YERRINTON & SON, PRINTERS.
1854.

Reports on fair results like this one were an important way of communicating with those who had produced items for the fair and of highlighting the progress of the antislavery cause. (Boston Athenæum)

efforts as our Fairs," the circular claimed, "had so greatly modified public sentiment that Slavery is half abolished. Let us then receive your aid to complete the good work so begun."[41]

The connection between the labor of individuals and small groups and the goal of emancipation was not always obvious during the 1840s, however. Frances Drake read the notice for the 1843 fair to women in Leominster, but "somehow our people cant understand an address unless it is directed especially to them. I have read again, and again the address by your committee, to the ladies, but they dont seem to feel it means them." Requesting an appeal directed specifically to the women of her town would help. But the fact that the work done the previous year had never been acknowledged was an additional obstacle. The women who had contributed to the fair expected polite recognition for their efforts and information about how their work had made a difference. "There were several who gave something that said at the time they gave," Frances wrote, "they *did not see what good it was or going to do* . . . because they have not seen the result of our labour, they have no faith to do anything more. Therefore, when you write us I hope you will send us a very emphatick Thank you Ladies."[42]

A notice for the 1841 Boston fair acknowledged the various circumstances facing possible contributors to the fair. Some lived in communities where an antislavery society still existed to structure collective efforts. Others lived in places where there was no society, or where the one that technically existed was, in fact, dead. In these situations, women were urged not to abandon the cause because of "protracted struggle and unanticipated perplexities" but to unite their efforts. "In many places," however, the circular recognized, "the laborer bears alone the heat and burden of the day. To such we would say, be resolute and self-sustained. You do but *seem* to be alone. Within your call are true and faithful hearts. . . . Help shall arise by your side soon, and at the eleventh hour the ranks will be full."[43]

While the circular accurately identified the different circumstances that shaped the work that could be done for the fair, the scenario of help at the eleventh hour was much too optimistic. Many women who wished to aid one of the large fairs found it difficult to get assistance. In North Attleboro, Sarah Rhoads thought the people were "in great measure asleep in regard to slavery," although she was planning to get a sewing circle to meet and work for few weeks. "I hope I shall get something," she wrote, "and I will do all myself considering the little time I can possibly spare on account of my own business." In Worcester the same year, Caroline Bartlett had a frustrating time trying to interest women in the fair. She had called on people with the plan of setting aside one day a week for work. No one came to the first meeting. The second meeting was only minimally more successful, with one old lady in attendance whose skills were such that she "could only sew a plain seam." In all, Caroline managed to round up only five people willing to help.[44]

Indifference, of course, was just one of the reasons that organizing for a fair was so difficult. Division, clerical opposition, and alternative ways to work for antislavery also played a part. In Taunton, Mrs. Woodward had a raft of excuses for her refusal to contribute to that year's fair: "She did not feel that interest in the cause that she used to, they were bedeviled, She did not know what they did with the money, and among other things, she said Mr. Emery (the minister) had not said one word on the subject for more than a year." Frances Drake faced opposition from evangelical abolitionists who advised members of the female society not to cooperate with her fair efforts. To Frances's disgust, they had some impact. "All those who were not thoroughly abolitionised, or were deficient in moral courage," she complained, "were so foolish as to be influenced by them and were so ungenerous as to even send in some work *unfinished*." Although Frances considered these women unenlightened, they had not abandoned abolitionism. They had merely chosen to work for the Canada Mission for fugitive slaves rather than for the fair.[45]

Frances Drake remained firmly committed to Garrisonian abolitionism, and her letters written over a series of years give insight into what working for the fair meant on a personal level. They also suggest why abolitionist women often felt beleaguered during the 1840s. Her first extant letter from late in 1842 described the divisions within Leominster that left only a few women interested in joining her. The sewing circle to which she had belonged actually had thirty members. But when it had changed its constitution to favor the "New Organization," she had withdrawn. Although that circle remained active, she had no sympathy for the group and chose to labor alone.[46]

The following year, Frances was hoping to form a Garrisonian antislavery society, knowing the name would keep out any but those whom she could accept as committed abolitionists. The New Organization now dominated the Leominster Female Anti-Slavery Society, and Frances was working with some "poor common people" who could do "only plain needlework." This modest success was enhanced by an agreement she had worked out with some local shopkeepers to take farm goods in exchange for the English articles and fancy goods her workers needed. Just before the Boston fair, she sent in greens for decoration but feared that the items from Leominster would arrive too late. She could not get anyone to finish the goods with her and had, in fact, more materials than she could use. "But I cannot raise help for love or money," she lamented. "I now have to sit up till one oclock at night to get them ready. . . . Every one I have asked to assist (with one or two excepts) has refused. . . . I am at time almost disheartened, when I see what I have to do, with my poor feeble eyes, and my little ones to care for, I find it next to an impossibility for me to complete the work."[47]

Frances did not give up her struggle to arouse the indifferent women of her community. Nor did she fail to work for the Boston fair. Even in 1848, when for the first time she could not spare a cent for the fair, she sent greens to Boston and offered to cook such country delicacies as applesauce and doughnuts. In 1850, she had extended her efforts all over the county and managed to get enough women to cooperate to sponsor a country table at the fair.[48]

As the example of Frances Drake makes clear, many women persisted in their fair work despite many obstacles. When J. W. Thomas sent in fair goods from Kingston, she gave some hint of the feelings she and her friends had experienced as they labored for the fair. "Some few among us have persevered under all discouragements from the lukewarm and the indifferent," she wrote, "and have devoted an afternoon of each week for some time past in working for the fair." [49]

Fair work demanded more than persistence and sociable afternoons of sewing in one another's houses, however. Women had to coordinate work, observe timetables, and assess who could make what. A certain amount of publicity might be necessary, as it was in Rochester, New York. The work group there, concerned by its invisibility, decided to publish a notice of its existence in the newspapers. But even more public work in the community was necessary. Because "as yet we make a poor show of begging," a Rochester woman wrote, the women were buying nearly all of their materials. Now they must approach storekeepers and individuals to plead for supplies. [50]

Dunning merchants and others for free merchandise was a chore that was often part of ensuring a successful fair. Worcester women formed a committee "to solicit every family in town for aid, whether of money, refreshments or other arts." Some women were uncomfortable with the task of approaching the public for donations. When Eliza Follen asked for fruit for a fair refreshment table, she had to overcome her sense that the request was improper. "I was on the point of asking you to excuse me for this seeming freedom," she wrote to her potential benefactor, "but as fellow workers in a holy cause there should not be any [im]propriety in my doubting your entire approbation of the confidence I have shown in asking." [51]

The surviving lists of articles prepared by different groups of women only begin to suggest the effort and skills involved and the scale of work on the local level. For the Salem fair of 1839, women in Ipswich contributed two quilts, shirts, aprons, bosoms, and dickeys, nightcaps, cuffs, a muslin cape, a child's frock, a cushion, three bags, eighteen needlebooks, and a scissor chain. From Danvers came aprons, boxes, pocketbooks, needlebooks, rollups, cuffs, mittens, hose, and penwipers. The bill the Salem society paid for goods, including thread, spotted and figured lace, ribbon, calico, linen, and muslin, serves as a record of its members' activities. [52]

When local women and groups succeeded in working together for a fair, they often enlarged the antislavery network by recruiting helpers. In the process, their effort gave some form of community to those who had no formal local antislavery society upon which to depend for fellowship. Just as important, the work and the correspondence it entailed linked women to the greater antislavery world. Organizers of the great Boston fair explicitly encouraged communication. Women were told to write to the fair's organizers and to one another. Their letters could elicit warm sympathy and helpful assistance, "for it may often be in the power of all the friends of the cause, mutually to aid each other by the interchange of materials and labor, and by furnishing the newest patterns of articles of dress, or models of articles of furniture." Even after the fair was over, ties were maintained through sending along leftover goods. As Abby Kelley remarked when she requested such items for a fair planned in Rochester, "You are well aware of the beneficial effect of the interchange of work and sympathy." [53]

While the essential function remained the same, to provide a sense of personal connection and acquaintance, the network that began to take shape in the 1830s continued with a new focus and purpose in the 1840s. At the end of her account of her small efforts for the fair, Deborah Palmer added an appeal to Maria Chapman. "Excuse me dear madam," she wrote, "I had almost forgotten that I was writing to a stranger so I have given you my thoughts just as they rose to my mind[.] I have hardly begun to write, what I feel that I could say if I could have the pleasure of a personal interview with you." Particularly for women who felt isolated and alone in their work, this network gave a sense of companionship and friendship that were otherwise lacking. [54]

In 1837, Julianna Tappan, the corresponding secretary of the Ladies' New-York City Anti-Slavery Society, wrote to Anne Weston that the New York society was having silk stamped with different scenes: a slave kneeling under a tree with a woman at work in the distance, a mother sitting under a tree with a sick child, various vignettes of slavery as it had existed in the West Indies. The silk would be used for reticules, and, since Julianna could get a good price, would the Boston women be interested in acquiring some for their handwork projects? [55] Julianna's offer not only shows the female antislavery network in use but also points to the role of women in creating material goods that served as propaganda for the cause. The material culture of antislavery has not survived, for the most part, but descriptions women gave of their work and lists of goods sent into fairs suggest what kinds of things they made. Depictions of slave scenes printed on material and made into work bags and other useful articles were popular. Mottoes either printed or stitched by individual women adorned needlebooks, penwipers, and anything that the imagination could devise. Maria Child attracted laughter for "putting mottoes on all her things," including a bachelor's bag with needles, thread, tape and "a skreed of doctrine." [56]

Mottoes captured abolitionist beliefs in abbreviated and simplified form and thus educated buyers about the essentials of the creed and the duties of an abolitionist. Penwipers instructed their owners to "Wipe out the blot of Slavery," while quills, "Weapons for Abolitionists," reminded their possessors of their responsibilities as advocates of immediate emancipation. The visual images that adorned handiwork appealed to the emotions. Scenes depicted the cruelty of slavery and undercut the southern insistence on the lower nature of slaves by emphasizing the humanity and even dignity of slaves. Representations evoking the triumphs of the abolitionist movement (emancipation in the West Indies, for example) suggested the feasibility of emancipation. Women proved to be able propagandists, both original (they might write their own mottoes, for example) and derivative (they built upon the iconography of British antislavery). Either way, they demonstrated their modern understanding of the dynamics of successful propaganda.[57]

In 1839, Mary White of Boylston mentioned in her diary that she had "assisted in getting the bed quilt at the Hall for the Antislavery cause." Boylston women, in fact, contributed two quilts that year, one for a bed, the other for a cradle. Maria Child also contributed a cradle quilt embellished with the words: "Think of the negro-mother / When *her* child is torn away." While the message of the quilts was not always so clear, familiar designs were given new meanings. Jacob's Ladder, for example, symbolized not the Old Testament story but the Underground Railroad. The most private household article, used to cover a bed, had taken on a clearly political message.[58]

As one fair circular suggested, such items were "useful in a double capacity." While the sale of these goods brought in money, their creation and use hammered in the basic antislavery message. As women made the articles, they continually recalled the purpose of their work. Those who bought them were reminded in the course of simple, daily tasks—wiping one's pen, doing mending, writing letters—of the necessity of emancipation. Recipients of letters sealed with a motto, or even guests at an evening party who glimpsed a velvet or silk reticule adorned with the image of a slave, might think about how their own lives contrasted with those of the poor slaves. While few scholars have seen the fragile material culture as particularly important, its value as omnipresent propaganda (as opposed to the visit of the lecturer) was great. Moreover, it is significant that women produced this material culture. By the act of making goods designed to carry a political and public issue into the household as well as into less private places, antislavery women, perhaps unconsciously, once again made elastic the definition of their sphere.[59]

While the subtle mingling of the private and public worlds suggested by material productions did not raise questions of propriety, the entry of women into the marketplace did. Elizabeth Gay, who lived on rural Staten Island, described herself working for both the Boston and Philadelphia fairs in these terms: "All I can do here is to sit alone . . . and stitch stitch hoping my little aid may do something for the cause." This depiction of herself sewing alone at home was accurate, for sewing was a domestic activity, and even antislavery sewing circles usually met at one another's houses. Mingled with such domesticity, however, was an involvement in the commercial world. Elizabeth, herself, gave a baldly economic description of fairs in 1857 when she wrote, "There is a set of producers who will supply the market, and a set of consumers who will come and buy." In a similar spirit, another woman ended her letter about fair business with these revealing words: "Make 'heaps of money.' "[60]

The commonly expressed desire to make goods that were both "saleable and profitable," as a New Bedford woman described them, entangled abolitionist women in the world of fashion and taste. Even the smallest items should conform to fashionable norms. As Elizabeth Gay had learned in her fair work, there was "a vast difference between such little things well & tastefully made, and such as I have thrown under the table very often at our Fairs in Phila[elphia]." Evelina Smith was equally aware of what standards she should meet, writing for a pattern for dickies "in [the] most approved fashion for Boston folks," knowing that it would be folly to make frumpy dickies for the fair. The exchange of patterns put women in touch with one another and served as the means for instructing and acquainting them with sophisticated norms of taste.[61]

Fair workers not only asked for advice and learned about the genteel market but also tried to build up sales experience from a distance. When they worked for one of the big fairs, the women often inquired about what had sold in the past and the prices specific items had commanded. It was with these concerns in mind that Silva Jones asked to know whether the table mats made by women in Ashburnham sold and what price the buyers had paid, for place mats were one of the principal items sent into the Boston fair from that town.[62]

The pricing issue was important. Fair managers wanted the women who made goods to price them as well. Women undertook what was initially an unfamiliar chore and sent in boxes of goods uncertain about their success in understanding marketplace values. Ellen Russell struggled with appraising articles, feeling that she had "probably made many errors, over-rating some things and undervaluing others." A cape, knit of spool cotton, was "a very serviceable article" she had not marked at all, for she had "no idea of its value." Quaker women in Nantucket also debated prices. Their first attempt at pricing had set the values too low, some of the women felt, so they had raised prices. Charlotte Austin was one who "should pronounce some of [the prices] extravagant." But the point was, as one women in East Bridgewater put it, to sell goods "for what they will fetch."[63]

Over time, women developed a sense of their intended market. In Boston, managers carried useful goods, but clearly the ornamental and fancy goods drew the crowds. In Nantucket, however, these sorts of items, sent on after a Boston fair, were "too expensive for . . . [the] market." Similarly, in Worcester, "a very different set of persons" attended the fair "from those they have at the Boston fairs, . . . so of course the sale of really costly articles is rare."[64]

The market dictated what women made and what fair managers solicited in terms of goods and buyers. When Elizabeth Gay learned that her baskets "did not go off, as I would wish at Boston" but were "eagerly sought for" at Phila[delphia]," she decided to make "them for that market this year." Managers of the Lynn fair planned to provide the toys, children's stockings, and mittens that they knew would meet with a ready sale, while, in Concord, New Hampshire, women determined to sell clothing "suitable" for Irish workers and "to stir round these Irish and get them to the fair if possible."[65]

The Concord fair, with its clothing for Irish immigrants, was quite a different affair from the Boston extravaganza, where tables were piled with tempting and elegant goods, including, in 1839, many different styles of " 'Parisian Necklaces' for the promenade or drawing room." Despite their varying character, however, all antislavery fairs raised questions and occasionally exposed tensions among women who worked for them. Susan Hayward of Uxbridge, Massachusetts, was mildly uncomfortable about the connection between her moral commitment and the values of a cash economy when she sent in her "trifling" contribution to the fair. She begged that her interest in the noble cause not be measured "by *value received*."[66]

Other women worried about other fundamental issues fair work raised. For instance, a woman who had pledged a donation of money to the Boston fair declined to pay, for she became "convinced that Fairs are wrong." An undated fair circular suggested that the argument "against the moral tendency of fairs" focused on "improprieties in the management." A fair was not in itself wrong, the flyer asserted, "unless the same can be proved of the act of selling and of purchasing." But the act of buying and selling was, indeed, centrally related to the problems some people perceived in fairs.[67]

The ranks of abolitionist women included those from the city and country and from evangelical and nonevangelical denominations; they attracted both Quakers and non-Quakers, and those with scant means and others more comfortable; so fairs were bound to bring out differences in attitudes toward commercial activity. Mary Gilbert, writing from West Brookfield, Massachusetts, described a clash between standards of Christian plainness, self-denial, and rural usefulness and urban elegance, self-indulgence, and frivolity, and between a just price and an usurious price. The debate, triggered by the market and industrial revolution, was not confined to abolitionist circles;it was part of a broader cultural discussion about the threat the cash-oriented, consumer-driven economy posed to the "traditional" self-sufficient farmstead and the evangelical household. "You are doubtless aware," wrote Mary, "that many persons are scrupulous in regard to . . . *Fairs* generally, on the ground that most of the articles offered . . . possess little or no intrinsic value and are sold at exorbitant prices." New Yorker Julianna Tappan had raised similar concerns years before. "There is so much time consumed, and so much consulting of fashion, and conformity to the world, that I doubt much whether fairs, *as they are conducted* are pleasing to God."[68]

Managers of the Boston fair explained that "the interest of our clients, the honor of our cause, and our credit as its advocates, above all bid us demand the highest market price." But charging high rather than fair prices for goods that had no useful purpose seemed unethical to some abolitionist women who viewed themselves and their cause in moral terms and who deprived themselves in order to contribute to abolitionist causes. In Walpole, Massachusetts, Mary Manter had decided she would "rather dress plain and poor and live on plain and cheep food then to have the slaves in bondage." She argued that "if people would only deny themselves of some unneedful things and be less careful to adorn their poor bodies," they might be of greater use to the cause. Mrs. May took action when she worked at the Boston fair. She "fought every step about the marking. She struggled to give away every thing & *would* privately catch up a thing & mark it without saying a word. We resisted . . . but it is hard to fight over every article."[69]

In the PFAS, Quaker members were initially hostile to the whole idea of a fair. As Sarah Pugh explained, "by that Society, Fairs were regarded with much suspicion, if not absolute disapprobation. So strong were these sentiments that it was difficult to get agreement on raising money in such a way." To calm anxieties, the PFAS called its first fair an "Anti-slavery Sale," and sold only "plain and simple" goods. In time, the Philadelphia fair became an annual event and the focus of the women's work. Members acknowledged that fairs were "one of the readiest measures for increasing . . . funds" and "a means of enlisting the interest of such as need some excitement of the kind to call forth benevolence."[70]

Questionable practices at some fairs raised further scruples and questions. Fair managers sometimes sponsored raffles. One Cincinnati woman made her objections to this practice clear in her letter to a Boston fair manager. "Do discard *Raffles* from your Bazaar," she wrote. "It *is* gambling." If not gambling, selling chances could be seen as a form of trickery, encouraging people to spend money for nothing. Other practices, while not specifically mentioned, raised the issue of impropriety. As the New York *Tribune* hinted, Boston fair managers drew attention and buyers by "advantageously posting" attractive young women in the hall. The paper noted the careful way in which "good looks and good spirits are judiciously distributed throughout the hall." The interest in securing a sale might also lead to questionable behavior on the part of the women in charge of the tables. While no one ever suggested that Elizabeth Gay acted in a cajoling or seductive fashion, her own account of the way she handled her sales is evocative:

> The great thing is to know our customers and at a Boston table I should be almost as raw a hand as the greenest of your country sellers. I could work however because nine years of bitter experience has taught me how. At a Phila[delphia] table I flatter myself I am *au fait* at all the tricks of trade. I can almost take my Quaker affirmation that a man or woman has money in his pocket . . . as soon as he enters. But in Boston my sagacity would fail me. I don't know your nabobs nor your spending people from your close-fisted short pursed ones.[71]

Some of the questions raised by women's support of and work for antislavery fairs were doubtless rendered less powerful by the unmistakable morality of the cause of emancipation and the profitability of the fairs themselves. Because fairs were events with multiple meanings, anxieties about buying and selling might be stifled. While the spectacle of women hawking abolitionist wares might be offensive to some, the way fairs functioned as elaborate pieces of propaganda for the antislavery cause in addition to the rituals and myths that they created for the movement helped to justify them as suitable activities for women.[72]

Fairs were, of course, marketplaces or bazaars. The spectacle mounted in the town hall by Lynn women in 1838 was far less elaborate than that offered by city fairs, yet the effect was sumptuous and inviting. The fair did not feature furniture for the upper-class drawing room, but it did offer a profusion of small tempting items suitable for those Lynn residents who desired goods that symbolized genteel middle-class taste. For sale for the parlor were a special English writing case for the center table, finished with pencil drawings, paintings of American scenery, wax flowers, lamp and vase stands, screens and portfolios, inlaid boxes, and glass and wood workboxes, some highly finished. There were more items ranging in usefulness from a gilt and lacquered tea caddy, to blotting books, paper, quills, and writing apparatus, needlebooks, and letter racks. Many articles were bits of finery that Lynn shoppers could afford: tippets, bags, and reticules "of every color, shape and material," capes, cuffs, and collars in a richly embroidered style, net and lace caps for the bonnet, "in a style not yet seen in the shops." Buyers could purchase eau de lavande and German cologne and the stands (one of them of Sevres porcelain) upon which to place them. Numerous toys and clothes for infants and children were for sale, and ample refreshments tempted shoppers.

Held on January 1 and 2, the fair contributed to the process of commercializing the holiday season. It invited visitors to buy New Year's presents or to acquire small luxuries for themselves. Sold by women, most of the goods seem to have been intended for women and children. In this vision of the fair women were at once the producers, the sellers, and the intended recipients of the cornucopia of articles in the town hall. The commercial nature of the fair placed women squarely in bustling world of buying, selling, and consuming.[73]

On another level, fairs operated as giant mechanisms for propaganda. Fair managers did not expect their goods to attract only abolitionists. The idea was to have a tempting enough display to bring in those who did not yet understand the need for immediate emancipation. For this audience, the fair was not just about buying but about the abolitionist cause.

The setting itself was pregnant with meaning. Anyone attending the Bangor fair in late August 1840, for example, must have been impressed with the scene the women had created. The fair took place in a hall "beautifully decorated" with paintings, flowers, and evergreens. If visitors missed the symbolism of the decoration (greens symbolizing rebirth and renewal were ubiquitous at fairs), they could hardly misunderstand the banners adorned with mottoes. In Bangor, messages like: "Emancipation," "Let My people Go," "Liberty," and "Loose the Bonds of Wickedness" were pithy and bold. Individual purchases carried these and other mottoes, reminding fair visitors long after the event had ended of the importance of abolitionism. The tables furnished by towns from all corners of Maine suggested the power of the movement and its inevitable triumph. When fair managers were able to obtain goods sent by women in the British Isles, the message was even stronger, for these goods symbolized the international dimensions of antislavery and reminded Americans that the English efforts to abolish slavery had succeeded.[74]

At the Salem fair, held in the basement of the Mechanics Building, the display at the entrance featured "wrought shoes, watch-cases, aprons, caps +c. neatly executed by the colored children." The handiwork highlighted the skills and industry of the African American youngsters and suggested their ability to become productive members of society. The center of the table—with "a barge splendidly carved by a native of Africa, filled with dolls of various sizes, with the inscription, 'We are free,' upon its pennant"—was at once an exotic evocation of a noble not servile Africa, of the tragic middle passage and enslavement of Africans, and of the heritage of freedom that abolitionists were claiming for black Americans.[75]

The tables stocked with goods made by women of Salem and other towns testified to the dedication and commitment of female abolitionists to this cause. The piles of "overwrought collars," "rich silk aprons," and "splendid knit bead workbags" offered proof of the middle-class credentials that women insisted upon so often. Even the diverse crowds, made up of Calvinists, Unitarians, Whigs, Democrats, and Liberty Party men, gave out a message about the cooperative nature and power of the cause. The presence of blacks reminded people of what the struggle was all about and made a statement against what Frederick Douglass called "the green-eyed monster—prejudice against color." But perhaps one of the most significant messages fairs proclaimed was that of free labor, freely given. In contrast to slaves who had no choice but to work, and in contrast to wage earners who worked for money, the abolitionist women had toiled freely and selflessly. The example of labor untainted by base desire for personal gain, free from the ignominy of the lash, made a powerful moral statement, one that resonated with northerners' understanding of their historical heritage.[76]

Information about fairs mounted by black women is sparse and provides little of the detail that has survived for the fairs discussed here. Given the economic circumstances of most free blacks, the fairs must have been far less lavish than the major urban fairs. The bazaar black women in Frankfort, Ohio, organized in 1847, for example, took place in Rilla Harris's home, not a rented hall. But even this modest event carried messages: about the domestic industry of black women, their status as ladies, and the capacity of blacks to rise to an equality with whites. The handbill for the Frankfort fair assured the public that "all the delicacies of the season will be served up in the most palatable style—such as *Ice Creams, Cakes, Lemonades, Jellies, Fruits, Nuts, etc. etc.*" The Women's Association of Philadelphia, which sponsored fairs to raise money for Frederick Douglass's paper, the *North Star*, provided the fair with respectable middle-class credentials by its support for "the elevation of the Colored People in the United States." Members of the association were, presumably, already elevated.[77]

New York African American women put on the most elaborate and lucrative fair of the prewar period in 1860. The managers, mostly the wives of clergymen, rented "a spacious and . . . elegantly lighted" room. Managers "were all decked in pretty calico gowns, all, or nearly all, of the same stripe, giving thereby a most picturesque effect." The goods were "very beautiful" and sales realized over $1,000 to benefit the Colored Orphan Asylum. The gay and elegant crowd stunned the white people who attended the fair, and the newspaper account of the event suggested that the appearance of so many genteel and well-dressed blacks dealt a blow to prejudice. The paper quoted approvingly the comments of one white visitor who remarked, "I wish . . . that the entire white population could, by some means, this night see this people. They would go from hence divested of most, if not all of their foolish prejudices."[78]

Fairs served yet other purposes, for they helped to create the rituals and history that sustained the movement for decades. Whether scheduled for the Christmas–New Year season or for the late summer, times of the year laden with meaning and sometimes marked by festivities, fairs imposed an antislavery stamp on the secular calendar. The throngs, the elegant goods, the bustle, and the noise, the mottoes and decorations—the excitement surrounding all aspects of the fairs—created a special atmosphere quite different from both everyday routines and holiday celebrations. For abolitionists, the ritual activity was less the act of purchasing goods than meeting, greeting, and, reaffirming ties with other like-minded abolitionists, both male and female. These occasions, repeated over time, helped to integrate abolitionist workers and visitors into a communion of believers. Especially for those who felt they were working alone, fairs were important moments of connection.

A young African American woman, Charlotte Forten, who breathlessly recorded in her diary that she had spent a day at the Boston fair, is an example of a woman energized by these moments of connection. "Had the good fortune," she wrote, "to be made known to three of the noblest and best of women; Mesdames Chapman, Follen, and Child. . . . Saw all the most distinguished champions of our cause." She would not soon forget "the kind pressure" of Wendell Phillip's hand and his "beaming smile." Charlotte's excited reaction highlights the role fairs played in providing opportunities to see and perhaps even shake the hand of the leaders of the movement, whether they were Liberty men, evangelical clerics, newspapers editors, or imposing women like Maria Chapman or Abby Kelley. As Charlotte's words suggest, the occasion was more than just a social one. Fairs, in fact, helped to create heroic figures by providing the audiences and admiring throngs for them. The 1847 fair broadside for the National Anti-Slavery Bazaar suggested the importance of this function when it pointed out that one of the most edifying aspects of the bazaar had been the sights of the "famous" that it had provided.[79]

In other ways, the fairs reinforced the stature of abolitionist leaders. The crayon portrait of Garrison a woman drew for one fair, and the letter written by Garrison surrounded by a wreath and leaves at another contributed to the process of heroizing him. Most fairs featured a post office where visitors could purchase letters written by leading abolitionists. At the Salem fair, many who declined to buy other items at the fair were willing to pay for a letter at the post office. Presumably, these documents were carried home to be proudly displayed or carefully preserved as sacred souvenirs. Also available for purchase at many fairs were anniversary books like the *Liberty Bell* (published by the Boston Garrisonians), the *Star of Emancipation* (published by the non-Garrisonian Massachusetts Female Emancipation Society), and the *Antislavery Autograph* (published by the Rochester Ladies' Anti-Slavery Society). Such books were partly intended to spotlight abolitionist leaders. As Julia Griffiths explained, the Rochester volume would "record the testimony of as many distinguished persons" as possible "against the great sin of our age." The *Liberty Bell* was filled "with pieces (either grave or gay—lively or severe as the muse dictates) from those whose names are dear to the abolitionists." The books both acquainted abolitionists with the names of significant figures and helped to make them beloved.[80]

Seen in symbolic terms, the tables sponsored by other towns and even by women in Great Britain placed abolitionism and its leaders in an American and British context. The tables representing work donated by women from many different communities suggested the democratic setting in which abolitionists operated. The English tables signified a historical pedigree for a movement that was relatively recent.

Even the dollars earned by fairs contributed to mythmaking. In a report on one of the Boston fairs, the *Liberator* argued that the fair's profitability proved false the claim "that abolitionism is *fast dying away in Boston*." In fact, dollars could be construed as proof of the successful progress of abolitionism. Certainly the presence of the crowds that often included "worldly people" seemed to indicate the strides abolitionism was making in reaching out to an ever-increasing audience.

Although fairs were the most dramatic and visible indications of women's work in abolitionism during the 1840s and 1850s, and represented crucial links for those involved in antislavery, other avenues of commitment existed, some of them individualistic and carried on outside of any organized network. In 1843, Maria Child, like others distressed by the controversies plaguing abolitionism, concluded that her feelings were "completely and forever alienated from the anti-slavery *organization*." She decided that she would "work in my own way, according to the light that is in me." It was in this spirit that Maria one week paid a "poor way-worn" fugitive's railroad fare to Hartford, with an introductory letter to a friend, and the next week gave another fugitive slave a dollar and again a "cautiously worded" letter. Not hearing from either of them, she worried that "the poor fellows were captured on the way," despite the discreet message she had provided to help them to freedom. With similar sympathies, Mary White noted in her diary in 1843 that she and her daughter had prepared a box of clothing "to send to Canada for the relief of runaway slaves," and she recorded giving lodging to "Mr. Washington a colored man." [81]

Offering hospitality or courtesy to African Americans often brought a storm of criticism down upon the women. Frances Drake learned that the reason that women would not cooperate with her on the fair was because she walked and rode with members of the Remond family (a noted black abolitionist family from Salem) when they came to Leominister. Village women reportedly said that she could be just as good an abolitionist "and still not treat niggers so familiarly." When she was asked if she would consider marrying a black man, she reported, "I answered very *frankly*. . . . Yes—if he was just as worthy in every respect as a white man ought to be. You can have no idea what a talk it has made all over town." In Utica, Paulina Wright's courtesy to one of the Remonds resulted in social ostracism. "There is scarcely a woman in the city that will speak to me because we went to the Falls with Remond[.] [T]hey are really making a worse fuss about that than anything else[.] I do sometimes feel the want of female sympathy and society." [82]

The criticism that often followed social gestures to African Americans makes clear that women who followed such advice had overcome some of the common antipathies of the day and transgressed community racial norms. Mary Manter attributed her lack of prejudice to the influence of the *Liberator*, which Garrison sent to her for free. In its pages she "learnt the cause of humanity, how to feal for the oppressed, and by reading . . . I lost entirely my prejudice against colour, and can feal just as well in the company of a coloured brother or sister as if their skin was the same colour as my own, and can sign a petition for the reapeal of that part of the Law, that makes a distinction on acount of colour, (heart and hand) wither it be to marry or ride together." Although Mary attributed her views to reading the *Liberator*, evangelical women heard the same message elsewhere. The 1849 Annual Report of the American and Foreign Anti-Slavery Society condemned prejudice as "mean and unchristian" and encouraged all to demonstrate that they were "exempted from its turpitude." It was not surprising, however, that abolitionist women, like both men and women in our own times, often unconsciously expressed their sense of black inferiority. When Maria Child met one of the Remonds, she found herself "extremely pleased" with him. Remond was the first African American she had met "who seemed to be altogether such an one as I would have him." Her comment suggests that she could best accept African Americans when they met her white expectations of what a black person should be.[83]

Although genuine acceptance was limited, and few white abolitionists confronted the tremendous economic problems facing free blacks, white and black abolitionist women did make some efforts to work together toward equality. In the Midwest, they participated in petition drives aimed at destroying state black laws. In the East, they sought signatures to overturn antiblack legislation. Some challenged discriminatory laws and practices directly. New Bedford women refused to adhere to racial policies during an 1841 train trip and invited an African American missionary into the white car with them. When the conductor ordered the man to leave the white car, the women told the conductor "what we thought. . . . Arnold, Ann, Mary and myself—all, joined, the girls forgetting that [they] were out of their 'appropriate sphere,' in their eagerness to protect an insulted brother, did their part and our poor conductor not expecting such opposition, retreated, leaving us in possession of the field."[84]

In such encounters, white women ran the risk of insult and possible injury. Blacks, however, bore the greatest responsibility for confronting injustice and were far more likely to experience bad treatment than white women, especially when they were acting alone. When Mary Green, the secretary of the Lynn Female Anti-Slavery Society, got on a white car in Lynn and refused to leave it, "she was dragged out of the car . . . in a very indecent manner with an infant in her arm, and then struck and thrown to the ground. Her husband, when he arrived at the scene, was also beaten for daring to interfere for her protection." Despite the rough treatment, Mary appealed to the railroad's stockholders in a letter. "I think I have a right, in common with others," she said, "to go in any car I choose. When I behave disorderly, it will be time to order me out." When Sarah Walker Fossett, a well-known hairdresser in Cincinnati, tried to ride the street car in that city, the conductor shoved her back into the street. She pursued her cause in court.[85]

Even undramatic individual attempts to help blacks could create a distance between a white abolitionist woman and her neighbors. Elizabeth Gay suggested as much when she wrote her friend, Lizzy, in Hingham and encouraged her to stand her ground. Lizzy's efforts with the "poor creatures . . . so long . . . considered the outcasts of society" included trying to find them employment. Phoebe Jackson was involved in a shelter for African American children in New Bedford. Her work there had finally conquered the "wicked prejudice" she had felt "in regard to color" but hardly endeared her to others.[86]

Simple occasions offered opportunities to make statements to the community. For her black scholars' picnic in Toledo, Ohio, Laura Haviland helped organize a parade through the town. The banner at the head of the procession proclaimed, "Knowledge is Power." The banner's motto explained Laura's decision to teach black children and their interest in going to school. Education was a transforming process, but most states provided little or no public education for free blacks. As a result, teaching became a way of expressing an abolitionist commitment.[87]

An early foray into black education occurred in Cincinnati, Ohio. In the mid-1830s, a group of young men and women, inspired by a call in the *New York Evangelist* and helped initially by the Tappan brothers, set up schools for blacks in that city. They hoped to prove wrong those who claimed that "the blacks can never be raised here, etc." [88] The teachers tried to inculcate their students with the moral, intellectual, and domestic standards of their middle-class white world. The transformation that they hoped to instigate was ambitious and daunting. Phebe Matthews reflected that the work was "*difficult*, . . . *arduous* but still pleasant and delightful," while one of her colleagues thought that "ours is not the work of a week or a year. . . . It looks more like *work* of *time* than it did when we commenced yet we feel not the least disheartened." The women's continued refrain of good cheer suggested that their task had its moments of profound discouragement.[89]

"Young and inexperienced," in "a little isolated company" in an unsympathetic white city, the white teachers made sacrifices for their work. They missed contact with "all literary and refined society" and felt keenly the difference between themselves and their students. The children were not habituated to school discipline, and many frequently missed classes because they had to work. Susan Wattles obviously chafed at the "daily hourly contact with a people whose moral sense is blunted[,] whose intellect is dimmed, and every faculty of body and mind degraded by a system of the cruelest oppression." She was further dismayed by what she saw as indifference in the families of her pupils. "I never saw a colored family who were willing to dispense with tea and coffee that they might buy books for their children," she claimed.[90]

Black women, usually from the middle class, also taught in cities all over the North. Few received the respect they believed was their professional due. Sarah Douglass, for example, dissolved into tears during a Quaker meeting after a Friend asked her, "Does thee go out ahouse cleaning?" And because they were constantly aware of the necessity of establishing their own credentials as respectable ladies and because they recognized (and sometimes overemphasized) the connections between black ignorance and white prejudice, African American teachers shared some of white teachers' dismay over their pupils' behavior and seeming lack of interest in education. Like white teachers, they frequently underestimated the way free blacks' worsening economic situation undermined educational goals.[91]

Black teachers, as did their white counterparts, often needed financial help to keep their schools open. The PFAS assisted Sarah Douglass, who ran the only academy for black girls in Philadelphia. Over the years, they provided her with an outright stipend, paid rent for her schoolroom, and bought a stove to keep it warm. White members of the society felt a genuine interest in Douglass's school, but Douglass apparently had problems with the arrangement. Perhaps she felt she was being too closely scrutinized. Whatever the reason, she refused the society's stipend after a few years, although she accepted the indirect help that came from the rent the organization paid for using the schoolroom for meetings. Other black teachers faced obvious prejudice. During an exhibition at the African Free School in New York, for example, whites ordered the black women not to sit "upon a platform that was reserved for the *trustees*."[92]

On a smaller scale than that of full-time teaching, other women established Sabbath schools and domestic skills classes for black young people. Betsy Cowles, employed as a teacher at Portsmouth Seminary in Ohio, gathered a Sunday school class of ten girls in 1842, who she remarked were "guilty of this crime, what think ye it is? why of possessing real black skins; & for this crime, have been excluded from Sabbath School." The two Stearns sisters, belonging to no society, labored on their "own responsibility" with their school for African Americans in Springfield. They had commenced their efforts after neighbors had responded to their speeches on behalf of "the *sufferings* of the poor slave" with the taunt, "Why do you not look after the colored people right here?" Like the Cincinnati teachers, the Stearns found that the cultural peculiarities they encountered in the "poor, wretched" African American neighborhood of "Hayti" made them uncomfortable. Did they experience relief or disappointment when "the worst families" and their children moved away, leaving the women with only a biweekly prayer meeting? They did not say so specifically, but they reported satisfaction with their prayer meetings: "Blessed good times, we can say just what we have a mind to." [93]

White women who dared to challenge racial norms by working among African Americans had to put up with criticism, gossip, and often loneliness. One New Hampshire woman called her opponents "*wolves*" poised to "*devour*" her little band. Writing from Harrisburg, Pennsylvania, Agnes Crain did not even have the companionship of like-minded abolitionists. She so feared "the influence of Society on my sentiments and feelings" that she stayed at home, and "thus I lose the opportunity of knowing who is disposed to learn the truth." Although she confessed that in her "single endeavors" she "got much discouraged," she persisted in her efforts to circulate abolitionist literature. [94]

Some of the material she lent may well have been written by other abolitionist women. Active propagandists, women used all the avenues of their print culture to spread the abolitionist message. Poems, songs, memoirs, short stories, novels, tracts, firsthand accounts of slavery, letters to newspapers, and pieces for fair giftbooks all were vehicles for women writers. Oddities, like the poetical alphabet a Philadelphia woman composed for the fair ("You are very young, tis true / But there's much you can do"), attest to women's inventiveness. [95]

Despite the prominence of literary women like Maria Child and Caroline Kirkland, writing for publication under their own names created for some women the familiar struggle between propriety and duty. Sarah Shaw, whose husband had agreed to contribute to the Boston fair's giftbook, the *Liberty Bell*, felt "a stronger objection than ever, to making any public acknowledgement of my principles or feelings." Her reluctance puzzled her, for her antislavery principles were growing stronger as time passed. She concluded that having her name in print was "against my taste, and my nature which is decidedly retiring." [96]

By using pen names, other women wrote abolitionist propaganda and retained their principles. As one woman explained, "I have never out of my

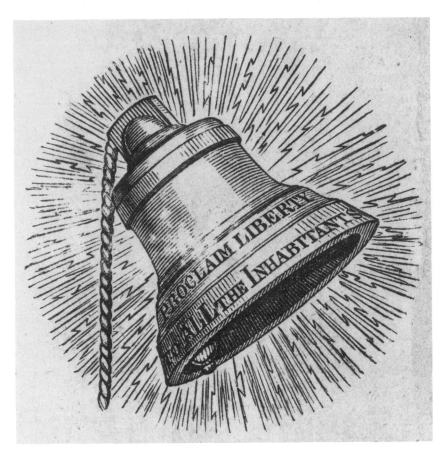

Emblem that appeared in The Liberty Bell, *the giftbook produced for the Boston fair. Giftbooks helped to highlight the importance of abolitionist leaders and offered a place for the work of abolitionist writers. They also made money for the cause and carried the abolitionist message into individual households. (Boston Athenæum)*

immediate family, allowed it to be known whom that name represents. If it should ever be divulged accidently, there will be an end to all literary effort on my part." Over time, some women were able to overcome norms that dictated female modesty and privacy. An acquaintance of Lucretia Mott's, for instance, had long "composed many little songs for her children in order to imbue them early with Anti-Slavery principle" and had used a pseudonym when her material appeared in print, but she agreed to have her real name appear in the *Liberty Bell*. The cause was sufficiently important for her to lay her qualms aside. And in what was a somewhat daring move, a Connecticut woman was willing to allow personal letters to be published in the *Liberator*. "They are, perhaps, of too private a nature for the general taste," she admitted, "but are . . . not some minds better reached in this familiar way than by a more personal address?"[97]

Phoebe Stearns was unable to send in either money or articles to one of the big antislavery fairs but was glad to use her pen to "aid [the] cause" in any way possible. Her narrative, which she thought could appear in tract form or in a giftbook, was true "in every particular" (although real names were, of course, not used). A woman from the evangelical wing of abolitionism also relied on facts that she asked Amos Phelps to supply. Despite the press of the domestic duties that interfered with her writing, she was eager for "narratives of runaway slaves, and [for] facts respecting the treatment of these poor creatures in different states" for her literary efforts.[98]

While some women stuck to facts, many imaginative treatments of slavery appeared. The male abolitionist who welcomed "the novelty of seeing abolitionism in a work of fiction" because he thought the public hungered for "every new view in which the important subject is presented" overstated the public's interest in the subject. But he was right to point to the power of fiction to engage the sympathies of readers and to attract an audience that loved to read even if it did not love the slave. Novelist Sophia Little was quite conscious that, while her writing was perhaps not "a work of art," it could "reach the people."[99]

Unlike male writers, who emphasized slave rebellion as a theme and who frequently produced abstract and ideologically oriented work, women writers used the techniques of sentimental fiction to arouse readers to the horrors of slavery. "See the young mother," counseled a piece in the *Envoy*, a Rhode Island giftbook. "Whisper in her ear / Tales which might chill to the life to hear."[100] Persuaded that their audience must not merely understand the facts of slavery but empathize with the enslaved, women writers sought to move readers without offending their genteel sensibilities. In the spirit of the first female antislavery societies that had adopted immediate emancipation as a means of reaching out to suffering sisters in bondage, women writers tended to emphasize the tragedies besetting slave families and the plight of noble female slaves who honored, in so far as they could, the values of purity and fidelity so cherished by middle-class culture. The focus on slave women and their families coupled with the desire to expose the sexual rapacity of white masters required some literary gymnastics. Caroline Healy Dall, author of a short story for the 1858 *Liberty Bell*, explained, "I could not write the story as he[r informant] told it. If I were to use the English tongue with the nervous strength that he did when he told the bitterest portion of his tale, all the women in the land would tear the pages out of the fair volume: Yet, alas! if we but knew it, when we mention the word slavery, we sum up all possible indecencies as well as all possible villanies."[101]

Caroline's efforts to move her readers without offending them were just one example of the varied and significant work women undertook in the abolitionist cause in the 1840s. Although many women bemoaned the divisions that beset the movement and were discouraged when former associates became disinterested or gave their loyalties to other branches of abolitionism, women of all stripes continued to labor in their own ways for immediate emancipation. From a modern vantage point, it is not decline or the retreat of timid women from, but the proliferation of opportunities to work for, the slave and the overlapping nature of many of their efforts that stand out.

In the 1840s, women were also boldly confronting strategic issues facing abolitionists. While some abolitionist women involved themselves in associational business, worked for fairs, taught black children and sometimes their parents, and published material about slavery, others were far more concerned about the state of the Union and the state of the American churches. In 1841, "Cora" from Rhode Island reported on the election there. In her opinion, the election showed "what may be effected by abolitionists in the way of political action." When Garrisonian activist Mary Clark of Concord, New Hampshire, died, one of her last acts was writing a piece for the *Herald of Freedom*. In it she attacked the clergy for supporting slavery and threatened them with divine retribution. Striking the same note, but in words composed to be sung, Almira Seymour called out, "O, purify thy churches, / Throughout this sinful land; / Let justice, truth and mercy / Beside thy altar stand." These published pieces point to further areas of interest in 1840s: politics and religious reform, topics that will be discussed in detail in Chapter 4.[102]

Chapter 4
Women Confront Their Churches and the World of Politics

Now we'll give the foe no quarter,

At the ballot-box or altar, -

She is Babylon's foul daughter,

And our work, it must not pause,

And we'll fight for freedom,

And we'll fight for freedom,

And we'll fight for freedom,

True religion and just laws.[1]

As a young woman Sarah Otis Ernst had joined the Boston Female Anti-Slavery Society, and, in the controversies that wracked that association and the American Anti-Slavery Society in the late 1830s, she had given her loyalty to the Garrisonians, female equality, and moral suasion. Nine years' residence in Cincinnati had not eroded these commitments, although she now felt increasingly marginal in a movement that itself appeared marginal. Writing in 1852, Sarah Ernst reflected that "all nominal abolitionists here for the last nine years (since it has been my home) have been either *Liberty Party* . . . [or] so called *Christian* Abolitionists, meaning those who will labor for the slave in and with *their* church but not *out* of it." As for Garrisonians, she claimed, "I scarcely know any *old organization* abolitionists here except for myself." No place needed "pure Anti Slavery influence" more than Cincinnati, Sarah concluded, and she determined to gather "a kind of nucleus . . . [of] females if there were any—who would labor for something besides politics and churches." She succeeded in starting up a sewing circle to help the fugitives who passed through Cincinnati on their way north to freedom. But while such labor was useful, Sarah was restless and dissatisfied, not convinced "that by it we advance real Freedom one step."[2]

Although Sarah scorned political and Christian abolitionism as merely "nominal," her letter highlights the different paths available to antislavery men and women during the 1840s and 1850s. Like Sarah Ernst, some abolitionists would cling to moral suasion but abandon hope of reforming the American churches or cooperating with a corrupt state. Others would agree with the founders of the American and Foreign Anti-Slavery Society (AFAS) that moral suasion might still bring the churches and benevolent associations around to condemning slavery. Still others, including eventually many members of the AFAS, would decide that the time had also come to attack slavery through the ballot box. Political tactics better suited the changing realities of American life, they believed, than sole reliance on propaganda and persuasion.[3]

Although there is no way of knowing for sure, Garrisonians probably constituted the smallest group of abolitionists in the two decades before the Civil War. Sidney Gay, editor of the *National Anti-Slavery Standard*, concluded in 1848 that "antislavery as represented by the old org. is without any visible influence, & but little outside of Massachusetts, Eastern Pennsylvania, & to a slight degree in Ohio." Lecturer Abby Kelley had even raised questions about the strength of Garrisonian abolitionism in western Massachusetts. On a speaking tour in 1844, she remarked that she had "frequent cause to blush at the laziness and inefficiency of the old organization."[4]

The recognition that most immediatists adopted political and/or religious tactics can lead to a historical narrative in which abolitionist women all but disappear. Such a story is quickly told. The radicalism of Garrisonian abolitionism frightened most women away from the only group that offered them equality. Many abandoned abolitionism altogether. Those who retreated into their churches to pursue the cause meekly accepted clerical direction and their subsidiary role. In synods, General Assembly meetings, and clerical conventions, however, churchmen struggled to force the major denominations to condemn slavery. Eventually the debate carried on in these male forums contributed to the division of churches into northern and southern branches, a rift that heightened sectional hostility and contributed to the coming of civil war. Meanwhile, political abolitionists busied themselves with the Liberty, Free-Soil, and Republican Party affairs and success at the polls, matters from which women were excluded.[5]

While such a picture is not entirely inaccurate and reflects the evidence found in many of the official sources, like the minutes of religious associational meetings and electoral results, women participated in the changing forms of antislavery work even if they did not always leave obvious clues of their activities. At the 1852 anniversary meeting of the AFAS, a resolution called upon "the women of this country" to continue "their persuasive influence in the great work of emancipation." The resolution recognized the reality of female involvement in antislavery and the composition of the audience. Over two-thirds of the 2,000 people present were women.[6]

That women could get keenly involved in antislavery politics and in efforts to cleanse their churches, even when these commitments meant entering into the public arena, is not as startling as it might appear at first glance. Why should women not embrace the party that espoused a politics of morality or scrutinize their church's stance on slavery when they felt that religious duty itself demanded female involvement? Why should campaign events be alien to women when their character so often resembled a revival camp meeting, where women felt at home?[7]

Recovering traces of these forms of female activism is not easy, however, and involves careful reading of private sources and painstaking scrutiny of printed sources like newspapers. Rarely do these materials describe white women's activities in much detail, and they overlook black women's religious and political work almost entirely. The meager evidence for white women is suggestive, not definitive, and leaves much to the imagination. An 1840 letter from one Ohio woman to her friend, Betsy Cowles, for example, merely hints at her political interests. Critical of abolitionists who refused to involve themselves in politics, she asked about Betsy's political views. "All Ladies have *politics now*," she remarked without elaborating. Just a few months later, a Dover, New Hampshire, woman writing on fair business only gave clues about her possible activities when she sealed her letter with a pink sticker that proclaimed:

The minister
who defends slavery
defends sin, and IS FALSE
To
HIS TRUST.[8]

Once it is acknowledged that women were involved continuously in new forms of antislavery work, however, it is tempting to see them as conservative in terms of women's rights and marginal to the efforts they supported.

These women are implicitly or explicitly contrasted to those few women in the radical Garrisonian camp who were active organizational leaders, fund-raisers, propagandists, and, sometimes, feminists. But labels of radicalism and conservatism do not entirely capture the nature of women's involvement in political and religious abolitionism. Women who would not adopt Garrison's definition of female rights, or approve of Abby Kelley lecturing to audiences of men and women, or hold office in a mixed antislavery society were willing to stand up and confront religious authorities in public. They courted clerical disapproval, withstood community censure, and undermined the social and religious status quo when they abandoned their churches, refused to contribute to benevolent causes because they condoned slavery, and even helped to establish antislavery churches. Politically, of course, women could not express their opinions through the ballot, a fact that frustrated Maria Child during the election of 1856. "It seemed as if my heart would burst, if I could n't *do* something to help on the election," she told her husband. Not only could Maria not vote, but she and other women were excluded from party deliberations and planning. Yet, while women had little access to leadership roles, they did not entirely lack influence in the political realm. Women who supported political abolitionism took advantage of opportunities ranging from the ornamental to the useful. Maria Child's propaganda pieces, including the "Song for the Free Soil Men" and her story "The Kansas Emigrants" published in the *New York Tribune* at election time, gave her the voice that she so desired.[9]

The character of American Protestantism during the decades of abolitionist activity shaped women's involvement in religious abolitionism. The disestablishment of churches in the years following the American Revolution had altered the religious landscape profoundly. In a sense, disestablishment created a free market economy in religion. Every denomination now faced the necessity of attracting enough adherents to support its operations financially. Each strove to maintain its moral and religious influence in this free market where people were able to choose which church to attend and even whether to attend church at all.

The need for adherents and the desire for influence encouraged the use of revival techniques even in mainline denominations like Congregationalism. As the Second Great Awakening's most prominent revivalist, Charles Finney, demonstrated time and time again, skillful preaching stirred emotions and moved listeners to the desired climax of conversion and Christian commitment. The number of new members who flocked into the churches during the Second Great Awakening proved the wisdom of evangelical techniques even as it highlighted the new requirements for successful ministry. "There must be excitement sufficient to wake up the dormant moral powers and roll back the tide of degradation and sin," Finney explained.[10]

It was no longer enough or perhaps even desirable for pastors to emphasize theology in their sermons. In the pulpit, the successful preacher aroused emotions, encouraged conversions, and made real the congregation's connection to God. Nor was it sufficient to confine pastoral efforts to sermonizing alone. Ministers became organizers of a panoply of events, prayer meetings, Sabbath schools, and concerts of prayer for specific objects, all intended to entangle members in a dense web of associational life, lead them toward conversion, and ensure denominational loyalty. The pastor was now judged and supported on the basis of his ability to meet his congregation's expectations. By the 1840s, one historian suggests, congregations were in the position of powerful clients who determined whether the services of their clergy were satisfactory or not.[11]

As the religious landscape changed, the relative position of Protestant denominations shifted as some proved more adept than others at attracting new adherents. Methodists and Baptists, once despised outcasts, proved to be the most successful at building up institutional strength. They became the nation's largest churches in the antebellum era, while Presbyterians and Congregationalists, despite the gains from the Second Great Awakening, lagged behind.[12]

In this new competitive religious world, denominational authorities and clergy recognized the danger of divisive issues like immediatism. Controversy drove members away, destroyed congregational harmony, and drowned out the pastor's voice. Financial consequences of dissension were real, endangering not only the position of individual clergy but also the future of collective efforts to spread the gospel, which many believed constituted the real work of the church. Members of denominations like Methodism, a sect having only recently achieved respectability, were hesitant to lose it in a fanatical debate. While most northern churches actually took positions that were critical of slavery and endorsed mild remedies like voluntary manumission and colonization, they were reluctant to condemn slaveholding as a sin. In its 1842 Annual Report, the Salem Female Anti-Slavery Society castigated the equivocal stance "of the American church, and its benevolent and religious societies, which cries union and peace before purity." The women further labeled "as antichristian the spirit which attempts to christianize far distant heathen, at the expense of heathen at home." [13]

Other forces unleashed by the Revolution and revivalism itself threatened denominational health and power at the same time that it supported religious independence and fragmentation. The democratic ideas spawned by the Revolution and its aftermath mingled with basic Protestant beliefs in the spiritual equality of all souls before God, the possibility of direct communication with God, and the importance of individual reading of Scripture. Anticlericalism, the weakening of religious authority, and the birth of new religious sects testified to the explosive combination of political and religious ideas. Evangelicalism, with its emphasis on an individual's conversion and the intimate connection with the divine, further contributed to spiritual autonomy and supported a critical stance toward organized religion.[14]

Even as revivals gathered in new members, it was clear that the bonds of denominational loyalty had weakened. Caroline Sloane's religious odyssey demonstrates that she was more interested in following her own voice of conscience than in blindly supporting any one religious institution. Born in Connecticut about 1810, Caroline early professed her faith and joined the Congregational Church. She married and continued as a Congregationalist until she moved with her husband to Holland, Connecticut, around 1837. There she learned about Methodism and, during a revival, "professed to experience the blessing of full salvation." From her new spiritual vantage point, her youthful conversion and Congregational affiliation now represented something less than the blessing of full salvation. Apparently, Congregational doctrine had not fully satisfied her, for one of the attractions of Methodism was that it "more particularly" agreed "with her own views." So "she cast in her lot with them." But not for long. Only five years after Caroline Sloane joined the Methodists, she abandoned that church because of its lukewarm stance toward slavery. "I have never for one moment regretted that step," she declared. "I feel God approves." Sometime during her religious odyssey, Caroline also managed to persuade "her once infidel husband . . . to acknowledge the truth of religion and to embrace Christ" by imitating her "consistent" or, perhaps more accurately, her meandering, religious course.[15]

Sarah Ernst's description of religious abolitionists as those "who labor for the slave in and with *their* church but not *out* of it" obscures the complex relationship between religious abolitionists and their churches. As Sarah Ernst implied, many religious abolitionist women did work for the slave in denominational organizations. Sometimes there was no conflict between abolitionism and religion. In Illinois, where the Congregationalists took an advanced stand on slavery, abolitionist women easily combined their interest in the slave with Congregational fellowship; in other less comfortable situations, abolitionist women determined to purify their churches. Purification entailed both the official condemnation of slavery as a sin and also the expulsion of slaveholders as members. These actions, religious abolitionists believed, would bring the church into accord with divine will, signify to all Christians the necessity of joining the abolitionist crusade, and even force southerners to accept immediate emancipation. Initially, women, like their fellow male church members, had expected the churches to move naturally to these decisions. Accepting abolitionism as a Christian duty, they could not envision a situation in which church leaders refused to act upon seemingly clear religious imperatives.[16]

Yet their confidence in their churches faltered as time passed. The reluctance of the Methodists, the nation's largest denomination, to take action that would interfere with its expansionary religious mission, or run the risk of driving southerners out of the church, was instructive. In 1836, the Methodist General Conference went on record as being "decidedly opposed to modern abolitionism, and wholly disclaim[ed] any right, wish, or intentions to interfere in the civil and political relations between master and slave." A subsequent letter to Methodist churches instructed the faithful "to abstain from all abolitionist movements and associations, and to refrain from patronizing any of their publications." Four years later, the General Conference came out in support of the Colonization Society. So laggardly was the progress of the Methodist Church toward purification that, in 1843, abolitionists broke away to form the Wesleyan Methodist Church. Two years later, southern Methodists withdrew into the Methodist Episcopal Church South.

Other denominations were hardly more eager to adopt an unequivocal (and divisive) stance on slavery. While Presbyterians separated into the New and Old Schools in 1837, partly over the slavery issue, another twenty years passed before the New School splintered again on the issue of fellowship with slaveholder. Meanwhile, the Old School's General Assembly rejected slavery as a topic for future discussion and refused to accept petitions from antislavery presbyteries. In the long run, however, schisms encouraged southern churches to argue that slavery was a positive good, a stance that contributed to the slow growth of antislavery sentiments among northern clergy.[17]

Despite their early interest in abolitionism, Quakers also disappointed abolitionists' hopes. At the AFAS's 1851 annual meeting, leaders "lamented that this ancient and respectable association does not more generally and extensively emulate the example of their brethren in Great Britain, in taking prominent and efficient action on the subject of slavery." Not only were

Friends reluctant to take a public stand on the question of slavery, but they were also unwilling to have members involved in antislavery associations with non-Quakers. The traditional Quaker emphasis on the importance of separating oneself from society at large seemed to forbid such mingling. In Rochester, abolitionist Amy Post was informed that she was "fast getting out of the quiet," and the committee charged with talking to her reproached her for "her attitude working with the 'world's' people." These sorts of tensions between abolitionism and the discipline of the Society led to separation from and division in meetings all over the North.[18]

Surprisingly, even black churches avoided committing themselves until the 1850s. There were certainly outspoken ministers, but, like their white counterparts, black religious leaders had no wish to lose support in and access to the South. Furthermore, some southern slaveholders were African Americans, and the existence of a group of black slaveowners contributed to foot-dragging. The African Methodist Episcopal Church (AME), the largest black denomination, managed to avoid all action until 1856. Even then, although the General Conference condemned slavery, it did not expel slaveholders from fellowship.[19]

While women abolitionists, like their male counterparts, wished to see national leaders adopt a clear position on the immorality of slavery, they saw the need to act in their own communities. Local churches and congregations needed purification and abolitionist commitment. The efforts to accomplish these ends forced women both to confront their formal exclusion from power and to make use of the informal power at their disposal. With the exception of the Society of Friends, most Protestant denominations prohibited women from holding governing positions. Women were neither elders, deacons, nor vestry members; and they were certainly not ordained ministers.

Although they stood outside the circle of official decision makers, church women had less tangible assets. By characterizing women as naturally moral and religious, middle-class culture lent power to their views and actions. Moreover, in the busy organizational church life spawned by revivalism and in the work of revivalism itself, women played an important, indeed, often a central, role. They held prayer meetings, visited potential converts, circulated religious literature, and taught Sabbath school. In the Society of Friends, separate women's meetings, female preachers, and more egalitarian notions of the two sexes endowed Quaker women with even more influence than their evangelical sisters. Even though women lacked the financial clout of wage-earning men, they were adept fundraisers. The donation parties they sponsored for the benefit of local clergy and their families, for example, contributed materially to clergy comfort and standard of living. They raised money for charitable and benevolent causes. Most important, women made up the majority of church members. Estimates of nineteenth-century Protestant membership suggest that there were two women for every man belonging to a Protestant church. They may have made up as much as 70 percent of Congregational membership. It was this informal power that made the High Street Congregational Church in Providence, Rhode Island, available to a July 4 antislavery service in 1837, despite the pastor's hostility to the gathering.[20]

While women may have composed the majority of church members, of course, a majority of churchgoing women were not likely to be abolitionists. When Eliza Gill surveyed Fitchburg's churches in 1839, she found few abolitionists and such strong ministerial opposition that "it seems almost futile to contend against it." Among the Unitarians, she counted only one or two female abolitionists. The Calvinist clergy were hostile to abolitionism, and except for "a very few valuable exceptions," most of the female members were under clerical influence. Although Fitchburg "hearers who cannot bear dictation" were leaving Mr. Ballard's society, the majority of the women heeded his heavy-handed sermons about what activities they should avoid. Lucy Furber was more typical of women in the pews than Eliza Gill and the small number of independent women in Fitchburg. Hearing an abolitionist lecture in 1855, Lucy responded negatively to the sarcasm "& many hard thrusts at ministers in particular & religion generally." She rejected the argument that "*everything* must bend and give place to the *one great thing*—the *Abolition of slavery*—men's laws & God's ordinances if need be."[21]

Even a small group of energetic and articulate women, however, could be influential in this setting and affect both pastoral decisions and congregational behavior. Harriet Aldrick's three-year campaign to convince the clergy and laity in the Ludlow, Massachusetts, Methodist congregation of "the defects in the government and policy" of the church did not succeed, but her persistence meant that everyone in the church had to consider her point of view. In Rev. Jacob Manning's church, abolitionists pressed the pastor hard. He recorded in his diary "some accusing experiences in regard to not reading Mrs. Stows appeal," and remarked that "my Opinions on Slavery are fished after." When abolitionists succeeded in making individual churches centers of abolitionism, or when groups broke away to form antislavery churches, one can safely assume that women like Caroline Sloane, who was the religious leader in her family, played an important role in the course of events. Although studies of denominational schisms over

"Who in God's sight is holy."

Written for the Anti-Slavery Melodies.

BY MISS ALMIRA SEYMOUR.   TUNE—"MORNING LIGHT IS BREAKING."

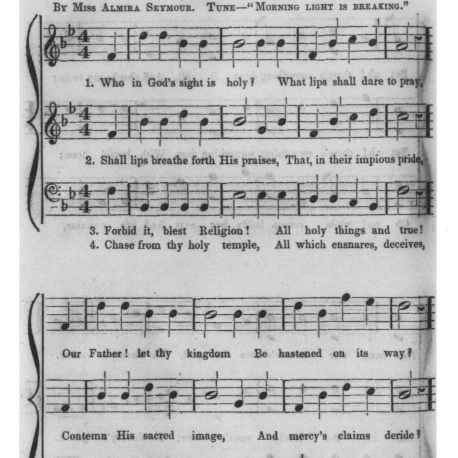

1. Who in God's sight is holy? What lips shall dare to pray,

2. Shall lips breathe forth His praises, That, in their impious pride,

3. Forbid it, blest Religion! All holy things and true!
4. Chase from thy holy temple, All which ensnares, deceives,

Our Father! let thy kingdom Be hastened on its way?

Contemn His sacred image, And mercy's claims deride?

And, Father! O forgive them, They know not what they do.
And let thy house, no longer, Be as a den of thieves;

The text of this antislavery song, written by a woman, testifies to
the efforts to purify the American churches. (Boston Athenæum)

slavery emphasize the deliberations and decisions of men, given the overwhelming female character of Protestantism, it seems likely that female pressure helped to precipitate and support men's actions.[22]

Some evidence suggests such an interpretation. In Talmadge County, Ohio, women, thinking "it important that our ecclesiastical bodies consider this subject," circulated a memorial that they intended to send to the General Assembly of the Presbyterian Church. In the Red River Conference of the Methodist Church, members of a local church also signed a petition and memorial objecting to the proslavery position of the conference. Some women attended their denomination's General Assembly meetings. "I have never so fully realized the meaning of 'outside pressure,' " a Cleveland woman reflected, "as when I saw, day after day, that body surrounded in church and gallery, by eager listeners, intent to hear their discussion."[23]

As abolitionist clergy began to hold interdenominational meetings, women got involved. Between 1851 and 1855, the Ladies Anti-Slavery Circle of Cincinnati actually sponsored conventions bringing all stripes of political and religious abolitionist together. These well-attended conventions promoted "pure" abolitionism by supporting the exclusion of slaveholders from church fellowship.[24]

The fact that abolitionism would demand a certain kind of religious activism was not at first evident to many women who supported immediate emancipation. In 1836, in the heyday of antislavery organizing, fifty-seven women of Uxbridge, Massachusetts, gathered to adopt a constitution and form a female antislavery society. Like so many other female associations, the Uxbridge women considered abolition a sacred duty. Their "faith, in the fulfillment of the blessed promises contained in the Holy Scriptures," made women abolitionists hopeful about the eventual triumph of their cause. But they soon realized that they needed to take an active role in harnessing the power of religion to immediate emancipation and in forcing local clergy to commit themselves on the question. Signs of commitment included such seemingly simple actions as making the church available for an antislavery lecture, or reading a notice of one from the pulpit, or preaching the pure doctrine of antislavery and refusing communion to slaveholders.

The struggle might easily begin over the issue of announcing abolitionist lectures. Publicizing an abolitionist lecture from the pulpit helped attract an audience, but, just as importantly, it appeared to validate the cause. For an abolitionist, therefore, reading an announcement became a test of a clergyman's position on abolitionism. Efforts to garner clerical backing precipitated what often became a public contest of wills. While Anne Weston confined her criticism of Deacon Gulliver to a family letter (he had "*omitted* to give notice at the Free Church *not daring* to do so. . . . [and was] a perfect coward"), others appealed to a wider audience. In Rhode Island, Sophia Little prepared a piece for publication accusing the clergy of cowardice. "The . . . respectability of your cause is your idol," she wrote scornfully.[25]

Deborah Weston undertook an aggressive campaign to publicize the news of an abolitionist lecture through "every thing calling itself a church" in New Bedford. Sending a male colleague to "attack" one of the more problematic clergymen, she confronted the city's prominent Baptist clergyman herself. Cornering him on the street a few days before the Sunday service, she used his own claim to be "a most devoted abolitionist" to pressure him to break his policy of refusing to announce abolitionist lectures from the pulpit. Her challenge, presented on a public thoroughfare, caused him to reflect. Deborah then put indirect pressure on the pastor through his sister. Though not all of New Bedford's ministers announced the lecture, the Baptist cleric did. Deborah was satisfied, for she had "carried my points, & hd two of the most intractable churches in town."[26]

In Seneca Falls, New York, Rhoda Bement's efforts to force her Presbyterian pastor, Reverend Horace Bogue, to read a notice of an upcoming abolitionist meeting in 1843 sparked an acrimonious controversy. Bogue, who had links with the American Colonization Society, disapproved of slavery but was hardly willing to give immediatism his seal of approval from the pulpit, especially since an antislavery speaker had attacked him in a recent lecture. When, for the second week running, Bogue failed to read the notice Rhoda had prepared, she accosted him in the church vestibule after the service. He excused his silence by claiming that he had not even read her note. Did he not habitually open notices to see whether they should be announced? she asked. The conversation was turning into a public event, with members of the congregation observing the heated interchange.

Later, Rhoda described Bogue's attempt to use the power of his position to silence her. Your "course is a very improper one from the beginning," he apparently said. "I think you very unchristian, very impolite and very much out of your place to pounce upon me in this manner." Rhoda thought differently. "I thought I had a right to put the notices on the desk & to ask him why he didn't read them," she responded. Now excited, Bogue accused his parishioner of questioning his honesty. Her scornful reply challenged both his veracity and his reputed antislavery credentials. "Mr. Bogue I'll tell you why I doubt [your veracity]," she recalled saying. "You told me you was an abolitionist & I supposed if you was an abolitionist you would read abolition notices that were bro't here."

Although Rhoda later maintained that she had not intended the argument to turn into a public event, privacy was unlikely, especially given the volatility of the issue and the location of the conversation. Tongues were soon wagging in Seneca Falls. Such matters quickly became the topic of conversation. Not long before, another abolitionist, Olivia Savage, had withdrawn from the Methodist Church and undertaken a house-to-house campaign to discuss religion and moral reform. Gossip tarnished Olivia Savage as "crazy."[27]

Religious women who dared to confront church authorities gained courage from the conviction that their cause was holy. "It matters little whether Dr. Channing or Dr. Beecher or any other Dr. in the land thinks as we do on the subject of slavery . . . [for] the Lord is on our side," explained one women. Such an attitude encouraged religious abolitionists to subject the words and actions of local clergy to minute examination. In Bedford, Massachusetts, Lavinia Hosmer reported on the Unitarian minister whom she regarded as lacking true antislavery feeling. She was willing to suspend final judgment because she understood "brother Woodward has spoken a word for the slave to-day before the people," and perhaps "may yet take up the highest antislavery ground." She would be sure to follow him closely.[28]

Many religious abolitionists found their study of clerical behavior sobering. "It is above two years since my confidence in *ministers* or *at least* some of them began to be shaken," confided Maria Rice in 1842. In Fitchburg, Massachusetts, Eliza Gill and her husband reported they "usually attend[ed] church but derive very little comfort or spiritual benefit from preaching[.] And again—it troubles us, that our children should thus constantly listen to such *conscience searing sentiments.*" Ultimately, some individuals would be driven to action, agreeing with Maria Rice, that "with the Bible before me though a fool I need not err." Elmira Swett, a Georgetown, Massachusetts, woman registered her public contempt for her pastor's preaching by clicking her knitting needles together during his sermon. Her behavior resulted in her bodily removal from the church and arrest for contempt of worship. Martha Barrett was satisfied with her Salem clergyman, but her diary made clear what she would do if he did not preach the truth. "I could not consistently attend church where a proslavery clergyman performs," she wrote. "I cannot call it worship for can the worship of an oppressor, or apologist for oppression, outrage & wrong be acceptable to a liberty-loving God of purity and truth?"[29]

"Woman's voice must not be hushed while the clergy are recreant to the poor slave," declared Patsy Newton, of Worcester, Massachusetts, in 1840. "It is enough to break a heart of stone to see with what indifference those who profess the gospel treat the subject of slavery." Her attendance at a ministerial convention recently held in the town had been most distressing, and she was passing along her opinion of it in her correspondence. Women relied upon letters and the spoken word to spread the news about ministerial dereliction. Mary T. Burrage, in Fitchburg, "expostulated with individuals" and wrote to her minister requesting "an opportunity for conversation." Members of the Portland Anti-Slavery Society debated their views of the church in their association meeting, leaving some recoiling from the accusations of religious guilt. Gossip also carried the tale of supposed clerical shortcomings, as it did when Rhoda Bement and her minister clashed.[30]

Sophia Little, a resident of Newport, where southerners traditionally summered, was unwilling to converse with church members whom she thought were basically unsympathetic to her criticism of a proslavery church. "The spirit will not suffer me to do it," she confessed. "I cannot speak on religious things freely to them." But she felt few inhibitions about expressing herself freely in other ways: "The pen or the conference is my *sphere* where there is none to throw me into a nonplus by arguing with me." Like Sophia, other women were willing to move into print to communicate their dissatisfactions with religious leaders. Critical resolutions about churches became part of the published annual reports of women's associations. Women also sent resolutions from their meetings to the newspaper. In Byfield, Massachusetts, Eleanor Jewett, censured for her abolitionist zeal by her "proslavery" minister, drafted a set of resolutions and presented them to her antislavery society for approval. "I have been told that my resolutions are strong," she reported. "I know it, & I also know that the giant sin of slavery is strong." Her resolutions eventually appeared in the newspaper. Individual letters to antislavery newspapers also expressed criticism of clergy. Phebe Blackmer, once a member of the Second Congregational Church in Plymouth, Massachusetts, began one such letter, saying, "I should like to appear as a witness against one branch, at least, of the great American Church." After detailing her case on the moral failure of the Plymouth church, she concluded, "If the publication of this article shall contribute anything toward helping public opinion in a right decision of the church, I shall have accomplished my object in appearing before the public."[31]

Controversies and challenges emerged when women judged their clergy cowardly or misguided on the subject of slavery. When abolitionists and clergy were in harmony, working for the slave within and through the church became a real possibility. In some places, working with the church was the only institutional option for abolitionism. While a majority of evangelical clergy were satisfied with a partial commitment to antislavery at best and considered abolitionists troublesome fanatics, there were still many clergy, both black and white, who were sympathetic to the call for immediate abolition. Indeed, despite Garrison's condemnation of American churches, most members of Garrisonian antislavery societies after 1840 were clergy and church members, as were those supporting other avenues of abolitionist activity. In the 1850s, legislation like the Fugitive Slave Act and turmoil in Kansas combined with the southern defenses of slavery to draw more clergy to the abolitionist cause.[32]

Mary White of Boylston, Massachusetts, had the good fortune of having a committed abolitionist as her pastor. Her membership in the antislavery society, her work in petitioning and in preparing items for the Boston fair, and her attendance at antislavery lectures meshed with antislavery sermons and strong ministerial support for her activities. But the experiences of Evelina Smith, whose minister, Mr. Stearns, was also a staunch abolitionist, dramatized how, over time, a religious abolitionist could find herself marginalized because of community indifference or hostility.[33]

When Stearns, an "anti-Slavery Pastor," arrived in Hingham in 1841, Evelina was delighted. Because the congregation was proslavery, with separate pews for African Americans and a policy of excluding antislavery lecturers, she anticipated some kind of "ordeal." It unfolded slowly. An antislavery convention held in Hingham in 1842 heightened the anxieties of church members who were already uncomfortable with Stearns's prayers for the slave. An air of crisis prevailed. Knots of men stood on street corners, in shops, and offices talking about religion. Women ran back and forth "to exchange words of sympathy, & to hear the latest development of the individual opinion of men whom they despise perhaps, but who have the power to vote." On one occasion, two men stalked out of the church during the service, and many stayed away to protest Stearns's abolitionist sermons. Evelina was unperturbed, even willing to see a "sifting" of membership, "if [only] Mr. Stearns does not go away." Six months later, the commotion showed no signs of dying down. Other ministers entered into the fray. In their services, they too began to pray for the oppressed. Evelina suspected that their supplications were meant to wake people up so that they heard the prayer that "the offending abolitionists" learn the prudence and discretion necessary for walking in "brotherly love." By the following year, however, Stearns had caved into the pressure. His sermons went "round & round slavery without mentioning the term," and he seemed intent on keeping *the parish together*" and pleasing all. Abolitionists had been turned out of the Sunday school in the interests of banishing "all discordant notes," and Stearns was encouraging religious enthusiasm with some success. Evelina was dismayed. Rather than the other members of the church being sifted out, she found herself on the fringes, avoiding the weekly prayer meetings at Stearns's house. In her words, "I have never been but once & found it then so stupid that I shall not go again I think."[34]

Stearns, doubtlessly, feared not only the division of his congregation and shrinking financial support but also the ultimate loss of his position. His fears were real. When Freewill Baptist Elder Martin Cheyney preached antislavery sermons in his Providence church, several prominent male parishioners withdrew their pledges of financial support. Only because of the fund-raising of a few determined women was Cheyney able to hold on to his post.[35]

As Stearns and Cheyney both discovered, congregations often reacted negatively to the antislavery message. Alice March expressed one of the reasons for such a response. Abolitionism raised scandal in the community, she believed, especially among the unchurched. "What can the irreligious think of those who profess to be Christians denounce so entirely—those who sit at the same communion table and their own minister," she wondered. Lucinda Storrs, writing from Lebanon, New Hampshire, thought that members had religious rather than antislavery matters on their minds. "The church members are more engaged to promote a revival of religion among ourselves than to have the oppressed go free, or to have the traffic cease in the District of Columbia," she complained.[36]

Those who tried to push the matter in their churches faced hostility and angry efforts by clergy, church officers, and members to discipline and silence them. Perhaps a sense of betrayal fueled clerical anger. Women formed the backbone of the church and, by their nature, were supposed to support rather than oppose their religious leaders. New Hampshire clergy, wrote one woman, thought it was woman's "duty & our only duty, apparently, to supply all their bodily wants and pray for their souls." Instead, fractious women were holding "them up to the scorn & contempt of the world."[37]

Rhoda Bement not only questioned her minister's veracity, "a very unchristian outrage" and a clear example of "disorderly conduct," but had also refused to drink communion wine. Further compounding her treachery, she had attended "in a conspicuous manner upon the exhibitions made by Abby Kelley on the first Sabbath of Aug. last between the hours of 5 and 8 o'clock P.M. & while the church to which . . . [she] belongs were attending upon divine service." So seriously did Rhoda challenge the authority and the peace of the church, that the church session brought her to trial in late 1843. During the proceedings, Rhoda stubbornly refused to acknowledge any wrongdoing and questioned the intent of her accusers. Was not the trial "an attempt to bind the conscience & deprive me of Christian liberty?" she asked. Did not the church's actions "look more like an attempt to *crush* than to reclaim an erring member (if I have been guilty of error)?"[38]

The session found Rhoda guilty of slander, but she remained defiant even when she appeared before the governing body itself. At this final meeting, she showed her contempt for clerical power. She would not appeal "unto Caesar," the corrupt worldly authorities whom her church leaders represented, she proclaimed, but to God. Suspended from communion until a confession was forthcoming, Rhoda was excommunicated when the session discovered that she was attending services with the Wesleyan Methodists, who broke away from the Seneca Falls Methodist Church in 1843.[39]

Rhoda Bement had not intended to part from her Presbyterian brothers and sisters so dramatically. She had even tried to argue that the trial itself was inappropriate since the church had not "labored" with her over her supposed sins. But although she could not have anticipated the course of events, she deliberately challenged prevailing religious norms in such a way that her departure was all but inevitable. She refused to back down before clerical and lay leaders, and she refused to be silent. She followed out the logic of her commitments to God and to the slave.[40]

While church records detail Rhoda's conflict with church authorities, less plentiful evidence suggests that other women pursued similar goals with the same sorts of personal consequences. Eleanor Jewett's minister considered her a "very disorderly member" of his church because of her antislavery activities, and he lectured her for "four or five hours at one time, & two hours at another time, for my improper conduct & overheated zeal." In 1844, L. M. Robbins, knowing that her minister considered her on a "downward course," received an unwelcome visit from a female parishioner, possibly sent by her pastor. Her uninvited guest pressed Robbins "to think better of Successors of the Apostle" and warned her darkly about the loss of her "spirituality of mind." "Anti-Slavery [should not be] the touchstone of character," she argued, and it had brought neither slaves nor free blacks to their savior. Robbins, accusing her visitor of being a racist, denounced "the unfaithfulness of the Church & Clergy." Her guest left with little attempt to be cordial. When the news of the interview became of matter of community discussion, Robbins ran the risk of social and religious ostracism.[41]

Other women boldly introduced the issue of slavery during regular services and church meetings, even when they knew they had little support. As one New Hampshire woman had informed her "clerical teachers, I shall speak in religious meetings." This boldness was not easy for many women. Despite the Quaker tradition of female preaching and speaking, Elizabeth Chace dreaded addressing her meeting about policies that counseled members "to keep in the quiet, . . . and not to unite with people outside of our religious society, in public undertakings." Finally, her dissatisfaction forced her to act. With her heart throbbing "violently" against her side and hoping "that the meeting would close" before she had a chance to make her remarks, she summoned up the strength to proclaim that acceptable worship was impossible so long as members were "living in indifference to the sufferings of our brethren and sisters in slavery." New York Quaker Sarah Gibbons adopted an even more confrontational position before a monthly meeting at which she accused its members of being hypocrites. "I believe it my religious duty to raise high my standard and declare to all the world, as far as I can, the wickedness of such proceedings," she told her sister. "Neither Minister, Elder, Overseer, Sect, nor Association should prevent me from thinking, acting, or speaking as a free woman."[42]

Bold actions could have unexpected consequences. Sarah Gibbons escaped bodily harm when she challenged Quaker authorities, although some women were not so lucky. One Quaker woman was thrown out of the meetinghouse into the street "sometimes with rough and merciless hands . . . for speaking . . . the truth." Maria French was carried out of Salem's Congregational Church for her refusal to obey the minister's order to sit down and be silent.[43]

Other women bore witness to the inadequacies of their church's stance on slavery by their refusal to give to the church or benevolent societies and by their conspicuous absence from worship. Some confronted racial practices and norms sanctioned by the church.[44]

Many congregations demonstrated a "proslavery" spirit by having segregated seating. Sarah Douglass's mother endured the humiliation of separate seating at the Philadelphia Quaker meeting she attended (but could not join) for years. While moral suasion might succeed in putting an end to such a practice, some evidence suggests women used more dramatic tactics. Sophia Little, not surprisingly, sent a letter to the newspaper to urge clergy to "class your white and colored children together in your Sabbath schools, though your halls be deserted." Another woman, a member of a Newport Baptist Church, flaunted her rejection of racial mores by inviting a black member into her pew during the service. When she was criticized for her behavior, she refused to pay her pew rent. Instead, she carried a stool into the church, placed it in the aisle next to her former pew, and occupied it during the service. Few black women put up with the discrimination Sarah Douglass's mother experienced; they left white congregations and joined black churches.[45]

Some white women challenged racial mores, as earlier chapters have suggested, by their demeanor in public places. They walked, even arm in arm, with African Americans and invited them into segregated railroad cars or steamship salons. While only a minority of women had both the opportunity and courage to demonstrate their racial views so publicly, when they did so, they were seen to be offending both community and religious norms. Thus, in Lynn, the minister of Gulielma Estes's church questioned her about her walks with an African American man. In a hostile fashion, he asked her the loaded question: Would she be willing to marry a black man? What might have cowed a more timid woman did not subdue Gulielma. She challenged his racial views and announced that she would be willing to marry a black man if his character were suitable. At the interview's conclusion, the minister warned that Gulielma should either "leave the church or, come before them and acknowledge your wrongdoing and promise never to commit the same offenses."[46]

Offending community racial and religious norms carried its costs. Mary Smith reported that her Exeter neighbors taunted her, calling her crazy. "I am *branded* with such *names* as *Elect Lady. Comadore* and willing to *sleep* with *niggar* children to marry them etc., etc." Mary put on a brave face and claimed the taint of scandal and the loss of respectability did not bother her. She had even prepared a letter to send to her church, presumably announcing her withdrawal from a body determined to control her behavior or hound her out. Asa and Anna Fairbanks in Providence absented themselves from their "so called church." Neighbors labeled them fanatics and stayed away from their house.[47]

Like the Fairbankses, Sophia Little was decidedly of the opinion that a "living Christian abolitionist" could not enjoy fellowship in a proslavery church. "If the church is wrong," said another woman, then "my conviction of duty is, come out of it until it is right." Other women ultimately agreed and made the final condemnation of their churches and fellow Christians by withdrawing from their churches. Some, like Lizzy Neall, did not feel the move was too painful, particularly because she was disgusted by the religious "cant" and caution she found in her Quaker meeting. Since she had not chosen her religious affiliation but had been born into it, and since she could not approve of its discipline, she resolved to dissolve her connection. "Who could wish to belong to such an organisation," she wondered?[48]

The address Thomas Stove gave to Salem women in 1852 suggested, however, that separation from a church could be a wrenching experience. "Some of you, perhaps, have met that deepest of sorrows, not the sneer of the world, nor the coldness or hostility of friends," Stove declared, "but the interruption of religious communion. Within the church, from which you had drawn a faith dearer than the blood of your own hearts; from the pulpit, to which that faith had trained you to look with reverence . . . you found . . . something else." [49]

Coming out of a church was a difficult and agonizing step. As one woman explained, she had been taught that religious authorities were "almost infallible." It took her five years to conclude that "our Evangelical churches" were proslavery. It appears that most supporters of immediate emancipation were unwilling or unable to cut ties with their community's most important social institution and its familiar cluster of associations. In Rhode Island, Sarah Gould found the whole idea that abolitionists should leave their churches "oppressive." She, like so many others, remained in the church, still hopeful that it might eventually "be aroused." [50]

Abandoning the church and all its sacred and human connections demanded a heightened sense of duty and a considerable spirit of independence. Come-outers weighed individual religious convictions against religious obligations proclaimed from the pulpit and espoused by friends and neighbors. They faced possible social ostracism. Even though Agnes Crain was confident that she had properly severed her religious connection, for example, she confessed that it was "hard to have those whom I most loved and honoured alienated from me." Her 1847 letter poignantly expressed her sense of loss: "Though I no longer meet my former friends in the prayer meeting or lecture room, in the sectarian Sunday school, or the teachers meeting, though they always see my seat in church empty, and when I meet them and their Pastor or to those of his church become the subject of conversation. I could no longer join in it." [51]

Women chose different ways of leaving their churches. Some did so quietly, writing personal letters conveying their decision. But others were intent on creating a public commotion. R. W. Stearns wanted to provoke her Springfield, Massachusetts, church to action. "I waited till October in hopes of being turned out," she revealed, but "was obliged at last, to turn myself out. The act cost me many a struggle, but *I am glad it is done*." Elizabeth Wheelwright capitalized on the fact that she was a thorn in the side of her congregation and anti-abolitionist minister. In her letter to the session, she used the desire of the church to have her gone as a means of ensuring that her criticisms would have yet another public hearing: "I requested . . .

[that my letter] might be read in the presence of the Church, that they might understand I entirely disapproved the course they had pursued; It *was* read, but would *not* have been had I not stated it was the only ground on which I would consent to receive a letter of dismission." Abby Gibbons, who realized that if she merely handed her letter to the clerk it would remain on his desk, read her own letter aloud "in a tone that might be heard at the farthest corner" of the meetinghouse. In it she announced her withdrawal from her Quaker meeting and condemned its failure to disavow the great evil of slavery.[52]

A woman who had the courage to separate herself from her church, whether in such a public manner or more privately, was both asserting the superior morality of her own beliefs in abolitionism and exposing the corruption of the institution that should have had morality and Christian duty at its center. Her brave challenge drew its strength from her conviction that women possessed virtues that men, even clergymen, did not posses in equal measure. When a guardian of morality gave witness to her beliefs, the action had power and might influence others to examine their own convictions and loyalties.[53]

Some of the women who acted upon their convictions found a welcome peace of mind. Elizabeth Chace rejoiced that she was no longer "responsible for the pro-slavery attitudes of the Society" of Friends. Like many Garrisonians, she never joined another church. Feelings of relief often mingled with less exuberant reactions, however, for the meetinghouse or church frequently formed the social center of women's lives. Sophia Little and her daughter were living in "hermit like seclusion from all spiritual communities" and were not happy in their lonely situation.[54]

The desire for religious fellowship led to the formation of antislavery churches. In upstate New York and western Massachusetts, religious abolitionists established more than forty "union" congregations, inclusive bodies without specific denominational ties. In northern Ohio, Indiana, Illinois, and western New York, many New School Presbyterian ministers and their churches adopted a congregational affiliation that allowed them to bar slaveowners as members. Disgruntled Methodists and Presbyterians withdrew from their national churches to form new denominational bodies. In many parts of the North, mid-Atlantic, and Midwest, Quaker meetings divided as Friends withdrew or were ejected from their meetings because of their abolitionist zeal. At least one black church, in Boston, divided. By 1850, one historian has estimated, membership in come-outer groups and in "traditionally antislavery" denominations, like the Freewill Baptists, totaled 241,000.[55]

Beyond the significance that leaving a proslavery church symbolized for the individual, come-outer sects gave collective testimony about the sin of slaveholding and intended to be "the means of reforming other churches from the foul stain of slavery." Although the racial practices of new congregations are not known, some evidence also suggests new churches made efforts to overcome prejudice. The Fulton, New York, Wesleyan Methodist Church, for example, welcomed into their congregation black members who had no place to worship. In Springfield, Massachusetts, the Wesleyan class meetings included several African American members who spoke and were reportedly "treated the same as any other persons."[56]

New sects were more than exemplars of a more perfect religious and racial order, however. They drew members and resources away from mainline denominations. Joining the Wesleyan Methodist or the Free Presbyterian Church represented a means of pressuring mother churches to adopt a stronger antislavery stance by reducing human and financial resources. New missionary associations and publishing endeavors similarly weakened the financial health of major denominations. Joining an antislavery church was not only an expression of the voice of individual conscience but also part of a collective effort to influence American Protestantism.[57]

Although no figures break down membership by sex in abolitionist churches, since the majority of all church members were women, it is likely that they also constituted a majority of members of the new abolitionist bodies. Perhaps the records of the Wesleyan Methodist Church in Leicester, Massachusetts, reveal a common pattern. The male church secretary recorded the founding events of the group and provided information about the thirty-seven Methodists who formed a Wesleyan congregation. Of the thirty-seven, nineteen were women; seven joined the new church with husbands or fathers; the remaining women came alone or with a female relative.[58]

Of the new antislavery churches, the Wesleyan Methodist connection was the most important. Its dramatic departure from the nation's largest denomination made a powerful antislavery statement, and its rapid growth testified to the lure of Christian abolitionism. In 1843, the year in which the division with the Methodists occurred, 6,000 left the mother church for the new sect. Within two years, another 9,000 had joined. By 1850, the church claimed 20,000 members and began to publish its own paper, the *True Wesleyan*.[59]

The Leicester church records also provide insights into the contentious process of schism. On March 1, 1845, Methodists met in the church vestry to discuss the differences between the Methodist and the Wesleyan Methodist Churches. A majority of those present voted to sever their connection with the Methodists. "This was followed by a violent opposition from the authorities of the Methodist Episcopal Church," the secretary noted. "After a warm discussion on both sides the following persons agreed to throw off the Episcopal yoke and enjoy the Liberties of the Wesleyan Methodist connection." What part, if any, the nineteen women played in the debate the secretary did not record.[60]

In the opinion of one historian, the Wesleyan Methodists made up part of the "blurred periphery" of the abolitionist movement, members of the rank and file about whom not much is known. His study suggests that ministers, artisans, and farmers between the ages of twenty-six and forty-five were well represented among Wesleyan Methodists. While there is no particular reason to believe that women came from different social backgrounds or age groups from men, the number of unattached women joining the Leicester church should serve as a caution about extrapolating information about women from data about men.[61]

The *True Wesleyan* describes the religious but not the social background of some of the women joining the Wesleyans and suggests the personal significance of the move. In some cases, husbands and wives came into the new church as a couple. But, as the Bradleys' example makes it clear, wives did not necessarily take religious cues from husbands. Harriet Bradley charted her own religious course; while her husband, Stephen, attended Martha's Vineyard's Congregational Church, Harriet followed her own conscience as a Methodist. In May of 1843, each left his/her respective church and together organized a Wesleyan congregation. "I believe we are the first that have thus publicly come out on this island," Stephen reported. While the Bradleys' communication does not reveal the personal dynamics involved in the joint action, the decision to organize a Wesleyan Methodist congregation suggests the importance of Harriet's Methodist leanings if not her leadership.[62]

What proportion of women came into the antislavery church from denominations other than Methodism cannot be ascertained. It is clear, however, that for many women a church's stand on slavery was more important than doctrine. "Anti-slavery Quakers can stand Anti-slavery Methodism," the *True Wesleyan* pointed out in 1849. Obituaries published in the paper contain information showing that individual women followed their consciences about religion and made decisions based on their convictions about the sinfulness of slavery. Diana Bentley from New York State experienced conversion at the age of fifteen, joined the Baptists, and remained with them for thirty-five years, despite her marriage (probably her second) to a

Methodist cleric. The "pro-slavery character" of the Baptist Church finally drove her out, and both she and her husband became Wesleyan Methodists. Mary Jane Hunt, of Syracuse, had formerly been a Congregationalist; Elizabeth Hiatt, of Hamilton County, Indiana, had been a Quaker; while Harriet Whitney of New York City had been reared as a Presbyterian and then converted to Methodism. All three became a Wesleyan Methodists.[63]

Former Methodists must have constituted the core of the new church. Obituaries show lifelong Methodist women severing their connections over the question of slavery. A few suggest how traumatic the experience could be. One of the most detailed pictures is of Mary Stanford, an Ohio woman who was converted to Methodism at a camp meeting at the age of sixteen. The event, probably occurring in 1809, came during the time when many people "despised" Methodism; but social disapproval did not deter young Mary. Willing to be the only Methodist in her neighborhood, she persisted in her newfound faith, which her family soon adopted. When she moved to Indiana in 1817, the year in which she married, her cabin became the home for many itinerant clergy. But just at the moment that Methodism was beginning to flourish, rumors of the slaveholding nature of the church and of bishops who held slaves began to circulate. "Having always lived in a free State," Mary "knew but little of the workings of slavery in the church. At first she looked upon the charge as foul slander." But eventually the actions of the General Conference convinced Mary that the charges were not slanderous, that they were true. The discovery was painful. "That the Church of her early choice, that she had so long cherished, instead of being opposed to slavery as she had supposed it to be, should be convicted by its own testimony, of being guilty of that sum of all villainies, was a shock she was not prepared to meet." But she could not avoid the necessary consequences of her discoveries. "She bid adieu to her old home and friends . . . for conscience sake. And was one of the first who united in organized Wesleyan Methodist Church in her neighborhood."[64]

Once they had made the new commitment, women in the Wesleyan Methodist connection, as well as in other come-outer congregations, undertook antislavery projects quite similar to those of their abolitionist sisters in mainline denominations. But, as reflected in the pages of the *True Wesleyan*, there was considerable uncertainty about the appropriate role for women. The energy that led women to break religious ties with churches they viewed as "proslavery" and to challenge the status quo was admirable but could prove problematic in the antislavery church as well. The paper thus contained stories and articles featuring pious domestic women as well as female obituaries praising the private nature of deceased women's lives. At the same time, amidst the tributes to conventional womanhood and female piety, letters from ministers, and accounts of conventions and camp meetings, the paper also included news of women who pursued anti-slavery aggressively. The paper encouraged women's petitioning and even reported favorably on an 1851 speech by Antoinette Brown on women's rights, expressing regret that such a remarkable woman was not a Wesleyan Methodist.[65]

Unsure of just what the parameters were for women's work as Christian abolitionists, the paper left the way open for women to determine for themselves their best course of action. Some of the women may have been radical advocates of equal rights and members of Garrisonian antislavery organizations. The Executive Committee of the Western Anti-Slavery Society claimed in 1847 that no religious sect in Ohio had "furnished as many members of the proportion of their number, that are ready to embrace ultra abolitionism, as the Wesleyan Methodists." Most women were probably not Garrisonians, however, and felt comfortable in gatherings in the evangelical mainstream. The newspaper described an antislavery concert held at the Lowell's Wesley Chapel in January 1844. For the first two hours, fifteen children, doubtless coached by women, held the audience of over 1,000 "in almost breathless [and tearful] silence" as they gave orations about the horrors of slavery. Music, a sermon, and a prayer meeting followed. By the end of the five-hour service, twenty or thirty people pressed forward as seekers of Divine favor. "Thus we see that the anti-slavery cause and revivals of religion go hand in hand," the paper commented. Given the dominance of women in the Lowell workforce, they must have played an active part in creating the emotional intensity that rendered the evening's blend of abolitionism, prayer meeting, and revivalism so powerful.[66]

If woman's moral voice for the slave and for sinners was being raised in ways even a timid evangelical woman might find acceptable, there were occasional hints of more unusual vocal contributions. In an obituary for Harriet Whitney, wife of an itinerant minister, and, with her husband, a convert to Wesleyan Methodism, the writer deliberately contrasted her upbringing in the Presbyterian Church to the needs of her new faith: "She had much to overcome concerning female labor in religious line." Specifically, she had learned reticence in her Presbyterian Church and had to conquer her habit of silence. When she did so, she was able to "scatter the precious seeds of truth" throughout New England and New York State. Ellen Elam of Granville, Ohio, at the instigation of her Wesleyan Methodist brethren, also spoke out. "Although I labor under considerable embarrassment on account of the prejudice that exists in the mind of many people in this country, with reference to female preaching," she explained, "yet I have had generally very good congregations."[67]

Newspaper articles sometimes criticized the methods women used to raise funds for the church, but female fund-raising skills were more valuable than ever. The Wesleyan Methodists had left behind in Methodist hands the buildings and financial resources that undergirded institutional health. In this context, women experimented with new ways to bring in needed cash. The Tea Meeting was one such experiment. The women of Boston's First Wesleyan Church in 1843 sponsored the first one described in the *True Wesleyan*. Prayer, singing, and a talk by a former slave combined with "the cheerful bustle and pleasant music peculiar to the tea table." All this entertainment and instruction came with an entry fee. As one critic of Tea Meetings remarked disapprovingly, "Some men and women will not come and contribute their one quarter of a dollar apiece . . . unless they are tempted by some good things to eat and drink." Why not entice them to a prayer meeting, he asked, misunderstanding how skillfully the women had attracted the public to an event that combined social, religious, and antislavery themes.[68]

Methodist itinerant clergy traditionally carried books and tracts with them on their travels. After the schism, Wesleyan Methodists established a new book concern to make religious and antislavery materials available. While women were not major contributors to this venture, they supported the book concern with their own money and sums gathered from friends and neighbors. Sister Morrow in Ohio collected $5 after only an hour or two of canvassing. Her success and the ever-shaky nature of the publishing venture prompted the paper to appeal to all women. "If our sisters would take hold of this enterprise in good earnest," it asserted, "in a few weeks the work would be done, for there are very few men that would turn away without subscribing something for such a godlike object when represented by this class of society."[69]

Although Sarah Ernst dismissed those who labored "for the slave in and with *their* church but not *out* of it," the activities that groups of church women established provided a major outlet for female abolitionists. The history of secular antislavery associations has overshadowed that of antislavery church societies, but it may well be that church groups had greater longevity than secular societies. In New York City, women formed a religious antislavery society in 1836 that apparently outlived the Female Association of Chatham Street Chapel and the Ladies' New-York City Anti-Slavery Society. By their society's seventh anniversary in 1843, its members claimed to be the only functioning female abolitionist group in the city.

At the anniversary meeting, the AFAS's Lewis Tappan read the society's annual report that detailed the many different projects the organization supported. Women had collected money for fugitive slaves in Canada and the Vigilance Committee, had made clothes, and had visited over 300 black families. The society's managers expressed approval of black families' attempts to "take care of themselves" and "to maintain a reputable standing." Demonstrating further their interest in promoting respectability, the women had obtained thirty-five signatures for the temperance petition. While the emphasis on middle-class values can be seen as narrow and biased against working-class and African American norms, it also reflects a realistic assessment of some of the roots of racial prejudice and the New York women's desire to eliminate it.[70]

The fact that the association had Lewis Tappan read their annual report highlighted the women's seeming acceptance of female norms of reticence and modesty. But their actions suggested a forthrightness on the slavery issue. Although the organization had originally been open only to Methodist women, the report proclaimed that "the indifference to anti-slavery subjects . . . [from] the ruling church powers" had led the church women to "drop our distinctiveness as Methodists, and labor as anti-slavery and Christian women."[71]

Wesleyan Methodist women's groups worked for the slave in ways similar to the New York women. Many busied themselves with assisting African Americans. Yearly reports from the Dorcas Anti-Slavery Society of Troy, Ohio, demonstrate a growing involvement with fugitives. In their First Annual Report, published in 1845, the society detailed making clothes for the destitute, the clergy, and fugitive slaves. The bulk of assistance went to the local poor. By the following year, priorities had shifted in favor of making clothing and bedding for the "poor, shivering, panting fugitive from the Southern prison-house of bondage." By 1847, the women felt a powerful connection with their clients, conjuring up in their imaginations the figure of "the poor trembling fugitive who had but just escaped." This vision of the helpless slave overcome with "joy and gratitude" for "the fruit of our industry" was emotionally powerful, if not always accurate. The evocative image amply repaid the women for their labor. They agreed that, "while we might find enough to engage us at home, almost every Northern breeze bears on it the intelligence of the misery and destitution of thousands who have fled." An appeal was made to work even more systematically in the following year, and each member was encouraged to clothe one child. "Let it enter into our calculations as we do in providing for ourselves. Let us make it our business. . . . Let us now put our shoulders to the work."[72]

The *True Wesleyan* featured frequent articles and letters about the settlements of former slaves living in Canada. Wesleyan Methodist women, like other female religious abolitionists, realized that former slaves needed assistance if they were to flourish in the free air of Canada. Their success or failure would provide the evidence that both the friends and foes of slavery would use to prove their case about the capacities of black people. Supporting the Canadian Mission was a way to do something both concrete and symbolic for the slave. It encouraged women, many of whom had only passing acquaintance with free blacks or fugitives, to think realistically about what might happen if emancipation ever became a reality. In many ways, the efforts to aid fugitives in Canada were the precursors to the work with freed people during and after the Civil War.

Articles from Canada laid out the scope of the task of turning former slaves into free men and women. In white reporters' minds, the religious beliefs of African Americans were unorthodox, hardly surprising given the lack of what white observers saw as an educated clergy. Schooling was difficult but necessary since most former slaves could neither read nor write. The material circumstances of many families were poor, and each family needed its own land. Of particular interest to women who had underscored the plight of the abused slave woman since the earliest days of antislavery was the situation of wives and mothers. An article in the *True Wesleyan* addressed to the "Christian Women of America" reminded female readers that sisterhood now extended to the women who had escaped from slavery and who were not yet "qualified for their proper station in life as wives and mothers." White women must be prepared to sacrifice for the moral, spiritual, and material betterment of black women. "If we would have our fellow sisters raised to an equality with ourselves we must deny ourselves some of the luxuries of this life," like well-trimmed bonnets, jewelry, or extra caps and gowns.[73]

Women responded by raising money to support education and religion and to provide necessities. They made clothes and bedding, and, like abolitionist women working for fairs, became part of a female network. Itinerant clergy, like fair managers, helped to connect women. Abolitionists in Millford, Michigan, put together part of a subscription for Canada. The circuit rider delivered their work to a female sewing society in Green Oak, whose members "made them up into the garments as they thought best."[74]

While there was no record of any contributions to the Canadian Mission from Anna Fellows, she was known as a staunch abolitionist in her Methodist Wesleyan congregation in Lysander, New York. Determined to "bear a faithful testimony for the suffering slave," she had been among the first to leave the Methodist Church. She held others up to her high standards, finding special reason to criticize men who were inconsistent on the subject of slavery. "She looked with pity and expressed her abhorrence for . . . a man who prayed for the slave and professed to be opposed to the institution of slavery, and yet voted for one who could even apologize for the 'vilest system that ever saw the sun.'" [75]

Anna Fellows's judgmental words show that her interests extended beyond religion to antislavery politics. She believed that voting and praying were related activities for abolitionist men. Voting offered a means of countering the economic and political power of slaveholders; praying and purifying the church would dramatize the slaveholders' sin. Although women did not seek to vote, some abolitionist women embraced political activity as well as prayer. [76]

Although no unanimity on the character of women's participation in political abolitionism existed, many clearly chose to participate rather than to sit on the sidelines. Some, like Anna Fellows, had probably already been involved in religious abolitionism or had belonged to a local or state antislavery association. But for others, like Harriet Wood of Sherburn, Vermont, political abolitionism represented a first step into antislavery. Harriet, sick "of the Harrison excitement," decided in 1842 to "be an Abolitionist. I believe the third party are the best." Studies of Liberty Party strength indicate that support for the party came from areas not previously involved in abolitionism. Similarly, at least in some regions, the Free-Soil Party drew new groups of people into antislavery. This pattern suggests that as political abolitionism drew in supporters, it may have recruited new female as well as male adherents to the cause. [77]

Political action encompassed far more than casting a vote at election time. The activities and events that supported and led up to the culmination of the ballot box were ones in which women took part, sometimes in passive roles, at other times in a more active capacity. Like men, women helped to create the public culture of the new mass participatory politics, even if historians have neglected to see the signs of their involvement in a world that they have defined as exclusively male. Two communications from non-Garrisonian women of Massachusetts show a transition to a modest but active interest and involvement in politics. In 1839, Mary Parker, former member of the Boston Female Anti-Slavery Society, appealed to the women of New England. No one, she argued, could accuse women of "being swayed by church spirit and tyrannous machinery of party hostilities." Just four year later, however, the Massachusetts Female Emancipation Society, of which Mary Parker was one of the first members, was urging women to forget their "unreasonable fastidiousness" about politics. "In the revolution, women and sisters bound armor upon their husbands and brothers," she now cried. "Shall not their '*cheers*' be heard by those who seek the deliverance of whipped and manacled women, by the peaceful and sacred power of the ballot." [78]

The move toward political action resulted partly from the perception that moral suasion alone could not lead to an end of slavery and partly from the intersection of national events and decisions made in Washington. The admission of Texas to the Union, the Mexican War, and the acquisition of new territories in the trans-Mississippi West fueled anxieties over the westward expansion of slavery. By 1846, congressional attempts to prevent slavery's extension (the Wilmot Proviso) signaled the opening round in an ongoing struggle in Congress over slavery, free soil, and territorial expansion. Clearly, the way to influence the course of congressional debate lay through politics.[79]

In 1840, the majority of abolitionists supported the Whigs as the party of reform. The commitment of the Liberty Party to abolish slavery and the insistence that voting was a moral duty never resulted in impressive votes at election time. Election results suggest the continuing minority position of abolitionists and the reluctance of antislavery Whigs to help proslavery Democrats by throwing away their votes on a third-party candidate. But the impact of the Liberty Party extended beyond ballots cast. Propaganda, lectures, and party rallies (all of which involved women) influenced thousands of people who did not vote a third-party ticket and kept the issue of slavery before them. The Liberty Party forced the issue of slavery into the arena of politics, where it stubbornly remained. Southerners reacted with fury to the politicization of their peculiar institution, and southern anger eventually fed the growth of antislavery sentiment in the North.[80]

During the 1850s, both the Free-Soil Party and the Republican Party were suspect from a pure abolitionist standpoint. Neither proposed to eliminate slavery in the South but only to prevent its extension. They focused on the rights of white men, not the plight of slaves. Not surprisingly, neither supported equal rights for African Americans. Each party moved beyond a single issue and put together platforms that could and did appeal to a wider constituency than the Liberty Party. Despite the inadequacies that abolitionists found in the Free-Soil and Republican Parties, many eventually came to support one or the other. Frederick Douglass, who announced in his newspaper in 1855 that "the Republican Party is Anti-Slavery as far as it goes; but . . . it does not go far enough in the right direction," came out in support of the Republican candidate, Fremont, in 1856. As he explained, "there is no chance whatever in the present contest of electing better men" than Fremont and his running mate.[81]

While abolitionists could be found among both Whigs and Democrats, the new third parties anticipated drawing support mainly from the Whig Party. As party managers realized, women already comprised an important part of Whig Party culture. Leaders promoted and valued female partisanship. There was no sense that men and women were the same. It was because women were different, because they represented middle-class respectability and morality that their loyalty was desirable. The Democrats followed the Whigs' lead, even in a conservative state like Virginia. The third parties thus built upon emerging political patterns in their utilization of women. But for a new party forging a new identity and a new mission, the support of the ladies was more important than it was to the two major parties.[82]

The character of mass politics in the antebellum period was theatrical rather than merely participatory. While the events that built up the enthusiasm that would lead to or reinforce commitment were carefully orchestrated, there was little agreement about the extent or meaning of female involvement. One female writer to the Ann Arbor *Signal of Liberty* made the claim that an unmarried woman was "on a perfect equality" with men. Mrs. E. Little, in her letter to the *Free Soil Republican*, had far more traditional ideas. In her opinion, women's rights were none other than meekness, love, faith, and patience.[83]

Involvement in party affairs varied in different places. In Ohio, Frederick Douglass observed in 1847, "The political Anti-Slavery meetings, are generally regarded as meetings with which women have nothing to do, and they can do little or nothing toward quickening their energies or expanding their intellects." Lucy Chase noted in her diary a political abolitionist convention that she "did not attend . . . as I supposed *women* would not be admitted." Yet newspaper accounts and other sources do show women at meetings, conventions, and other party functions. In 1844, the Illinois State Liberty Committee deemed it "not only appropriate but highly desirable that women" attend all its meetings. Maine "Liberty men and women" were urged to come to the Oxford County Anti-Slavery Society annual meeting in South Paris, Maine, and were assured that residents at South Paris would take care of all expenses, including those of their horses. Similarly, Maine men and women were "particularly invited" to "A Great Liberty Meeting" and "Rally for LIBERTY" in Turner Village.[84]

In 1847, a member of the Philadelphia Female Anti-Slavery Society resigned from the group, explaining that "she sympathized in the views and measures of a society lately formed to advocate the principles of the Liberty Party." Women from Michigan to Massachusetts took similar steps to support the Liberty Party by forming their own organizations. In Michigan, Liberty Party leaders encouraged the process, telling women to ignore "idle taunt[s]" that asked "what can a woman do in a cause so interwoven in the political framework of society." Although initially leaders had modest expectations for Liberty women, by 1846 some in Michigan concluded that women, like blacks, should vote.[85]

Of course, as Lucy Chase and Frederick Douglass both noted, women continued the supportive work for which they were responsible in all camps of abolitionism. Lucy recorded attending "a meeting of the liberty party sewing circle," and Douglass observed that Ohio women were involved in mounting fairs. The efforts survived the demise of the Liberty Party. In later years, Ohio women would be sponsoring Free-Soil fairs. This sort of ongoing work meant that women's views could not be completely ignored by male managers.[86]

Female involvement in the public party rites ranged from symbolic to active. Even their symbolic efforts created rich meaning for politics. During the 1856 election, women staged numerous tableaux in which thirty-one women dressed in white represented the existing states while one woman draped in black signified Kansas, where southerners battled to entrench slavery. On a subliminal level, the colors that draped the women also dramatized the existence of black slavery in white America. As pillars of morality, women blessed political efforts and adorned them with appropriate pageantry. Hearkening back to the tradition of offering banners to men marching to war, third-party women often made and presented banners to the men facing the fury of political battle. The flag from the women of Hallowell, Maine, bearing the names of presidential and vice presidential Liberty candidates in 1844 fluttered its message from the top of one of the town's buildings. The flag proclaimed "not the name of *slaveholders*! but the names of the honored representatives of Liberty, BIRNEY and MORRIS."[87]

In June 1842, the Maine paper, the *Liberty Standard*, criticized Abby Kelley, the Garrisonian lecturer. "She has no idea that a woman should learn in silence in the public assembly," was the waspish comment. Of course, these sorts of disparaging remarks and the lack of agreement about the boundaries of female participation meant that some women avoided raising their voices. In Dundee, Illinois, in 1847, men read presentation remarks and presented banners with women standing silently to the side. Yet, as one New Hampshire women pointed out, "We as females, cannot vote, but we can speak, and we will do that, let public or popular opinion be against it." Hallowell women addressed a large gathering in the town hall, expressing their love for the cause and encouraging Liberty men to remain faithful to the cause "until the slaves repose in serenity beneath . . . [their banner's] folds." In Milwaukee, women supporting the Republican candidate John C. Fremont also made speeches as they presented their banners.[88]

In 1854, at a July 4 celebration at the campgrounds in East Livermore, Maine, women provided clear political statements through the medium of their banners. One proclaimed, "We are all for freedom, John P. Hale for President in 1856"; another, "Equal infamy to Douglas and his followers"; and a third, "The Daughters of Freedom opposed to the Nebraska Bill" (a piece of legislation that potentially opened the trans-Mississippi West to slavery). Presiding over the meeting was Esther Gibbs, president of the newly organized state antislavery society, who had rejected as "absurd" the idea that "the ladies can do nothing." This gathering was remembered as "the first political meeting in the state in which a woman presided and was its acknowledged leader." The following year, in Augusta, the capital, after an address from an African American woman, Esther Gibbs led a procession to the governor's mansion, where a tower-shaped cake, more than four feet high, was presented to him. On the cake were a melange of political slogans: "We detest and resist oppression. . . . Liberty and pursuit of Happiness. . . . A governor with a backbone. The People Rule." The cake, which suggested women's skills in the private sphere, had been transformed into a public and political statement in a ceremony that had a ritualistic significance as well.[89]

Even though women did not vote, many were aware that casting a ballot was only the final step in a long process of forging commitment to an antislavery political party. As Frederick Douglass pointed out in his newspaper in 1852, the way to win votes lay in education. "We would not give a snap of our finger for one who begins and ends his antislavery labors on election day." The *Liberty Standard* made the same point about the necessity for working for a proper vote long ahead of election day and highlighted special contributions women might make. They could "undertake to raise a small sum" to procure copies of stirring addresses, and they could circulate Liberty papers, almanacs, and other antislavery material that offered "simple, thrilling eloquence for suffering humanity." In reality, women were more instrumental than the paper suggested. When the *Liberty Standard* faced a financial crisis in 1845, funds to keep the voice of liberty afloat came from a successful donation party. Women in the Rochester Ladies'

Anti-Slavery Society provided needed support for Frederick Douglass's paper, which encouraged political action.[90]

Women bought and circulated antislavery materials that dramatized the platform of the Liberty Party. Such work would have been particularly important, if, as the *True Wesleyan* reported in 1846, "the liberty party . . . does not incline to keep agents in the field for the sake of books or to lecture." Recognizing the necessity for reading materials, Liberty men urged women to take on projects, although it is by no means clear that women needed male encouragement. In 1843, for example, Maine women paid for the printing of 5,000 copies of a piece that illustrated the nature of slavery in Washington, D.C. Three years later, the *Liberty Standard*, explaining that the sale of a fugitive slave account "would do great good to the cause," described the task as "*just the work*" for women. The link between this sort of propagandizing and voting was made clear in a long letter to the paper. The writer's wife was indefatigable in her efforts to spread tracts and papers. As a result, people were more willing to discuss abolitionism and read about it. "I shall be much disappointed if fall elections do not prove that they are more fond of voting on the subject," her husband declared.[91]

In 1851, Maine women established an organization called the Daughters of Freedom. Its special work was the circulation of antislavery literature, especially copies of *Uncle Tom's Cabin* with Stowe's explanatory key. But a "no less effective" part of members' task was "to follow that with their personal and organic appeals to all to enlist in behalf of the slave and of Liberty, especially to men to give the cause their ballots." On election day, women further encouraged voting by putting appropriately lettered banners in front of their houses and on the streets.[92]

During the election of 1856, women were urged to be even more political. "Ignorant or evil men may tell [women] . . . they are precluded from any concern with questions of public morality and social happiness because they have become political," the *Portland Inquirer* observed. "But no consideration whatever should be given to such stupidity." Not only were women encouraged to sell material about Kansas and copies of political speeches but to pass out campaign literature. The New York *Independent* thought that "women may be even more efficient than men" in carrying out such tasks. Over the years, abolitionist women had had plenty of practice circulating information in their communities, although their activities became more politically pointed in 1856.[93]

While many abolitionist women were probably content to leave politics to men, at least some women seized upon the opportunity to influence men's voting. It was not out of place, of course, for women to try to use their influences within the walls of their households. In an article entitled "HOW WOMEN MAY VOTE FOR COL. FREMONT," appearing in the *Independent*, a Maine woman highlighted the importance of women's influence over their husbands. Wives might decide the election, she declared. But the new possibilities for participation in the political culture and the strong belief in the crime of slavery encouraged a more ambitious effort. At the very least, women should, as Sallie Holley told her classmates at Oberlin in 1850, "be ready to counter-act the pernicious influence of such speeches as Clay's and Webster's on the plastic minds of all our young men and women." More useful in terms of the ballot box were conventions that women sponsored. Abolitionist speakers at an event, like that planned in New Bedford in 1852, "coming as it will be on the eve of an election," had the chance of making "its influence . . . felt." [94]

When the Free-Soil and Republican Parties successively replaced the Liberty Party as the diluted voice of political abolitionism, the efforts of abolitionist women took on a somewhat different significance. Female efforts to spread the antislavery message helped to legitimate the parties' shaky credentials. "The ladies ought to be here," Senator Joseph Hoxie insisted in 1856. The language of party publications that made specific gendered appeals to women further acknowledged the importance of female influence in cementing loyalty to the party. [95]

The line between presenting banners with propaganda slogans and creating more ambitious messages was an indistinct one. Betsy Hudson, writing from Oberlin, Ohio, in 1846, stated emphatically that "*I* for one have yet to be convinced that the Liberty party is not the heaven-appointed means for the overthrow of that most vile and heaven-insulting system of slavery." She inquired whether she could contribute "an article on the importance of Political Action" to the book that was being compiled for an upcoming antislavery fair. Popular writers like Maria Child and Harriet Beecher Stowe, who presented an abbreviated version of the Republican platform in her 1856 novel, *Dred*, were more firmly abolitionist than the parties they endorsed. [96]

In the 1850s, Maria Child became an enthusiastic supporter of the Republican Party, not only writing pieces to generate support for it but also speaking out forcefully to men who could vote. She chastised an acquaintance who was leaning toward the American Party candidate, telling him that the "moral distinction" between the Democratic and American Party candidates was "so small, I did n't wonder he plumed himself upon his sagacity in perceiving it." As she wrote to a friend, "I shall not live to see women vote, but I'll come and *rap* at the ballot-box. . . . I never was bitten by politics before; but such might issues are depending on *this* election, that I cannot be indifferent."[97]

Republican Party managers realized that the situation of political flux meant that many voters were uncertain about their votes and were open to influence. They also observed how many women there were at party rallies. In New York State women comprised half of those attending rallies. Obviously, women were not indifferent to the results of the 1856 election, which Maria described as "the death-grapple between Slavery and Freedom." Whether the all-female Jessie Band (named after Fremont's wife) that played at a rally in Dover, New Hampshire, or the female singers who warbled "Fremont and Victory" after a picnic in New Haven, or the women who formed Ladies Meetings did so at the bidding of men is not clear. What is clear is that their willingness to contribute to the excitement that whipped up party loyalty was evident and useful.[98]

Democrats and Republicans alike accepted the notion that women wielded influence over male voters. As one New Hampshire Democrat grumbled, "The Clergy and old women" were responsible for encouraging "the Church members to go" for Fremont. In efforts to gain female loyalty, Fremont's biography was tailored to appeal to women, and party propagandists exploited the supposed achievements and views of his wife, Jessie. And in a clear bid for abolitionist support, campaign literature described Jessie as a decided foe of slavery. In keeping with the character of the campaign, a speaker at a Westchester County, New York, rally tried to strengthen the credentials of his candidate by saying, "All the women of the West are for Fremont, and you know their power." His audience cheered and applauded approvingly. A campaign poem was even more explicit:

The Ladies' aid we shall secure,
For slav'ry's laws, They'll ne'er endure,
They'll think, they'll write, they'll print, they'll *speak*,
Till tyrants' hearts with fear shall quake.
United, led by Jessie brave,
They'll cheer us on, our land to save;
While they've a *tongue*, you'll hear in front,
'Free Speech, Free Kansas, and Fremont.' "[99]

The political world was one of competition and struggle. Because third parties were entering the competition from a position of weakness, they valued not only the practical assistance women could give but also the moral luster the ladies could provide for their party. While women adapted to changing opportunities in both the political and religious realms, however, there were significant continuities in their activism. They continued to engage in moral suasion. Without changing people's minds about slavery, no political or religious tactic would succeed. They persisted in their efforts to raise money for the cause. Many continued to ply their needles, for the fairs and for the fugitives. And many women discovered, to their surprise, that their testimony about the sinfulness of slavery demanded an unexpected public forthrightness. When there was a clear conflict between individual duty and socially sanctioned behavior, many women found the courage to risk reputation and stand for what they believed was right.

Chapter 5
Crisis and Confidence
The 1850s

The fearful storm—it threatens lowering,

Which God in mercy long delays;

Waves yet may see their masters cowering,

While whole plantations smoke and blaze! . . .

And ye may now prevent the ruin,

Ere lawless force with guilty stride

Shall scatter vengeance far and wide—

With untold crimes their land embruing.

Have pity on the slave;

Take courage from God's words;

Pray on, pray on, all hearts resolved these

captives shall be free[1]

Elizabeth Earle traced her involvement in abolitionism back to "earliest childhood," when her father taught her "to lisp" antislavery poetry. As a young woman in the 1830s, she felt her commitment to *the oppressed* deepen and was hopeful that the cause was advancing. Although her expectations about the rapid progress of abolitionism were dashed, she never wavered in her support for immediate emancipation. In the 1850s, Elizabeth was still working for the cause as the main organizer of Worcester's Anti-Slavery Bazaar. She singlehandedly raised money to pay the fair expenses by soliciting every store and office along the city's Main Street and provided the leadership needed to make the fair a success. Made anxious about the future by the events of the decade, she used the fair as a way of alerting others to the growing dangers of Slave Power. In the published fair announcement for the 1856 bazaar, she warned readers that "the powers of slavery are no longer content with self-defence—they are active and aggressive." The next year, she reviewed the triumphs of slavery over the eight years of the bazaar's history and clarified the purpose of abolitionism. "Our object is not merely to save Kansas, or to exclude slavery from the free States," she explained, "but to wage against it increasing warfare wherever it exists on the national domain."[2]

In the late winter of 1858, Elizabeth died unexpectedly. The women from Worcester and nearby communities who had long depended on her "wise counsels and indefatigable efforts for the cause" were uncertain whether to hold the bazaar. Only three people turned out for the initial meeting to decide upon the bazaar's fate. In the end, although filled with "misgivings and fears," the women decided to go forward with the annual event. While the Worcester Bazaar was a modest affair compared to the Boston extravaganza or the less showy but still very profitable Philadelphia fair, it was an important abolitionist fund-raiser in central Massachusetts. The results of the bazaar far exceeded the women's anxious expectations. More people came to the fair than had been the case for some years, and the proceeds were gratifying.[3]

With Elizabeth gone, the notices for the 1858 bazaar provided no interpretation of national events that might spark or renew enthusiasm for the abolitionist cause. But silence did not suggest complacency. Not since the 1830s had abolitionists felt such urgent commitment to immediate emancipation.

Elizabeth Earle was well known locally but hardly famous or important enough to attract much attention outside of her hometown; yet her life and her death suggest some significant truths about abolitionism in general and the situation of antislavery in the 1850s in particular. The length of her commitment to abolitionism marks her as belonging to a stalwart core of women who continued their antislavery activities despite disagreements, divisions, and lack of success. Whether as members of societies or sewing circles, secular or religious in orientation, black or white, some women, and we have no way of knowing how many, never dropped out of abolitionism. They were not professional reformers like Garrison, Frederick Douglass, or Maria Chapman; they did not spend most of their time working for the cause. Rather, these women wove their commitment into the fabric of annual routines, responding to antislavery's yearly cycle of work and celebration. While they were not unified by affiliation to any one organization, they were connected by both their belief in immediate emancipation and the types of activities they undertook. Without the possibility of making third-party politics an all-consuming interest, abolitionist women pursued their varied tasks with the same focused earnestness, whether it was an election year or not. Their ongoing work may well have rooted them more securely in antislavery than politics could for their male counterparts.

The fair notices that Elizabeth Earle wrote for publication indicated her determination to participate in the public debates of the 1850s. She was not content to leave the interpretation of events to others more important than she. Like Elizabeth, women, both black and white, insistently and more frequently than before, claimed the right to discuss and debate the issues swirling around slavery. A few women became public lecturers, but many more, like Elizabeth, published their views or argued the case for abolition with friends and strangers. As they did so, they adopted the new style and the vocabulary of the more aggressive abolitionism of their decade and thereby contributed to sectional tensions. But they also continued to employ the moral, religious, and empathetic rhetoric that had marked abolitionism from its early days in the 1830s. In the new climate, reminders that emancipation of the slave was a moral and religious duty and that slavery was a sin acted as antidotes to the increasing emphasis on free land and free labor.[4]

Elizabeth's death also marked an important moment in the history of antislavery. When she had first become active in the movement, she had been a young women in her thirties. By the 1850s, she and other women of her generation were aging and passing from the scene. While Lucretia Mott would continue her reform commitments for years to come, she recognized that younger women were assuming leadership. "I have great hope of these new recruits, who have youth on their side," she remarked. "Some of us older warriors may begin to retire from the field and give place to them." These new "warriors" would find that the experience of abolitionism differed dramatically from the experiences of those women who had been active since the 1830s. Abolitionism had changed, and so too had the times.[5]

The numbers of people who thronged the 1858 Worcester Bazaar, even without Elizabeth's expert management, the gratifying profits of $360 and the lecture the "Orthodox Congregational" minister presented there, all hinted at the changed status of antislavery. So too did the new societies formed during the decade. While there are no statistics, impressionistic evidence suggests that, after a decade of associational decline, a spurt of organizing and reorganizing occurred during the 1850s. Reports from antislavery lecturers who spoke to large and attentive crowds confirm the picture of renewal. Not just in New England or New York, but in the Midwest as well, there seemed to be greater interest in abolitionism than there had been just a few years before.[6]

As public attitude shifted during the 1850s to a greater tolerance, if not acceptance, of abolitionism, women who had dropped out of organized abolitionism became active once again. Maria Child and others returned to antislavery with new energy and enthusiasm. Maria's attendance at the Boston fair symbolized her renewed interest and marked the beginning of her vigorous efforts to undermine slavery, assist settlers in Kansas, work for the Republican Party, and dislodge Garrisonians from pacificism. As the context of abolitionism changed, the psychological experience of commitment did as well. Although there were moments of great discouragement for abolitionism during the 1850s, abolitionists no longer saw themselves as marginal. Still conscious of being in minority, they nonetheless felt increasingly heeded, at the center rather than on the periphery of events, prophets increasingly honored rather than cast out into the darkness.[7]

The political events of the decade shaped the antislavery experience and its work and eventually encouraged greater sympathy and support for its activities and messages. The shift in public opinion was gradual and halting. While the Compromise of 1850 later appeared to be the first step in the process, at the time, abolitionists despaired. Most northerners welcomed the compromise, fervently hoping that it would remove the issue of slavery from political debate. But the Kansas-Nebraska Act, the Dred Scott decision, open warfare in Kansas, the caning of Senator Charles Sumner, and John Brown's raid, along with the explosive rhetoric these incidents inspired, made it clear that the controversy over slavery could not be avoided. Many people found themselves for the first time sympathetic to abolitionists or to the "moderate antislavery" that the Republican Party represented.

While abolitionists found the Compromise of 1850 no compromise at all, the agreement did address some northern concerns. The slave trade in Washington, D.C., was terminated, but not slavery itself, despite the numerous petitions submitted to Congress urging its elimination there. California came into the Union as a free state, thus upsetting the balance between free and slave states. The measure that stuck in the throats of abolitionists and even some moderates, however, was the Fugitive Slave Act.

The need for new legislation to replace the Fugitive Slave Law of 1793 was obvious to southerners. The 1793 law was ineffective outside of the South. Many northern states had directly defied the law's intent by passing personal liberty laws. Northern courts all too often decided for the fugitive rather than for the slaveholder. In many northern communities, the likelihood that a slaveholder could recover an escaped slave was remote. As one Northampton, Massachusetts, woman pointed out in an 1847 letter, the family of fugitives living in that town felt "perfectly safe . . . as the Southerners are about giving up the idea of looking up their slaves so far

North." In many northern cities like Boston, African American communities harbored large numbers of former slaves. Perhaps a quarter of the Boston's adult black residents came from the South; most had fled slavery. Although they were far more vulnerable to slave hunters than fugitives in New England, most of the 45,000 blacks living in the Old Northwest in 1850 had also escaped from slavery.[8]

Features of the new law tilted power to the slaveholder and denied those accused of being fugitives of the most elementary civil rights. Southern whites who laid claim to former slaves appeared before U.S. commissioners in an administrative rather than a judicial hearing. The alleged fugitive had no right to a lawyer and no right to testify during the hearing; nor was there a jury to evaluate the evidence. Although the lucky few might have someone who could swear to their free status, many had no time or opportunity to get help after they were captured. Blacks could be and were swiftly remanded to the South on the word of the slaveowner alone. The law obligated northerners to help in recapturing fugitives, and, if they refused to cooperate, they faced fines or even prison. The cards were stacked in favor of reclaiming fugitives. Commissioners received twice as much remuneration for deciding a case in favor of the slaveholder than for an accused fugitive.[9]

Congressional debate on the bill provoked criticism from some northern evangelical leaders, who characterized the proposal as contrary to divine law and civil procedures. Methodist newspapers, the most widely circulated of the evangelical papers, discussed the bill's progress in a disapproving fashion, but writers showed no agreement on possible responses. Most evangelicals, in fact, accepted the compromise. Ministers informed their congregations from the pulpit that they were obligated to obey congressional dictates. Northerners who were worried that the Union might dissolve over the question of slavery celebrated that the country had survived.[10]

The responses to the Fugitive Slave Act among abolitionists of both races and free blacks offered a stark contrast to the relieved enthusiasm of northern crowds. White abolitionists interpreted the bill's passage as yet another triumph of the Slave Power. In black communities all over the North, free men and women and former slaves gathered to protest the legislation and to form militias and vigilance committees. Determined to resist the implementation of the law, they began to raise money for legal fees.[11] Thousands of African Americans lost whatever sense of security they might have had in their new lives in the North and headed for Canada. The 300 who left Pittsburgh in 1850 defiantly armed themselves for their journey, determined to oppose any attempt to reenslave them. During the decade, as many as 11,000 emigrated to Canada and freedom.[12]

Southern supporters of the legislation had never expected that the new law would result in the recovery of most of the South's fugitives, and they were right. Although approximately 1,000 slaves escaped every year, only about 330 fugitive slave cases were heard between 1850 and 1860. About 260 alleged fugitives ended up being returned to the South. For southerners, the goal was less about numbers than about the clear message they wished to send about an owner's right to reclaim property. In this regard, the legislation succeeded, with long-term results that southerners could hardly have anticipated. Enough slavehunters, owners, and federal marshals appeared in northern towns and cities to alarm many who had welcomed the compromise.[13]

Growing discomfort with the Fugitive Slave Law provided an opening for abolitionist propaganda, while the enforcement of the legislation created the material for a persuasive case against slavery. The argument Elizabeth Earle had made in her 1856 fair announcement, that the South was aggressive and determined to destroy liberty, corresponded well enough to local and national incidents and activated deep-seated republican fears about the fragility of freedom.[14]

The inhabitants of Harrisburg, Pennsylvania, experienced a change of heart over the Fugitive Slave Law that suggests the ways in which attempts to enforce the legislation backfired. Only forty miles from the Maryland border, Harrisburg had a stream of fugitives passing through the city. Citizens, however, were not sympathetic to organized abolitionism or Free-Soil politics, and only a few whites and members of the black community assisted fugitives before 1850. Initially, the legislation aroused little interest in Harrisburg, but events in the city brought the meaning of the law home. In a little over a year, seventeen runaways were apprehended in Harrisburg, and several kidnapping attempts were foiled. In 1852, an accused fugitive was killed. By mid-1853 public opinion in the town had shifted from indifference to hostility to the law and those enforcing it. The papers expressed the new mood, and citizens voted three of the four constables helping to administer the law out of office. While the circumstances of Harrisburg were unique, other northern communities that found slavehunters and federal marshals in their midst were uncomfortable with their presence. One Indiana residence long remembered the "arrogant and boastful" behavior of slavehunters, "their whips, handcuffs, and ropes tied to their saddles, and their pistols belted around them."[15]

The passage of the Kansas-Nebraska Act in 1854 could be construed as another victory for a rapacious Slave Power. Illinois senator Stephen Douglas developed the concept of popular sovereignty as the basis for determining whether the states formed from the Nebraska Territory would enter the Union as slave or free. The idea that a majority of settlers could decide for or against slavery overturned the Missouri Compromise's exclusion of slavery in this part of the trans-Mississippi West and was the price Douglas had paid for southern Democratic votes.[16]

In Massachusetts, Hannah Robie did not believe the bill would pass, but she reported that "some people think even if it should, the consequence would be that it would rouse to still greater activity the antislavery spirit." Her words were prophetic. Throughout the North, enraged and worried citizens gathered to protest the betrayal of the Missouri Compromise, which had supposedly established the ground rules for settling the trans-Mississipppi West. The Protestant press attacked the legislation. Northern clergy thundered against the proposal from the pulpit, leading one northerner to observe that "the ministers all pray & preach one way." Over 3,000 New England clerics signed petitions to register their disapproval of the law's provisions. Many told their parishioners to exchange the usual politics of "coaxing smiles" for more radical political approaches. In Michigan, the *Adrian Expositor* estimated that "from Maine to Nebraska, four-fifths of the clergymen of all denominations have . . . stood up boldly for freedom and against slavery." [17]

Renewed agitation over the Fugitive Slave Law was one indication of northern anxiety about southern political victories. Many northerners decided that the politicians' betrayal of the Missouri Compromise legitimated defiance of the legislation.[18]

The conflict in Kansas between settlers who would make it into a slave state and those determined to have it free energized abolitionists and provided them with new propaganda. But warfare there also resulted in the broadening and diluting of the antislavery message. Many who passionately supported a free Kansas were no friends of the southern slave. The future of the free laborer rather than the need to emancipate the slaves captured their attention. The threat of Slave Power rather than the retribution of a God angry over the sin of slavery compelled attention.[19]

Bloodshed also brought the issue of violence into the forefront of consciousness. Although not all abolitionists who believed that moral suasion or politics could bring about emancipation abandoned their positions, many sensed that violence was the only way to crush slavery. Maria Child, who had "always dreaded civil war," now concluded, "If there is no *other* alternative . . . I am resigned to its approach. In fact I have become accustomed to the thought that it is inevitable." In a similar frame of mind, Mary Ann Darnes, an African American student who made a brief speech after the presentation of a flag to the black Attaucks Guards in Cincinnati in 1855, warned that "the time is not far distant when the *slave must be free*; if not by moral and intellectual means, it must be done by the sword. Remember, gentlemen, should duty call, it will be yours to obey, and strike to the last for freedom."[20]

In 1857, the Dred Scott decision appeared to put the final nail in the coffin of the Missouri Compromise. By deciding slaveowners had the right to take their slaves anywhere in the United States and its territories, the majority of the Supreme Court rejected the idea that Congress possessed the power to decide upon the question of slavery in any part of the nation. Slavery rather than freedom was universal. The southern-dominated Supreme Court had delivered yet more evidence for the accusation that the Slave Power was determined to destroy liberty.[21]

The response of Connecticut's General Assembly to the Supreme Court decision was but one indication of a changing northern public opinion. In the 1830s, abolitionists had considered Connecticut hostile to the message of immediate emancipation. Now, in a series of 1857 resolutions, the state General Assembly rejected the Dred Scott decision and passed a version of personal liberty law. Connecticut citizens were exhorted to resist the extension of the slave system.[22]

Other less dramatic trends and events affected the climate within which abolitionists operated and contributed to growing interest in its messages. Manufacturers had initially been hostile to abolitionism because their financial interests were so tightly connected with southern cotton. Now northern manufacturing had diversified beyond cotton goods. Profits might be combined with conscience as the dependence on the South diminished.[23] In the Northeast, the development of the railroad allowed antislavery lecturers and their published materials easier and faster access to potential recruits. And as rural areas were integrated into the modern cash economy and changed under its impact, a message hostile to slavery and oppression struck a chord among working men and women who themselves felt oppressed as they struggled to accommodate themselves to new economic conditions.[24] The Great Revival that fed evangelical fires in 1857 and 1858 was no doubt connected to the hard times that hit at the end of the decade. By encouraging northerners to attend to moral and religious problems like slavery, revivalism contributed to growing sectional tensions. It probably also heightened the northern sense of self-righteousness, for the revival never made much progress in the South.[25]

At the beginning of decade, however, the growth of interest in abolitionism was still in the future. Abolitionists and even fugitive slaves lent themselves to ridicule. During her June 1851 tour of Vermont, Maria Thorp attended an exhibition in Burlington. There she enjoyed "a good burlesque on the present state of things in our country." Various national foibles and events were held up for the amusement of the audience. Maria carefully recorded that "the Abolitionists were also remembered as the fugitive . . . was captured and whipped most unmercifully etc. etc. etc."[26]

The fact that a New England audience laughed about the plight of fugitives is a commentary on the indifference of many northerners toward abolitionism and slaves. Yet sympathy for and assistance to fugitives had characterized the work of some abolitionists well before the 1850 legislation. For Abigail and Lydia Mott, two Quaker sisters in Albany, New York, assisting fugitives was a principal expression of their abolitionism. In the early 1840s, Abigail Mott and her sister worked as shirtmakers and routinely sheltered fugitives in their home. Having only modest resources, they undertook the difficult and unpleasant task of soliciting their neighbors for support. In the 1840s, the reception might be quite hostile. Abigail was reduced to tears by one neighbor's threatening words. "Rather than . . . give one cent for their relief," he told her, he would give "fifty dollars to know where they were that he might deliver [them] back to their masters." Black women, not part of any organized abolitionist movement, also aided fugitives. Less affected by genteel female notions than Abigail Mott, they did not hesitate to resort to threatening and distinctly unladylike behavior. One "old" woman in the Midwest forced bounty hunters into a corn crib by threatening them with a knife, thus allowing two fugitives to flee. In 1848, Cincinnati black women armed themselves with washboards and shovels to fend off slavehunters while Boston women flung stones.[27]

The new law brought the plight of the fugitive slave into the foreground of abolitionists' consciences and shaped the activities they undertook during the decade. It caused the organization or revival of urban vigilance societies, led to renewed efforts on the part of those who had occasionally helped fugitives in the past, and encouraged many newcomers to work for the fugitives individually and collectively. "Is it not also important that we be acquainted with the wants of thousands of fugitives?" asked a Foxboro, Massachusetts, woman in 1850. "Shall we not make an effort to save their lives, supply their wants, raise, cultivate and improve their long neglected intellects, [and] instruct their children?"[28]

Not all white abolitionists answered her questions in the affirmative, however. Assisting fugitives used up scarce resources and did nothing to weaken slavery directly. Many felt that it was a diversion from the real task at hand. Lucretia Mott expressed this point of view in an 1856 meeting of the Philadelphia Female Anti-Slavery Society. She told members that, while she thought the tales of escaping slaves were both interesting and exciting, she wanted to remind them "that relieving the necessities of these was not properly Anti Slavery work." Garrison was also doubtful about the validity of fugitive slave work. But he found opposing aid to fugitives difficult to maintain and eventually took the position that assisting fugitives was an abolitionist duty. While the American and Foreign Anti-Slavery Society was not particularly active in the 1850s, it strongly supported an evangelical commitment to the fugitive. The 1850 legislation made demands on individuals "to which they cannot yield." "We consider it a privilege and a duty to shield . . . [fugitives] from assault, arrest and annoyance, and to aid them in securing an asylum," the society announced unequivocally.[29]

Black abolitionists harbored no doubts about the necessity of disobeying the Fugitive Slave Law, nor did they have any illusions about the fragile nature of black freedom. Assisting fugitive slaves might be a duty for white abolitionists, but the law was, for the most part, external to their everyday realities of life. For black people, the issue was personal and pervasive. Because the Fugitive Slave Law gave the accused no rights, it could ensnare a free black individual as well as a former slave. Because there was no statute of limitations preventing slaveowners from trying to reclaim a slave who had fled years before, all blacks in the North were vulnerable. Mistakes in identifying supposed slaves who could have been children at the time of their escape were all too possible. In 1851, for example, a slaveowner seized Euphemia Williams in her own home, claiming that she was his slave who had been missing for over twenty years. Stories of attempts to bypass the law altogether through kidnappings further reinforced a sense of basic insecurity among northern blacks.[30]

During the 1850s, blacks not surprisingly participated in underground railroad activities more often than whites. As one black leader explained, the work represented "practical" abolitionism. Self-interest and self-preservation drew many working-class blacks into abolitionist activities for the first time. Chance also played a role. The Fitzgerald family of Chester County, Pennsylvania, "were not joiners of reform movements." When slaves from the South sought shelter in their barn, family members "met the issue squarely" and gave assistance to the fugitives. Black leaders encouraged broad participation, conscious that it provided an opportunity to undermine negative stereotypes of free blacks as indolent and incapable.[31]

The underground railroad was never so organized as mythmakers would suggest, nor were the numbers involved so large, nor white participation so dominant. In a few areas of heavy fugitive traffic like Delaware, south-east Pennsylvania, parts of Ohio, Indiana, and Illinois, workers developed a loose organizational structure. In general, however, the underground railroad mostly depended on the energy and commitment of a few people who might or might not have contacts with similarly committed people elsewhere. In some places like Delaware, blacks and whites worked together. In other locations where blacks were rare, white abolitionists obviously took the lead. Cities with substantial black populations furnished many blacks willing to do what was necessary for the fugitive. Black abolitionist William Still was the primary force in Philadelphia's vigilance operation, while in Pittsburgh, blacks were most active in underground railroad work.[32]

As Still pointed out, "the safety of all concerned called for still tongues." Because few kept records, the actual numbers of those who used the underground railroad or who labored for it are unknown. It is not even clear how many slaves fled north as opposed to staying in the South. One historian has calculated that, of the 40,000 blacks living in Canada West (the main destination for fugitives) in 1860, 30,000 were fugitives; some of these had migrated to Canada before 1850, and others were free blacks who left northern communities during the hazardous days of that decade.[33]

Most fugitives depended on their wits and only occasional assistance from others during their escape. An 1861 estimate suggests that three-quarters of those escaping did so without significant help. During the early part of their flight in the South, they were cautious about revealing themselves to anyone. Once out of the South, many slaves were distrustful of white people and reluctant to approach white households. "I have no confidence whatever in white people," for they were "only trying to get us back into slavery," remarked Ellen Craft, who, with her husband, had engineered a daring escape from bondage. Such suspicions led fugitives to take refuge with black families rather than white. Not all black households, of course, were willing to run the risk of sheltering escaped slaves, nor were all blacks trustworthy. On one occasion, Still visited three or four Philadelphia families searching for separate hiding places for six fugitives. After learning of the danger, they all made excuses. "This was painful," Still recalled, "for the parties had plenty of house room, were identified with the oppressed race, and on public meeting occasions made loud professions of devotion to the cause." On some occasions, blacks even betrayed the fugitives.[34]

Although many of the stories about conductors on the underground railroad highlight the role of men, black women, like their white counterparts, did much of the routine work upon which the smooth operation of the underground railroad depended. Most northern blacks lived in cities, and a majority of them were women. Because household income was low, both married and single women worked for wages, often outside of their homes. Assistance to a fugitive slave came in addition to daily domestic labor and the drudgery of low-paying jobs. Nonetheless, black women took fugitives into their homes and boardinghouses. When Still could not find hiding places for his six fugitives, Ann Laws, a poor widow, welcomed them all and kept them for several days. Her circumstances were precarious enough that the vigilance committee felt bound to pay the expenses.[35]

Working in the underground railroad was more often exhausting than exciting. Women prepared meals, hiding places, and clothes for disguise or for the trip north. Albro Lyons, proprietor of a Colored Sailors's Home, in a rare acknowledgement of women's contributions, estimated that he had helped "a thousand persons, thanks to . . . [his wife Mary's] devotion and discretion." Women coped with arrivals at all hours and ministered to them. One Quaker correspondent of Still's suggested what faced a woman who harbored fugitives. "Thy wife must not sit up washing and ironing all night again," she wrote. "She ought to have help in her sympathy and labors for the poor fugitives."[36]

Because they often worked outside their homes as domestics, black women served as the eyes and ears for fugitives and urban vigilance committees. As they went about their daily chores, they overheard conversations and noted suspicious southern visitors in hotels and boardinghouses. Freer to walk the streets alone than middle-class white women, they collected information and observed strangers. In New Bedford, Massachusetts, a southerner tracked down a slave family who had been living there for almost a year. But "the colored people of that town" discovered his presence and "communicated with some of the few Abolitionists . . . [so that] the man was hurried off to Fall River."[37]

Some African American women were in the position to take on more daring tasks. Mary Meyer, the owner of a Philadelphia bakery, concealed fugitives in her shop, and on one occasion, received a fugitive delivered in a box. Henrietta Duterte assumed her husband's undertaking business when he died and used caskets to hide the fugitives for whom she was responsible.[38]

As more blacks settled in Canada, a few records show black women in the States trying to help fugitives at the end of their flight. From Wilmington, Delaware, Elizabeth Williams, a free black woman active in the underground railroad, maintained a correspondence with her niece in Canada. Her 1858 letter concerned a female fugitive whose owners lived in Baltimore. The fugitive's situation was an uneasy one, for "there is a Coulred man living in fall river that knows her owners and She lives in continuel dread of him." The woman was planning to go to Canada in the spring, but perhaps as a woman alone, with no family to welcome her to Canada, she was fearful about her future there. Elizabeth took it upon herself to inquire about employment possibilities and to arrange a place for her. Could "she . . . make a living by her neadle there?" Elizabeth asked. And would her niece "be willing to let her come to your house for a short time . . . [and] be willing to ade her . . . when She first Comes out there?" [39]

Despite the poverty in the black community, black women also undertook fund-raising to support fugitive work. Existing women's church groups provided an organizational base for these efforts. In New York, black women sponsored a yearly fair at the Broadway Tabernacle to benefit the city vigilance committee, charging an entry fee of 12½ cents. Women also contributed money to support Harriet Tubman's daring forays into the South, where she rescued about 300 individuals from slavery. [40] In some places, the recognition of black women's importance in their communities resulted in appointments to vigilance committees. Four of the nine members of the all-black vigilance committee in Cleveland were women. The committee was an active one, sending 275 slaves north between April 1854 and January 1855. [41]

Although white abolitionist women made up the less important part of the underground railroad, it is somewhat easier to recover their experiences than it is to retrieve those of black women. Ironically, in William Still's book on the underground railroad in Delaware and Pennsylvania, he gave more details about white women than about black women, including his own wife. Whatever their color, however, women who took an active part in the work needed to be flexible, committed, discreet, energetic, and organized. On occasion, they had to be daring and able to carry off deceptions. The wife of Levi Coffin, a major figure in Cincinnati's underground railroad, often had the care of several fugitives at one time in her Cincinnati home. She was adept at concealing her activities from inquiring eyes. Her husband described her as having "a quiet unconcerned way of going about her work as if nothing unusual was on hand." When she brought food to her hidden guests, she put it in the bottom of a basket and then covered it with freshly ironed clothes. During a visit to Canada, she was approached by an old man who reminded her of a more impromptu and desperate attempt to protect a fugitive. "La me! Misses," he said. "Don't you 'member when day was close after me to take me an' you had me in de feather bed and saved me?" [42]

Still also emphasized the participation of Quaker women in the underground railroad in his book. Fugitives, he asserted, were reasonably secure in areas of Quaker settlement. The Quakers' historic antipathy to slavery certainly encouraged participation in the underground railroad, although conservative Quakers were troubled by the secrecy, deception, and illegality connected with the work. Like other committed Christian abolitionist women, especially Wesleyan Methodists and Reformed Presbyterians, however, Quakers who supported underground railroad activities decided that God's law outweighed any laws of men. At least some satisfied their consciences by taking care to learn no details from their fugitive guests. If questioned, they could give honest but unrevealing answers.[43]

In Schoolcraft, Michigan, Mrs. Thomas was apparently not a Quaker herself, but a Friend brought fugitives to her household. Over a twenty-year period, Mrs. Thomas estimated that she and her husband sheltered 1,500 fugitives who came in groups of six to twelve. Her husband's task was to transport them to the next stop, and perhaps his responsibilities were more dangerous than hers. But Mrs. Thomas's were more exhausting. As she recollected, "They brought much hard work to me and great expense to my husband. Often after my little ones were asleep and I thought the labor of the day over, Friend Shugart would drive up with a load of hungry people to be fed and housed." While most of Mrs. Thomas's guests probably stopped only briefly at her house, depending on the place, time of year, and situation of the fugitives, some women found themselves hosting fugitives for considerably longer periods. One family in West Chester, Pennsylvania, took in a woman and her two children who had fled during the winter, and the family who sheltered them thought the weather too bad to send them on. They stayed for several weeks before proceeding to Philadelphia.[44]

In some cases, women found themselves nursing very sick fugitives. Hannah Gibbons, a Quaker woman who, with her husband, received fugitive slaves in Lancaster County, Pennsylvania, discovered that one of them had smallpox. She took entire responsibility for nursing, and when the man recovered he spent over a year with the family. In Danvers, Massachusetts, Sarah Baker remembered the arrival of a fugitive whose back was raw from beating. Her parents melted brown sugar, then laid "the old negro upon it to heal his back." He required nursing care in the upper chamber for several weeks.[45]

When Charles Thompson dreamed about fleeing from his master, he "had often thought that I would be in a bad condition to come here, without money and clothes." But in the end, "I made up my mind to come, live or die." Thompson's comments suggest some of the needs that women tried to meet. Fugitives who, like Thompson, often arrived in rags had to be equipped. Even those whose clothes were still serviceable needed warmer clothing for the Canadian climate. If there was any danger that the fugitive might be recovered, he or she might need to move on almost at once. Women had to produce garments in short order for people whose size and sex could not be known ahead of time. Elizabeth Chace remembered that in such a situation, "We had no time for anything more than to pick up what we could find, whether it fitted them or not, for we dared not keep them longer than was absolutely necessary." A Manchester, Massachusetts, woman "worked nearly all day Sunday, repairing an overcoat that happened to fit" a thinly clad fugitive arriving during a cold, rainy spring. Individual women and groups of women also raised money to pay for outfitting fugitives. Abigail Goodwin, an elderly widow in Salem, New Jersey, whose antislavery efforts stretched back to the 1830s, sent stockings she had made to William Still and told him she would send more clothes as soon as she could earn enough money to buy materials.[46]

Most women expanded their domestic routines to accommodate fugitives. But occasionally they also took on more visible and daring roles. Women in one Michigan community were responsible for giving out the warning if slavecatchers came into the neighborhood. Their signal was the toot of a horn. "If the sound of a tin horn is heard it is understood a few miles, each way . . . just what it means." Levi Coffin's wife proved herself adept at disguising fugitives so they could get to their next stop. On one occasion, she dressed a young woman as a nursemaid, put a rag baby in her arms, and then donned fashionable clothes herself. Playing lady and maid with baby, the two strolled right by suspicious neighbors without discovery. Others also disguised fugitives (Quaker dresses with heavy veils were often used because they were so concealing) and accompanied them to complete the deception. Laura Haviland, one of the more extraordinary white female abolitionists connected with the underground railroad in the Midwest, was especially bold and imaginative. She even led a female fugitive through the streets of Cincinnati, where people were discussing the woman's escape across the Ohio River and the reward for her capture. In rural Pennsylvania, Sarah Marsh, daughter of abolitionist and Free-Soil parents, used her market wagon to transport slaves, sometimes disguised as Friends, to their next stop. Before the passage of the Fugitive Slave Act, she traveled during the day, but after 1850, she made her trips at night.[47]

The numbers of those who broke the law through their direct and personal involvement with fugitives were probably few compared to the numbers of women who adapted familiar activities to new purposes. Sarah Ernst, distressed that abolitionists in Cincinnati had only political and religious agendas, was one of the women who for years met at Levi Coffin's house every week to sew for fugitives. The group supplied a clothes deposi-tory for outfitting those passing through the city on their way to Canada. William Still often received letters from women's sewing circles offering to send their work to Philadelphia. Indeed, the plight of fugitives seems to have fostered the organization of women's groups and provided them with a tangible purpose. In Topsham, Vermont, the sewing circle, composed of "mostly ladies," wrote to Still, explaining that "we want to give the little money raised, in such a way that the fugitives who are really needy will be benefitted." In rural Vermont, the organization did not have an easy time attracting members. "Fugitives are never seen here," the president informed Still. "Indeed the one half of the people have never seen more than a half-dozen of colored people. There are none in all this region." If Still could send "another long letter in detail of interesting fugitives . . . I would have it read before the circle. Your last letter was heard by the ladies with great interest." Difficult as it was to sustain their circle, the women recognized that the fugitive issue provided a powerful reason for association. Without fugitives, there probably would not have been an abolitionist society there at all.[48]

As longtime fund-raisers for antislavery, women were also involved in supporting fugitive work financially. The two Osgood sisters in Medford, Massachusetts, found "that the very moderate care for the poor fugi-tives which devolves upon ourselves, in our comparatively retired position, forms a constantly increasing item in our expenses." The financial bur-dens led some women to solicit individually, while others cooperated in their ventures. Women predictably turned to the familiar device of the anti-slavery fair. Just as there was some debate as to whether general assistance to the fugitive was appropriate antislavery work, so too was there discus-sion about using fairs for this purpose. The decision to assign some of a fair's profits to helping fugitives could acerbate relations between women for whom aid to fugitives had become a priority and those who worried that the true cause, the abolition of slavery, was being neglected. Lizzie Gay did not favor using money from the New York City fair for the fugi-tives but failed to persuade others. "When I who opposed it on the ground that the money might be begged on the streets," she wrote, "was asked if I would go out and get it, and was [told?] *The money must be had* and we can get it with ease and all fair and right" through the fair. In Cincinnati, ten-sions arose not only over fair proceeds but the purpose of women's handi-work. Sarah Ernst complained that at the weekly sewing meetings nothing was done for the bazaar. All the sewing was for the clothing depot.[49]

Women, like men, exploited the inherent drama of fleeing slaves to create propaganda highlighting the evils of southern slaveholding. Harriet Beecher Stowe's *Uncle Tom's Cabin* was only the most famous example of the power of images connected with the fugitive. Stories of successful or unsuccessful attempts to recapture slaves and the tales fugitives themselves told all made excellent material for women who shaped it for the public. Even before the 1850 law was passed, some women had recognized the potential of the material. In 1848, Mary Thomas wrote an account of the recapture of a young black woman living with her family. "I feel so much excited by the attendant circumstances of this daring and atrocious deed, as scarcely to be able to give a coherent account of it; but I know that it is my duty to make it known, and I therefore write this immediately." Despite her professed difficulty in expressing herself, Mary ably portrayed the incident in language designed to shock her readers in the *Pennsylvania Freeman* and the *Liberator*, the papers to which she sent her narrative. She described the slavehunters "lurking" about the household, waiting to accomplish "their horrid errand," their "deliberate invasion of our house," a "thing unimagined." She made sure her readers understood the meaning of this incident. "There is no need to preach about slavery in the abstract; this individual case combines every wickedness by which human nature can be degraded."[50]

Although Julianna Tappan, the daughter of the abolitionist leader Lewis Tappan, apparently dropped out of organized antislavery because of Garrisonians' radical views of women's role, his second wife, Sarah, modestly contributed to the public discussion of the evils of slavery. Sometime in the 1850s, she wrote an account of a fugitive's escape for *Frederick Douglass's Paper* (formerly *North Star*). In a similar fashion, Elizabeth Chace recorded James Curry's story of his escape for the *Liberator* and subsequently wrote and published a poem about his mother who fled to Canada. Maria Child, who had heard plenty of fugitive stories, helped shape Harriet Jacobs's book-length account of her miseries in slavery and her escape from her lascivious master. "I have taken a good deal of pains to publish it, and circulate it, because it seemed to me calculated to take hold of many minds, that will not attend to *arguments* against slavery," Maria explained. Local events made especially good copy, as Sarah Ernst realized. "Deeds have been done in our midst that warn us not to relax our efforts," she pointed out in her notices for the 1854 Anti-Slavery Convention in Cincinnati.[51]

In 1857, Maria Child explained the value of her connection with fugitives over the years. Although she had dropped out of all antislavery organizations, she credited her "frequent interviews with fugitives" with keeping abolitionism "so *near* . . . [her] heart" over a twenty-five-year period. Depending on individual and local circumstances, each woman drew her own meaning from her contact and work with fugitives. For Elizabeth Chace, the occasional arrival of a fugitive in her Rhode Island home brought the excitement, the sense of danger, and the possibility of dramatic sacrifice for her beliefs that her other more mundane abolitionist efforts could not. Years later, she could vividly remember the "hourly fear and expectation of the arrival of the slave-catcher" that accompanied hiding a fugitive and the practice of keeping the "doors and windows fastened by day as well as by night, not daring to let our neighbors know who were our guests, lest some one should betray them." Tied down as she was by the care of her children and household chores, sheltering fugitives allowed her to make a political statement within the confines of her own home. Each time she hid a fugitive she broke the law and defied Congress. Her underground railroad activities also provided a way for her to dramatize for her children the cause and the possible consequences of commitment.[52]

Esther Moore had strong antislavery credentials. She had rejected the advice from her Quaker meeting "that she had better let these questions of Slavery alone, and leave it for God to settle . . . in his own good time," and had become the first president of the Philadelphia Female Anti-Slavery Society. But participation in the work of the organization became increasingly unrewarding as the once energetic group narrowed its focus to the yearly fair. Although the society supported vigilance operations in the 1840s, many of the members, including Lucretia Mott, did not see relieving the wants of fugitive slaves as the proper focus for antislavery. Esther withdrew from the society because she was "more interested in the Vigilance Com[mittee] operations and such like departments of the cause" than she was in society work. Cooperation with the vigilance committee provided an opportunity for personal interactions that made abolitionism come to life. Asking the vigilance committee to inform her of every fugitive who arrived in the city, she "delighted" in meeting with them, welcoming them to freedom, and listening to their stories. William Still noted the emotional character of Esther's connection with fugitives, the tears she shed when she heard of their sufferings in slavery, the wrench she experienced when it was time for them to move on. The gold dollar that she pressed in each fugitive's hand kept the personal link alive even after fugitives had left Philadelphia. Her identification with the work of the underground railroad led her to efforts that many mainline abolitionists rejected. Just a month before her death in 1854 at the age of eighty, she was going from house to house collecting money to ransom a family of slaves.[53]

Even if helping fugitives escape did not undermine the institution of slavery, each act represented an individual political and personal statement that provided meaning to the term abolitionist. Esther Moore was not the only woman for whom the fugitive became an all-consuming commitment. Abigail Goodwin, a New Jersey widow, did not have Esther Moore's financial resources, but poor as she was, she contributed steadily to the cause. Mourning that "scarcely anybody seems to think about" the fugitives, she habitually denied herself. Her clothes were so worn that one of her friends claimed that beggars who approached her door were better dressed than Abigail. "Giving to the colored people was a perfect *passion* with her." [54]

Working with fugitives also provided some women with a sense of power. The planning and execution of escapes, even the furnishing of food and clothing, reinforced female capabilities and authority. But the work could also generate feelings of superiority that had racist overtones. Levi Coffin's wife routinely provided fugitives with new names, as did Laura Haviland, as if the fugitives were incapable of selecting names for themselves. Devoted as he was to his work, Levi Coffin disparaged the abilities of Cincinnati's black community, the largest in the Midwest. Blacks were "not shrewd managers" in work of sheltering fugitives, he suggested. [55]

White abolitionists helped to create the stereotype of the thankful slave, particularly in their accounts of visits to fugitive settlements in Canada. If genuine gratitude was ever tinged with some resentment of whites' unconscious sense of superiority, abolitionists did not realize it. Perhaps most fugitives did not recognize the limitations of their white conductors, but, during the 1850s, many black leaders, including Frederick Douglass, found white abolitionists prejudiced and struck out on an independent course.

Race shaped the experiences of abolitionism. Despite the course of events in the 1850s, white abolitionists found themselves energized as the decade proceeded. Abolitionist history and contemporary affairs suggested all the obstacles to immediate emancipation. Yet many white women were determined rather than discouraged. The women of Maine were caught up in a wave of organizing new antislavery societies called The Daughters of Freedom. The commitment they expressed hearkened back to the faith of women's societies in the 1830s. As one group in Palmyra explained in 1855, "The ladies often feel that anti-slavery is a cause in which they cannot be too much engaged." Other women meeting at Steep Falls pledged themselves "to labor for the slave until he is free, or its members are numbered with the dead." [56]

White women reshaped and redirected familiar activities and jumped into the controversies of the period. In Dover, New Hampshire, the Anti-Slavery Sewing Circle recruited seventeen new members, bought and distributed tracts, raised money for Kansas settlers, called a citywide meeting on behalf of Kansas, and took Frederick Douglass's newspaper in 1855. The next year, the society charged the corresponding secretary to discover whether Kansas settlers needed money or goods. The association sent $35 to Owen Lovejoy's mission in Kansas. In a similar fashion, other women combined fund-raising with political statements. "The Ladies of Stoughton" held a Kansas "Levee," as did Portland women, who got up "splendid Tableaux . . . in aid of suffering Kansas." Maria Child gathered both orthodox and Unitarian women to make winter clothing for Kansas settlers. She stitched "as fast as my fingers could go" and cut and made up more than sixty yards of cloth with the assistance of her friends.[57]

The Kansas-Nebraska Act provided ample opportunities for women not only to work but also to make statements. Ohio women sent Stephen Douglas thirty pieces of silver, a symbolic gesture that other women replicated for other "Judases." One of the banners at a large woman's rally in Maine proclaimed, "Eternal infamy to Douglas and his followers." In the *Liberator*, a woman signing herself only as "Old Woman" chided men and suggested their responsibility for the turn of events. Would the Nebraska bill or the Fugitive Slave Law have passed "if all the friends of humanity . . . had used their political power?" she asked. Obviously not. "Be up and doing," she continued. "Resume our political rights! . . . It is political and legislative action which is needed now."[58]

Each crisis generated vigorous responses. As rhetoric became more heated, abolitionist white women resorted to more extreme language. One Ohio woman compared slavery to a vampire, an omnipresent monster, a force almost all-powerful. She had given up on politics and was no longer in the habit of "reading congressional reports and speeches, having ceased to look for much good from them, and seeing so much of evil." Emeline Hogeboom, in Ghent, New York, had not given up on politics but had given up on the Union. She was circulating a petition for its peaceable dissolution. During a visit to Rev. Cornell, she and a friend tried to present an argument for the measure, but Cornell "flew into a towering passion" and "flourishing his hands . . . over our heads," used "sundry disagreeable epithets" before forcing the women out his house.[59]

John Brown's raid on Harpers Ferry threw Maria Child into a frenzy of activity, but less well known women also hailed the failure as a victory for "the heroic old man." Sarah Mason, in Springfield, Massachusetts, was moved to write a book so that "all, even very little children, should understand perfectly the *principle* for which he died." She planned the book to be a modest affair so that ordinary people would be able to afford to buy it.[60]

Black abolitionists interpreted the decade's events in a much more negative way than their white counterparts. Although there was little agreement on appropriate responses to the crises, blacks called for more radical and even violent action than they had in earlier years. Some concluded that present conditions meant that there was no future for them in the United States.[61]

Only a handful of black women rose to leadership positions in abolitionist circles and were able to contribute to the debates carried on in them. Most black women had neither the education nor the time to devote to activities that could win a hearing for their opinions. Although Harriet Tubman was able to combine occasional domestic work with her forays to free slaves in the South, she was an exception. As had been true since the 1830s, the few women who gained influence usually came from middle-class backgrounds. Like the new generation of black male leaders, however, they did not owe their prominence to their social position within the black community but to the abolitionist credentials they established.[62]

Mary Ann Shadd Cary was one of the women achieving public prominence in the 1850s. Shadd Cary was born in Wilmington, Delaware, to successful free black parents with good abolitionist credentials. She attended a Quaker private school for free blacks in Pennsylvania and went on to teach in black schools for twelve years. At twenty-eight, she moved to Canada West with her brother and father, intending to work with fugitives. In 1854, she became an editor of the *Provincial Freeman*. The first black woman to hold such a position, she used it as a vehicle for entering into debates that divided black abolitionists in the 1850s.[63] Like other black leaders, Shadd Cary condemned the paternalism of white abolitionists. In a biting 1854 editorial, she attacked "the disposition to make black appear white," which she considered "the most prominent feature of the times" and a characteristic of white abolitionism. This attempt to force white standards upon blacks, like the victories of Slave Power, stripped "the mis-called free colored man . . . of all rights" and turned Shadd Cary into a staunch supporter of emigration to Canada. Realizing some black leaders opposed emigration in the 1850s for the same sorts of reasons that immediatists had rejected colonization in the 1830s, she tried to persuade them that times had changed. "Look calmly and without prejudice at your position anti-emigration brethren," she wrote, "and you too who are indifferent! Not only are your hands tied against your own redemption from political thraldom, but you encourage a people to remain, and you remain and accumulate wealth, the very taxes upon which are . . . put into the United States Treasury, and used to maintain a government cemented with the blood of your brethren." The conclusion was obvious. "Determine to remove to a country or to countries, where you may have equal political rights," she advised, and "thus be *elevated at once*." [64]

Occasionally, Shadd Cary lectured before audiences in Canada and the United States. In her public appearances, she was careful to observe gender conventions. Her 1856 speech in Elkhorn, Indiana, was "modest, and in strict keeping with the popular notions of the 'sphere of women.'" When she spoke to the Colored National Convention on the necessity of emigration that same year, delegates, who had spent considerable time debating whether to allow her to address them, praised "the earnestness of her manner and the quality of her thoughts." Her audience found her "a superior woman." [65]

The fact that black men had spent precious convention time discussing whether they should allow even a "superior" woman to speak to them suggests that some black male abolitionists were as conservative as some of their white counterparts when it came to female participation in antislavery work. *Frederick Douglass's Paper* criticized Shadd Cary's opponents, one of whom was a "rough, uncouth, semi-barbarous fellow" who recalled early opposition to female lecturers in his sarcastic question of whether "we would admit Abby Kelley also." The desire of black male abolitionists to keep women in their place could be seen as a legitimate response to the negative sexual stereotyping of black women that allowed them no claim to woman's sphere. It also was an assertion of black masculine superiority in a society where it was very difficult for black men to prove their masculinity. Yet, conservatism burdened black women with white notions of ladylike behavior, whether they were appropriate or not. As always, gender conventions could be used as a weapon to silence women. Ironically, some black leaders were just as engaged in making "black appear white" in terms of imposing standards of gentility on black women as the white abolitionists Shadd Cary decried. [66]

Despite her strong views, in public appearances, Shadd Cary shaped her behavior to conform to expectations. She was less careful in her blunt and often caustic public writing. Henry Bibb, one of the targets of her vituperative pen because of their disagreement over integration, appealed to middle-class norms in his feud with her: "Miss Shadd has said and writes many things we think will add nothing to her credit as a lady." When she finally abandoned the editorship, her male successor suggested that convention had triumphed. "A wrongly developed public sentiment that would crush a woman whenever she attempts to do what has hitherto been assigned to men" had driven her from her job, he explained. [67]

The independent course many black abolitionists charted and the presence of a woman as abolitionist editor and speaker highlighted some of the alterations that had taken place in antislavery circles. The movement had reached middle age, with many of its adherents conscious of the passage of the years. "How changed from Old times!" Lizzie Gay observed. The women, like Lizzie, who had organized societies and circulated petitions as young women were no longer so young. Although she had not wavered in her abolitionist commitment, Lizzie was now a mother and frequently harried. As she told a friend, "I have such a sense of the utter helplessness of [a] mother's—I mean in the way of commanding time or quiet, or anything." Susan Lesley, writing from New Jersey in 1858 described herself as "rooted and grounded in Anti-slavery principles" but bored by their familiarity. "I don't care to hear much more discussion of them," she admitted. "It is stale to me." She had heard all the arguments before.[68]

Other women, although no longer youthful, drew strength from the dramatic events of the decade. Maria Child responded to the various crises and milestones with renewed determination and a changed perspective on the meaning of her abolitionist commitment. "We old abolitionists may well feel repaid for twenty five years of labor, discouragement, unpopularity, and persecution, since our principles, at *last* begin visibly to sway the masses. I, for one, thank God that I live to see it," she reflected before the 1856 election. Even the failure of John Brown's raid on Harpers Ferry invigorated her. "Before this affair," she told a friend, "I thought I was growing old and drowsy, but now I am as strong as an eagle."[69]

Maria Child began to attend the Boston fairs in the 1850s but had little interest in formal associations. She had never been comfortable in the Boston Female Anti-Slavery Society and saw no reason to change her mind. Although a few of the early female associations had maintained an organizational identity since the 1830s, some were definitely showing their age. The Philadelphia Female Anti-Slavery Society could pride itself on its longevity and its successful fair. In the 1850s, the society indulged in some modest propagandizing, buying space in the newspapers for antislavery material that the papers refused to publish in their regular columns. No longer much interested in recruiting new members, however, the association added only twenty women to its rolls between 1849 and 1853. For the small group of aging white and black women, the familiar routines sufficed as an expression of their abolitionist sympathies.[70]

For the young women who had grown up in abolitionism, the experiences and reference points were very different from those of their elders, who remembered mobbings, social isolation, and rudeness from disapproving neighbors. The early years of abolitionism had become the old days, and its early supporters heroes and "pioneers of the cause." Martha Barrett, a working-class woman from north of Boston, wrote admiringly in her diary of the Merills, who had achieved the status of "sterling abolitionists. true-hearted reformers. In the midst of a fluctuating community they have kept straight on never swerving." At the annual antislavery meeting in Boston, she admiringly described the speakers as "the *champions*." [71]

The contrast between the generations was apparent in the experiences of Elizabeth Chace and her daughter Lillie. As a young woman, Elizabeth Chace had helped form one of the earliest female antislavery societies (in Fall River) and had continued her involvement in antislavery affairs since that point. She had experienced the agonies of leaving her Quaker meeting and continued to work for the cause in Rhode Island when the organized movement was in the doldrums. For the Chace children, however, abolitionism was not a choice but a given. There was no need to renounce Quakerism, for it had already been replaced. As Lillie later recalled, "Antislavery held the place in our family life which had been withdrawn from the occupancy of church influences, since they had been deemed tainted by the spirit of moral compromise. We made no jest and no play about anything concerned with Abolitionism." Her mother's commitment shaped education and leisure. Friends came from other like-minded families, and many family high points were connected with abolitionism. The presence of abolitionist lecturers who routinely stayed in the Chace household when they visited Rhode Island acquainted the children with important figures. The occasional fugitive slave provided excitement and drama. The possibility of discovery led the Chaces to instruct the children on what to do if their parents were carried away to jail and prompted the children to form heroic plans of "how . . . they would take care of everything." Antislavery conventions in Providence were special enough occasions that no one in the family would want to miss them. Lillie wrote to her brother away at school to reassure him that the he would be "at home time enough for it." [72]

Without any anguished examination of what her duty might be, Lillie slipped into the role as her mother's helper. During the 1850s and early 1860s, Elizabeth arranged for speakers to come to Rhode Island, and Lillie wrote many of the letters for her mother. Just as naturally, she undertook other antislavery tasks. As she informed her brother, "We have got petitions out for the abolition of the colored schools and some to make R.I. free soil it has failed in Massachusetts but that is no reason why it should fail in R.I. [Those] who are old enough to understand it can sign these petitions under the heading of nonvoters. I have signed it."[73]

As a member of the prominent Forten-Purvis family of Philadelphia, Charlotte Forten also grew up in the cause. As a black woman, her experiences were both similar to and different from those of Lillie Chace and other young white women who were coming to maturity in the decade before the Civil War. Because she could not attend public school in Philadelphia, Forten came to Salem, Massachusetts, to finish her education. She stayed with the Remonds, a well-known black abolitionist family, and took part in Salem's abolitionist social life. She went to lively sewing parties, where there was pleasant talk, antislavery meetings, and evenings of abolitionist conversation. She was an avid consumer of the lectures that the Salem Female Anti-Slavery Association still sponsored, and she filled her diary with evaluations of the various speakers' styles, their messages, and the size of the audience. A well-attended lecture by Mr. Prince, for example, was excellent, even though he "had not *quite* so much enthusiasm as I like." The radical and eloquent lecture of Rev. Appleton, on the other hand, "had my entire sympathy and approbation." In 1855, she joined the Salem Female Anti-Slavery Society.[74]

The high points of her year were trips to the Boston fair and antislavery anniversary meetings. Like Martha Barrett, she idolized the prominent people she met there. At the 1857 fair she "saw Sumner, Emerson, Wendell Phillips, all in the air at once. It was *glorious* to see such a trio. I feasted my eyes." She treasured handshakes and greetings. When Wendell Phillips spoke to her "*very* kindly," her "heart was too full to say much." Abby Kelley Foster, "that most excellent of women, gave me so warm and kind a greeting that I was quite touched. She pressed my hand with great fervor and said most earnestly, 'God bless you, my dear, I am most happy to meet you.'" In an extension of her hero worship, she began to write to her idols, "dear noble" Garrison, Charles Sumner, and others, asking for their autographs. In her diary she confessed that her behavior was daring, even presumptuous, but she felt powerless to curb her desire for contact with the greats. When Wendell Phillips wrote her, she fantasized "how delightful it would be to be admitted to his society; Alas I can never hope to be fitted for that great privilege. — But I *can* love and admire him."[75]

Some of the attention she received was what the younger members of any family with an impressive abolitionist lineage might expect. But race also played a part. When she received a parcel of autographed speeches from Charles Sumner, a "stranger," she acknowledged, "I have to thank my color for it." Perhaps she even capitalized on her ancestry. After seeing work sent to the Boston fair by Harriet Martineau, she wrote to her, rationalizing that the famous women might like to hear "from a young colored girl in a distant land." [76]

Consciousness of race brought more than special favors. Despite her comfortable background, Forten identified with slaves in ways that no white person could. She had not experienced slavery firsthand, but she certainly had encountered prejudice. Although her family sheltered her from the worst expressions of racial hatred, Philadelphia's policy of segregation had affected her directly. Antislavery lecturers spoke not only for the enslaved, she realized, but also on her "behalf." Her habit of evaluating lecturers came partly from her sense that they spoke for her and partly from her recognition that a powerful address could alert white people to "the terrible sin" of slavery and cause them to "think rightfully." Charlotte, herself, needed no instruction to think "rightfully." But she did need the emotional fervor that a strong speech provided, the renewed "strength" that made her "feel equal to any labor, for the ennobling of mankind." [77]

Expected by her family to continue in a leadership role, she struggled in Salem to improve herself, "to prepare . . . for the responsible duties of a teacher, and to live for the good that I can do my oppressed and suffering fellow-creatures." Her sense of obligation shaped her early literary efforts and determined her subject: a story about "prejudice against color." Conscious of transgressing boundaries, she even "*dared*" to write to an antislavery lecturer "(anonymously, of course)," informing him of the exclusion of blacks from the hall where he was to lecture. After finishing her own schooling, she began teaching, the career used by other women in her family to improve the situation of blacks. She had a difficult initiation. In September 1857, she felt "*desperate.* . . . This constant *warfare* is *crushing*, killing me." Yet she never considered doing something more enjoyable. "I will try not to forget," she told herself, "that, while striving to improve myself, I may at least *commence* to work for others." [78]

Despite the trials of her introduction to teaching, Forten continued to enjoy the routines of antislavery social life. Like Martha Barrett, she attended the Salem lecture series faithfully. Antislavery lectures offered opportunities for instruction and for social and intellectual interactions between young and old abolitionists and the curious public. [79]

By the 1850s, lectures had become such a popular form of entertainment and instruction that many places organized lyceum committees to arrange lecture series. Improvements in recording and publishing speeches broadened the lecture audience by allowing the reading public to participate

Yᴱ ABOLITIONISTS IN COUNCIL—Yᴱ ORATOR OF Yᴱ DAY DENOUNCING Yᴱ UNION, MAY, 1859.

This rather unsympathetic depiction of an abolitionist meeting appearing in Harper's Weekly *in 1859 features the presence of women, who are mainly recognized by their bonnets, and African Americans. (Boston Athenæum)*

vicariously in such events. This expansion of interest and audience encouraged local antislavery societies like the Salem Female Anti-Slavery Society, the Rochester Ladies' Anti-Slavery Society, and the Portland Anti-Slavery Society to sponsor public lecture series, and prompted state societies and the AAS to hire antislavery agents. The popularity of the medium, the stirring events of the decade, and the familiarity and longevity of abolitionism as a reform all contributed to good attendance, attentive audiences, and even reunions between different groups of antislavery activists. Frederick Douglass recognized the new context, remarking that the antislavery lecturer now "speaks to a different audience, moves in a different atmosphere, and treads a less rugged pathway."[80]

Twenty years earlier, male lecturers like Amos Phelps had faced the possibility of mobbing and worse when they attacked slavery in public. When women addressed mixed audiences, they did not risk tarring and feathering, as did some male lecturers, but the risks for transgressing gender conventions and upholding an unpopular cause were real. Maria Stewart,

Crisis and Confidence   197

a black woman who was the first female abolitionist to lecture before a mixed audience in the early 1830s, soon abandoned public speaking. She explained that it was "no use for me as an individual to try to make myself useful among my color in this city," for "it was the nature of man to crush his fellow." The Grimké sisters' speaking tour occasioned a major clerical rebuke, while Abby Kelley was branded as a Jezebel during her tour of Connecticut in 1840. Ellen Smith, who lectured in a church in Maine in 1843, left a vivid account of her hostile audience "howling, stamping, kicking, slamming . . . pew doors, and pounding . . . the pews with their fists." Boys sitting in the church's galleries threw hymn books at her, and she was lucky to escape without injury.[81]

The same year that Ellen Smith confronted the rain of hymn books, the women of Essex County, Massachusetts, held a female antislavery convention. One of their resolutions expressed their conviction that they must be ready at all times to speak out on the subject of slavery. Despite the hazards of public speaking, women continued to advocate publicly the emancipation of the slave in the 1840s. By the 1850s, with the expansion of the lecture field and the changing political and social environment, audiences were more receptive to women's voices on the lecture circuit than they had been earlier. While women lecturers were still a novelty, even a possible advantage in attracting a crowd, as Sallie Holley observed, "the days of clubs and stones are past." Occasionally women lecturers faced a disapproving audience. In one church, men registered their opposition to their speaker by depositing their chewed tobacco quids in the collection plate. But eloquent women often disarmed their listeners and reported that "a great amount of prejudice against female speaking . . . found a grave" by the time they had finished making their case against slavery.[82]

Black lecturer William J. Watkins characterized the "effectual Reformer" in an 1854 article in *Frederick Douglass's Paper*. The work of agitation, he suggested, required "a strong nerve, and potent arm, determined will, moral courage, strong powers of analysis, depth and breadth of comprehension, indomitable perseverance, correct judgment, and a worldwide heart, full of hope and love." Additionally, the reformer's pen must "manufacture words of fire," and his tongue "should sting like a thousand scorpions."[83] Watkins doubtless had a male reformer in mind when he listed the traits needed for successful agitation. The women who became agents and lecturers possessed many of the qualities Watkins thought necessary. But they had to find words that stung without conjuring up images of scorpions. They needed to develop strategies capable of disarming audiences and pressing home the abolitionist message without raising objections based on gender.

Although historians of abolitionism have not given Sallie Holley much attention, perhaps because she did not become an active feminist, Sallie was a well-known and popular abolitionist lecturer in the 1850s. Her career provides valuable insights into the ways in which a few women participated in the public debate during the last decade before the Civil War and into the changed environment of antislavery.

Sallie Holley was a second-generation abolitionist. Her father, Myron Holley, an early proponent of the Liberty Party in New York State, had done some lecturing for the New York Anti-Slavery Society. When Sallie was in her early twenties, her father died. His death transformed him into a heroic figure for his daughter, and she came to view him as he had viewed himself: as a martyr for abolitionism. Wishing to continue his work in some way, she was disillusioned about marriage by her firsthand view of her sisters' domestic drudgery. After doing some teaching, she started the ladies' course at Oberlin at the age of twenty-nine. During the summer of 1850, she heard Abby Kelley Foster speak at an antislavery convention and began to consider the possibility of becoming a lecturer herself. Abby was encouraging and wanted to start her off at once. Sallie decided to finish her Oberlin course but assured Abby that she would take up the invitation when she graduated.

Sallie had more preparation for lecturing than many women who spoke publicly in the 1850s. As a member of the Oberlin Young Ladies' Association, she had some practice with speaking in front of groups. In her final year at Oberlin, public sentiment against the Compromise of 1850 brought her an opportunity to try lecturing before a mixed audience in Litchfield, Ohio, and a gathering of free blacks in Sandusky. She felt that she had succeeded well, and after graduation, she joined Abby Kelley Foster for her first formal lecture tour. Lecturing provided a way for her to act upon her abolitionist commitment and to support herself. Feeling both useful and independent, she symbolized her new status by changing the spelling of her name from Sally to Sallie.[84]

Although her first speech in her hometown of Rochester, New York, elicited both praise and criticism for her departure from the "acknowledged sphere of women," Sallie told friends that "I have at last found out my 'sphere.'" For the rest of the decade, she lectured throughout New England, New York, the Midwest, and the mid-Atlantic and raised money for the cause. For the most part, she faced few of the difficulties earlier speakers had confronted. Abolitionist friends usually made the necessary arrangements for her engagements, ranging from posting and publishing notices of the lectures to securing space. In the spring of 1853, Frances Drake, long active in central Massachusetts and a stalwart worker for the Boston fair, was busy trying to set up Sallie's visit in Leominster. She hoped to secure one of the churches for her lecture, thereby saving the cost of both renting and heating a space (the church would be still warm from the service). In the end, the Unitarians offered only the vestry, "low, unpleasant, and ill-ventilated," and a disgruntled Frances had to rent the Town Hall for the lecture.[85]

Sallie reported having large and attentive audiences, and observers who wrote to abolitionist newspapers agreed. In Plymouth, Massachusetts, she spoke for two hours to a group sitting in "perfect silence." In New York State, over 500 people turned out in the midst of haying season to hear her during the furor over the Kansas-Nebraska Act. Increasingly she felt as if she was reaching ordinary people. "Now, as in Jesus's time," she commented, "it is the common people who hear the truth gladly." By 1855, she reported that "hearts are softening" and "abolitionists find more willing attendance upon their teachings than formerly." The next year, she noted "a deeper earnestness in the people for the great idea of Anti-Slavery." Her reception and her sense that the cause was advancing reinforced her career choice and fed her self-confidence and sense of usefulness.[86]

Listeners responded respectfully and with interest because Sallie Holley's message did not sound particularly radical in the 1850s and seemed, in fact, to be proven by the crises of the decade. She also had the abilities without which no speaker could succeed: a voice able to carry in large spaces and an energetic delivery. But Sallie, like other successful female abolitionist lecturers, appealed to audiences because she developed a style of discourse capable of delivering the antislavery case without raising too many gender-based objections. While not all female orators used the same approach, common features connected their oratorical strategies.

All women were operating within the general mode of nineteenth-century public discourse. During the first decades of the century, a new style of oral communication arose to replace the formal, refined, and re-served oratory favored by gentry speakers of the eighteenth and early nineteenth centuries. This "middling" style, characterized by bluntness, informality, and exaggeration, suited the rough-and-tumble world of politics. It established easy contact rather than distance between speaker and listeners. While it might be vulgar, colorful, insulting, and not particularly truthful, it could be persuasive and moving.[87]

Women who, like Abby Kelley, adopted some of the unrestrained aspects of the middling style were likely to provoke the wrath of their listeners who chided them for speaking in public. By the 1850s, women were both more familiar on the lecture stage and more adept at modifying the middling style in ways that allowed them to address audiences without offense. As Sallie Holley pointed out in a letter to Abby Kelley, perhaps with her mentor's style in mind, she did not speak with "fury might and thundering power of indignations." Successful female orators during the 1850s were direct but not vulgar, they used inflated language that was spiritual or poetic, and they established a connection with their audiences through various rhetorical devices rather than inappropriate informality. Despite the emotional rapport they established, these women managed to convey to their audiences that they were still refined ladies.[88]

Female abolitionist speakers were praised for speeches that were "free from offensive boldness, . . . gentle, calm, dignified, earnest." They were neither pretentious nor aloof but showed "simplicity of manners and modest deportment, . . . [and] gentleness of speech." No one "could possibly complain of the language . . . used." Within such parameters, Sallie Holley developed her own distinctive approach and voice. Reporting on an early speech in Nantucket, the *Nantucket Weekly Mirror* described her strategy: "Each discourse was preceded by readings from the Scriptures, and prayer." Her talks had "all the characteristics of a sermon. They were pervaded by a devout religious spirit, and her highest appeals were to the sentiments of justice and mercy as exemplified in the life and teachings of Jesus Christ." Her decision to use the familiar evangelical model not only made most listeners feel at home with her as a speaker but also encouraged the emotional response she sought. At a lecture given in Salem, her address was "calculated to move deeply . . . the feelings and excite the sympathies of her hearers." In Newport, Rhode Island, an appreciative abolitionist suggested, "We should call her a preacher . . . rather than a lecturer . . . an Anti-Slavery Revivalist." Such a characterization corresponded to Sallie's view of herself as preaching "the everlasting gospel" and saving her listeners.[89]

The revivalist structure and language Sallie Holley employed disarmed her listeners and rendered more effective her antislavery message. Her success attests to the continuing importance of the religious impulse in attracting people to abolitionism, despite many other possible appeals. Her reliance on familiar themes, like the suffering of women under slavery and the innate sinfulness of slavery, and her use of hallowed vignettes of slave life point to the long-lived appeal of central abolitionist images and ideas. As the decade wore on, however, Sallie, like other abolitionists, increasingly exploited current and local events to highlight the threat of the Slave Power. She also sought to bring the various camps of antislavery closer by not harping upon "the points of difference." But she did not dilute the emancipation message. "I urge no compromise with Slavery and direct assault upon the foul institution," she told Abby Kelley Foster. Her presentation "would have been found to be as radical as any speech of the most 'ultra' abolitionist," one listener explained. "Much depends upon the manner in which the truth is presented in its taking hold of the heart and conscience," he added. Abby Kelley Foster made the same point when she said that Sallie's "sword is very much colored." [90]

That Sallie often worked closely with ministers and spoke in their churches was a sign of the change in public opinion . Even those who disapproved of her presence frequently read the notices of her meetings. In one Vermont town in 1858, the Presbyterian and Congregational ministers, feeling the pressure of national events, "clubbed together and agreed that they had better give out the notice of my lectures for fear of being considered proslavery." Clerical assistance did not reduce her criticism of the institution, however. Like other women who accused the church of sin, Sallie was bolstered by "the great thought of God, and the excellence of anti-slavery truth." [91]

Although Sallie had crafted her appeal to move the emotions, saying that the point of her lectures was "to effect a *mighty change* in the hearts of your people," she also relied upon argument and impromptu reasoning. During each lecture, she gave opportunities for people in the audience to raise objections and ask questions. When one man disagreed with her about the necessity of dissolving the Union, "Miss Holley spoke a few words, and put the matter right about Henry Clay." The success of this question and answer format depended upon the speaker having an assortment of facts at her disposal, quick thinking, and good debating skills. [92]

"How much happier and richer my life has been than I ever expected it to be!" Sallie exclaimed in the early years of her lecturing career. There were many rewards for public antislavery work in the 1850s, but there were also trials that led Sallie to remark that same year, "The fact is, I am very tired of this rough and tumble kind of life." [93]

Lecturing for antislavery took a toll, though hardly comparable to the toll it took in the 1830s. The schedule of speaking for as long as two hours several times a week was hard on the voice. Sallie, like other female lecturers, had periods when her chest bothered her and her voice was damaged. Traveling in the East was certainly much easier than it had been two decades before, but even train travel was not particularly comfortable. In the winter, one might either freeze or roast, depending on whether one was sitting near the central aisle, where the stove was placed, or not. During the summer, when windows might be shut, open doors let in air and sparks and dust. In the Midwest, a stagecoach without springs served as a very uncomfortable form of transportation.[94]

Perhaps more stressful than the rigors of travel was the necessity of staying with strangers. The antislavery lecturer, Sallie wrote, "always advances with some doubtfulness to the strange house mapped out." On the one hand, the policy of arranging for antislavery lecturers to reside with abolitionists saved money and could result in warm friendships. On the other hand, Sallie had to put up with conditions that offended her genteel standards. Her letters are peppered with descriptions of awful accommodations. "I have encountered more filth in the last year than in all the other years of my life," she wrote a friend in 1852 from "a dreadfully dirty" house. "Oh, *so* untidy!" Beyond the problems different ideas of housekeeping presented, the curiosity and attention that came along with being a public person was sometimes a trial. "I wish the art of 'letting alone' was better understood," she remarked. All too often after a lecture and hard travel, she was "expected to entertain."[95]

Despite the constant attention, the lecture circuit could be a lonely place, as Sallie discovered when she was on her own. Sallie occasionally traveled with other antislavery agents but more often with her Oberlin friend Caroline Putnam, whom she persuaded to accompany her. Less confident than Sallie, Caroline was content to stay mostly in the background. Because both women were staunch second-generation abolitionists, however, they agreed that Caroline should also have her antislavery work. She became a colporteur, responsible for circulating tracts in the villages and towns where Sallie spoke. Her shyness did not shield her from engaging in public discussion. She was expected to counter ignorance, prejudice, and indifference, and the responsibility was almost too much. "I stand on the steps of this door or that," Caroline wrote, "with my little handful of Tracts thinking over the message I am to stammer out to the inmates when bidden to enter. How their objections & incredulity—and indifference and ignorance will tempt me to despair of any good I can do."[96]

Caroline's timidity came partly from her conception of herself as "a plain, awkward little, not young! country girl." While Sallie had much greater self-confidence than Caroline and defended her rights to speak as a woman, she also experienced misgivings that stemmed from her gender. Her stage fright, which she never completely outgrew, and her discomfort when she first saw her name in print suggest the price she paid for entering so openly into public dialogue. The newspaper notices made it clear to the world and to herself just how far she had departed from the private sphere. "I think I can never forget the sudden, intense, and overwhelming emotion, I experienced on seeing my name for the first time in a public newspaper," she recalled in 1865. "It seemed that every drop of blood in my body, and every feeling of my soul rose up in 'terrible rebellion'—I can never forget the day, the hour, and the spot where it happened."[97]

Ingrained notions about female gentility may have caused a certain amount of tension, but they did not prevent Sallie from feeling competitive with other female agents. She envied Lucy Stone's "self-possession," calling her "a little, independent piece." But gender did intersect with her status as a second-generation abolitionist to produce insecurities that limited her scope. She regarded the early days of abolitionism as "the old chivalric days of Anti-Slavery" and, like other young women, heroized its leaders. She was fearful of appearing before them, having "nothing good enough to say." Her colleagues were dismayed at Sallie's feelings of inadequacy. Samuel May wrote to Caroline Weston, urging that "if anything human can be done by you to remove or lessen that dreadful nervousness which makes her so painfully conscious (!) of her own inferiority to everybody in New England, at least to everyone whose names she heard before coming here, it would be a work of great mercy and utility." Unfortunately, Caroline and others never could remove Sallie's self-doubt, and she avoided engagements that would expose her to her heroes.[98]

At the end of the decade, Sallie supported an effort in Rhode Island to eliminate "caste schools." Although abolitionists had once sought separate schools for black children, often because they were the only schools available, the expansion of the public school system made all-black schools an expression of racial prejudice. Sallie wrote a reasoned memorandum to the legislative committee considering the change. She decided not to read the memo before the committee herself, however, believing that a young black woman who was prevented from attending the high school in Providence would have a greater impact on the committee than a white person.[99]

The recognition that black speakers might make the abolitionist case more effectively than a white speaker lay behind the appointment of black women as antislavery lecturers and agents in the 1850s. While to some extent their experiences resembled those of their white counterparts, race played a role in shaping their situation.[100]

Frances Ellen Watkins Harper, like Sallie Holley, was born into abolitionism. The uncle with whom she lived after the death of her parents was a prominent free black abolitionist in Baltimore. Reputedly, it was his in-

This picture captures the magnetic character and presence of Frances Watkins Harper, who was so successful as an abolitionist lecturer during the 1850s. (Boston Athenæum)

fluence that caused Garrison's change of heart about colonization.[101] Watkins's established position in Baltimore's free black community allowed him to provide members of his family, including his niece, with the many of the advantages of middle-class life. Watkins Harper received a solid education in her uncle's school, but the fact that she left school at thirteen suggests one of the differences between the white and black middle class.

Black middle-class families were economically more fragile than white families. Because black men ordinarily earned meager salaries, families needed the income of women and older children to maintain a middle-class life. Watkins Harper, like her cousins, was expected to enter the labor market in her early teens, and she did so. She took one of the few jobs open to a young black girl and became a nurse and seamstress for a white family. Her employers recognized her exceptional literary leanings and allowed her to read in her spare time.[102]

At the age of twenty-six, Watkins Harper moved on to one of the other opportunities open to black middle-class women, school teaching. She became an instructor of embroidery and plain sewing at Union Seminary, a school for free blacks in Ohio. She was the first female teacher and faced hostility from male faculty, who thought her out of her place. Her principal commented on how "firmly" she "braved the flood of oppression which . . . manifested itself from the beginning—and . . . [he took] great pleasure in commending her." Such an experience could hardly have made teaching seem a very desirable occupational choice. Nevertheless, Watkins Harper moved on to another school in York, Pennsylvania. Despite her conviction that "the condition of our people, the wants of our children, and the welfare of our race demand the aid of every helping hand," she found the burdens of teaching fifty-three children too heavy. Exposed to the underground railroad and some of the abolitionists who were involved with it, like William Still, she began to contemplate other ways to help her race. In the end, she decided that "it may be that God himself has written upon both my heart and brain a commission to use time, talent and energy in the cause of freedom." [103]

Watkins Harper accompanied a cousin to Boston, met leaders like Garrison, and then went on to New Bedford, where she gave her first public speech. She chose as her topic one stressed by other black abolitionists, "the Elevation and Education of our People." Several more successful lectures followed, leading the Maine Anti-Slavery Society to offer her a position as an antislavery agent.[104]

Watkins Harper enjoyed success in her tour in Maine. Her color was a drawing card, as an article in the Portland *Advertiser* noted. "Miss W. is slightly tinged with African blood, but the color only serves to add a charm to the occasion which nothing else could give." Negative stereotypes of black women as different from white "ladies" apparently also played a role in legitimating her speeches, for the article went on to note that her color disarmed "the fastidious of that so common prejudice which denies to white ladies the right to give public lectures." In addition, Watkins Harper attracted audiences because she could give firsthand witness to the horrors of the Slave Power and the institution of slavery. While her voice could not be as authentic as a former slave, she had had the opportunity to observe slavery in Baltimore and to hear fugitives' stories in Pennsylvania.[105]

In its barest outlines, Watkins Harper's route to the antislavery platform had qualities similar to Sallie Holley's: an abolitionist family, a commitment to emancipation, and trial years of teaching before deciding upon a career as antislavery agent. But the differences were dramatic. Watkins Harper entered the workforce as a girl. There was no Oberlin education for her. And while her commitment to the cause may have been no more deeply felt than Sallie's, her connection with antislavery was embedded in her person and her color. Her work was helping her people, "a people over whom weary ages of degradation have passed." "Whatever concerns them, as a race," she said, "concerns me." Events that touched her directly reinforced her decision to enter the public debate. In 1853, Maryland passed legislation forbidding free blacks from the North to come into the state. The fate of one man who did so and ended up being sold as a slave led her to pledge herself "to the Anti-Slavery cause." Slavery had robbed her of her home. "I might be so glad," she wrote, if "I could go home among my own kindred and people, but slavery comes up like a dark shadow between me and the home of my childhood." [106]

Like Sallie Holley, Watkins Harper perfected an acceptable version of the middling style. "Few speakers surpass her in using language and arguments so potently, in impressing and charming her audience," declared the *Provincial Freeman*. She was articulate, dignified, and composed, and, while often "fiery," her passion showed not "the slightest violation of good taste." Whereas Sallie Holley depended on revivalistic techniques, Watkins Harper relied on poetry (probably her own) and pathos to move her audience "to tears." Reading a poem like "The Slave Auction" affected listeners not only because of Watkin Harper's eloquent and pathetic delivery but also because her color allowed people to see her as a representation of her subject. Her other device—recitations of the wrongs of the slave, use of the fugitive slave theme—were no different from those white lecturers employed, but they became more powerful and real because her color encouraged imaginative connections with her subject.[107]

As a traveling lecturer, first for the Maine Anti-Slavery Society, and then as an agent in Pennsylvania and the Midwest, Watkins Harper faced the same sorts of conditions as her white counterparts. But as a black woman, the experience of lecturing was bittersweet. On the one hand, there was the gratification of appreciative audiences, both white and black, who listened to her and bought her book of poems. Her success reinforced a positive view of black ability. She had the satisfying sense of doing her duty. As she wrote to Still from Maine, "My life reminds me of a beautiful dream." Acceptance and approval from white abolitionists pleased her. In Maine, she traveled with the agent of the state antislavery society, "a pleasant, dear, sweet lady. . . . We travel together, eat together, and sleep together (she is a white women.)." On the other hand, as her parenthetical aside implied, there were strains involved in moving in white abolitionist circles. She was always on view, always an example of what the black race could be. To be black as well as female was a double responsibility. Perhaps this was the meaning behind her comment to Still that "I have not been in one colored person's house since I left Massachusetts."[108]

The lecturing circuit hardly provided an easy or comfortable existence, but for Watkins Harper, it was less easy and comfortable because of her efforts at self-denial, prompted by her identification with slaves. She observed the principle of free produce, for "how can we pamper our appetites upon luxuries drawn from reluctant fingers." She deprived herself in order to send money to be used for escaping fugitives.[109]

Whether the occasional violence she encountered in the Midwest and Ohio was related to race is impossible to say, for Lucy Colman, a white lecturer, faced similar hostility. Watkins Harper reported an incident of "rowdyism" in Columbiana, Ohio, and elsewhere; and while she was in Churchill, someone "removed some linch pins from our wagon. It was, however, discovered in time to prevent any injury to life or limb."[110]

If there was some ambiguity about the motivations of Ohioans, there was none about the residents of Pennsylvania. Watkins Harper considered the state "the meanest of all, as far as the treatment of colored people is concerned." Unlike white lecturers, she was subjected to rude behavior in everyday situations. In one place, the conductor tried to eject her from a trolley car. A mediator suggested that she sit in a corner, but she refused to move from her seat. "When I was about to leave," she recalled, the conductor "refused my money, and I threw it down on the car floor." And this was hardly the only time she was "insulted." "The shadow of slavery, oh how drearily it hangs," she reflected.[111]

At the end of the decade, despite the greater receptivity to the abolitionist message apparent in the northern public, both racism and the continued existence of slavery showed how far abolitionism still had to go before its supporters could proclaim victory. But many abolitionists suspected that the means to that victory would more likely be violent than peaceable and that violence would come sooner rather than later. When Elizabeth Chace draped her front door with black crepe streamers to mark the execution of John Brown, and when African American men and women in Detroit held a concert to raise funds for a monument to John Brown's black associates, they were taking steps away from moral suasion toward more ominous strategies for abolitionism and for the country at large.[112]

Chapter 6
Emancipation at Last

Strike grandly, in his hour sublime,

A blow to ring through endless time!

Strike! for the listening ages wait!

Emancipate! Emancipate![1]

In the winter of 1840, in Dover, New Hampshire, a group of women signed the constitution for an antislavery sewing circle, thereby pledging themselves to work for the cause of immediate emancipation "by discussion, collecting and disseminating information on the subject of Slavery and raising funds in aid of the Anti-Slavery cause." Over the years, their activities reflected the changing rhythms of abolitionism. They contributed money and clothing to the Canadian mission for fugitives, listened to former slaves, one of them "with the *branded hand*," describing the evils of slavery, sustained an antislavery concert of prayer for decades, circulated and signed petitions, distributed antislavery tracts, and contributed to the American Missionary Association (AMA), an evangelical antislavery organization founded in 1846. In the 1850s, the Dover women supported the free settlers in Kansas and organized a citywide meeting on the subject. When war finally came in 1861, the members of the sewing society, like so many other women in the North, made bandages for soldiers and formed a soldiers' aid society. But their work for white soldiers did not replace their interest in the slave. As increasing numbers of southern blacks fled across Union lines, the women grew anxious about the plight of the contrabands and their future as free people. Their concern led to a name change and new focus. The Dover Anti-Slavery Sewing Circle became the Dover Anti-Slavery and Freedmen's Aid Society.[2]

The minutes of the Dover Anti-Slavery Sewing Circle reveal the ways in which women in that community carried their abolitionist commitments into wartime. While the records are silent about how the women felt as their causes became more acceptable in the North, they may well have shared the elation of two members of the Philadelphia Female Anti-Slavery Society. Wrote Mary Grew, "After 30 years of persecution . . . abolitionists . . . see with joy their own arguments and phraseology adopted" by the city's "prominent journals." Sarah Pugh reflected on the wondrous fact that her society could make money by holding an antislavery lecture. "To think that the day has come to supply our Treasury instead of emptying it on such an occasion. What next?"[3]

The feeling of being in the mainstream was all the sweeter for the hostility that had preceded it. Tolerance for abolitionism had grown during the 1850s, but, when southern states began to secede from the Union after Lincoln's election, abolitionists suffered renewed unpopularity. Desire to keep the Union intact and to avoid bloodshed was strong. Many blamed abolitionist agitation for the South's secession. Levi Coffin, the Quaker conductor of the underground railroad in Cincinnati, noted that all the churches were holding meetings "to pray that . . . the awful calamities of war [be] averted. Acknowledgements were made of our sins, such as intemperance and Sabbath-breaking . . . but the sin of slavery was not mentioned." In several northern cities, workers held huge meetings urging Lincoln to compromise with the South. Unfriendly crowds once again broke up abolitionist meetings. Reflecting the timing of her own entry into abolitionism in the 1850s, Susan B. Anthony described the mob actions during the winter of 1861 as "unprecedented" and harmful. Not only had they prevented lecturers from presenting the abolitionist perspective on events, but they had also had made it impossible for her to meet expenses. Antagonism had taken on a personal character when opponents paraded effigies of Susan and her abolitionist colleague Samuel May engaging in sexual activity.[4]

In Boston, an unfriendly throng prevented Frederick Douglass from delivering an address honoring the "martyrdom" of John Brown. In what was one of the more remarkable features of the tumultuous meeting, women abolitionists seated in the balcony entered into the fray without any concern for decorum. They cheered Douglass, hissed and shouted at his opponents, and were disorderly and abusive when the police forced them out of the auditorium. One woman, a newspaper reported, told the policeman who was hurrying her down the stairs, " 'I am a mother, but if I had you in a good place wouldn't I give it to you.' (Down the stairs she went with a jump.)" [5]

With the outbreak of war, antipathy toward abolitionists died away to be replaced eventually with respect and acceptance. From the abolitionist viewpoint, however, the new acceptability did not warrant a cessation of antislavery efforts. Much needed to be done. Lincoln, like most northerners, went to war to save the Union, not to end slavery. The immediate challenge, therefore, was to make the emancipation of the slaves first a war goal and then a reality. Along with their male counterparts, women abolitionists took part in this campaign as well as in the other endeavors the conflict generated.

Women abolitionists' activities during the war represented a culmination and expansion of the varied efforts they had undertaken during the preceding thirty years. White women had created and circulated propaganda, raised thousands of dollars for the cause, made speeches, petitioned the government, assisted fugitives, taught blacks to read and write, opposed segregation, and lobbied their churches to take a public stand against slavery. African American women had joined white women in some of these efforts but, because of prejudice and a difference in focus, had more frequently struggled on their own to improve the situation of freed and fugitive black men and women.

During the war, female abolitionists relied upon many of the tactics that had served them in the past, but they often employed them on a larger and more public scale. Some work that had never been central for most women, like support for black education, now became so. While some criticism of women's activities continued (the New York *World* called the organizing meeting for a large petition drive a "witches Sabbath"), abolitionist tactics often attracted praise and even emulation. The large sanitary fairs mounted by northern women during the war may well have been inspired by the profitable antislavery fairs that had been held for so many years. Women speakers gained new respectability. In the congressional elections of 1863, Republican politicians in several states vied for the talents of abolitionist lecturer Anna Dickinson to make the party's case to voters.[6]

The outbreak of the war drew the various factions of abolitionism closer together. In Rochester, New York, the evangelically oriented Ladies' Anti-Slavery Society cooperated with Garrisonian female abolitionists to support contraband relief. At the national level, as prominent abolitionists like

EXPULSION OF NEGROES AND ABOLITIONISTS FROM TREMONT TEMPLE, BOSTON, MASSACHUSETTS, ON DECEMBER 3, 1860.

The disorderly nature of this antislavery meeting and the unrestrained behavior
of the women in the audience are apparent in this 1860 illustration for
Harper's Weekly. *(Boston Athenæum)*

Frederick Douglass rejoined its ranks, the American Anti-Slavery Society took on renewed importance as the voice of abolitionism.[7]

As had been true for many years, however, abolitionists continued to work in a variety of settings and styles. Long-lived antislavery societies and sewing circles were joined by new local and national organizations like freedmen's aid societies and the Woman's National Loyal League. The American Missionary Association, founded to do missionary and anti-slavery work at home and abroad, took on an educational mission among freed men and women. Some organizations adopted the methods of efficiency and business; others operated on familiar benevolent principles, resisting attempts to force them into new modes of operation. While collective opportunities proliferated, some abolitionists continued to prefer working for the common goal of emancipation and freedom as individuals rather than as members of any organization.[8]

The literature on the Civil War is immense, and this chapter, which sketches the involvement of abolitionist women during the conflict, is meant to be suggestive rather than exhaustive. While much research remains to be done, evidence points to the close connections between the past efforts of abolitionist women and their contributions during the war years. Abolitionist women's wartime projects built upon and extended activities pursued over three decades. Unlike most northern women, women abolitionists needed no encouragement to enter the public realm, for they had been operating there for years. Many were experienced and relaxed in their role as advocates of change and suffered few of the conflicted feelings that had accompanied early forays into antislavery work. Younger women who had grown up with the movement had precedents to guide their activism and to embolden them to work on a larger, businesslike scale. Often able to mantle their actions in the rhetoric of patriotism, they lobbied politicians, made their case before the public, and proved instrumental during political campaigns. While few of them were feminists, their activities suggested how the climate for female activism had changed and how the role that abolitionism of all stripes had played in encouraging women to adopt public activities and advocacy.[9]

The fact of war with the South and the restricted nature of the war's purpose—to restore the Union with slavery apparently intact—made the necessity of operating in the political arena obvious to most abolitionists. As Lucretia Mott pointed out, "Those in power" had to be forced to recognize "how unavailing is their pro-slavery conservatism." Women embraced the task of encouraging northern public opinion, politicians, and especially Lincoln to accept emancipation of the slaves as the war's goal. As the *Liberator* emphasized, it was "in character for *women*, not only to aid and comfort the soldiers . . . but to urge on government to follow up the present most righteous war with magnanimous offer of assisting to extinguish slavery."[10]

"I am all the time sending paragraphs and collections of facts to the newspapers, to help public opinion on in the right direction," wrote Maria Child to a friend. Sympathetic to the policy of the Boston Emancipation League, founded in September 1861 by abolitionists, Republicans, and former supporters of John Brown, Maria developed materials to prove that slavery not only lay at the heart of the conflict but also assisted the South's efforts to establish independence. Emancipation of the slaves, she argued, would weaken the southern war effort and lead to northern victory. Eager to have mainstream papers publish her materials without the slightest taint of fanaticism, she sent her contributions "under cover," or, anonymously. She urged others to barrage the public with similar messages. Realizing that "nothing on earth has such effect on the popular heart as Songs," she encouraged the poet Whittier to write lyrics for the soldiers that would make clear "what they went to fight for . . .—home, country, and liberty, and indignantly . . . [proclaim] that they did *not* go to hunt slaves." The song that captured the imagination of troops and the home front alike while it made the case for freedom was not a composition of Whittier's, however, but Julia Ward Howe's moving "Battle Hymn of the Republic." Julia, dismayed that she could give little to the cause—her husband was too old and her sons too young—took to heart her abolitionist minister's suggestion that she write some "good" words to the tune of "John Brown's Body." That very night, inspiration came to her, and, as she "lay waiting for the dawn, the long lines of the desired poem began to twine themselves" in her mind.[11]

Anna Dickinson, a young Quaker abolitionist, began an astonishing lecturing career by pointing out the necessity of emancipation as a war goal. "We have no war cry—no noble motive," she argued in an 1861 speech before the Pennsylvania Anti-Slavery Society. "While the flag of freedom waves merely for the white man, God will be against us." Using the same basic reasoning about the connection between slavery and southern persistence as Maria Child, Anna made an effective and melodramatic case that moved audiences. As the *Providence Press* noted in 1862, "With the tongue of *a dozen women*, she combines the boldness of forty men." Anna Dickinson became the most popular female abolitionist speaker of the war years, but others, like Hannah Cutler, who stumped the Midwest with a lecture entitled "The Christian Policy of Emancipation," presented powerful reasons to endorse emancipation.[12]

In Rhode Island, Elizabeth Chace also found herself energized by the need to change the war's focus. In the early days of the war, she had told her children confidently that "slavery will be destroyed." But when Lincoln did nothing to make emancipation part of the war effort, she went into action, securing speakers for public meetings, raising money to support antislavery work, and, as she had in the 1830s, circulating petitions. Even her children were recruited to go "on expeditions from house to house" to get signatures on petitions urging the necessity of emancipation.[13]

Once again, petitioning became one of the major vehicles for abolitionist women to express their opinions. "You ask why they, at Washington, wait? They wait for us to speak," declared one woman in the pages of the *Liberator*. Wartime petitioning seems to have begun almost spontaneously. As early as July 1861, American Anti-Slavery Society lecturer Josephine Griffing was collecting signatures supporting emancipation as she traveled through Michigan. She reported that many signed, and some expressed deep commitment to abolitionism as they did so. Said one women, "I have sent my only son to the army, and precious as his life is to me, I willingly risk it for the liberty of the slave, and the freedom of the country." This woman's sense that as a mother of a soldier she had a right to be heard was a point petition drives emphasized. The argument clearly resonated with female signers. By 1862, Senator Charles Sumner had presented his colleagues with petitions with over 23,000 women's names.[14]

In 1863, a group of abolitionist women who were now taking on leadership positions founded the Woman's National Loyal League to coordinate petitioning at the national level. Appealing to the notion that women had a moral duty to confront the evils of slavery, a duty that had supported female abolitionism from the beginning and still touched a powerful chord despite the emphasis on the part of some war workers on "masculine" values, the new organization coordinated a vast petition drive that dwarfed previous efforts. The petitions, to be signed by women over eighteen (and eventually by men as well), asked Congress to "pass, at the earliest practicable day, an Act emancipating all persons of African descent held to involuntary service or labor in the United States." Elizabeth Cady Stanton, one of the major forces behind the league, hoped to secure over a million signatures.[15] Petition gatherers also tried to collect at least a penny from each person who agreed to sign the petition. Although the National Loyal League was never as popular as more conservative organizations like soldiers' aid societies, the contributions showed widespread grassroots support for the petitioning efforts and sympathy for its objectives.[16]

Organizers drove home the message of their campaign with the badge worn by supporters. On the badge was a slave, rising to his feet, breaking his chains. "We have had the negro in every variety of posture—hopeless, imploring, crouching at the feet of the goddess of Liberty. But now, in harmony, with our own day, *our* negro is striking the blow himself with his own right hand. I wish every loyal woman in the nation would wear this badge," Elizabeth Cady Stanton said.[17]

In early 1864, Sumner presented his colleagues with petitions bearing 100,000 signatures, 65,601 of them female. "These signatures represent, mothers, wives, sisters & daughters of honest men who have fought and died for our country," the letter accompanying the petition explained. Because "the 'Right of Petition,'" the letter continued, "is woman's only political right under our government, it is the sacred duty of her representatives to give this petition earnest careful consideration." Ultimately, women collected 400,000 signatures, more than had ever been secured for one purpose before. One scholar's estimate that one of every twenty-four northerners signed a petition suggests the scope of the effort and its importance as an expression of public opinion. The results of the campaign supported the argument that the North was willing to wage war on new terms and helped to push politicians and the president toward acceptance of the emancipation of slavery as a war goal.[18]

The Philadelphia Female Anti-Slavery Society, like a number of other local abolitionist groups, cooperated with the national petitioning drive. At least two of the three women on the committee charged with circulating the petition were black. In Chicago, the auxiliary of the National Loyal League included women of both races. But for the most part, the National Loyal League was a white organization. Although black members were not barred, neither were they encouraged to join. Given the goals of the league, its founders' failure to make it biracial was an ironic commentary on the limitations of white abolitionism and perhaps of the focus of black women's past efforts on elevating free blacks in the North. Although black women certainly favored the emancipation of the slaves and the attainment of black legal and civil rights, and although black and white women did cooperate during the war, black and white abolitionist women continued to pursue many of their objectives, whether shared or not, independently of one another.[19]

When war broke out, white women, abolitionist and nonabolitionist alike, involved themselves in war work. They made bandages, established sanitary societies, and began to organize ways to supply the soldiers' needs. Since blacks could not yet serve in the army, these activities were irrelevant to the concerns of black women. Moreover, many shared the hesitation of their white counterparts to support a war whose objective was to bring the South and its system of slavery back into the Union. But when thousands of slaves, many of them women and children, fled to Union-held territories, black women found a focus for activism. Contrabands often arrived in pathetic condition. Describing what was a common sight in the contraband camps, Maria Mann noted men, women, and children "covered with vermin [and] . . . open sores and consumed with diarrhea." Inadequate clothing and housing, as well as poor sanitation, contributed to suffering and disease. Responding to the needs of their own race, black women in many communities established female associations with titles like "Colored Ladies Freedmen and Soldiers Aid Society" and "Society of Colored Ladies of Syracuse."[20]

Sattira Ford Douglas, a free black woman from Illinois, left suggestive evidence of her activism. Ford Douglas's solid education and middle-class status set her apart from the majority of African American women. Many black women, if not most, however, probably shared her growing understanding of the measures that were needed to improve the situation of American blacks, whether born free or enslaved. Ford Douglas's wartime efforts grew out of an established interest in abolitionism. As a teenager, she had pursued antislavery causes and collected subscriptions for the *Provincial Freeman*, the Canadian emigrationist newspaper edited by Mary Ann Shadd Cary and H. Ford Douglas, Sattira's future husband. When war broke out, H. Ford Douglas enlisted in the Illinois Infantry Volunteers, thus becoming one of the few blacks to join a white company. During his absence, Sattira Ford Douglas cooperated with those organizations supporting her reform interests. At first she confined herself to local and familiar activities and people. Working within the decades-old tradition of abolitionist sewing circles, Ford Douglas and the other members of the Chicago Colored Ladies Freedmen's Aid Society met several times a week to prepare clothes and other items needed by contrabands in the Mississippi Valley and Kansas. Inevitably, they also found themselves raising funds. As the organization's treasurer, Ford Douglas must have been involved in the decision to generate income by sponsoring lectures in the black community and to reach beyond Chicago by hiring Mary Ann Shadd Cary as a financial agent. By 1864, Ford Douglas had decided to involve herself personally in refugee work. Backed by Chicago's racially mixed auxiliary of the Woman's National Loyal League, she went to Kansas to teach in a school for freed people. As she assessed the needs of the contrabands, she called upon her former associates in the Chicago Colored Ladies Freedmen's Aid Society for assistance and broadened her base of support by sending accounts of her work to the *Weekly Anglo-African*. Sattira Ford Douglas's ability to make her case to a variety of abolitionist organizations and audiences, both black and white, made her a successful advocate for the needs of freedpeople.[21]

As in Chicago, black women in the capital saw the plight of contrabands as their own particular responsibility. Contrabands poured into Washington, D.C., overwhelming governmental resources. The situation prompted forty of the city's black women to organize a Contraband Relief Association in 1862. Members pledged "to do all we can to alleviate . . . [the] sufferings" of "the hitherto oppressed people of a portion of God's race to be cast among us in a most deplorable condition." Despite the women's "limited means," the president, Elizabeth Keckley, hoped to reach into the pockets of "well-to-do colored people" to help "the suffering blacks." Making the organization a center for the collection of funds and goods, the women linked up with black churches, fugitive aid societies, and individual donors in their own city as well as in communities like Boston, Brooklyn, and New Haven. Elizabeth Keckley also undertook fund-raising tours.[22]

When African Americans became eligible for military service, some women joined black leaders in urging men to enlist. Sattira Ford Douglas, writing for both the *Weekly Anglo-African* and the *Christian Recorder*, argued that service would bring the recognition that black people needed to win respect and rights. "If they do not now enroll themselves among those other noble men who have gone forth to do battle . . . it will only prove the correctness of the aspersion indulged in by our enemies, that we are unworthy of those rights that they have so long upheld from us," she explained. "Colored men have everything to gain in this conflict: liberty, honor, social and political position." As a paid recruiting agent, Mary Ann Shadd Cary traveled throughout the North and Canada West to make the case for enlistment. Her success as a recruiter led one person to observe, "It takes a woman to pick out a good man." [23]

Once blacks entered military service, black women, like white women, set up a network of soldiers' aid societies. The double standard that paid black soldiers less than their white counterparts lent special importance to this aid work, which extended to the families of black soldiers as well. Maria Child attended a fair held to help the widows and children of African American soldiers. The organizers' decorative scheme brought home the message that black soldiers, like white citizen soldiers, had done their patriotic duty. "The colored ladies who presided over it had decorated [the hall] . . . very tastefully with stars and stripes," Maria observed. She also noted how many longtime abolitionists lent their support to the fair's goal and its rationale by coming to the fair. Other white abolitionists also proved themselves sensitive to the problems posed by black military service. The great Northwestern Sanitary Fair of 1864 had as its object the families of black soldiers. As an article in the *Liberator* explained, the service of black soldiers was responsible for saving the life of many a white woman's husband. [24]

"We are having at our Pace St. meeting-house an exciting time just now, having formed a Freedmen's Association, after the example of our Orthodox Friends," wrote Lucretia Mott in 1864. While their commitment did not grow out of a sense of racial identification, white abolitionist women also gathered in local freedmen's aid societies to sew and collect supplies for contrabands. Some societies operated independently, preferring to make their own decisions and to direct their own aid as they saw fit. Other societies and many individuals cooperated with national secular relief efforts or with their denominations or the evangelically oriented AMA. [25]

During the 1840s and 1850s, most antislavery women had sympathized with the evangelical and political camps of abolitionism. It was not surprising, then, that when the war broke out individual women started to send donations to the AMA, the organization that became the "natural successor" to the American and Foreign Anti-Slavery Society in the 1850s. Wrote one woman from New York, "I pray this may be the beginning of the emancipation of the African race." Added another, "Be sure and take good care of the poor 'contrabands' for God has opened up a new field." One Freeport, Maine, seamstress, demonstrating her willingness to sacrifice for the freed people, contributed $50 to the AMA. The size of her gift was unusual. Most gave only a small amount, suggesting both interest in the future of black people and their modest circumstances.[26]

The needs of contrabands far outweighed resources. To increase revenue, the AMA began to send speakers of both races to make the case for the contrabands. At least one black woman, Edmonia Highgate, canvassed for the AMA. Her inclusion in the roster of speakers indicated how much antislavery had changed. Years earlier, Lewis Tappan, one of the leaders of the evangelical organization, had left the AAS partly in protest over the full participation of women. Now, in 1864 and 1865, Highgate was speaking and collecting funds for the AMA in upstate New York.[27]

Revenues had almost tripled by the time of Highgate's tour. As a nominally nonsectarian but avowedly evangelical and missionary organization, the AMA tapped into the still powerful religious commitments that had nourished abolitionism and established profitable connections with several denominations. Longtime sympathizers with abolitionism, including Quaker and Wesleyan Methodist congregations, among others, began to collect money for the AMA. The women of these churches also rounded up supplies to send to the AMA.[28]

From one perspective, contraband work was merely an extension of the efforts women had made to assist fugitive slaves in the United States and in Canada. But their new work was on a scale that was unprecedented. In the early years of the war, Orthodox Friends in Philadelphia spent $6,000 on clothing for contrabands and made 7,000 garments. In central and western New York State, sewing circles, representing different stripes of prewar abolitionism, now cooperated to meet the needs of Alexandria's contraband population. Other groups of abolitionist women matched these efforts.[29]

Not only were the demands on women's time, money, and energy greater in wartime, but the connection with the former slave was also closer. Northern groups often solicited and received detailed reports from the field. Rachel Jackson, a member of the Philadelphia Female Anti-Slavery Society, informed society members about the conditions she encountered in a Washington contraband camp; Julia Wilbur, the agent for the Rochester

Ladies' Anti-Slavery Society, reported what she had seen to that organization and to more radical abolitionist women as well. The Philadelphia society also carried on extensive correspondence with other field workers. Detailed accounts about former slaves and the conditions in which they lived also appeared in northern papers and journals. Except for concrete assistance to fugitive slaves, working for emancipation had often been an abstract moral duty. Now that abstract duty became concrete and compelling. As Lewis Tappan's wife, Sarah, pointed out, "God never laid so great a work upon one generation as he has on this."[30]

As had been true so often in the past, fund-raising constituted an important aspect of women's work. While abolitionist women continued to raise money to support general antislavery activities, they also took on new projects. Northern societies not only solicited and prepared goods like clothing, bedding, and books, but they also collected money to support educational and relief efforts among the contrabands. Some female societies sponsored a teacher in the South, taking on the responsibility for her salary and classroom activities. Other groups supported assistance to refugee slaves. Quakers in Philadelphia sent Harriet Jacobs, an escaped slave herself, to nurse contrabands in Alexandria.[31]

Relief work attracted an unknown number of single, widowed, and married women away from their homes and placed them in challenging and complex situations. Laura Haviland, a founder of and teacher at the Raisin Institute, an integrated school in Michigan, and an active member of the underground railroad, made several tours south. While she was more famous and perhaps more aggressive than most, Laura's exertions suggest the many-sided character of women's relief efforts during the war years and the continued power of the identification of women with religious and moral duty.

Laura combined her soldiers' aid work with assistance to refugee slaves. Although she ultimately became a paid agent of the Freedmen's Aid Commission, she began her work in the familiar guise of a volunteer. Well organized and articulate, Laura was adept at both dealing with men in authority and utilizing the network of female societies and church groups to raise funds and supplies for her trips. Her conception of her mission, "to inquire after the health of this people, body, soul, and spirit," combined secular help with spiritual advice and was doubtlessly particularly appealing to evangelical abolitionists.[32]

Laura's secular task was to distribute to former slaves the basic necessities of life. The gratitude that they routinely expressed was deeply satisfying, as was her realization that she was meeting her donors' expectations of

PRIMARY SCHOOL FOR FREEDMEN, IN CHARGE OF Mrs. GREEN, AT VICKSBURG, MISSISSIPPI.—[SEE PAGE 398.]

The varied ages of the pupils in this Mississippi freedmen's school begin to suggest some of the challenges facing women who volunteered to teach former slaves. (Boston Athenæum)

her. How pleased they would be, she reflected, if they could "see me with open boxes, taking out garment after garment" and presenting them to the destitute recipients who exhibited the grateful behavior Laura thought appropriate. Her spiritual mission also brought rewards. Contrabands, she believed, responded to her moral homilies "to live soberly and honestly in the sight of all men." Often invited to speak during Sabbath services or at Sabbath schools, she mingled spiritual exhortations with fervent denunciations of slavery. Certainly her spirited condemnations of the slave system, if not her advice on the good life, elicited responses from her listeners. On one occasion, she reported proudly, the black preacher compared her to "an angel dropped down 'mongst us," and so many shook her hands that they were swollen for days.[33]

The educational work among freed people began in late 1861, the first year of the war when blacks at Virginia's Fort Monroe established a school. While education represented an extension of benevolent and abolitionist sympathies, it also had an important political purpose. "Upon our alleged inferiority is based our social ostracism and political proscription," Frances

Harper Watkins had declared when she described teaching as "some of the best anti-slavery work that can be done in this country." The goal first of emancipation and then of political and civil rights for freedmen depended on weakening or even destroying the stubborn belief in black inferiority. Abolitionists needed to present concrete "proof" of black achievement. In 1861, Mary Putnam, a Massachusetts women, had published anonymously a powerful and influential argument for black equality. Although the *Record of an Obscure Man* supposedly drew upon real life events to demonstrate black abilities, its author had actually depended on her imagination and logical skills to make her case. In late 1861, when Union forces occupied South Carolina's Sea Islands, where thousands of slaves lived, abolitionists finally had a major opportunity to base their case on facts not fancy. As Laura Towne, one of the first abolitionists to go to the Sea Islands, explained, "We have come to do anti-slavery work, and we think it noble work and mean to do it earnestly." [34]

When the war ended in 1865, over 900 northerners were teaching in the South. Twenty-seven-year-old Sarah Ann Dickey from Ohio was one of them. Unable to read or write until her teen years, Sarah had struggled to obtain an education and teacher's credentials. Her own journey from illiteracy to literacy undoubtedly made her sympathetic to the educational needs and ambitions of the contraband, but her interest in the slave went back to her own childhood, when she had dreamed of teaching slave children. In 1863, her dream became a reality. The Church of United Brethren in Christ chose her as a teacher for their school in Vicksburg. [35]

Like Sarah Dickey, most of the teachers who went south were female. Their sponsors included female antislavery societies, the nondenominational AMA, black and white church congregations, individual denominations, and secular freedmen's aid societies. What percentage of them were, like Laura Towne, avowed abolitionists is unclear. One scholar has estimated that only 8 percent of a sample of 560 teachers from New York had abolitionist sympathies. But his definition of abolitionism excludes those whose sense of moral duty rather than commitment to racial equality drew them south. Thus, he did not consider as an abolitionist Harriet Arnold, who felt "it the highest honor to occupy the most humble place in my masters vineyard teaching the poor downtrodden outcasts of humanity the way of salvation." Given the importance of duty as a motivating factor for abolitionists over the decades and their flawed commitment to racial justice, his definition probably excludes many of those who considered themselves abolitionists. [36]

In any case, avowed abolitionists were among those going south. Like

Laura Towne, they were motivated by abolitionist zeal and an awareness of the political and social significance of their work. Some had abolitionist credentials dating back to the early days of abolitionism. Abigail Gibbons, who had been the sole white member of a black women's abolitionist society in New York in the 1840s and who had come out of her Quaker meeting, became a nurse and worker in the contraband camp next to the hospital. Josephine Griffing, an AAS lecturer, was another old-timer who pursued aid and educational efforts in Washington, D.C. Others, like Lucy and Sarah Chase, two Quaker sisters from Worcester, Massachusetts, had come of age in abolitionism during the 1840s. Like the Chases, the majority of female teachers were women no longer youthful, seizing the opportunity for independence and usefulness in the antislavery cause. One study has established the average age of women teachers as just over thirty years.[37]

While most women who moved south to teach had taught school before taking on their new assignment, they were hardly prepared for the challenges awaiting them. Despite all they might have read or heard about the condition of slaves, reality stunned them. "It certainly takes great nerve to walk here . . . and not be disgusted or shocked or pained so much as to give it all up," exclaimed Laura Towne. Her colleague, Harriet Ware, pointed out some of the problems: "We are not used to these people—it is even very difficult to understand what they say." Another teacher recalled her bewildering situation. All her charges "were black as ink. . . . They all looked alike to me." Neither children or adults knew the basic rules of classroom behavior that the teachers had taken for granted in their previous schools. Classrooms were inadequate, and because so many former slaves clamored to learn reading and writing, classes were often large and crowded. Other demands on pupils' time meant irregular attendance as well.[38] Physical conditions in many of the camps undermined educational objectives, and teachers found themselves not just teaching reading, writing, classroom manners, values, and skills but doing relief work as well. They became expert at juggling responsibilities. To be successful at their posts, teachers often needed considerable managerial skills in addition to pedagogical expertise and a commitment to the freed people among whom they lived.

Lucy Chase's experiences with contrabands suggest some of the frustrations and rewards involved in work with freed people. In her early days on Virginia's Craney Island, Lucy was both elated and sobered by what she encountered. After years of activism, she rejoiced at the tangible nature of her task and its importance. "We are to give them a *chance*! which they never have had," she told her family at home. But the obstacles were formidable. The physical condition of the contrabands was serious but perhaps less so than what Lucy judged their moral and social inadequacies. Despite her Quaker background, Lucy disapproved of the character of slave religion. The prayer meeting she attended was a "painful exhibition of . . . barbarism. Their religious feeling is purely emotional; void of principles, and of no practical utility." Lucy was determined that former slaves learn to "worship aright," and to do so meant knowing "what is *right*!" Her missionary impulse was not purely religious or moral, for she also hoped to teach middle-class values and behavior and gender-specific norms. Much to her distress, the women, who had been mostly field hands, were ignorant of their domestic duties as she understood them. Inculcating them with proper ideas of their roles as mothers and wives was one part of her mission.[39]

Despite the "barbarous assaults" upon her "patience and forbearance," and the long hours that made her feel that her work was never done, Lucy was happy. She and her sister were "in at the birth!" and successful at meeting great needs. They tackled all sorts of problems, including soliciting aid from northern societies for clothes, simple domestic articles, and educational supplies like slates and books. Lucy supervised the manufacture of beds and the making and mending of clothes, the latter task done while the sewers learned their ABCs. Although she did not abandon her middle-class standards, she was able to overcome her misgivings and enjoy warm interactions with her pupils. She attributed what she saw as defects not to any inherent racial weakness but to the slave system itself.[40]

As time passed, priorities shifted. As had been true in the efforts to help fugitives in Canada, concern grew that charity would sap recipients' sense of industry and independence. One of Lucy's Worcester relatives explained that the women in her society wanted parents to pay something for the children's clothing they were sending. "They will value the articles more[,] will learn more self reliance and feel more self respect than if they depend entirely upon charity," she explained. "But we would not have [relief workers] . . . fail to *give* wherever they are really destitute." This directive accorded with Lucy's sense that former slaves needed to become self-sufficient. "We further honor them by *leaving them alone*," she told friends at home.[41]

The desire to make former slaves independent in a short period of time may have been unrealistic, given their long experience with a system of forced labor and the limited economic opportunities actually available to them. But the need to demonstrate that African Americans were capable of emulating the virtues valued in northern society and of operating as free persons was politically necessary. Lucy, like other teachers, realized the importance of destroying old stereotypes that could justify denying black people rights. Despite long hours and fatigue, she wrote lengthy, detailed letters intended to circulate to family and members of contraband societies. Submissions to newspapers broadened her audience. Frances Gage, who became a correspondent for the *Herald Tribune*, and Charlotte Forten, who wrote for the *Atlantic Monthly*, were among the other women providing northerners with accounts of the progress that their pupils made.[42]

As teachers sought to shape northern public opinion, they discovered how stubbornly southerners clung to familiar race and gender norms. Because teachers and refugee workers were assisting former slaves, southerners angrily lashed out against them. According to some southerners, the women had forfeited any rights they once might have had as ladies. Abigail Gibbons received a letter warning her that she was "not needed at this place and you had better leave double Quick. . . . You old nigger lover yea worse an old hypocrit the devil has his house full of better people than ever you were you old Hell hound." Women, as had often been the case when they worked with free blacks in the early days of the abolitionist movement, drew criticism for having "negro[es] on the brain," for elevating blacks *"above the whites."* Threatening behavior sometimes reinforced abusive language. Lydia Montague, disparaged as a "nigger teacher," discovered her schoolroom ravaged by those hostile to her work. While much of the violent behavior may have been the work of local men, southern women also turned a cold shoulder on the interlopers.[43]

While a majority of teachers were white, black women, in proportions exceeding those in the northern population, also joined the effort to elevate former slaves. Their motivation drew upon shared racial bonds as well as a recognition of the importance of the task to all black people. As one black editor stressed, "We have got to do our own work. . . . The process of transforming three million of slaves into citizens requires the aid of intelligent colored men and women. We are nearer to them than another class of persons; we can enter into their feelings and attract their sympathies better than any others can." Letters of application to the AMA echoed this point of view. Ellen Garrison Jackson, writing from Newport, Rhode Island, asked, "Who can feel the sympathy that we can who are identified with them?" Sarah Stanley, a Cleveland woman, saw herself bound to former slaves "by the ties of love and consanguinity; they are . . . my people."[44]

The belief that northern free blacks and freed blacks had a natural sympathy for southern freedpeople may often have proved true and lay behind the AMA's interest in recruiting blacks. But, in their new situation, some northern black women found themselves as uncomfortable initially as any white teacher. The American Missionary Association's policy of recruiting cultivated black women as teachers may have contributed to early awkwardness between black teachers and their pupils. Despite her strong sense of duty, Oberlin-educated Sarah Stanley expected her charges would be ignorant and degraded. Charlotte Forten, a member of Philadelphia's black elite, initially described former slaves as "certainly the most dismal specimens I ever saw." Although she soon had a more positive impression, Charlotte's view of freedpeople as "poor creatures" suggests the distance she initially felt from her charges.[45]

While black and white teachers experienced similar reactions to their work and faced similar conditions as they tried to bring black people into freedom, race shaped their experiences. Idealism and a sense of duty prompted both white and black abolitionist women to volunteer for teaching assignments, but black women had pressing economic imperatives. Those who applied to become teachers with the AMA were well educated but, like most free black women, in very modest circumstances. Sarah Stanley described herself as "possessing no wealth and having nothing to give but my life to the work." Some prospective black teachers were not only supporting themselves but often helping family members as well. Some found the pay insufficient to meet their obligations. As one applicant explained, "I would consider [the salary] a liberal remuneration if it were not that I have a mother, towards whose support I am obliged to contribute to some extent."[46]

When the white Chase sisters began to consider whether their "mission" demanded war work, their Quaker father merely asked whether their experience, constitutions, and health were equal to camp life. Money played no apparent role in their decision to work with contrabands. Other white women came from families of artisans, shopkeepers, and farmers, however, and were less affluent than the Chases. Although struggling, these families owned property and were in a position to help their daughters. Eventually Laura Towne accepted a salary, but for the first few years she taught in the South she did so as a volunteer.[47]

For white teachers, the journey south could be a pleasurable experience, but for black teachers the trip often turned out to be an exercise in humiliation. Clara Duncan was initiated into what it meant to be a black AMA teacher in the South during her train journey to Virginia. Called a "nigger wench," she was barred from sitting or dining with whites. Once in the South, she and other black teachers, like their white counterparts, faced unconcealed hostility. Ellen Jackson described an incident that took place on a sidewalk in Port Deposit, Maryland. Not content with simply stepping on her dress, a white man lashed out at Jackson, calling her "a nigger" and warning her "he would not have any of my sass and . . . would slap me in the mouth." Jackson claimed this threatening behavior had not cowed her: "I have found out one thing about these people if they attack you be careful to stand your ground and they will leave you[,] but if you run they will follow."[48]

Sarah Stanley discovered that some of her white coworkers were prejudiced against her despite her Oberlin credentials and the "slight admixture of negro blood in . . . [her] veins." She and the other black teachers who came to Norfolk had inferior teaching conditions compared to those of white teachers, and they were housed separately. When they joined white associates in the mission house in 1864, they found the resident missionary took "an especial pleasure in advocating the inferiority of 'negroes' and the necessity of social distinction, with special application to colored missionary teachers." The matron was equally prejudiced. "Oh!" exclaimed Stanley, "if we could have in this work only earnest, humble, true-hearted Christians—regarding all mankind as brothers; feeling not that the great desire of all hearts should be to wear a Saxon complexion, how blessed it would be." Problems between black and white teachers pointed to the difficult future of race relations and the stubborn force of prejudice even among some of those laboring to elevate freed people. When racial relations were cordial, black teachers could feel very lonely. As Charlotte Forten wrote in her diary, "Kindness, most invariable . . . I meet with constantly[,] but congeniality I find not at all in this house."[49]

Despite the difficult conditions, black teachers persisted. Their decision to educate freedpeople represented more of a long-term involvement than was the case for most white women. On the average, black teachers from New York stayed at their posts for over four years, compared to white women's tenure of about two and a half years. Blanche Harris, from Michigan, stayed in the field far longer than the New York figures suggest. Her first appointment was in 1863 in Norfolk, Virginia. Within a few months, her health was "declining," and she felt "compelled to resign my position as missionary teacher, hoping that my field of usefulness is not entirely [over]." Nine months later, recovered, she applied to the AMA once again. She taught in Natchez, Mississippi, until 1867, then went on to North Carolina under the auspices of a Quaker organization, where she taught until her marriage in 1871.[50]

One white teacher, Susan Walker, decided she was "not prepared to accept" teaching former slaves as her "life-work" because she did not feel "a drawing towards it." Worn out by a heavy schedule of teaching or interested in pursuing other interests, most white teachers left the field. Confusion over the essential meaning of abolitionism also contributed to that pattern of retreat and had ramifications for all those men and women who had considered themselves abolitionists.

Most of the women who had accepted the unpopular cause of emancipation were responding to the stern demands of moral duty. Few had bothered to explore what emancipation really signified and what freedom for black people might mean. The constitutions of early antislavery societies had often spoke of the need to elevate the character of blacks, to correct "prevailing and wicked prejudices," and to secure for them "an equality, with the whites of civil and religious privileges." While white women made some modest efforts to realize these goals, few considered them primary. Black women's organizations always were more attuned to the difficulties facing free black people and less to the abstract requirements of moral duty than their white counterparts. With the passage of time, women of both races had turned to assist fugitives as they adapted to freedom in Canada. But the Canadian settlements were remote, and the news about the progress and problems of former slaves was mostly secondhand. Thus, as the likelihood of emancipation and freedom came closer, few had explored the meaning of basic assumptions and terms.[51]

The milestones in the struggle to end slavery came, forcing abolitionists to confront difficult questions. What signaled the end of slavery? Lincoln's Emancipation Proclamation? The Thirteenth Amendment? The North's victory? Some other event or trend like a decline in racial prejudice? What was the real meaning of freedom for former slaves? As early as 1862, Maria Chapman, one of the driving forces during the first decades of abolitionism, declared "that the work of Abolitionists—specifically is done: in that the Nation has answered to the question." "This," reported William Nell to Rochester abolitionist Amy Post, "is the position she now occupies not but that there are many branches of usefulness for antislavery reformers to work in but their main mission is completed and hence she retires from active participancy." Most women did not retire so precipitously. The year after Maria's decision, Lucy Stone argued that "there is a great deal of proslavery sentiment yet to be rooted out."[52]

The difficulty of deciding when the movement had accomplished its purpose called into question the future of abolitionism and its organizations. What was the relationship between freedmen's aid societies and antislavery societies? Should the latter be disbanded? Garrison himself, although recognizing the need to continue work among freedmen, urged members to dissolve the American Anti-Slavery Society in 1865. As he told Maria Child, since "slavery is being abolished, and the rebellion at last suddenly suppressed, we are now in an anomalous and very complex condition."

Despite his belief that "much of the old slaveholding spirit remains," he was hopeful that there was "irresistible" progress toward freedom and free institutions. Most of the members of the American Anti-Slavery Society disagreed with his assessment. Lizzie Gay reflected the majority viewpoint in her letter to Philadelphian Sarah Pugh: "I lean very much to the side of those who would carry it on. Better keep on the safe side. When Slavery is everywhere in this country actually wiped out, then we can say our work is done." The American Anti-Slavery Society and other societies, like the Philadelphia Female Anti-Slavery Society, continued on into the 1870s. One of the last efforts of the Philadelphia women focused on eliminating segregation in the city's streetcars.[53]

Even when societies disbanded, some men and women questioned the move. Former lecturer Sallie Holley could hardly accept a future without the sociability and support yearly antislavery meetings provided. But more serious than her personal loss was the meaning of dissolution for the former slaves. Antislavery societies had acted as watchdogs for African Americans. "The mere fact that the coloured race has such friends and guardians is a strong defence and high tower of deliverance from more wrongs and insults," she pointed out. "The American Nation is not good enough to be trusted with the care of the black race—The blacks still need their long-tried and faithful of the American Anti-Slavery Society, which is a very different individual from the Nation."[54]

Midway through the war, Frances Gage had optimistically looked to the future and the role women would play at that time. "If our army is victorious," she had said, "every womanly energy will find an outlet in this noble work" among freedpeople. However, the loss of the old simple focus on emancipation, the dissolution of antislavery societies that had taken some formal responsibility for the plight of black people, and the disappearance of collective events that had kept the faith alive all dealt a blow to continuing involvement in the affairs of black Americans. The reality of southern resistance to new racial arrangements and persistent northern racism and indifference all contributed to lassitude. As time passed, many women lost their enthusiasm for the work. Young women who had grown up in abolitionism, like Lillie Chace, felt lost and struggled to find a compelling interest to replace it. Some, perhaps most, eventually discovered other causes—moral reform, suffrage, and homes for veterans, widows, and orphans—and hoped for the best in terms of the former slaves.[55]

The choices of some of the better-known women are suggestive. Elizabeth Chace, Lucy Stone, and Elizabeth Cady Stanton, all Garrisonians, used their expertise and experience in working for women's rights. Doubtless the temperance movement and women's church groups, like missionary associations, also attracted some of those who wished to improve the world after the war had ended. Lucretia Mott recognized the new realities. "The claims of the Indians—so long injured & cheated & wronged in so many ways," she observed, "seem now, with many of our Friends, to take the place of the Freedmen, so that we can hardly collect money eno' to pay our 8 or 10 teachers [in the] South." [56]

Further research is needed to reveal the specific paths and causes the women who formed the basis for this study pursued after the war. But it is quite possible that most of the women whose activities were so important to the success of abolitionism appear in the historical record only because of their involvement in the movement. When the abolitionist newspapers published their last issues, when antislavery fairs and petitions that had energized informal communication networks ceased, when antislavery societies held their final meetings, the traditional outlets for these women's voices were gone.

A cadre of women, both black and white, did continue to work in the South or among northern blacks, but their efforts did not gain widespread support. Mary Still, an African American who had started her teaching career with a school for northern black children in the 1840s, became a teacher for the American Missionary Association during the war and taught after the war in AMA schools in South Carolina and Florida. Former lecturer Sallie Holley and her companion, Caroline Putnam, ran a school for blacks in Virginia for many years. In 1874, abolitionists gathered in Chicago to recall "the period of self-sacrifice, when Anti-Slavery principles were advocated in faith and hope; the progress of the reform and its growth in public opinion; and its final triumph; with congratulations at the success which we have been permitted to realize." Mary Still was probably not invited to the celebratory event, and Sallie Holley was too busy to attend it. As Sallie explained in a letter, she was engaged in "hand to hand conflict with the remains of the Old Slave Power." She had little time or energy for "congratulations or review of the past triumphs of the Anti-Slavery cause." [57]

Thus, the great efforts woman had made on behalf of immediate emancipation and the slave either came to an end or sputtered on here and there. The call of moral duty that had seemed so clear and compelling to abolitionist women for decades, that had taken them so demandingly from hearth and home, that had exposed them to ridicule and rudeness, grew silent before the ambiguities of race relations in the United States. There were other moral causes, to be sure, as Lucretia Mott had realized, and an expanded range of opportunities for professional and volunteer activities.

But most reformers focused on other peoples and problems, not the former slaves.

In time, most people would forget the great contributions women had made to abolitionism just as others would minimize the role northern women played during the Civil War. If the war represented a crisis in gender relations, as some scholars have suggested, many men and women were eager to put brakes on female activism. Even during the years when women were so important in sustaining the cause, some male abolitionists, perhaps uncomfortable with the reality of female involvement and the ways in which women interpreted "the plain commandments of God," refused to acknowledge the work women were doing. One Michigan abolitionist concealed the dimensions of female activism even as he acknowledged its importance. "Woman's influence," he wrote, "distilling like the dew of Heaven, gentle, constant and no less effectual, fertilizes and refreshes where it goes, and steals over the heart with irresistless power, which prompts to action." [58]

Women's involvement in abolitionism far surpassed the gentle, constant influence this man described. The Providence Female Anti-Slavery Circle conveyed the character of women's commitment more accurately in a resolution adopted in 1837: "Remember that our rights are sacred and invincible, and founded on the liberty of the gospel, that great emancipator for *women*." In this spirit, women had faced mobs to listen to abolitionist lectures, formed societies and spread antislavery doctrine in their neighborhoods, circulated petitions, sewed for fugitives and fairs, mounted financially and symbolically important antislavery bazaars, challenged church authorities, and helped to sustain antislavery churches. They had rallied to the third-party banners they had made and presented, passed out political propaganda, and argued with men about how to cast their votes. They had housed fugitives, raised funds to meet some of the needs of free black communities, and delivered antislavery lectures. Abolitionism had provided an emotional and moral focus for the activism of some, while it was only a passing interest for others. [59]

Above all, abolitionism had tested women's understanding of what it had meant to be female. In 1836, women in Andover, Massachusetts, had given the challenge, "Now let [woman] . . . use her tongue to speak on slavery." Over three decades, women had responded and rejoiced in their "strong minds and vigorous intellects . . . willing to labor in the cause." [60]

Notes

ABBREVIATIONS

AAS   American Anti-Slavery Society
AFAS   American and Foreign Anti-Slavery Society
AmAS   American Antiquarian Society, Worcester, Massachusetts
BFAS   Boston Female Anti-Slavery Society
BL   Bentley Library, University of Michigan, Ann Arbor
BPL   Boston Public Library, Boston, Massachusetts
BrFAS   Brooklyn Female Anti-Slavery Society
CLAS   Canton Ladies Anti-Slavery Society
CSL   Connecticut State Library, Hartford
EPI   Essex-Peabody Institute, Essex-Peabody Library, Salem, Massachusetts
GFP   Gay Family Papers, Butler Library, Columbia University, New York
HL   Houghton Library, Harvard University, Cambridge, Massachusetts
HSP   Historical Society of Pennsylvania, Philadelphia
KSUL   Kent State University Library, Kent, Ohio
LASD   Ladies Anti-Slavery Society of Dover
LFAS   Lynn Female Anti-Slavery Society
LHS   Lynn Historical Society
LOC   Library of Congress, Washington, D.C.
MHS   Massachusetts Historical Society, Boston
NHHS   New Hampshire Historical Society, Concord
PFAS   Philadelphia Female Anti-Slavery Society
SFAS   Salem Female Anti-Slavery Society
SL   Schlesinger Library, Radcliffe College, Cambridge, Massachusetts
WRHS   Western Reserve Historical Society, Cleveland, Ohio

INTRODUCTION

1. Quoted in Quist, " 'Great Majority of Our Subscribers,' " 337.
2. *Liberator*, October 19, 1847; quote from Stevens, " 'From Generation to Generation,' " 344.
3. In her essay, "The Political Activities of Antislavery Women," in *Majority Finds Its Past*, 112–28, Gerda Lerner did some fundamental work on female abolitionism and pointed out the challenges to recovering women's activism. Nancy A. Hewitt, "On Their Own Terms: A Historiographical Essay," in Yellin and Van Horne, eds., *Abolitionist Sisterhood*, 24–25; David Brion Davis, "Reflections on Abolitionism," 812, 813–28. See also Ashworth, "Relationship between Capitalism and Humanitarianism," 813–38.
4. Barnes and Dumond, eds., *Weld-Grimké Letters*, 287.
5. Douglass quote in Lutz, *Crusade for Freedom*, frontispiece.
6. *Liberator*, May 31, December 13, 1850.
7. William E. Gienapp, "Abolitionism and the Nature of Antebellum Reform," in Jacobs, ed., *Courage and Conscience*, 36.
8. Quote from Stevens, " 'From Generation to Generation,' " 332.

9. Nancy A. Hewitt, "The Social Origins of Women's Antislavery Politics in Western New York," in Kraut, ed., *Crusaders and Compromisers*, 208, 212.

10. Constitution of the LASD, February 9, 1835, LASD Records, NHHS. Historians have made some attempts to explain the abolitionists' failure to think about what might happen if the movement to free the slave succeeded. As Robert H. Walker points out in *Reform in America*, 87, the program of the American Anti-Slavery Society was largely a negative one; its energies were devoted to destroying slavery. He also argues that few abolitionists suspected that emancipation would not solve the race problem (180). I agree with Walker that abolitionists were often vague about the future, but their work with fugitive slaves, with black education, and eventually with freed people, alerted some of them to the likelihood that emancipation by itself would not solve the problem of racism. Steven Mintz makes a point related to Walker's about the AAS's negative goal in *Moralists and Modernizers*, 141, when he suggests that abolitionists saw their task as awakening Americans to the necessity of immediate emancipation and saw the task of politicians as providing the actual solutions (see also xxi).

11. In her study of religious abolitionism in Illinois, Linda Jeanne Evans argues that blacks paid little attention to the idea of sin and that most of their public statements stressed the importance of winning economic and legal rights for African Americans ("Abolitionism in the Illinois Churches," 43–44). Hewitt, "Feminist Friends," 30.

12. Evans, "Abolitionism in the Illinois Churches."

13. Ginzberg, *Women and the Work of Benevolence*, 98–99.

14. Ripley, ed., *Black Abolitionist Papers*, 4:38–40.

15. Letter from Deborah Palmer to Maria Chapman, December 1, 1839, Chapman-Weston Papers, BPL.

16. As John Kasson points out in *Rudeness and Civility*, 117, the ideal governing women's behavior in public was that she was to be as inconspicuous as possible. For essays on the crisis in gender during the Civil War, see Clinton and Silber, eds., *Divided Houses*.

17. Chambers-Schiller, *Liberty, a Better Husband*, 116; Ryan, *Women in Public*, 20–23, 26–35.

18. The best sources for understanding the emergence of the middle class and its fluidity are Blumin, *Emergence of the Middle Class*, and Ginzberg, *Women and the Work of Benevolence*. Catherine E. Kelly has explored the question of class in rural New England in her unpublished paper, " 'A Certain Tone of Sincerity and Self Respect': Community, Sociability, and Class in Rural New England, 1790–1830," delivered at the annual meeting of the Society for the History of the Early Republic, Cincinnati, Ohio, July 21, 1995. Karen V. Hansen explores the rural working class in *A Very Social Time*, 1, 6–8, 137. Hansen suggests the existence of a social sphere where men and women met to work and socialize. She shows that working-class men and women both attended town meetings, lectures, and lyceums, and argues that church was both private and public. See also her article " 'Helped Put in a Quilt,' " 334–54. Elizabeth D. Leonard describes the shifting gender boundaries during the Civil War in *Yankee Women*.

19. White Diary. Jane Carter, "The Avery Farm in America, 1893," in AmAS. Gray, "Diaries of Caroline Barrett White," 38. A word is perhaps needed as to my use of first names rather than last names for the women who appear in this book. While some people feel that the use of first names trivializes women, I disagree. I feel that a woman's Christian name is her only name for life, and referring to a woman by her father's name or her husband's name somehow robs her of her individuality. Some abolitionist women obviously had such a point in mind when they refused to use Mrs.

20. Colman, *Reminiscences*, 5–6, 11–13, 20, 24, 32–43, 56, 63; *Liberator*, March 6, April 17, 1857, August 26, December 2, 1859.

21. Some correspondence from Frances Drake includes letters to Maria Weston, August 6, 1843, December 10, 1850, and to Miss Weston, December 10, 1850, in Chapman-Weston Papers, BPL. See also letters from Frances Drake to Wendell Phillips, October 2, 1850, August 21, October 12, September 8, November 19, 1856, Blagden-Phillips Papers, HL. *Liberator*, April 1, 1853, August 15, September 19, 1856, August 29, 1862.

22. Letter from Abigail Goodwin to Mary Grew, June 6, 1837, PFAS Records; Still, *Underground Rail Road*, 617–22.

23. Letters from Sarah Ernst to Anne Weston, July 28, 1850, February 1, November 14, 1852, January 13, 1856, Chapman-Weston Papers, BPL; letter from Christian Donaldson to William Lloyd Garrison, November 19, 1852, Antislavery Papers, BPL.

24. Ripley, ed., *Black Abolitionist Papers*, 4:58–59; Black Abolitionist Papers, reel 13, no. 526, reel 15, nos. 524, 601, 640, 769, 858, LOC.

25. Aptheker, *Abolitionism*, 77.

CHAPTER ONE

1. Song entitled, "Christian Resolution," by Caroline Weston, in Eaklor, ed., *American Antislavery Songs*, 37.

2. *Liberator*, August 20, 1831.

3. Stewart, *William Lloyd Garrison*, 35–36; McKivigan, *War against Proslavery Religion*, 28; Ripley, ed., *Black Abolitionist Papers*, 3:8–9; quote from Hochreiter, "*Pennsylvania Freeman*," 84.

4. As Steven Mintz points out in *Moralists and Modernizers*, 125, American abolitionists learned from the British experience that becoming too specific about how emancipation should come about only confused the question.

5. Stewart, *Holy Warriors*, 22–25; Mintz, *Moralists and Modernizers*, 122.

6. Stewart, *Holy Warriors*, 26–27; William E. Gienapp, "Abolitionism and the Nature of Antebellum Reform," in Jacobs, ed., *Courage and Conscience*, 24–25.

7. Hugh Davis, *Joshua Leavitt*, 41–46; Mintz, *Moralists and Modernizers*, 121; Stanley Harrold, *Gamaliel Bailey*, 9.

8. Fladeland, *Men and Brothers*, 193–94; Friedman, *Gregarious Saints*, 29, 25, 27; Stewart, *William Lloyd Garrison*, 35–44.

9. Hochreiter, "*Pennsylvania Freeman*," 18; Ripley, ed., *Black Abolitionist Papers*, 3:7. Quote from Stewart, *William Lloyd Garrison*, 42, 39–43.

10. *Liberator*, August 20, 1831.

11. Donald M. Scott, *From Office to Profession*, 76–91; Gienapp, "Abolitionism and the Nature of Antebellum Reform," in Jacobs, ed., *Courage and Conscience*, 25.

12. Both evangelical Christians and Quakers shared a belief in the efficacy of moral action. As George M. Thomas points out in *Revivalism and Cultural Change*, 15, moral imperatives are rooted in assumptions about reality. In the case of both Quakers and evangelicals, important moral assumptions were the same. Hamm, *Transformation of American Quakerism*, 2–3; Karlyn Kohrs Campbell, ed., *Women Public Speakers*, 126–27; Hochreiter, "*Pennsylvania Freeman*," 19.

13. Hewitt, "Feminist Friends," 36, 30; Brown and Stuard, eds., *Witnesses for Change*, 94–100.

14. Stewart, *William Lloyd Garrison*, 42; Daniel Walker Howe, "Evangelical Movement," 1223.

15. *Liberator*, March 31, 1832, February 26, 1831. *Advocate of Freedom*, January 31, 1839.

16. *Liberator*, January 7, 1832.

17. Ibid., August 20, May 28, May 7, 1831.

18. Margaret Hope Bacon, "By Moral Force Alone: The Antislavery Women and Nonresistance," in Yellin and Van Horne, eds., *Abolitionist Sisterhood*, 277–79; Hine, ed., *Black Women in America*, 266–67.

19. *Liberator*, May 28, 1831, January 28, 1832.

20. Ibid., May 28, 1831.

21. Ibid., September 17, 1832.

22. Lutz, *Crusade for Freedom*, 3–16; Bass, " 'Best Hope of the Sexes,' " 24, 28; letter from Elizabeth Chandler to "Dear Aunt," May 19, 1829, Chandler Papers, BL.

23. Letters from Elizabeth Chandler to Jane Howell, [August/September?] 1831, October 28, 1833, Chandler Papers, BL.

24. Letter from Elizabeth Chandler to Sarah Chandler, June 28, 1831, and letter from Elizabeth Chandler to Jane Howell, August 30, 1832, both in Chandler Papers, BL; Bacon, "By Moral Force Alone," in Yellin and Van Horne, eds., *Abolitionist Sisterhood*, 279.

25. *Liberator*, March 24, 1832.

26. Chambers-Schiller, *Liberty, a Better Husband*, 116; *Liberator*, July 14, May 5, 1832.

27. *Liberator*, March 29, 1834; *Advocate of Freedom*, January 31, 1839.

28. *Liberator*, August 25, May 12, May 19, May 26, June 2, 1832; *Advocate of Freedom*, January 31, 1839.

29. "Appeal to Females of [the] North" (1838), 1, Vermont Historical Society, Montpelier. As this pamphlet suggests, women took on the role of encouraging other women to learn the facts and to become articulate. In her 1843 speech before an Ohio antislavery society, Betsy Cowles told the women, "We need to understand the subject—we want to acquaint ourselves with the sub-

ject of slavery in its length & breadth; height & depth. The character and consequences of slavery should be perfectly familiar to us; & the plans proposed for its discontinuance" (quoted in Geary, *Balanced in the Wind*, 48).

30. *Liberator*, May 19, March 17, 1832. Stewart, *William Lloyd Garrison*, 56.

31. For background on women's early organizational activities for charitable and benevolent causes, see Anne Firor Scott, *Natural Allies*; Anne M. Boylan's articles "Women in Groups," 497–523, "Timid Girls," 779–97, and "Women and Politics," 363–82; and Ginzberg, *Women and the Work of Benevolence*, chs. 1, 2. Presbyterian General Assembly quoted in Jeffrey, *Converting the West*, 21. *Liberator*, January 7, 1832; Midgley, *Women against Slavery*, 43–45, 49.

32. Letter from Evelina Smith to Caroline Weston, September 25, 1836, Chapman-Weston Papers, BPL.

33. *Liberator*, June 2, 1832.

34. McElroy, "Social Control and Romantic Reform in Antebellum America," 30; Ginzberg, *Women and the Work of Benevolence*, 19–20, 44; *Liberator*, May 9, 1835.

35. *Liberator*, May 19, May 26, June 2, 1832. An African American woman who submitted verses to Garrison that were published in the *Liberator* on March 3, 1832, observed female norms by her modest approach: "Should you think them worthy [of] a corner of your papers, you are at Liberty to insert them."

36. Letter from Elizur Wright to Amos Phelps, November 27, 1834, Antislavery Papers, BPL.

37. Letter from Lucinda Storrs to Martha Storrs, February 12, 1836, Storrs Papers, New York Public Library; letter from Rachel to Jeremiah Wilbur, June 20, 1834, Lambdin Family Papers, 1834–35, AmAS.

38. Letter from Louisa Phillips to Maria Chapman, July 31, 1837, letter from Anne Weston to Mary W.[?], October 27, 1835, letter from Grace Williams to Maria Chapman, July 23, 1839, and letter from Sophia Davenport to Caroline Weston, November 10, 1836, all in Chapman-Weston Papers, BPL.

39. Letter from Louisa Phillips to Maria Chapman, July 31, 1837, Chapman-Weston Papers, BPL. As will be discussed later in this chapter, the threat of violence was a real one. Samuel J. May recalled an address he was planning to make in Montpelier, Vermont. Placards were posted all around the village "admonishing 'the people generally, and ladies in particular, not to attend the antislavery meeting proposed to be held that evening in the Presbyterian church, as the person who is advertised to speak will certainly be prevented, *by violence if necessary*'" (May, *Some Recollections*, 154).

40. Myers, "Agency System," 44, 50, 90–92, 141–42; American Anti-Slavery Commission to Amos Phelps, 1834, Antislavery Papers, BPL.

41. Myers, "Agency System," 360, 365; American Anti-Slavery Commission, 1838, Antislavery Papers, BPL.

42. Letter from Mary Irwin and Fanny McDill to "Sister," March 1835, Hooker Collection, SL; letter from Sophia Davenport to Caroline Weston, June 5, 1835, Chapman-Weston Papers, BPL.

43. *Liberator*, May 2, 1835, September 8, 1832.

44. Ibid., September 8, 1832.

45. Ibid., February 1, 1834; letter from Lucretia to Brother Johnson, December 30, 1839, Antislavery Papers, BPL.

46. *Liberator*, April 18, 1835.

47. Pease and Pease, *Ladies, Women, and Wenches*, 64; *Liberator*, October 6, 1833.

48. White Diary, entries for May 21, June 10, 1837, AmAS.

49. *Advocate of Freedom*, February 8, 1840; letter from Abby Talbot to Maria Chapman, June 26, 1839, Chapman-Weston Papers, BPL.

50. *Liberator*, December 1, 1832, November 2, 1833.

51. Diary of Deborah Weston, entries for May 24, August 3, 1835, Chapman-Weston Papers, BPL; letter from Lucinda Storrs to "Dear Children," January 7, 1836, and letter from Lucinda Storrs to Martha Storrs, February 12, 1836, both in Storrs Papers, New York Public Library.

52. White Diary, entry for January 30, 1837, AmAS; Ladies Anti-Slavery Society of Dover Records, NHHS.

53. White Diary, entry for June 3, 1836, AmAS.

54. Ibid., June 9, 1837; letter from Deborah Weston to Caroline Weston, October 5, 1836, Chapman-Weston Papers, BPL; letter from Ruth Evans to Jane Howell, October 22, 1832, Chandler Papers, BL.

55. Letter from Mary Irwin and Fanny McDill to "Sister," March 11, 1835, Hooker Collection, SL; letter from Sarah Berrien to Betsy Cowles, July 14, 1835, Cowles Papers, KSUL.

56. Letter from A. A. Guthrie to Betsy Cowles, October 29, 1835, Cowles Papers, KSUL; letter from Hannah Cranch to Maria Weston Chapman, 1835[?], Chapman-Weston Papers, BPL; letter from Elizabeth Chandler to Jane Howell, August 30 through September 25, 1832, Chandler Papers, BL.

57. *Liberator*, November 3, 1837; letter from Louisa Phillips to Maria Weston Chapman, August 6, 1838, Chapman-Weston Papers, BPL; letter from Sybil Swetland to Jerome, October 31, 1839, Treadwell Family Papers, BL; Sophia Davenport to Caroline Weston, November 10, 1836, Chapman-Weston Papers, BPL; letter from Eliza and Antoinette Roote to Betsy Cowles, January 28, 1838, Cowles Papers, KSUL.

58. Ginzberg points out the radical nature of efforts to eliminate prostitution and highlights the antagonism these moral reformers felt toward men. Radical as it might have been to wish to change male behavior and to establish a single sexual standard, it was far more radical to wish to revolutionize economic, political, social, and racial relations in the North and South (Ginzberg, *Women and the Work of Benevolence*, 19–20). For the radical nature of antislavery, see Gerteis, *Morality and Utility in American Antislavery Reform*, xi, xiv, xv. Letter from Sophia Davenport to Caroline Weston, November 15, 1835, Chapman-Weston Papers, BPL. Meltzer and Holland, eds., *Lydia Maria Child*, 56–57. For an excellent discussion of the central importance of Lydia Maria Child as a propagandist and activist, see Karcher, *First Woman in the Republic*.

59. Karcher, *First Woman in the Republic*, 64.

60. Ibid., 57; letter from Octavia Gardner to Wendell Phillips, May 9, 1839, Blagden-Phillips Papers, HL; letter from Lucretia Cowings to Deborah Wes-

ton, March 21, 1838, and letter from Mrs. S. H. Kingsbury to Caroline Weston, August 6, 1838, both in Chapman-Weston Papers, BPL.

61. Letter from Experience Billings to Maria Chapman, June 28, 1839, Chapman-Weston Papers, BPL.

62. Letter from Betsy Newton to Mary Weston, July 28, 1837, and letter from Sarah Plummer to Anne Weston, March 31, 1838, both in Chapman-Weston Papers, BPL. Sarah Plummer remained active in the cause for years. Erasmus Darwin Hudson, in his journal of his antislavery work in New England and New York from 1842 to 1845, noted on July 4, 1842, that he had tea with the Plummers. He recognized "Mrs. P. [as] a very intelligent woman & [nearly] right—would be so if . . . not tied to sect" (Hudson Collection, Smith College Library, Northampton, Mass.). See also Experience Billings's letter to Maria Chapman, July 28, 1839, Chapman-Weston Papers, BPL.

63. Letter from Betsy Newton to Mary Weston, July 28, 1837, and letter from Louisa Phillips to Maria Chapman, July 31, 1837, both in Chapman-Weston Papers, BPL.

64. *Liberator*, March 15, 1834. The paper announced the formation of the societies listed here and many others in issues between 1832 and 1835. Letter from Maria Mills to Betsy Cowles, January 29, 1839, Cowles Papers, KSUL; Anne M. Boylan, "Benevolence and Antislavery Activity among African American Women in New York and Boston, 1820-1840," in Yellin and Van Horne, eds., *Abolitionist Sisterhood*, 125-28.

65. Letter from Sarah Baker to Wendell Phillips, 1839, Blagden-Phillips Papers, HL. Quote from Karcher, *First Woman in the Republic*, 175. Karcher points out the difficulties Maria experienced as she tried to reconcile public and private needs. Chambers-Schiller discusses the process of constructing a vocational identity in *Liberty, a Better Husband*, 52-69. She notes that abolitionism provided a sacred vocation and provided a sense of self-gratification.

66. Letter from Grace Williams to Maria Chapman, July 23, 1839, Chapman-Weston Papers, BPL.

67. Ripley, ed., *Black Abolitionist Papers*, 3:116-17.

68. Preamble to the Constitution of the CLAS, CLAS Records, WRHS. *Liberator*, January 17, 1834.

69. Ashtabula County Female Anti-Slavery Society Records, 1835-37, WRHS; BrFAS Records, CSL; CLAS Records, WRHS. See also Constitution for the SFAS reprinted in the *Liberator*, June 21, 1834.

70. Letter from Mrs. Kingsbury to Caroline Weston, August 6, 1838, Chapman-Weston Papers, BPL; postscript from Amy in letter from Marius Robinson to Emily Robinson, February 16, 1837, and letters of Marius Robinson, both in Robinson Papers, WRHS; letter from Sybil Swetland to Jerome, October 31, 1839, Treadwell Family Papers, BL. See also letter from Julia Tappan to Anne Weston, July 21, 1837, Chapman-Weston Papers, BPL.

71. Letter from Betsey Lincott to the BFAS, June 30, 1834, BFAS Records, MHS; Swerdlow, "An Examination of the New York City Female Anti-Slavery Societies," 72; Constitution of the BrFAS, BrFAS Records, CSL; *Liberator*, December 13, 1834.

72. *Liberator*, December 13, 1834; letter from Abby Cox to the BFAS, November 19, 1836, BFAS Records; MHS; letter from Martha Higginson to Hannah Robie, February 2, 1831, Robie-Sewall Papers, MHS. See also the Constitution of the LASD, February 9, 1835, LASD Records, NHHS.

73. See the identical constitutions for the Chatham St. Chapel Anti-Slavery Society in Swerdlow, "An Examination of the New York City Female Anti-Slavery Societies," and the BrFAS, in BrFAS Records, CSL.

74. The *Anti-Slavery Almanac* for 1836, 35, Sophia Smith Collection, SCL; Constitution of the BrFAS, BrFAS Records, CSL.

75. In her book *A Very Social Time*, Karen V. Hansen suggests that a social sphere existed where public and private, work and leisure mingled together.

76. Constitution of the BrFAS, BrFAS Records, CSL; quote from Bass, " 'Best Hope of the Sexes,' " 46.

77. Constitution of the BrFAS, BrFAS Records, CSL; Constitution of the CLAS, WRHS. As these constitutions make clear, abolitionist women were also a supporting vision of the family that was more egalitarian than the southern family. See McCurry, "Two Faces of Republicanism," 1252–54, and Pierson, " 'Free Hearts and Free Homes.' "

78. Sterling, *We Are Your Sisters*, 113; Linda M. Perkins, "The Impact of the 'Cult of True Womanhood' on the Education of Black Women," in Hine, ed., *Black Women in United States History*, 3:1067. Linda Jeanne Evans, in "Abolitionism in the Illinois Churches," 44, makes an interesting point about black abolitionists in that state. She points out that they did not emphasize the sin of slavery as did white abolitionists but tended to concern themselves with economic issues and civil rights. Not enough primary source materials from black women's antislavery associations remain to test her generalization.

79. Linda M. Perkins, "Black Women and Racial 'Uplift' Prior to Emancipation," in Hine, ed., *Black Women in United States History*, 3:1078–84. As Perkins points out, black women spearheaded the assault on intellectual inferiority.

80. Black Abolitionist Papers, reel 1, no. 203, LOC. James Oliver Horton disagrees with the view that free blacks were more interested in their own welfare and, therefore, less interested in slavery. He points out the many ways in which northern blacks felt connected to southern slaves. The threat of kidnapping or recapture, the recollections about slavery from family members, and the communication network that kept northern blacks informed about relatives and others in slavery all made abolitionism natural for free blacks, Horton argues (see his *Free People of Color*, 56–59, 73).

81. SFAS Records, vol. 1, EPI; Yee, *Black Women Abolitionists*, 33–39; letter from Sarah M. Douglas to Elizabeth Chandler, March 1, 1833, Chandler Papers, BL.

82. *Liberator*, July 12, 1834. As Anne Boylan points out in her essay "Benevolence and Antislavery Activity," in Yellin and Van Horne, eds., *Abolitionist Sisterhood*, 120, respectability was especially important for black women because they were so vulnerable to accusations of unladylike behavior.

83. Letter from Lydia Dean to Maria Chapman, April 25, 1839, Chapman-Weston Papers, BPL.

84. Studies that present information on membership in female antislavery societies

include Blumin, *Emergence of the Middle Class*; Boylan, "Women in Groups," 497–523, and "Timid Girls," 779–97; Brooke, *Heart of the Commonwealth*; Ginzberg, *Women and the Work of Benevolence*; Hewitt, *Women's Activism*; Debra Gold Hansen, "Bluestockings and Bluenoses"; and Swerdlow, "An Examination of the New York City Female Anti-Slavery Societies." Blanche Glassman Hersh characterizes some of the movement's leaders in *Slavery of Sex*. Edward Magdol deals primarily with signers of petitions but gives some information on membership in *Antislavery Rank and File*.

85. Debra Gold Hansen, "Bluestockings and Bluenoses," 103–33; letter from Caroline Weston to Mrs. L. R. G. Hammatt, April 15, 1835, Chapman-Weston Papers, BPL. Sterling, *Ahead of Her Time*, 39.

86. J. William Frost, "Years of Crisis and Separation: Philadelphia Yearly Meeting, 1790–1860," in Moore, ed., *Friends in the Delaware Valley*, 78; Debra Gold Hansen, "Bluestockings and Bluenoses," 103; Nancy A. Hewitt, "The Social Origins of Women's Antislavery Politics in Western New York," in Kraut, ed., *Crusaders and Compromisers*, 208–9; Swerdlow, "An Examination of the New York City Female Anti-Slavery Societies," 11, 14–15; Boylan, "Women in Groups," 512; McElroy, "Social Control and Romantic Reform in Antebellum America," 32.

87. Letter from Garrison to BFAS, April [?], 1834, BFAS Records, MHS; quoted in Yee, *Black Women Abolitionists*, 93; Friedman, *Gregarious Saints*, 163.

88. Hine, ed., *Black Women in America*, 918. Constitution of the PFAS, PFAS Records, HSP.

89. Winch, *Philadelphia's Black Elite*, 86; Lapansky, "Friends, Wives, and Strivings," 8–9; Yellin and Van Horne, eds., *Abolitionist Sisterhood*, 47, 57–58; letter from Anne Weston to Deborah Weston, April 18, 1837, Chapman-Weston Papers, BPL; Yee, *Black Women Abolitionists*, 18–19.

90. R. J. Young, in *Antebellum Black Activists*, argues that the majority of black women were not involved in or sympathetic to reform activities. He concludes, "The real dichotomy in the Northern African American community was between the activists and the mass of their people" (182–83). Because "the activists tried to discipline and mold the mass of African Americans into a respectable following," it was "an uphill struggle against both the prejudice of white society and the resistance of lower class African Americans." See also James Oliver Horton, *Free People of Color*, 110.

91. Moynihan, "Coming of Age," 90; letter from Garrison to BFAS, April [?], 1834, BFAS Records, MHS; Yellin and Van Horne, eds., *Abolitionist Sisterhood*, 57; *Liberator*, June 21, 1834; Yee, *Black Women Abolitionists*, 3, 88–90. One should not think that all-black organizations were open to anyone who wished to join them, Anne Boylan points out in Yellin and Van Horne, eds., *Abolitionist Sisterhood*, 128–30. These organizations not only required dues but also emphasized that all members had to have the proper moral credentials.

92. Letter from Eliza Earle to Abby Kelley, February 28, 1837, Kelley-Foster Papers, AmAS; Lovell, ed., *Two Quaker Sisters*, 113; letter from Lucia Weston to Deborah Weston, Sunday–Friday, 1836, Chapman-Weston Papers, BPL. Stevens, in "'From Generation to Generation,'" 27–30, outlines the exten-

sive family abolitionist network that reached from Philadelphia to Fall River to Leicester, Massachusetts. She suggests that these ties were vital in keeping female abolitionism alive when domestic duties drew women away from organized activities. James Oliver Horton, *Free People of Color*, 44–45.

93. Debra Gold Hansen, "Bluestockings and Bluenoses," 73–74, 106, 108–9; Boylan, "Timid Girls," 787–90; Pease and Pease, *Ladies, Women, and Wenches*, 10.

94. *Liberator*, March 30, 1833; "Members of the Blissfield Anti-Slavery Society," Chandler Papers, BL; *Old Anti-Slavery Days*, x, xi. As Hamm points out in *Transformation of American Quakerism*, 9–10, Quaker communities were tightly knit and kinship ties reinforced communal ties.

95. *Liberator*, March 30, 1833, January 4, 1834; letter from Hannah H. Smith to Abby Kelley, July 25, 1839, Kelley-Foster Papers, AmAS.

96. *Liberator*, January 17, 1834; letter from Elizabeth Wright to Harriet Foster, May 24, 1839, SFAS Records, EPI; letter from Pauline Garry to Maria Chapman, July 6, 1839, Chapman-Weston Papers, BPL; *Liberator*, January 4, 1834. Because it is often impossible to recover membership lists, discussion often has to be focused on those women who were officers as opposed to members at large.

97. Letters from Mary Clark to Anne Weston, June 13, 1837, from Pauline Garry to Maria Chapman, July 6, 1839, from Sarah Plummer to Anne Weston, March 31, 1832, and from Experience Billings to Maria Chapman, April 22, 1839, all in Chapman-Weston Papers, BPL; LFAS Records, June 21, 1837, LHS.

98. *Advocate of Freedom*, May 7, 1840.

99. Ibid.; letter from Rachel to Jeremiah Wilbur, June 20, 1834, Lambdin Family Papers, AmAS.

100. Letter from Hannah Robie to Martha Higginson, December 21, 1831, Robie-Sewall Papers, MHS; letters from Deborah Weston to Aunt Mary, November 6, 1836, June 15, 1837, and letter from Deborah Weston to Anne Weston, November 13–17, 1836, both in Chapman-Weston Papers, BPL.

101. Letter from Anne Weston to Caroline Weston, August 7, 1837, Chapman-Weston Papers, BPL.

102. LASD Records, 1835–46, NHHS; BrFAS Records, 1834, CSL.

103. Letter from S. Judson to the BFAS, May 7, 1835, BFAS Records, MHS; letter from Amos Phelps to Charlotte Phelps, March 25, 1836, Antislavery Papers, BPL.

104. Richards, *"Gentlemen of Property and Standing,"* 7–10, 14, 24, 30, 36, 40–41, 77–79, 84, 86–92, 157, 166–68; Anne Norton, *Alternative Americas*, 46–47.

105. Richards, *"Gentlemen of Property and Standing,"* 40; letter from Merriam Hussey to BFAS, August 23, 1835, BFAS Records, MHS.

106. Letter from Amos Phelps to Charlotte Phelps, November 16, 1834, Antislavery Papers, BPL.

107. *Liberator*, December 6, 1834.

108. Caroline Weston diary, entry for Monday (September), 1835, Chapman-Weston Papers, BPL.

109. Letter from Howard Gilbert to Barclay Gilbert, September 15, 1837, Lukens-Gilbert Papers, WRHS.

110. Letters from Marius Robinson to Emily Robinson, January 25, 29, 1837, Robinson Papers, WRHS; Karcher, *First Woman in the Republic*, 221.
111. Letter from Deborah Weston to "Aunt Mary," October 22, 1835, Chapman-Weston Papers, BPL; letter from the BFAS to Pittsburgh Female Anti-Slavery Society, July 5, 1835, BFAS Records, MHS.
112. Letter from Mary Clark to the PFAS, October 31, 1836, PFAS Records, HSP.

CHAPTER TWO

1. Song by Elizabeth Chandler in Eaklor, ed., *American Antislavery Songs*, 355.
2. Myers, "Agency System," ii.
3. Barnes and Dumond, eds., *Weld-Grimké Letters*, 287, 289. William E. Gienapp, "Abolitionism and the Nature of Antebellum Reform," in Jacobs, ed., *Courage and Conscience*, 32. As Thomas D. Hamm points out in *Transformation of American Quakerism*, 13, by 1843, the majority of Orthodox Quakers lived west of the Appalachians.
4. *Liberator*, October 15, 1836; Hewitt, "Feminist Friends," 30.
5. Hersh, *Slavery of Sex*, 16. The *Liberator* noted on August 20, 1836, that the Juvenile Anti-Slavery Society in Pawtucket, Rhode Island, was composed wholly of little girls and was directed by half a dozen young ladies.
6. Letter from Elizabeth Wright to Harriet Foster, May 24, 1839, SFAS Records, Correspondence 1834–39, EPI.
7. Letter from Louisa Phillips to Maria Chapman, July 31, 1837, Chapman-Weston Papers, BPL; letter from Maria Mills to Betsy Cowles, January 19, 1836, Cowles Papers, KSUL; Van Broeckhoven, "Abolitionists Were Women," ch.1, p. 18; ch. 3, pp. 10–11 (this and subsequent citations from this work are taken from the prepublication manuscript copy generously shared by Van Broeckhoven).
8. Myers, "Agency System," 224, 275; Ashtabula County Female Anti-Slavery Society Records, 1835–37, WRHS; letter from Abby Talbot to Maria Chapman, June 26, 1839, Chapman-Weston Papers, BPL; Deborah Van Broeckhoven, "'Let Your Names Be Enrolled': Method and Ideology in Women's Petitioning," in Yellin and Van Horne, eds., *Abolitionist Sisterhood*, 182.
9. Van Broeckhoven, "'Let Your Names Be Enrolled,'" in Yellin and Van Horne, eds., *Abolitionist Sisterhood*, 182–83.
10. *Liberator*, October 15, 1836.
11. Ibid., December 10, 1836.
12. Letter from Lucy Wright to Betsy Cowles, March 5, 1836, Cowles Papers, KSUL; Barnes and Dumond, eds., *Weld-Grimké Letters*, 259. In January 1834, Garrison wrote to Helen Benson, whom he would later marry, encouraging her to organize a female society in Providence, Rhode Island. Her reply to his letter suggests her own limitations and, by implication, what was involved in recruiting. She wrote, "You are not aware how extremely limited my influence is, and how inefficient my efforts would be in such a cause. There are only two families in the large circle of my acquaintances where I can feel the liberty of introducing the subject of slavery" (Merrill and Ruchames, eds., *Letters of William Lloyd Garrison*, 1:285).

13. LASD Records, 1835–46, NHHS; *Liberator*, August 27, 1836; BrFAS Records, 1834, CSL.

14. *Liberator*, April 9, 1836, October 6, 1837; CLAS Records, 1836, WRHS.

15. White Diary, entries for 1836, 1837, AmAS.

16. Letter from Mary Manter to Maria Chapman, 1840, Chapman-Weston Papers, BPL.

17. Letter from Sophia Davenport to Caroline Weston, June 5, 1835, Chapman-Weston Papers, BPL; *First Annual Report of the Dorchester Female Anti-Slavery Society*, 20, Dorchester Female Anti-Slavery Society, miscellaneous papers, AmAS.

18. Barnes and Dumond, eds., *Weld-Grimké Letters*, 283.

19. Hewitt, *Women's Activism*, 83; Ginzberg, *Women and the Work of Benevolence*, ch. 3; letter from Evelina Smith to Caroline Weston, December 11, 1836, Chapman-Weston Papers, BPL. Evelina Smith's comment may also be related to more than social class—to rural or small-town location as opposed to urban, for example.

20. Letter from M. P. Rogers to Maria Chapman, February 21, 1839, Chapman-Weston Papers, BPL; letter from Ann Buckman to Mary Grew, June 11, 1836, PFAS Records, HSP.

21. This important point is made in Van Broeckhoven, "Abolitionists Were Women," ch. 1, p. 10.

22. Records and letter from "DW" Bell to the BrFAS, July 28, 1834, BrFAS Records, CSL.

23. Letter from Mary Grew to the Reading Female Anti-Slavery Society, May 17, 1834, BFAS Records, MHS.

24. *Liberator*, February 25, 1837; letter from Mary Grew to the Reading Female Anti-Slavery Society, May 17, 1834, BFAS Records, MHS.

25. Richard D. Brown, *Knowledge Is Power*, 218–19, 234.

26. I encountered the phrase "imagined community" in "The Postal System, the 'Public Sphere,' and the Social Construction of Space in the Early Republic," a paper delivered by Richard John at the annual meeting of the Organization of American Historians, April 14, 1994, Atlanta, Georgia. It comes from Benedict Anderson's *Imagined Communities*. Letter from Melanie Ammidon to the PFAS, April 15, 1836, Antislavery Papers, BPL; *Liberator*, February 25, 1837.

27. Letter from Anne Weston to the New York Female Anti-Slavery Society, July 21, 1835, BFAS Records, MHS; letter from Lucy Wright to Betsy Cowles, March 5, 1836, Cowles Papers, KSUL. Another example comes from Sarah Plummer of Bangor, who "though personally unknown" to Anne Weston, subscribed herself as "your sister." As she pointed out, "when writing to an abolitionist I cannot feel that it is to a stranger" (Sarah Plummer to Anne Weston, March 31, 1838, Chapman-Weston Papers, BPL).

28. Swerdlow, "An Examination of the New York City Female Anti-Slavery Societies," 24.

29. Debra Gold Hansen, "Bluestockings and Bluenoses," 25–30; Pease and Pease, *Ladies, Women, and Wenches*, 128; BrFAS Records, 1837, CSL. In Lynn, Massachusetts, the constitution of the female antislavery society established a

meeting on the third Wednesday of every month to work (LFAS Records, 1837, LHS). LASD Records, 1835–46, NHHS.

30. Letter from Mary Clark to Anne Weston, June 13, 1837, Chapman-Weston Papers, BPL.

31. White Diary, entries for June 10, 19, 24, 25, 28, 30, July 14, August 23, September 29, 27, October 2, 3, November 1, 1837, October 10, 6, and passim, 1838, June 30 and passim, 1840, January 21, November 3, 1841, ASA.

32. Constitution reproduced in Swerdlow, "An Examination of New York City Female Anti-Slavery Societies"; Loudon Village Anti-Slavery Sewing Circle Records, 1840, NHHS; letter from Mary Manter to Maria Chapman, July 30, 1840, Chapman-Weston Papers, BPL.

33. Sterling, *Ahead of Her Time*, 38; LFAS Records, 1837, LHS.

34. Letter from Deborah Weston to Anne Weston, February 1, 1837, Chapman-Weston Papers, BPL.

35. Quoted in Yee, *Black Women Abolitionists*, 93; letter from Deborah Weston to Anne Weston, January 15, 1837, Chapman-Weston Papers, BPL; Robert L. Hall, "Massachusetts Abolitionists Document the Slave Experience," in Jacobs, ed., *Courage and Conscience*, 80.

36. Friedman, *Gregarious Saints*, 163; Parker quote from Lutz, *Crusade for Freedom*, 102; Sterling, *We Are Your Sisters*, 125; Anne M. Boylan, "Benevolence and Antislavery Activity among African American Women in New York and Boston, 1820–1840," in Yellin and Van Horne, eds., *Abolitionist Sisterhood*, 119–20, 130.

37. CLAS Records, 1836, WRHS.

38. Constitution of the PFAS, PFAS Records, HSP; Black Abolitionist Papers, reel 2, no. 283, reel 3, no. 42, LOC.

39. Black Abolitionist Papers, reel 1, no. 949, reel 2, nos. 10–11, LOC.

40. Quotation from the Ashtabula County Female Anti-Slavery Society Records, 1835–37, WRHS.

41. Letter from Lucretia Mott to Maria Chapman, November 30, 1842, Chapman-Weston Papers, BPL.

42. Meltzer and Holland, eds., *Lydia Maria Child*, 104; letter from Anne Weston to Eliza Mason, January 7, 1838, BFAS Records, MHS.

43. CLAS Records, 1836, WRHS.

44. This communication was probably from Caroline Weston. *Liberator*, April 13, 1838.

45. Ibid.

46. *Liberator*, January 11, 1839; letter from Lucy Wright to Betsy Cowles, May 20, 1836, Cowles Papers, KSUL; LFAS Records, June 21, 1837, LHS; CLAS Records, 1836, WRHS. Sarah Rugg, a member of the Groton Ladies Anti-Slavery Society, used similarly martial vocabulary. "We must pray more, & work less, we have neglected prayer too much, our armour has grown dull, restraining prayer we cease to fight" (Sarah Rugg to Anne Weston, February 6, 1838, Chapman-Weston Papers, BPL).

47. LFAS Records, 1837, LHS; *Advocate of Freedom*, September 13, 1838.

48. Letter from Mary Grew to the BrFAS, July 1834, BFAS Records, MHS.

49. Minutes of the PFAS, January 12, 1837, PFAS Records, HSP. Although the presence of Hicksite Quaker women, who did not subscribe to the polarized gender views of their society to the same extent as other Protestant women, might be seen as an explanatory factor, it is more accurate to see the ways in which the concept of duty allowed women to ignore inconvenient rules for conduct.

50. Letter from the Portage Female Anti-Slavery Society to the BFAS, August 11, 1836, BFAS Records, MHS; LFAS Records, 1837, LHS.

51. Letter from Deborah Weston to Anne Weston, January 15, 1827, Chapman-Weston Papers, BPL; letter from Hannah H. Smith to Abby Kelley, July 25, 1839, Kelley-Foster Papers, AmAS.

52. Letter from Lucinda Wilmarth to Abby Kelley, July 11, 1842, Kelley-Foster Papers, AmAS; letter from Pauline Garry to Maria Chapman, July 6, 1839, Chapman-Weston Papers, BPL.

53. LASD Records, 1835–46, NHHS.

54. SFAS Records, December 27, 1837, January 10, 1838, January 19, 1842, EPI.

55. Ibid., September 11, October 6, 1848, September 30, 1850, September 20, 1842.

56. BrFAS Records, 1840, CSL.

57. Letter from L. Dean to Maria Chapman, April 25, 1839, Antislavery Papers, BPL; letter from Lydia Dodge to Abby Kelley, April 9, 1838, Kelley-Foster Papers, AmAS. SFAS Records, vol. 1, EPI. Sewing circles were ubiquitous in female abolitionism. They took on numerous projects, from clothing poor students, black teachers, and fugitives to creating fancy articles for sale. The work itself acted as a motivator and provided satisfactions that kept women involved. Perhaps the specificity of female work made it easier for women to keep up their interest in abolitionism than men.

58. Letter from Sarah Rugg to Anne Weston, October 24, 1836, remnant of letter to Deborah Weston from [?], March 17, 1837, letter from Anne Weston to Caroline Weston, August 7, 1837, all in Chapman-Weston Papers, BPL.

59. Letter from L. Dean to Maria Chapman, April 25, 1839, Antislavery Papers, BPL.

60. Letter from Eliza Gill to Maria Chapman, April 28, postscript, May 25, 1839, Chapman-Weston Papers, BPL.

61. SFAS Records, vol. 1, January 9, 1839, EPI; letter from Lucia Weston to Deborah Weston, January 22, 1837, Chapman-Weston Papers, BPL.

62. LASD Records, January 29, 1851, July 28, 1852, NHHS; letter from Eliza Pope to Maria Chapman, September 28, 1840, Chapman-Weston Papers, BPL.

63. Letter from Mary Grew to the Reading Female Anti-Slavery Society, May 17, 1834, BFAS Records, MHS.

64. Letters from Sarah Plummer to Anne Weston, March 31, 1838, from S. W. Thomas to Maria Chapman, May 6, 1839, from Mary Manter to Maria Chapman, July 30, 1840, from Lucy Durrels to Maria Chapman, September 24, 1840, from Sophia Little to Maria Chapman, September 26, 1840, and from Harriot Minot to Amos Phelps, November 22, 1838, all in Antislavery Papers, BPL. Harriot wrote: "Our ladies are thinking much less of the wants of the famishing slaves, than of providing an abundance of pies for their households."

65. Letter from Pauline Garry to Maria Chapman, July 6 1839, Chapman-Weston

Papers, BPL; *Advocate of Freedom*, February 8, 1840; letter from Abby Talbot to Maria Chapman, June 26, 1839, Chapman-Weston Papers, BPL.

66. Letter from Elizabeth Wright to Harriet Foster, May 24, 1839, SFAS Records, Correspondence, 1834–39, EPI; letter from Frances Drake to Maria Chapman, June 11, 1843, Chapman-Weston Papers, BPL.

67. Swerdlow, "An Examination of New York City Female Anti-Slavery Societies," 127.

68. Ashtabula County Anti-Slavery Society Records, 1836, WRHS; letter from Mary Weston to Deborah Weston, October 24–29, 1836, Chapman-Weston Papers, BPL. Not all societies listened to a formal annual report. In Brooklyn it was not until the third annual meeting that the secretary made her first report, which "congratulated the So. on having the happiness of knowing that its influence had made converts to its doctrines beyond its own precincts." Certainly when there was a report, its reading became an important part of the ceremony marking the society's anniversary (BrFAS Records, June 13, 1837, CSL). The South Reading Female Anti-Slavery Society's First Annual Report expressed common themes: regret that members hadn't felt or labored as much as they should have and the hope of doing more in the coming year. Accomplishments were detailed: the membership had increased from twelve to fifty, partly as a result of two lectures; eleven meetings for work had been held; and some publications had been circulated. Confronting adversity also was celebrated. The South Reading women had survived the frowns of the indifferent as well as the caustic comments of critics who called the women fools and weak-minded. Members were reminded that while such enemies might rage on, God was on their side (*Liberator*, December 17, 1836).

69. *First Annual Report of the Dorchester Female Anti-Slavery Society*, 3, Dorchester Female Anti-Slavery Society, miscellaneous papers, AmAS.

70. Ibid., 4.

71. Letter from Ruth Evans to Jane Howell, October 22, 1832, Chandler Papers, BL; letter from Arza, Achsah, and Hannah Blanding to Anne Weston, March 9, 1837, Chapman-Weston Papers, BPL; letter from Betsey Lincott to the BFAS, June 30, 1834, BFAS Records, MHS.

72. BrFAS Records, June 16, 1835, March 1, May 19, 1836, June 13, 1837, and passim, CSL.

73. LFAS Records, May 27, 1836, LHS; BrFAS Records, February 2, 1836, June 13, 1837, CSL.

74. Letter from Sarah Rugg to Anne Weston, February 16, 1838, Chapman-Weston Papers, BPL; Ashtabula County Female Anti-Slavery Society Records, January 6, 1836, WRHS; LASD Records, NHHS.

75. Letter from Mary Weston to Deborah Weston, October 24–29, 1836, Chapman-Weston Papers, BPL.

76. Meltzer and Holland, eds., *Lydia Maria Child*, 104; letter from Louisa Phillips to Maria Chapman, July 31, 1837, Chapman-Weston Papers, BPL; Hewitt, *Women's Activism*, 84. As Paul Joseph notes, writing about a twentieth-century social movement, "Participation in grass-roots initiatives, cultivation of affinities, and direct action produce a vision that sustains local actions on the one

hand, and feelings of membership in a global community on the other. Here effectiveness is the creation of a sense of collective identity that transcends individualism" ("Direct and Indirect Effects," 172).

77. LASD Records, July 4, 1840, November 8, 1841, August 2, 1842, April 4, July 17, December 1844, NHHS.

78. Copy of letter from Melanie Ammidon to the PFAS, April 15, 1836, Antislavery Papers, BPL; LFAS Records, June 21, 1837, LHS.

79. LFAS Records, July 19, 1837, LHS; SFAS Records, vol. 1, June 12, 1834, EPI; LASD Records, December 1, 1852, NHHS.

80. Letter from Deborah Palmer to Maria Chapman, January 30, 1840, Chapman-Weston Papers, BPL.

81. Barnes and Dumond, eds., *Weld-Grimké Letters*, 263.

82. *Liberator*, October 17, 1835; BrFAS Records, June 13, 1837, CSL; letter from Lucia Russell to Maria Chapman, 1840, Chapman-Weston Papers, BPL.

83. Letter from Grace Williams to Maria Chapman, April 10, 1839, and letter from Charlotte Austin to Maria Chapman, October 9, 1840, both in Chapman-Weston Papers, BPL; *Liberator*, March 22, 1839; letter from Anne Weston to Deborah Weston, January 16, 1837, and printed letter to "Dear Friend," March 25, 1839, both in Chapman-Weston Papers, BPL; *Advocate of Freedom*, April 13, 1838. Myers, in "Agency System," ii, states that by 1838 there were six weekly abolitionists newspapers and two that appeared biweekly.

84. Letter from Experience Billings to Maria Chapman, April 22, 1839, and letter from Sarah Plummer to Anne Weston, March 31, 1838, both in Chapman-Weston Papers, BPL.

85. *Liberator*, August 27, 1836; letter from Marius Robinson to Emily Robinson, February 7, 1837, Robinson Papers, WRHS.

86. Minutes of the PFAS, December 4, 1834, September 8, November 11, 1836, PFAS Records, HSP.

87. LFAS Records, June 21, 1837, LHS; letter from A. B. Ordway to the Board, August 25, 1839, Correspondence 1839, SFAS Records, EPI. Mrs. Ordway was a milliner. Debra Gold Hansen, "The Boston Female Anti-Slavery Society and the Limits of Gender Politics," in Yellin and Van Horne, eds., *Abolitionist Sisterhood*, 61.

88. *Liberator*, May 10, 1834, December 17, 1836. See also *Advocate of Freedom*, September 13, 1838, which notes continued expenditures for the black community in Portland. Ripley, ed., *Black Abolitionist Papers*, 3:14–18.

89. Minutes of the PFAS, June 9, 1834, February 11, 1836, February 9, 1837, January 4, March 8, 1836, April 12, 1838, July 11, 1839, January 1, 1840, PFAS Records, HSP.

90. Letter from L. L. Dodge to Garrison, January 4, 1838, SFAS Records, EPI; letter from Caroline Weston to Mrs. L. R. G. Hammatt, August 1, 1835, and letter from Deborah Weston to "Mother," May 8, 1835, both in Chapman-Weston Papers, BPL. Meltzer and Holland, eds., *Lydia Maria Child*, 69–70. The Bangor Female Anti-Slavery Society, the Portland Sewing Circle, and the Newport Young Ladies' Juvenile Anti-Slavery Society together made it possible for black abolitionist Charles Remond to attend the 1840 World's Anti-

Slavery Convention and to lecture in the British Isles for a year and a half (Porter, "Remonds of Salem, Massachusetts," 275).

91. The January 25, 1839, issue of the *Liberator*, included a letter from Salem's corresponding secretary, informing Garrison of the $100 gift the society had voted to give him. Another reference to the work appears in the April 13, 1838, issue. See also *Advocate of Freedom*, July 19, 1838. Throughout this issue, the general agent of the Maine Anti-Slavery Society appealed to "warm-hearted persons," suggesting that they collect from each member of their societies twenty-five cents every quarter to be used for antislavery literature.

92. *Advocate of Freedom*, December 6, 1838; LASD Records, July 4, 1837, 1840, NHHS; letter from A. M. Houghton to Maria Chapman, April 15, 1839, Chapman-Weston Papers, BPL.

93. May, *Some Recollections*, 231.

94. Letter from Frances Drake to Maria Chapman, August 6, 1841, and letter from Eliza Gill to Maria Chapman, September 2, 1840, both in Chapman-Weston Papers, BPL.

95. Letter from Mary Clark to Anne Weston, June 3, 1837, Chapman-Weston Papers, BPL; LFAS Records, June 21, 1837, LHS; Hewitt, *Women's Activism*, 82.

96. Boylan, "Women and Politics," 364; McCurry, "Two Faces of Republicanism," 1245; Lerner, *Majority Finds Its Past*, 114; Van Broeckhoven, " 'Let Your Names Be Enrolled,' " in Yellin and Van Horne, eds., *Abolitionist Sisterhood*, 193.

97. *Liberator*, June 2, 1832.

98. Lerner, *Majority Finds Its Past*, 114–15; Edward Magdol, "A Window on the Abolitionist Constituency: Antislavery Petitions, 1836-1839," in Kraut, ed., *Crusaders and Compromisers*, 45–46; Ginzberg, *Women and the Work of Benevolence*, 82.

99. Letter of Caroline Weston to [?], July 14, 1835, Chapman-Weston Papers, BPL. For analyses of women's greater effectiveness, see Lerner, *Majority Finds Its Past*, 117–23, and Van Broeckhoven, " 'Let Your Names Be Enrolled,' " in Yellin and Van Horne, eds., *Abolitionist Sisterhood*, 187–93.

100. Van Broeckhoven, " 'Let Your Names Be Enrolled,' " in Yellin and Van Horne, eds., *Abolitionist Sisterhood*, 179; Black Abolitionist Papers, reel 3, no. 291, LOC.

101. Letter from Caroline Weston to "Dear Sir," 1836, Chapman-Weston Papers, BPL; *Advocate of Freedom*, November 8, 1838; letter from Julianna Tappan to Anne Weston, May 24, 1837, Chapman-Weston Papers, BPL.

102. Letters from Mary Clark to Anne Weston, June 3, 1837, from Mary Weston to Deborah Weston, January 22, 1837, from Charlotte Austin to Maria Chapman, July 26, 1839, and from Anne Weston to Deborah Weston, September 19, 1837, all in Chapman-Weston Papers, BPL. Charlotte Austin wrote, "I generally copy them but my time will not now permit."

103. LFAS Records, June 21, 1837, LHS; letter from Mary Grew to the BrFAS, March 17, 1837, CSL.

104. Letter from Mary Clark to Anne Weston, June 13 1837, Chapman-Weston

Papers, BPL. Mary Clark was one of the women who signed her society's constitution after a "noisy rabble" interrupted the address of George Thompson (*Liberator*, December 6, 1834).

105. Letters from Deborah Weston to Anne Weston, February 18, 1840, from Anne Weston to Deborah Weston, September 15, 1837, from Deborah Weston to Mary Weston, November 6, 1836, all in Chapman-Weston Papers, BPL. As Lee Virginia Chambers-Schiller notes in *Liberty, a Better Husband*, 116, "To sustain . . . [the abolitionist] commitment required strength of will, force of mind, and physical stamina."

106. Letters from Deborah Weston to Mary Weston, October 19, 1836, from Caroline Weston to Deborah Weston, March 3, 1837, from Sarah Rugg to Anne Weston, February 16, 1838, all in Chapman-Weston Papers, BPL; Minutes of the PFAS, January 4, 1838, PFAS Records, HSP. Meltzer and Holland, eds., *Lydia Maria Child*, 93.

107. *Advocate of Freedom*, January 31, 1839.

108. *Liberator*, May 24, 1839; letter from Julianna Tappan to Anne Weston, July 21, 1837, Chapman-Weston Papers, BPL.

109. Letter from Charlotte Austin to Maria Chapman, July 26, 1839, Chapman-Weston Papers, BPL; letter from Hannah Smith to Abby Kelley, July 25, 1839, Kelley-Foster Papers, AmAS.

110. For a few examples, see letters from Deborah Weston to Mary Weston, October 19, 1836, from Anne Weston to Deborah Weston, November 19, 1836, and from Louisa Phillips to Maria Weston, August 6, 1837, all in Chapman-Weston Papers, BPL. Lucy Chase, diary fragments, January 27, no year, Chase Papers, AmAS. For an example of a newspaper response, see Dorothy Sterling, *Ahead of Her Time*, 78.

111. Letter from Anna Cook to Maria Chapman, December 25, 1839, Chapman-Weston Papers, BPL. John Kasson, in *Rudeness and Civility*, 112–21, makes the point about the importance of being inconspicuous in public. Ryan, *Women in Public*, 3.

112. A list of petitions that was presented to Congress and reported in the *Liberator*, March 2, 1838, for example, shows that in the village of Lockport, New York, 371 women signed a petition asking Congress not to admit any new state into the Union if its constitution recognized slavery, 234 signed a petition against admitting Texas to the Union, while 405 signed the petition asking Congress to abolish slavery in the territories. Letter from Sarah Rugg to Anne Weston, February 16, 1838, Chapman-Weston Papers, BPL.

113. Muelder, *Fighters for Freedom*, 182; "1842 Circular of the Anti-Slavery Convention of American Women," Chapman-Weston Papers, BPL.

114. LFAS Records, June 21, 1837, LHS; *Liberator*, March 2, 1838; letter from Louisa Phillips to Maria Chapman, August 6, 1838, Chapman-Weston Papers, BPL.

115. Letter from Julianna Tappan to Anne Weston, July 21, 1837, Chapman-Weston Papers, BPL; LFAS Records, June 21, 1837, LHS; letter from Anna Cook to Maria Chapman, December 25, 1839, Chapman-Weston Papers, BPL. In *Old Anti-Slavery Days*, 42, Abby Diaz, former secretary of the Plymouth Juvenile

Anti-Slavery Society, recalled how she and her friends circulated petitions on their way to and from school. Schoolgirls, she pointed out, "had become skillful in anti-slavery argument."

116. Sterling, *Ahead of Her Time*, 78–79; letter from Anne Weston to Deborah Weston, January 6, 1837, letter from Deborah Weston to Mary Weston, November 6, 1836, letters from Louisa Phillips to Maria Chapman, July 31, 1837, and August 6, 1836, letter from Anne Weston to Deborah Weston, December 15, 1839, and letter from Anna Clark to Maria Chapman, December 25, 1839, all in Chapman-Weston Papers, BPL; *Liberator*, May 24, 1839.

117. Letter from Rachel Stearns to Maria Chapman, December 18, 1842, Chapman-Weston Papers, BPL.

118. *First Annual Report of the Dorchester Female Anti-Slavery Society*, 11, Dorchester Female Anti-Slavery Society, miscellaneous papers, AmAS.

119. Letter from Anne Weston to the Concord Female Anti-Slavery Society, July 22, 1835, BFAS Records, MHS; *Liberator*, September 15, 1837. For another reference to the American Revolution and the role of women, see the *Liberator*, December 17, 1836.

120. Sterling, *Ahead of Her Time*, 43–49; quotes on 44, 48, 49; Yellin and Van Horne, eds., *Abolitionist Sisterhood*, 10–15.

121. Sterling, *Ahead of Her Time*, 62–66; Yellin and Van Horne, eds., *Abolitionist Sisterhood*, 16–17, and Margaret Hope Bacon, "By Moral Force Alone: The Antislavery Women and Nonresistance," in ibid., 285–88, quote on 288.

122. Bacon, "By Moral Force Alone," in Yellin and Van Horne, eds., *Abolitionist Sisterhood*, 289–91.

123. Letter from Aroline Chase to Abby Kelley, May or June 1843, Kelley-Foster Papers, AmAS.

CHAPTER THREE

1. Song by unidentified abolitionist in Eaklor, ed., *American Antislavery Songs*, 244.

2. Letter from J. W. Thomas to Maria Chapman, November 15, 1841, and letter from Sarah Stearns to Maria Chapman, November 10, 1840, both in Chapman-Weston Papers, BPL.

3. Ginzberg, *Women and the Work of Benevolence*, 85–88; Yacovone, *Samuel Joseph May*, 66–68; Walters, *Antislavery Appeal*, 13; Hersh, *Slavery of Sex*, 23–25. William E. Gienapp, "Abolitionism and the Nature of Antebellum Reform," Jacobs, ed., *Courage and Conscience*, 24–26; Ripley, ed., *Black Abolitionist Papers*, 3:335–36.

4. Letter from Maria Child to Maria Chapman, April 10, 1839, Chapman-Weston Papers, BPL. Ronald G. Walters, "The Boundaries of Abolitionism," in Perry and Fellman, eds., *Antislavery Reconsidered*, 15–16; Ripley, ed., *Black Abolitionist Papers*, 3:13, 19–25. By 1840, less than 10 percent of all free blacks were able to vote.

5. Van Broeckhoven, "Abolitionists Were Women," ch. 3, pp. 25–27; Stevens, " 'From Generation to Generation,' " 94–96; letter from Emma Hart Willard to Wendell Phillips, May 25, 1845, Blagden-Phillips Papers, HL.

6. Quoted in Quist, " 'Great Majority of Our Subscribers,' " 338.

7. Ginzberg, in *Women and the Work of Benevolence*, 88, makes the point about non-Garrisonian women retreating from abolitionism. Implicitly, in the focus on politics as the major form of abolitionist activity in the 1840s, other historians make a similar point. See Chapter 4 for further explanation of my disagreement with this position.

8. Nancy A. Hewitt, "The Social Origins of Women's Antislavery Politics in Western New York," in Kraut, ed., *Crusaders and Compromisers*, 209–10; Minutes of the PFAS, October 8, 1846, PFAS Records, HSP.

9. Letter from Rhoda De Garma to Maria Chapman, January 26, 1845, Bladgen-Phillips Papers, HL. Hewitt, in Kraut, ed., *Crusaders and Compromisers*, 208, highlights the different social and economic backgrounds of Rochester's Hicksite abolitionists that may also have contributed to the sense of isolation.

10. Walters, *Antislavery Appeal*, 4–5. Walters points out that diversity encouraged the involvement of a maximum number of those who disapproved of slavery despite the ending of the early period of rapid growth. Jane H. and William H. Pease accuse Garrison, and by implication, Garrisonians, of "endless discourse, . . . limitless verbiage," and an avoidance of direct action in politics in *Bound with Them in Chains*, 36. I argue that such discourse was vital to turning the tide of opinion in the North. Letter from Louisa R. Beal to Abby Kelley, October 24, 1845, Kelley-Foster Papers, AmAS.

11. *Liberator*, October 20, 1848; letter from Eliza Boyce to Maria Chapman, December 1, 1839, Chapman-Weston Papers, BPL; letter from Aroline Chase to Abby Kelley, May or June 1843, Kelley-Foster Papers, AmAS; Foner, ed., *Life and Writings of Frederick Douglass*, 1:188.

12. Letter from Deborah S. Palmer to Maria Chapman, September 24, 1840, Antislavery Papers, and letter from S. H. Earle to Maria Chapman, December 27, 1841, Chapman-Weston Papers, both in BPL; Bonfield and Morrison, *Roxana's Children*, 15.

13. 1842 Annual Report, SFAS Records, EPI.

14. Ibid.

15. Letter from Lucretia to Brother Johnson, December 30, 1839, Antislavery Papers, BPL.

16. 1840 Annual Report, SFAS Records, EPI.

17. SFAS Records, June 12, 1834, March 7, 1838, January 9, 1839, EPI.

18. Sterling, *We Are Your Sisters*, 116; SFAS Records, April 1836, January 10, March 7, 1838, January 16, 1839, January 15, February 19, 1840, April 28, 1841, EPI; Lang, "Black Bootstraps," 115. Similarly, the black members of the PFAS won the society's support for the vigilance society and a temperance retreat for African Americans in Philadelphia (Minutes of the PFAS, September 9, December 9, 1841, February 10, June 23, 1842, PFAS Records, HSP).

19. Letter from Mary Kenney to William Lloyd Garrison, May 1, 1841, Correspondence 1840–44, in SFAS Records, and SFAS Records for January 21, April 28, 1841, all in EPI; letter from Lydia Dean to Maria Chapman, December 15, 1839, Chapman-Weston Papers, BPL.

20. SFAS Records, September 20, 1852, January 21, 1860, EPI.

21. LASD Records, October 29, 1839, and the Dover Anti-Slavery Sewing Circle Records, February 1840, in NHHS.

22. Dover Anti-Slavery Sewing Circle Records, February 1840, July 4, 1840, August 29, 1849, NHHS.

23. Dover Anti-Slavery Sewing Circle Records, February 1840, February 3, 1847, September 27, 1848, December 1, 1852, NHHS.

24. Dover Anti-Slavery Sewing Circle Records, August 2, 1842, November 19, 1845, January 25, March 4, September 30, 1846, November 14, 1848, August 29, 1849, December 5, 1850, NHHS.

25. On January 3, 1855, for example, the circle voted to send a contribution to Hiram Wilson in Canada. The reading of a letter from Mr. Whipple on March 1, however, caused the circle to rescind its vote and send the funds elsewhere (where they would still be used to assist fugitive slaves). Dover Anti-Slavery Sewing Circle Records, January 3, March 1, 1855, NHHS.

26. See ibid., January 3, 1849, January 2, 1850, November 1, 1855, May 29, September 3, 1856.

27. *Liberator*, June 22, 1838.

28. Letter from Maria Rice to Maria Chapman, January 21, 1840, and letter from Alvan Ward to Maria Chapman, July 23, 1840, both in Chapman-Weston Papers, BPL.

29. Portland Anti-Slavery Society Records, Preamble and Constitution, January 21, 18, 1841, Maine Historical Society. The secretary was N. A. Foster and not identified as either male or female.

30. Portland Anti-Slavery Society Records, February 25, March 10, 17, 24, April 7, April 14, August 10, August 30, September 28, 1844, July 11, 1845, Maine Historical Society.

31. 1850 Constitution of Portland Anti-Slavery Society, Portland Anti-Slavery Society Records for June 27, 1850, May 25, 1851, and letters from Elizabeth Montfort to Wendell Phillips, April 8, 1850, to C. L. Remond, April 29, 1850, and to Samuel May, May 5, 1850, Official Correspondence Letter Book, April 1850–May 1851, all in Portland Anti-Slavery Society Records, Maine Historical Society.

32. For a reference to African American women's fairs, see letter from "MTC" to Deborah Weston, July 26, 1840, Chapman-Weston Papers, BPL. The writer notes that she was informed "that the coloured women [of New Bedford] intended to assist us in preparing articles for the Mass. fair instead of holding a fair themselves." Elizabeth Gay wrote to Maria Chapman on July 1, 1857, about New York women "who held *not Anti-Slavery, but Fugitive Slave Fairs*" (GFP).

33. Hewitt, "Social Origins of Women's Antislavery Politics," in Kraut, ed., *Crusaders and Compromisers*, 222. Debra Gold Hansen, "Bluestockings and Bluenoses," 197; Lutz, *Crusade for Freedom*, 192; Jean R. Soderlund, "Priorities and Power: The Philadelphia Female Anti-Slavery Society," in Yellin and Van Horne, eds., *Abolitionist Sisterhood*, 83–84; Report of the Executive Committee, Seventh Annual Report, 1849, Papers of the Western Anti-Slavery Society, LOC.

34. Hewitt, "Social Origins of Women's Antislavery Politics," in Kraut, *Crusaders and Compromisers*, 223–24; Debra Gold Hansen, "Bluestockings and Blue-noses," 176. Elizabeth Gay made clear the difference between small and large fairs when she wrote to Boston's Maria Chapman: "If you have articles that are too tasteful or expensive for the smaller Fairs, left from your over-supplied tables, they would likely find a ready sale here" (letter of June 11, 1857, GFP). Even when women sent in goods to the larger fairs, they might still decide how they wanted the proceeds from their efforts to be spent. As E. D. Pillsbury, from Milford, New Hampshire, wrote to Maria Chapman, "they wish [the proceeds from the sewing circle's bundle] to be given to Frederick Douglass to aid him in conducting his paper" (letter of December 18, 1848, Antislavery Papers, BPL).

35. Debra Gold Hansen, "Bluestockings and Bluenoses," 196–97, suggests that fairs were a noncontroversial way to help a controversial cause. I am suggesting that fairs raise controversial questions focused on meaning and women's involvement. Ferrero, Hedges, and Silber, *Hearts and Hands*, 66–68; Hewitt, *Women's Activism*, 150.

36. Letter from M. P. Rogers to Maria Chapman, February 21, 1839, Chapman-Weston Papers, and letter from Mary P. Rogers to Henry Wright, September 8, 1842, Antislavery Papers, both in BPL.

37. Letter from Elisabeth Nile to Maria Chapman, August 28, 1839, and from S. W. Thomas to Maria Chapman, September 18, 1842, Chapman-Weston Papers, BPL; Western Anti-Slavery Society Fair, Clippings, Cowles Papers, KSUL.

38. Letter from Sarah Ernst to Anne Weston, January 13, 1856, Chapman-Weston Papers, BPL. In "'A Good Work among the People': The Political Culture of the Boston Antislavery Fair," in Yellin and Van Horne, eds., *Abolitionist Sisterhood*, 250, Lee Chambers-Schiller itemizes the many innovations introduced in the Boston fair. These innovations helped attract crowds of potential buyers to the sale.

39. Letter from Deborah Weston to Caroline Weston, December 27, 1839, and letter from Deborah Weston to "Aunt Mary," January 5, 1840, Chapman-Weston Papers, BPL.

40. Letter from Sarah Stearns to Maria Chapman, November 10, 1840, Chapman-Weston Papers, BPL. For a reference to goods from Minnesota, see letter from Mary H. Weston to Maria Chapman, November 14, 1857, ibid.

41. Letter from Deborah Palmer to Maria Chapman, December 1, 1839, letter from Evelina Smith to Maria Chapman, October 25, 1840, and Address of the Committee of the Tenth Massachusetts Anti-Slavery Fair, 1843, all in Chapman-Weston Papers, BPL.

42. Letter from Frances Drake to Maria Chapman, June 11, 1843, Chapman-Weston Papers, BPL.

43. Notice for the 1841 Boston fair, Chapman-Weston Papers, BPL.

44. Letter from Sarah M. Rhoads to Maria Chapman, October 11, 1840, and letter from Caroline Bartlett to Maria Chapman, July 23, 1840, Chapman-Weston Papers, BPL.

45. Letter from Jerusha Bird to Maria Chapman, November 1, 1840, and letter from Frances Drake to Maria Chapman, October 31, 1843, Chapman-Weston Papers, BPL.

46. Letter from Frances Drake to Maria Chapman, December 18, 1842, Chapman-Weston Papers, BPL.

47. Ibid., June 11, December 15, 1843, Chapman-Weston Papers, BPL.

48. Letter from Frances Drake to Maria Chapman, June 22, 1844, letter from Frances Drake to Anne Weston, November 17, 1848, and letter from Frances Drake to Miss Weston, December 10, 1850, Chapman-Weston Papers, BPL.

49. Letter from J. W. Thomas to Maria Chapman, November 15, 1841, Chapman-Weston Papers, BPL.

50. Letter from Amy Post to Abby Kelley, December 4, 1842, Kelley-Foster Papers, AmAS.

51. Letter from Abby Kelley Foster to Lydia Dennett, March 17, 1848, Blagden-Phillips Papers, HL; letter from Eliza Follen to Joseph Congdon, 1840s or 1850s, Follen Papers, Mss. A.F.667, SL.

52. Bills and Receipts, 1834–49, SFAS Records, EPI.

53. Circular of the Eleventh Massachusetts Anti-Slavery Fair, February 8, 1844; letter from Abby Kelley to Maria Chapman, January 23, 1843, Chapman-Weston Papers, BPL.

54. Letter from Deborah Palmer to Maria Chapman, September 24, 1840, Anti-slavery Papers, BPL. Hewitt, in *Women's Activism*, 63, describes the network of Hicksite women in the Western New York Anti-Slavery Society as reaching out to Boston, Philadelphia, New York City, and into the Northeast and Midwest.

55. Letters from Julianna Tappan to Anne Weston, May 26, July 21, 1837, Chapman-Weston Papers, BPL.

56. Letter from Lucia Weston to Deborah Weston, December 18, 1836, Chapman-Weston Papers, BPL.

57. Van Broeckhoven, "Abolitionists Were Women," ch. 2, p. 13; Lee Virginia Chambers-Schiller, "The Boston Antislavery Fair," in Yellin and Van Horne, eds., *Abolitionist Sisterhood*, 260; Bernard F. Reilly Jr., "The Art of the Antislavery Movement," in Jacobs, *Courage and Conscience*, 47–63.

58. White Diary, entry for October 4, 1839, AmAS; letter from Hannah Cotton to Maria Chapman, October 27, 1839, Chapman-Weston Papers, BPL; Karcher, *First Woman in the Republic*, 219; the verse, Karcher points out, came from Eliza Follen. Ferrero, Hedges, and Silber, *Hearts and Hands*, 69; Patricia J. Keller, "Methodology and Meaning," 2.

59. Another aspect, scarcely noted by scholars, that makes these artifacts important is that they were visually appealing. Anyone who has waded through inexpensive abolitionist tracts, usually composed of text without illustration, can appreciate the visual power of the objects the women made and their contribution to the cause.

60. Letter from Elizabeth Gay to Anne Weston, January 12, 1848, and letter from Elizabeth Gay to Sarah Pugh, July 2, 1857, GFP; letter from Anna Bailey to "Dear Friends," 1839, Chapman-Weston Papers, BPL.

61. Letter from Susan [Tabor?] to Deborah Weston, December 31[?], 1837,

Chapman-Weston Papers, BPL; letter from Elizabeth Gay to Lucia Weston, December 1, 1850, GFP; letter from Evelina Smith to Caroline Weston, July 21, 1839, Antislavery Papers, BPL. In a similar fashion, Charlotte Austin knew the shells her group had managed to collect would appeal to Boston buyers, for visitors to Nantucket eagerly sought after them "for cabinets and ornaments" (letter from Charlotte Austin to Maria Chapman, October 4, 1839, Chapman-Weston Papers, BPL).

62. Letter from Silva Jones to Maria Weston, December 15, 1837, Chapman-Weston Papers, BPL.

63. Letter from Ellen Russell to Maria Chapman, October 15, 1839, letter from Charlotte Austin to Maria Chapman, October 4, 1839, and letter from Hannah Something[?], October 17, 1839, Chapman-Weston Papers, BPL.

64. Letter from Charlotte Austin to Maria Chapman, December 5, 1841, Antislavery Papers, BPL; letter from Elizabeth Chapin to Elizabeth Gay, October 3, 1853, GFP.

65. Letter from Elizabeth Gay to Caroline Weston, December 15, 1847, GFP; letter from Eliza Boyce to Maria Chapman, December 1, 1839, and letter from M. Brooks to Maria Chapman, June 30, 1843, Chapman-Weston Papers, BPL.

66. Fair Announcement, 1839, and letter from Susan Hayward to Maria Chapman, December 13, 1857, Chapman-Weston Papers, BPL.

67. Letter from Lucinda Wilmarth to Maria Weston[?], 1839, Antislavery Papers, BPL; undated Fair Report, probably 1830s, Chapman-Weston Papers, BPL. Rochester women revealed their concerns when they insisted their fair would be "conducted with propriety." Letter from L.S.A. Burtis to Abby Kelley, January 17, 1842, Kelley-Foster Papers, AmAS.

68. Catherine E. Kelley, "Fashioning Consumption in the Countryside: Languages of Consumption in Provincial New England," paper presented at the annual meeting of the Society for the History of the Early Republic, Boston College, July 15, 1994; letter from Mary Gilbert to Maria Weston, probably December 1843, and letter from Julianna Tappan to Anne Weston, October 30, 1837, Chapman-Weston Papers, BPL.

69. *Liberator*, January 25, 1956; letters from Mary Manter to Maria Weston, July 5, July 30, 1840, Chapman-Weston Papers, BPL. Chambers-Schiller, "Boston Anti-Slavery Fair," in Yellin and Van Horne, eds., *Abolitionist Sisterhood*, 268–69.

70. Hallowell, ed., *James and Lucretia Mott*, 127; Minutes of the PFAS, March 3, 1840, PFAS Records, HSP. Hicksite Quaker Amy Post found that her fair work brought a visit from a committee of her meeting that advised "her in regard to her duty towards her family" (Nancy A. Hewitt, "The Fragmentation of Friends: The Consequences for Quaker Women in Antebellum America," in Brown and Stuard, eds., *Witnesses for Change*, 101).

71. *Liberator*, January 22, 1858; letter from Sarah Ernst to Miss Weston, July 28, 1850, Chapman-Weston Papers, BPL; letter from Elizabeth Gay to Caroline Weston, December 15, 1847, GFP; Deborah Bingham Van Broeckhoven, "The Political Economy of Massachusetts Women's Benevolent Fairs during the

1840s," paper presented at the annual meeting of the Society for the History of the Early Republic, Boston College, July 15, 1994, and session comments.

72. Van Broeckhoven, "Benevolent Fairs."

73. Schmidt, *Consumer Rites*, ch. 3; *Liberator*, December 28, 1838.

74. Willey, *History of the Anti-Slavery Cause*, 138–39.

75. Letter from Mary Kenney to William Lloyd Garrison, May 1, 1841, SFAS Records, EPI. Working with blacks to mount a fair could be problematic. Paulina Wright was anxious about the 1843 Utica fair because "colorphobia" was raging, and she felt it would hurt sales (letter from Paulina Wright to Maria Chapman, August 29, 1843, Chapman-Weston Papers, BPL).

76. "National Anti-Slavery Bazaar, January 1847," Chapman-Weston Papers, BPL; Foner, *Life and Writings of Frederick Douglass*, 2:15. In Philadelphia, not only was the labor of the women freely given, but at some fairs, only free produce materials were used (see Minutes of the PFAS, May 18, 1843, PFAS Records, HSP).

77. Sterling, *We Are Your Sisters*, 117; Black Abolitionist Papers, reel 6, no. 43, LOC. See also no. 128 for note of the large fair in Syracuse in 1849, and reel 7, no. 349 for mention of a Detroit Levee in 1852 that earned only $30. The levee may have only been an evening party, not a sale.

78. Sterling, *We Are Your Sisters*, 118–19. For a brief reference to other fair efforts, see James Oliver Horton and Stacy Flaherty, "Black Leadership in Antebellum Cincinnati," in Henry Louis Taylor Jr., ed., *Race and the City*, 79.

79. Billington, ed., *Journal of Charlotte L. Forten*, 74–75; "National Anti-Slavery Bazaar, January 1847," broadside, Chapman-Weston Papers, BPL.

80. *Liberator*, January 29, 1849, September 15, 1843; letter from Harriet Foster to Harriet Webster, January 9, 1839, SFAS Records, EPI; Debra Gold Hansen, "Bluestockings and Bluenoses," 191–93; letter from Julia Griffiths to Garrison, August 5, 1852, and letter from Maria Chapman to Elizabeth Pease, August 20, 1839, Antislavery Papers, BPL.

81. Meltzer and Holland, eds., *Lydia Maria Child*, 193, 194, 244; White Diary, entries for October 26, November 18, 1843, AmAS.

82. Letter from Frances Drake to Maria Weston, August 6, 1843, Chapman-Weston Papers, BPL; letter from Paulina Wright to Abby Kelley, August [?], 1843, Kelley-Foster Papers, AmAS.

83. Letter from Mary Manter to Garrison, April 23, 1842, Antislavery Papers, BPL; AFAS, *Annual Report*, 1849, 68; Meltzer and Holland, eds., *Lydia Maria Child*, 172.

84. Dillon, "Antislavery Movement in Illinois," 297–98; letter from unidentified woman to Deborah Weston, January 1, 1841, Chapman-Weston Papers, BPL. Ripley, ed., *Black Abolitionist Papers*, 3:19–21.

85. Mabee, *Black Freedom*, 115–17; Cheek and Cheek, *John Mercer Langston*, 365. See also Black Abolitionist Papers, reel 11, no. 650, LOC.

86. Letter from Elizabeth Gay to "Lizzy," March 22, 1846, GFP; letter from Phoebe Jackson to Helen Garrison, April 24, 1842, Antislavery Papers, BPL.

87. Haviland, *Woman's Life-Work*, 182; Lang, "Black Bootstraps," 5, 12, 15, 74–

75. Lang points out that while Quakers pioneered in black education, they did not educate for equality.

88. Barnes and Dumond, eds., *Weld-Grimké Letters*, 1:134, 178.

89. Ibid., 213, 215.

90. Ibid., 219, 211; letter from Susan Wattles to "Mary," June 25, 1838, Lukens-Gilbert Papers, WRHS.

91. Sterling, *We Are Your Sisters*, 131; Lang, "Black Bootstraps," 82, 85, 87, 89, 134.

92. Hine, ed., *Black Women in America*, 454; Sterling, *We Are Your Sisters*, 127–29; Lang, "Black Bootstraps," 109.

93. Letter from Betsy Cowles to "Mother," September 28, 1842, Cowles Papers, KSUL; letter from Rachel Stearns to Maria Chapman, December 18, 1842, Chapman-Weston Papers, BPL. See also Rachel's letters of November 29, 1843, and February 4, 1844, in ibid.

94. Letter from Mary Smith to Abby Kelley, August 16, 1841, and letter from Agnes Crain to Abby Kelley, March 26, 1847, Kelley-Foster Papers, AmAS.

95. See chapter 2 of Van Broeckhoven's "Abolitionists Were Women." She gives the example of the rhyming alphabet in "'A Determination to Labor . . .': Female Antislavery Activity in Rhode Island," in Finkelman, ed., *Articles on American Slavery*, 457. Whether this is the same alphabet mentioned by Lucy Chase in her diary fragments, in perhaps 1843, in Chase Papers, AmAS, is not clear.

96. Letter from Sarah Shaw to Maria Chapman, December 3, 1841, Chapman-Weston Papers, BPL.

97. Letter from "A. L. Otis" to Maria Chapman, December 24, 1857, and letter from Lucretia Mott to Maria Chapman, November 30, 1842, Chapman-Weston Papers, BPL; letter from Catherine D. Davis to Garrison, June 20, 1852, Antislavery Papers, BPL.

98. Letter from Phoebe Stearns to Maria Chapman, December 12, 1841, Chapman-Weston Papers, BPL; letter from Mary Torrey to Amos Phelps, June 1845, Antislavery Papers, BPL.

99. Letter from Edward Davis to Elizabeth Pease, February 15, 1842, and letter from Sophia Little to Samuel May, August 13, 1852, Antislavery Papers, BPL.

100. Karcher, *First Woman in the Republic*, 323. Quoted in Van Broeckhoven, "Abolitionists Were Women," ch. 2, p. 18.

101. Karcher, "Rape, Murder and Revenge," 323–24. See this article for a perceptive discussion of female literary strategies. Deborah Bingham Broeckhoven, "Female Antislavery Activity in Rhode Island," in Finkelman, ed., *Articles on American Slavery*, 451–53; Van Broeckhoven, "Abolitionists Were Women," ch. 2, pp. 4, 19, 26.

102. *Liberator*, April 10, May 21, November 19, 1841; Eaklor, ed., *American Antislavery Songs*, 65–66.

CHAPTER FOUR

1. Song by D. S. W. in Eaklor, ed., *American Antislavery Songs*, 253.

2. Letter from Sarah Ernst to Miss Weston, July 28, 1850, Chapman-Weston Papers, BPL.

3. McKivigan, *War against Proslavery Religion*, 64; Howard, *Conscience and Slavery*, 29–31; Stewart, *William Lloyd Garrison*, 111–12. Political and religious abolitionism were obviously not mutually exclusive. Many supporters of the Liberty Party had strong evangelical ties. See Volpe, *Forlorn Hope of Freedom*, xiii–xiv.

4. Quoted in Stewart, *Wendell Phillips*, 141. Ironically, though the Garrisonians were the smallest abolitionist group, they are probably the most studied. The availability of records for the Garrisonians has drawn historians to document their views and activities in some detail.

5. See, for example, Lori D. Ginzberg, *Women and the Work of Benevolence*, 86–88. Ginzberg writes that "political abolitionists who supported voting and church-oriented abolitionists who used the issue of women's visibility to limit the movement's radicalism thus allied, using the language of morality and femininity in their own behalf" (88). Women who supported these men, she suggests, moved on to other concerns as they recognized their marginality. Goen, *Broken Churches*, 6–9.

6. AFAS, *Annual Report*, 1852, 5; *True Wesleyan*, May 17, 1852.

7. Carwardine, *Evangelicals and Politics*, 51–52, 54.

8. Letter from A. D. Hawley to Betsy Cowles, July 6, 1840, Cowles Papers, KSUL; letter from Hannah Wilbur to Maria Chapman, December 21, 1841, Antislavery Papers, BPL.

9. Meltzer and Holland, eds., *Lydia Maria Child*, 295; Karcher, *First Woman in the Republic*, 390–400.

10. Quoted in Thomas, *Revivalism and Cultural Change*, 72.

11. Donald M. Scott, *From Office to Profession*, 43–46, 119–23.

12. Goen, *Broken Churches*, 50–53.

13. Hatch, *Democratization of American Christianity*, 206; Carwardine, *Evangelicals and Politics*, 141; 1842 Annual Report, SFAS Records, EPI.

14. Hatch, *Democratization of American Christianity*; Thomas, *Revivalism and Cultural Change*, 64, 67, 69.

15. *True Wesleyan*, January 10, 1846.

16. Howard, *Conscience and Slavery*, p. 39; John R. McKivigan, "Vote As You Pray and Pray as You Vote: Church-Oriented Abolitionism and Antislavery Politics," in Kraut, ed., *Crusaders and Compromisers*, 179; Evans, "Abolitionism in the Illinois Churches," 193.

17. Quoted in Goen, *Broken Churches*, 80; see also 75–76, 81, 66. Letter to the churches quoted in Fladeland, *Men and Brothers*, 233; Carwardine, *Evangelicals and Politics*, 153, 160; Blackett, *Building an Antislavery Wall*, 80, 91.

18. AFAS, *Annual Report*, 1851, 44; quote from Sterling, *Ahead of Her Time*, 165; Evans, "Abolitionism in the Illinois Churches," 268.

19. Ripley, ed., *Black Abolitionist Papers*, 3:195, 4:195; McKivigan, *War against Proslavery Religion*, 107–9.

20. Carwardine, *Evangelicals and Politics*, 31. Carwardine agrees that, although women lacked a formal vote, they by no means lacked power. Michael J. McTighe, in his study of Cleveland, *A Measure of Success*, 35, points out that, although women accounted for less than half the population of that city, they

still made up two-thirds of all church members. The figure for Congregational membership was suggested by Traci Hodgson in her paper "Egalitarian Transformations: Family Government, Religious Culture & Community on the Western Reserve of Ohio, 1800–1830" presented at the annual meeting of the Society for the History of the Early Republic in Cincinnati, Ohio, July 20, 1995. Van Broeckhoven, "Abolitionists Were Women," ch. 4, p. 1.

21. Letters from Eliza Gill to Maria Chapman, April 28, December 6, 1839, Chapman-Weston Papers, BPL; quote from Saum, *Popular Mood of Pre-Civil War America*, 173.

22. *True Wesleyan*, December 19, 1846; Jacob M. Manning diary entry, March 3, 1854, Manning Papers, MHS. Manning did not identify critics by gender. Volpe, *Forlorn Hope of Freedom*, 66; Evans, "Abolitionism in Illinois Churches," 9.

23. Letter from Patsy Newton to Maria Chapman, January 1840, Chapman-Weston Papers, BPL; letter from Lucy Wright to Betsy Cowles, March 5, 1836, Cowles Papers, KSUL; *Liberator*, November 18, 1842, July 31, 1847.

24. McKivigan, *War against Proslavery Religion*, 134.

25. Letter from Anne Weston to Mary Weston, October 27, 1835, Chapman-Weston Papers, BPL; Little quote from Van Broeckhoven, "Abolitionists Were Women," ch. 4, p. 35.

26. Letters from Deborah Weston to Anne Weston, April 14, April 26, 1842, Chapman-Weston Papers, BPL.

27. Altschuler and Saltzgaber, *Revivalism, Social Conscience, and Community*, 16–17, 43, 90–93; *True Wesleyan*, October 28, 1843.

28. Letter from Sophia Little to Maria Chapman, September 26, 1840, and letter from Deborah Weston to Caroline Weston, October 5, 1841, Chapman-Weston Papers, BPL; *Liberator*, June 14, 1844. Writing from Northampton, Maria Child expressed her disapproval of "a minister who receives $250 a year from a rich slave-auctioneer here" (Meltzer and Holland, eds., *Lydia Maria Child*, 89).

29. *Liberator*, March 12, 1836; letter from Maria Rice to Maria Chapman, October 3, 1839, and letter from Eliza Gill to Maria Chapman, April 28, 1839, Chapman-Weston Papers, BPL; Mabee, *Black Freedom*, 217. Elmira Swett was convicted but avoided going to jail when the jailkeeper would not accept her as a prisoner. Martha Barrett Diary, entry for June 30, 1850, EPI.

30. Letter from Patsy Newton to Maria Chapman, January 1840, Chapman-Weston Papers, BPL; Portland Anti-Slavery Society Records, August 10, 1844, Maine Historical Society. Karen V. Hansen, in *A Very Social Time*, 125, 132, 145, points out the importance of gossip and its relationship to religion.

31. Letter from Sophia Little to Maria Chapman, September 26, 1840, and letter from Eleanor A. Jewett to [?], January 5, 1840, Chapman-Weston Papers, BPL; Report of the SFAS, 1842, SFAS Records, EPI; *Liberator*, March 21, 1845, August 20, 1852.

32. Evans, "Abolitionism in the Illinois Churches," 3, 9; McKivigan, *War against Proslavery Religion*, 69–73; Ripley, ed., *Black Abolitionist Papers*, 4:195.

33. White Diary, AmAS; McKivigan, *War against Proslavery Religion*, 15–16.

34. Letters from Evelina Smith to Caroline Weston, September 9, December 12, 1841, July 10, 1842, and letter from Evelina Smith to Maria Chapman, June 25, 1843, Chapman-Weston Papers, BPL.

35. Van Broeckhoven, "Abolitionists Were Women," ch. 1, p. 26, ch. 4, pp. 3, 4. Rev. Daniel Foster wrote in his diary, "I feel a good deal anxious for I learn that some of this people are dissatisfied with my preaching because I make reference so often to slavery." It was only because of the support of his wife that he felt able to continue his course. Although originally a Congregationalist, he joined the Wesleyan Methodist connection because he could not get ordained in the Congregational church (diary entry, April 2, 1852, and clipping, "Rev. Daniel Foster's Address on Slavery," 1853, Daniel Foster Papers, MHS).

36. Letter from Alice Hale March to John March, April 23, 1838, March Family Papers, EPI; letter from Lucinda Storrs to "Dear Children," January 31, 1835, Storrs Papers, New York Public Library.

37. Bass, " 'Best Hope of the Sexes,' " 183; letter from Evelina Smith to Maria Chapman, June 25, 1843, Chapman-Weston Papers, BPL.

38. Altschuler and Saltzgaber, *Revivalism, Social Conscience, and Community*, 90, 93, 96, 99.

39. Ibid., 139–40, 143–44.

40. Ibid., 122.

41. Letter from Eleanor Jewett to Anne Weston or Maria Chapman, January 5, 1840, and letter from L. M. Robbins to Maria Chapman, March 16, 1844, Chapman-Weston Papers, BPL.

42. *Liberator*, March 6, 1840; Stevens, " 'From Generation to Generation,' " 70, 72–73; Emerson, *Life of Abby Hopper Gibbons*, 105, 107. Lucy Chase, in a diary entry for May 14, 1844, also recorded that a woman "wielded her tongue long and impressively," in the Quarterly Meeting and that she admired the woman's courage if not her speaking abilities (diary fragments, Chase Papers, AmAS).

43. Letter from Lucretia Mott to Maria Chapman, February 11, 1843, Chapman-Weston Papers, BPL; Mabee, *Black Freedom*, 217. Mabee calls such actions "speak-ins."

44. See *Liberator*, October 30, 1840.

45. Black Abolitionist Papers, reel 3, nos. 598–601, LOC; Van Broeckhoven, "Abolitionists Were Women," ch. 4, p. 35; Mabee, *Black Freedom*, 128, 137. By the time of the Civil War, the Boston *Courier* suggested that in New England such tactics had succeeded. But while New England churches may have banished segregation from houses of worship, apparently the practice continued elsewhere in the North.

46. Letter from Gulielma Estes to "Friend Wright," August 11, 1842, Antislavery Papers, BPL.

47. Letter from Mary Smith to Abby Kelley, August 16, 1841, and letter from Asa and Anna Fairbanks to Abby Kelley, October 11, 1841, Kelley-Foster Papers, AmAS.

48. Letter from Sophia Little to Maria Chapman, September 26, 1840, Chapman-Weston Papers, BPL; *Liberator*, August 20, 1852; letter from Elizabeth Neall to Elizabeth Pease, June 18, 1842, GFP.

49. Address of Thomas Stove, Salem, 1852, Sophia Smith Collection, Smith College Library, Northampton, Mass.

50. *Liberator*, August 20, 1852; quoted in Van Broeckhoven, "Abolitionists Were Women," ch. 4, p. 16, 47 n. 34.

51. Karen V. Hansen, *Very Social Time*, 137; letter from Agnes Crain to Abby Kelley, March 26, 1847, Kelley-Foster Papers, AmAS.

52. Letter from R. W. Stearns to Maria Chapman, November 29, 1843, and letter from L. M. Robbins to Maria Chapman, March 16, 1844, Chapman-Weston Papers, BPL. Emerson, *Life of Abby Hopper Gibbons*, 115–20.

53. Bass, " 'Best Hope of the Sexes,' " 210.

54. Lovell, ed., *Two Quaker Sisters*, 122–24; letter from Sophia Little to Maria Weston, September 26, 1840, Chapman-Weston Papers, BPL.

55. McKivigan, "Vote As You Pray," in Kraut, ed., *Crusaders and Compromisers*, 181; McKivigan, *War against Proslavery Religion*, 168; Evans, "Abolitionism in the Illinois Churches," 369; Ripley, ed., *Black Abolitionist Papers*, 3:423; Bradley, "Progressive Friends in Michigan and New York," 95. Divisions occurred in both Orthodox and Hicksite meetings.

56. *True Wesleyan*, January 7, 1843, June 1, March 23, 1844.

57. McKivigan, *War against Proslavery Religion*, 17; letter from R. W. Stearns to Maria Chapman, February 4, 1844, Chapman-Weston Papers, BPL.

58. Wesleyan Methodist Church Records, March 1, 1845, AmAS. In "Abolitionism in the Illinois Churches," 295–97, Evans provides some interesting figures on the First Baptist church in Chicago. The church divided in 1843 over the issue of slavery. Sixty-two members of First Baptist joined the new Tabernacle Baptist church. Evans does not provide the breakdown of the first group of come-outers, but by 1854 there were 120 male members and 235 female members in this abolitionist body.

59. Padgett, "Antislavery Rank-and-File," 64–66; McKivigan, "Vote As You Pray," in Kraut, ed., *Crusaders and Compromisers*, 181; McKivigan, *War against Proslavery Religion*, 92, 96–99.

60. Wesleyan Methodist Church Records, AmAS.

61. Padgett, "Antislavery Rank-and-File," 64, 74–76.

62. *True Wesleyan*, May 13, 1843.

63. Ibid., February 17, 1849, July 11, 1846, November 25, 1848, October 12, 1850, April 28, 1849.

64. Ibid., June 28, 1851.

65. For examples of conventional fiction and articles that supported middle-class gender norms, see *True Wesleyan*, January 21, 1843, October 24, 1846. For support of petitioning, see ibid., January 29, 1848, October 4, 1851.

66. Executive Report of the Western Anti-Slavery Society, 1847, Papers of the Western Anti-Slavery Society, LOC. McKivigan, in *War against Proslavery Religion*, 98, details the Wesleyan Methodists' "poor relations" with Garrisonians. *True Wesleyan*, January 13, 1844.

67. *True Wesleyan*, April 28, 1849, March 13, 1847.

68. Ibid., April 15, 1843, March 16, 1844. The critical article was reprinted from the *Baptist Advocate*, suggesting that church women were using the strategy

across denominational lines. An article published on February 27, 1847, described the event's committee as mixed, two women and two men. For information about a donation visit sponsored by African American women in Erie, see *True Wesleyan*, May 10, 1850. McKivigan, in *War against Proslavery Religion*, 15-16, points out that men raised money through soliciting individual contributions while women mounted campaigns. Collecting money was an enduring element of women's "invisible" career in the voluntary sector.

69. *True Wesleyan*, June 6, 1846.

70. Ibid., April 15, 1843.

71. Ibid.

72. Ibid., also January 25, 1845, January 17, 1846, February 6, 1847.

73. Ibid., July 4, 1846, December 9, 1848, August 1, 1846.

74. Ibid., December 21, 1850.

75. Ibid., January 20, 1849.

76. Volpe, *Forlorn Hope of Freedom*, 45.

77. Ibid., 62-63; letter from Joshiah, Judith, and Harriet Wood to Sister and Thomas Fish, November through December, 1842. Clement Papers, Vermont Historical Society, Montpelier; John L. Brooke, *Heart of the Commonwealth*, 369-70. Paula Baker, in "Domestication of Politics," 621-31, urges adopting a broad definition of political action, one that will include female activism. Women also took political action against third parties. A February 10, 1843, article in the *Liberator* described Sarah Sanbourn of Maine who disrupted a convention of "hirelings and politicians" interested in promoting the Liberty Party. Apparently she both spoke and tried to adjourn the meeting. The account says that priestly ingenuity tried "to confuse her and put a stop to her remarks. Cries of 'Order!' and votes to explain away the resolutions . . . and motions to adjourn" were offered by the men present.

78. Political historians are beginning to recognize the importance of political activities beyond voting and to create a political history that moves beyond the limits of formal politics. See McCurry, "Two Faces of Republicanism," 1245 and following. McTighe, in *A Measure of Success*, 137, discusses the formation of public culture. Carwardine, *Evangelicals and Politics*, 32-34, touches upon female political participation. *Advocate of Freedom*, November 23, 1939; *Liberty Standard*, January 18, 1843.

79. Stewart, *Wendell Phillips*, 135, 143. Stewart points to the irony of Garrisonian rhetoric. It condemned the Union as proslavery and thus encouraged antislavery voters to cast their ballots "for the first available Liberty man or Free-Soiler."

80. Volpe, *Forlorn Hope of Freedom*, 24-43; Foner, ed., *Life and Writings of Frederick Douglass*, 2:67; Kraut, ed., *Crusaders and Compromisers*, 4, 29; Gerteis, *Morality and Utility in American Antislavery Reform*, 44-45; Carwardine, *Evangelicals and Politics*, 103-4.

81. Richard H. Sewall, "Slavery, Race, and the Free Soil Party, 1848-1854," in Kraut, ed., *Crusaders and Compromisers*, acknowledges both racism and bolder commitments to racial equality than majority opinion in Free-Soil. He also sees many Free-Soilers believing that slavery was morally wrong. "A great

many abolitionists . . . found in the Free Soil Party a promising (if flawed) instrument of abolitionism and racial justice," he suggests. The party was a conduit for Liberty ideas that eventually passed to the Republican Party (see 101–8, 117–18). Foner, ed., *Life and Writings of Douglass*, 2:383, 396, 399. For a detailed account of the development of the Republican Party, see Gienapp, *Origins of the Republican Party*.

82. Elizabeth R. Varon, "The Ladies are Whigs: White Women and the Second Party System in Antebellum Virginia," paper delivered at the annual meeting of the Society for the History of the Early Republic, Cincinnati, Ohio, July 22, 1995. Ryan, *Women in Public*, 36 and passim.

83. Ryan, *Women in Public*, 137; quotes from Pierson, " 'Free Hearts and Free Homes,' " 101; see also 51–52.

84. Foner, ed., *Life and Writings of Douglass*, 2:264; Lucy Chase, diary fragment, 184[?], Chase Papers, AmAS; Evans, "Abolitionism in the Illinois Churches," 71; letter from Hannah Robie to "Brother," June 5, 1854, Robie-Sewall Papers, MHS; *Liberty Standard*, February 11, 25, 1847. Reinhard O. Johnson points out that Maine had one of the strongest Liberty Party votes in the country ("Liberty Party in Maine," 135).

85. Minutes of the PFAS, March 12, 1847, PFAS Records, HSP; Quist, " 'Great Majority of Our Subscribers,' " 338; Johnson, "Liberty Party in Maine," 246; Ripley, ed., *Black Abolitionist Papers*, 4:96.

86. Lucy Chase, diary fragments, November 16, 1844[?], Chase Papers, AmAS; Foner, ed., *The Life and Writings of Frederick Douglass*, 1:264. For a reference to a Free-Soil fair, see letter from Sarah Macmillan to Anne Weston, April 15, 1852, Chapman-Weston Papers, BPL. Nancy A. Hewitt, "The Social Origins of Women's Antislavery Politics in Western New York," in Kraut, ed., *Crusaders and Compromisers*, 214.

87. As Joel H. Silbey pointed out in " 'There Are Other Questions Beside That of Slavery Merely': The Democratic Party and Antislavery Politics," in Kraut, ed., *Crusaders and Compromisers*, 156, no party leader could afford to ignore what made a party unique in the minds of the voters. Pierson, " 'Free Hearts and Free Homes,' " 214; McTighe, *Measure of Success*, 5; comments of Harry Watson, in "New Approaches to the History of Jacksonian Politics," commentary delivered at the annual meeting of the Society for the History of the Early Republic, Cincinnati, Ohio, July 22, 1995. *Liberty Standard*, August 15, 1844. The connection between religious and political abolitionism is suggested by the formation of an antislavery Congregational church in Hallowell in the 1840s (Schriver, *Go Free*, 89).

88. *Liberty Standard*, June 1, 1842, August 15, 1844. Volpe, *Forlorn Hope of Freedom*, 56; Pierson, " 'Free Hearts and Free Homes,' " 216–17. In a slightly different context, but equally involved in speaking in public and in creating public culture, were the women of Andover, Massachusetts, at a July 4 event. There Miss R. Smith gave a lengthy address, parts of which were reported in the *True Wesleyan*, August 10, 1844. As Pierson points out (217), in Centreville, Connecticut, however, a man presented the banner to the Fremont Club. Gienapp, *Origins of the Republican Party*, 205.

89. Beedy, *Mothers of Maine*, 231–33. Beedy says that the work of this female society was taken over by "the leading political party of the state" in 1856. Schriver, *Go Free*, 37, 38–39, 45; Willey, *History of the Anti-Slavery Cause*, 443. The *Portland Inquirer*, March 1, 1855, notes that a male baker made the cake.

90. Foner, ed., *Life and Writings of Douglass*, 2:222; *Liberty Standard*, October 16, 1845; Schriver, *Go Free*, 52. Schriver does not say explicitly that women sponsored the donation party, but it is likely. Certainly, they did the work for it.

91. *True Wesleyan*, February 14, 1846; *Liberty Standard*, February 1, 1843, June 12, 1845, May 30, 1844.

92. Willey, *History of the Anti-Slavery Cause*, 423, 442–43.

93. Gienapp, in *Origins of the Republican Party*, 205, points out that Maine Republicans had adopted a radical antislavery platform in 1855. *Portland Inquirer*, August 2, 1855; Pierson, "'Free Hearts and Free Homes,'" 215.

94. Pierson, "'Free Hearts and Free Homes,'" 216–17; Chadwick, ed., *Life for Liberty*, 68; letter from Sarah Field to S. May, August 20, 1852, Antislavery Papers, BPL.

95. For a full treatment of this subject, see Pierson, "'Free Hearts and Free Homes.'" Hoxie quote is on 218. Hoxie, like other political men, was a bit uneasy with the implications of females in the political arena. "We do not expect them, to be sure, to go into the jury-box, or labor in the fields," he said. Kenneth M. Stampp, in *America in 1857*, 126, acknowledges the deep debt the party owed women for creating an effective moral climate.

96. Letter from Betsy Hudson to Betsy Cowles, February 27, 1846, Cowles Papers, KSUL; Pierson, "'Free Hearts and Free Homes,'" esp. 107–9, 132–36.

97. Meltzer and Holland, eds., *Lydia Maria Child*, 293, 191.

98. Pierson, "'Free Hearts and Free Homes,'" 132, 214–16.

99. Carwardine, *Evangelicals and Politics*, 34; Pierson, "'Free Hearts and Free Homes,'" 188, 194, 201, 202, 208–9, 214. Pierson points out the limitations of female participation and notes that at rallies they were often separately seated. I have seen no indication of separate seating in my research.

CHAPTER FIVE

1. Song by Mrs. J. G. Carter in Eaklor, ed., *American Antislavery Songs*, 169.

2. Letter from Eliza Earle to Abby Kelley, February 28, 1837, Kelley-Foster Papers, AmAS; letter from Sarah Russell May to Wendell Phillips, August 23, 1858, Blagden-Phillips Papers, HL; *Liberator*, September 19, 1856, August 14, 1857.

3. Letter from Sarah Russell May to Wendell Phillips, August 23, 1858, Blagden-Phillips Papers, HL; *Liberator*, October 22, 1858.

4. For an example, see Black Abolitionist Papers, reel 9, no. 112, LOC.

5. Letter from Lucretia Mott to Adeline Roberts, March 5, 1852, SFAS Records, EPI; Black Abolitionist Papers, reel 10, no. 487, LOC.

6. *Liberator*, October 22, March 26, 1858. Support for antislavery was doubtlessly helped by the migration from the Northeast to the Midwest.

7. Lawrence J. Friedman, in "'Pious Fellowship' and Modernity: A Psychosocial

Interpretation," in Kraut, ed., *Crusaders and Compromisers*, 244–45, points to the importance of economic changes that allowed entrepreneurs to sympathize more easily with abolitionism. He highlights the psychological impact of this sympathy on abolitionists. Fladeland, *Men and Brothers*, 284, suggests that by the 1850s abolitionism had become respectable.

8. Ralph A. Keller, "Methodist Newspapers," 323; Stanley W. Campbell, *Slave Catchers*, 14; letter from "Hattie" to Betsy Cowles, July 11, 1847, Cowles Papers, KSUL; Robert L. Hall, "Massachusetts Abolitionists Document the Slave Experience," in Jacobs, ed., *Courage and Conscience*, 80; Cashin, "Black Families in the Old Northwest," 452, 461–62.

9. On the Fugitive Slave Law's provisions, see Carwardine, *Evangelicals and Politics*, 178, and Sterling, *Ahead of Her Time*, 280.

10. Carwardine, *Evangelicals and Politics*, 178, 191; Yacovone, *Samuel Joseph May*, 137. Ralph A. Keller, "Methodist Newspapers," 320, 322; Ripley, ed., *Black Abolitionist Papers*, 4:308; Stewart, *William Lloyd Garrison*, 158. The Waterloo Yearly Meeting did not condemn the law until 1852 (Bradley, "Progressive Friends in Michigan and New York," 100).

11. Ripley, ed., *Black Abolitionist Papers*, 4:98.

12. Yacovone, *Samuel Joseph May*, 139; R. J. M. Blackett, " 'Freedom, or the Martyr's Grave': Black Pittsburgh's Aid to the Fugitive Slave," in Finkelman, ed., *Articles on American Slavery: Fugitive Slaves*, 36.

13. Blackett, " 'Freedom, or the Martyr's Grave,' " in Finkelman, ed., *Articles on American Slavery: Fugitive Slaves*, 128; Eggert, "Impact of the Fugitive Slave Law," 537.

14. Stange, *Patterns of Antislavery*, 38; *Liberator*, September 19, 1856.

15. Eggert, "Impact of the Fugitive Slave Law," 537–40, 546, 550–53, 568; Cockrum, *History of the Underground Railroad*, 60.

16. Sterling, *Ahead of Her Time*, 293; Stampp, *America in 1857*, 330.

17. Letter from Hannah Robie to "Brother," April 11, 1854, Robie-Sewall Papers, MHS; Lacy, "Protestant Newspaper Reaction," 65; quotes from Gienapp, *Origins of the Republican Party*, 74, 73; Carwardine, *Evangelicals and Politics*, 249; *Liberator*, June 12, 1857.

18. Carwardine, *Evangelicals and Politics*, 240–41.

19. Ibid., 242; Gienapp, *Origins of the Republican Party*, 76–77.

20. John Demos, "The Antislavery Movement and the Problem of Violent 'Means,' " in Finkelman, ed., *Articles on American Slavery*, 139; Clifford, *Crusader for Freedom*, 226; Lawson and Merrill, *Three Sarahs*, 284.

21. Stampp, *America in 1857*, 99, 105, 329; Strother, *Underground Railroad in Connecticut*, 179.

22. Strother, *Underground Railroad in Connecticut*, 179. Stampp, in *America in 1857*, 104, points out that most northern legislatures, dominated by Republicans, lodged similar protests.

23. Friedman, " 'Pious Fellowship' and Modernity," in Kraut, ed., *Crusaders and Compromisers*, 242–45.

24. Knights, *Yankee Destinies*, 15, 20; Christopher Clark, *Roots of Rural Capitalism*, 312–13.

25. Carwardine, *Evangelicals and Politics*, 194–95.

26. Maria L. Thorp, "Sketches of My Travels in the Month of June, 1851," Thorp Papers, Vermont Historical Society, Montpelier.

27. Letter from Abigail Mott to Abby Kelley, August 18, 1842, Kelley-Foster Papers, AmAS; Cashin, "Black Families in the Old Northwest," 472; Sterling, *We Are Your Sisters*, 222. R. J. Young, in *Antebellum Black Activists*, 129–33, 149, suggests there were two styles of black womanhood, with those she calls "folk women" less influenced by middle-class norms and less interested in literacy than the women who were black activists. James Oliver Horton, in *Free People of Color*, 36, notes that Boston's blacks formed the Freedom Association in 1845 as part of an effort to assist fugitives. Women probably provided many of the services for the fugitives.

28. *Liberator*, August 23, 1850.

29. Minutes of the PFAS, April 10, 1856, PFAS Records, HSP. Mabee, *Black Freedom*, 274; Gara, *Liberty Line*, 73. AFAS, *Annual Report*, 1851, 4; see also reports for 1849 and 1850.

30. Winch, "Philadelphia and the Other Underground Railroad," 3; Still, *Underground Rail Road*, 566–67; Ripley, ed., *Black Abolitionist Papers*, 3:23, suggests that there were two distinct types of abolitionism in the 1840s and 1850s: white abolitionism, where the issues were abstract, and black abolitionism, where the issues were concrete. See James Oliver Horton, *Free People of Color*, ch. 3, for a good discussion of the involvement of free blacks in the underground railroad.

31. Bacon, *Quiet Rebels*, 4, 300; Jane H. Pease and William H. Pease, "Ends, Means, And Attitudes: Black-White Conflict in the Antislavery Movement," in Finkelman, ed., *Articles on American Slavery*, 373; Benjamin Quarles, "Harriet Tubman's Unlikely Leadership," in Hine, ed., *Black Women in United States History*, 4:1137; Ripley, ed., *Black Abolitionist Papers*, 3:38. Lois Horton points out: "The potential power of an issue to mobilize a community and to sustain a long-term struggle appears to depend on the extent to which that issue is a part of the people's immediate experience and has an impact on the community at all levels of its organization" ("Community Organization and Social Activism," 183). James Oliver Horton, *Free People of Color*, 62–63.

32. Gara, *Liberty Line*, 90, 92; Mabee, *Black Freedom*, 274–75; Blackett, " 'Freedom or the Martyr's Grave,' " in Finkelman, *Articles on American Slavery: Fugitive Slaves*, 39–40.

33. Still, *Underground Rail Road*, 4; Gara, *Liberty Line*, 30; Hembree, "Question of 'Begging,' " 314.

34. Quarles, *Black Abolitionists*, 147–48; Mabee, *Black Freedom*, 274. Levi Coffin, in his *Reminiscences*, 297, remarked that, before his arrival in Cincinnati, fugitives almost always stayed with other blacks. Still, *Underground Rail Road*, 218–19. Laura S. Haviland, in *Woman's Life-Work*, 135, describes one incident when a fugitive was betrayed by another black whom she labels as a "Judas," "an idle, loafish mulatto."

35. Yee, *Black Women Abolitionists*, 20. Most boardinghouses were run by women. Hallie Q. Brown, *Homespun Heroines*, 27. Still, *Underground Rail Road*, 219.

36. Still, *Underground Rail Road*, 620; Sterling, *We Are Your Sisters*, 220–21. The daughter of Frederick Douglass likewise recalled the female role. Her father "enlarged his home" to accommodate fugitives. "It was no unusual occurrence for mother to be called up at all hours of the night, cold or hot as the case may be, to prepare supper for a hungry lot of fleeing humanity" (Lawson and Merrill, *Three Sarahs*, 302).

37. Ripley, ed., *Black Abolitionist Papers*, 3:38; Lovell, ed., *Two Quaker Sisters*, 129; Yee, *Black Women Abolitionists*, 12. Theodore Hershberg, in "Free Blacks in Antebellum Philadelphia: A Study of Ex-Slaves, Freeborn, and Socioeconomic Decline," in Kusmer, ed., *Antebellum America*, 199, suggests that 80 percent of black women in Philadelphia did day work.

38. Blockson, *African Americans in Philadelphia*, 21. *McElroy's Philadelphia Directory*.

39. Ripley, ed., *Black Abolitionist Papers*, 2:287–88. Elizabeth's niece was Mary Ann Shadd Cary. James Oliver Horton, in *Free People of Color*, 30, discusses the importance of networks in helping migrants adapt to new cities and situations.

40. Ripley, ed., *Black Abolitionist Papers*, 3:38. Quarles, *Black Abolitionists*, 158.

41. Linda M. Perkins, "Black Women and Racial 'Uplift' Prior to Emancipation," in Hine, ed., *Black Women in United States History*, 3:1081; Quarles, *Black Abolitionists*, 157.

42. Coffin, *Reminiscences*, 300; Blockson, *Underground Railroad*, 93.

43. Bacon, *Quiet Rebels*, 111–12; Coffin, *Reminiscences*, 303. In Delaware and Pennsylvania, Hicksite Quakers were involved in the underground railroad, but some found the official attitude toward abolitionism discouraging. In Pennsylvania in 1852, Hicksites established the Pennsylvania Yearly Meeting of Progressive Friends, which became a stronghold of abolitionist activism. Similar divisions took place elsewhere. Priscilla Thompson, "Harriet Tubman, Thomas Garrett, and the Underground Railroad," in Hine, ed., *Black Women in United States History*, 4:1369, 1372–73; Hamm, *Transformation of American Quakerism*, 32; Nancy A. Hewitt, "The Fragmentation of Friends: The Consequences for Quaker Women in Antebellum America," and "Documents," in Brown and Stuard, eds., *Witnesses for Change*, 102–12; Hochreiter, "*Pennsylvania Freeman*," 235. Gara, in "Friends and the Underground Railroad," 5, 8, 19, warns not to overemphasize Quaker involvement and suggests that the Friends' reputation was based on the efforts of a few active individuals. Gara emphasizes that blacks, Wesleyan Methodists, and Reformed Presbyterians were at least as active as Quakers. Wahl, in "Pennsylvania Yearly Meeting of Progressive Friends," 122, 131, highlights the importance of those Hicksites who became Progressive Friends.

44. Ndukwu, "Antislavery in Michigan," 114, 138. Nathan Thomas, as so often seems to be the case with underground railroad couples, was active in abolitionist politics. Still, *Underground Rail Road*, 207.

45. Smedley, *History of the Underground Railroad*, 55–56; Siebert, *Underground Railroad*, 53.

46. Still, *Underground Rail Road*, 149, 618. In a letter sent to Still in January 1855, Abigail enclosed $10, money she had made in two weeks. She wrote: "Of course it belongs to the slave. It may go for the fugitives or Canada slaves" (see 619). Lovell, ed., *Two Quaker Sisters*, 132. On the repair of an old overcoat, see *Old Anti-Slavery Days*, 74. Blockson, *Underground Railroad*, 241.

47. Haviland, *Woman's Life-Work*, 92, 124–26, 130–33; Coffin, *Reminiscences*, 336; Smedley, *History of the Underground Railroad*, 137–41.

48. Coffin, *Reminiscences*, 300–301, 310; Still, *Underground Rail Road*, 585, 587–88, and for other evidence of circles forming see 589; see also Ripley, ed., *Black Abolitionist Papers*, 4:272, and Blockson, *Underground Railroad*, 204, 271–72. In Franklin, New York, Lucia Stilson presided over an antislavery society of forty women who supplied clothing for the Fugitive Aid League in Syracuse. Her husband, Ansel, had been a promoter of the Liberty Party. Perhaps this marriage of male political abolitionism with male and female underground railroad participation was common. There are other references to such commitments. For example, see Smedley, *History of the Underground Railroad*, 55–61, 137.

49. Letter from Lucy Osgood to Rev. Stetson, October 20, 1851, Caleb Stetson Papers, MHS; letter from Lizzie Gay to Maria Chapman, June 11, 1857, and letter from Lizzie Gay to Sarah Pugh, July 2, 1857, GFP; letters from Sarah Ernst to Anne Weston, February 1, November 14, 1852, Chapman-Weston Papers, BPL; *Liberator*, February 17, 1851. For records of the Boston Vigilance Committee that show monetary contributions, see Black Abolitionist Papers, reel 6, nos. 619–44, LOC.

50. *Liberator*, May 26, 1848.

51. Ginzberg, *Women and the Work of Benevolence*, 88; Still, *Underground Rail Road*, 681; Stevens, " 'From Generation to Generation,' " 65, 68; Meltzer and Holland, eds., *Lydia Maria Child*, 378; *Liberator*, March 3, 1854; Wyatt-Brown, *Lewis Tappan*, 303–4. For one discussion of Maria Child's involvement in the Jacobs narrative, see Mills, *Cultural Reformations*, ch. 6.

52. Meltzer and Holland, eds., *Lydia Maria Child*, 313; Lovell, ed., *Two Quaker Sisters*, 133–34, 164; Stevens, " 'From Generation to Generation,' " 80, 101–3. As Stevens points out, Elizabeth Chace made her home the locus for political activism.

53. AAS, *Proceedings of the American Anti-Slavery Society at Its Second Decade*, 24; Yee, *Black Women Abolitionists*, 99–100; Jean R. Soderlund, "Priorities and Power: The Philadelphia Female Anti-Slavery Society," in Yellin and Van Horne, eds., *Abolitionist Sisterhood*, 69, 81–86; Minutes of the PFAS, September 19, 1841, June 2, 1842, June 12, 1845, April 10, 1856, PFAS Records, HSP; Still, *Underground Rail Road*, 613–16.

54. Still, *Underground Rail Road*, 617–19; Blockson, *Underground Railroad*, 241–42.

55. Coffin, *Reminiscences*, 297. To be fair to Levi, he thought that many whites were "too timid, . . . not willing to risk the penalty of the law or the stigma on their reputation" (see 297–98). Haviland, *Woman's Life-Work*, 212; Block-

son, *Underground Railroad*, 92; Middleton, "Fugitive Slave Crisis," 23. Gara, in *Liberty Line*, 94, asserts that free blacks, in fact, did most of the work.

56. *Portland Inquirer*, May 31, 1855.

57. Dover Anti-Slavery Sewing Circle Records, May 29, September 3, October 25, 1855, January 29, April 9, 1856, NHHS; Notice, December 2, 1856, Swan Family Papers, MHS; *Portland Inquirer*, November 6, 1856; Meltzer and Holland, eds., *Lydia Maria Child*, 295.

58. *Liberator*, April 14, March 10, August 18, 1854; Schriver, *Go Free*, 38.

59. *Liberator*, June 20, August 15, 1856.

60. Meltzer and Holland, eds., *Lydia Maria Child*, 342, 335–36, 362–64; letter from Sarah Mason to Wendell Phillips, January 2, 1860, Blagden-Phillips Papers, HL.

61. Ripley, ed., *Black Abolitionist Papers*, 3:53.

62. Ibid., 27. At the end of the 1840s, 46 percent of Philadelphia's black women toiled as washerwomen, an occupation that must have made it very difficult to rise to a leadership position (Hine, ed., *Black Women in America*, 5).

63. Ripley, ed., *Black Abolitionist Papers*, 2:192; Yee, *Black Women Abolitionists*, 70.

64. Ripley, ed., *Black Abolitionist Papers*, 2:350, 285–86, 330–41.

65. Yee, *Black Women Abolitionists*, 119, 118.

66. Ripley, ed., *Black Abolitionist Papers*, 2:285; Sterling, *We Are Your Sisters*, 170, 172; James Oliver Horton, *Free People of Color*, 95–96, 103, 116.

67. Yee, *Black Women Abolitionists*, 117–18, 127.

68. Letters from Lizzie Gay to Sarah Pugh, February 24, April, 1857, GFP; Ames, *Life and Letters of Peter and Susan Lesley*, 1:357.

69. Meltzer and Holland, eds., *Lydia Maria Child*, 292, 330. For another indication of energy, see letter from Hannah Robie to S. B. Robie, June 5, 1854, Robie-Sewall Papers, MHS. Fladeland, *Men and Brothers*, 374.

70. Soderlund, "Priorities and Power," in Yellin and Van Horne, eds., *Abolitionist Sisterhood*, 80–88. As Soderlund points out, "The Philadelphia women chose to be a tiny band of moral reformers rather than the organizers of a mass movement" (87).

71. Martha Barrett Diary, entries for February 22, February 1, 1851, EPI; *Liberator*, January 30, 1857.

72. Stevens, "'From Generation to Generation,'" 90, 125, 97–106, 128–31, 134. Lillie recalled her youth during both the 1850s and 1860s. Lovell, ed., *Two Quaker Sisters*, 134.

73. Lovell, ed., *Two Quaker Sisters*, 134, 54.

74. Billington, ed., *Journal of Charlotte L. Forten*, 42, 51, 55, 63, 67, 98.

75. Ibid., 98, 78, 100, 101, 77–78.

76. Ibid., 101, 76.

77. Ibid., 45, 42. 52, 55, 74.

78. Ibid., 95, 79, 82, 97, 109–10; Lapansky, "Feminism, Freedom, and Community," 12–13, 4, 7–8; Sumler-Lewis, "Forten-Purvis Women of Philadelphia," 232–86.

79. Erving Goffman, in *Forms of Talk*, 187–88, suggests that lectures provide an

audience with a ritualistic access to the subject matter. Certainly for those who attended antislavery lectures over the years the experiences were not only social and intellectual but also ritualistic.

80. Stewart, *Wendell Phillips*, 179–85; *Liberator*, October 24, 1851; Foner, ed., *Life and Writings of Frederick Douglass*, 2:448. In 1852, Douglass wrote to the president of the Rochester Ladies' Anti-Slavery Society that it was the society's responsibility "to call conventions, secure the attendance of eloquent speakers, and make all the needful arrangements for the spread of Anti-Slavery truths here. . . . At the present you have the field to yourself" (159). The Rochester ladies supported Douglass's causes faithfully over the years.

81. Karlyn Kohrs Campbell, ed., *Women Public Speakers*, 340. Campbell points out that women entered into public dialogue as early as 1787 (xi) and notes the importance of Quaker women in the early days of female lecturing (xiii); Sterling, *Ahead of Her Time*, 118–19; *Liberator*, January 13, 1843.

82. *Liberator*, November 3, 1843, August 18, 1854, July 9, 1858, September 2, 1859. The collection to which men donated their chewed tobacco quids as well as buttons and other articles occurred in 1852 in response to an attack on the Baptist church's stand on slavery. Herbig, *Friends for Freedom*, 177. Jane Gray Swisshelm made the same point about being able to speak freely in her *Crusader and Feminist*, 41–42.

83. Ripley, ed., *Black Abolitionist Papers*, 4:212.

84. The only full-length modern study of Sallie Holley is Herbig's dissertation, "Friends for Freedom." For background information, see 2–4, 13, 22, 28–36, 44, 51–52, 74–76, 78. See also Chambers-Schiller, *Liberty, a Better Husband*, 53–54, 39, and Sterling, *Ahead of Her Time*, 276–77.

85. Herbig, "Friends for Freedom," 2–4; *Liberator*, April 1, 1853. Herbig points out the very material help that Abby Kelley Foster provided for her protégé and the way she often wrote ahead to make sure that proper arrangements would be made (see "Friends for Freedom," 110–11). The amounts of money Sallie raised were not large, although Stevens, "From Generation to Generation," suggests that, in the end, the sums were significant (196–97). Stevens says, "Holley and Putnam were the slightly more visible tip of an invisible army of antislavery workers who kept the abolitionist movement alive." Sterling, in *Ahead of Her Time*, 86–87, describes how Abby Kelley often had to make arrangements for herself.

86. *Liberator*, September 3, 1851, August 18, 1854; Herbig, "Friends for Freedom," 104, 178; letter from Sallie Holley to Abby Kelley Foster, July 19, 1856, Kelley-Foster Papers, AmAS. Christopher Clark, in *Roots of Rural Capitalism*, 312–13, analyzes the link between economic changes in the Connecticut Valley and sympathy for antislavery and Free-Soil. He suggests that antislavery covered over fissures in rural society. See also Brooke, *Heart of the Commonwealth*, 389–90. Lucy Stone noted the importance of scheduling antislavery lectures when there were no competing events (Wheeler, ed., *Loving Warriors*, 152).

87. Cmiel, *Democratic Eloquence*, 17, 25, 30, 55–58, 62, 69–71; Karlyn Kohrs Campbell, ed., *Women Public Speakers*, 221–24.

88. Letter from Sallie Holley to Abby Kelley Foster, July 19, 1856, Kelley-Foster

Papers, AmAS. Other successful women speakers were Lucy Stone, Antoinette Blackwell, and Frances Watkins Harper. Lucretia Mott continued to be a popular and well-received lecturer. Antoinette Brown did not succeed so well. Lizzie Gay, in a letter to Sarah Pugh, June 10, 1855, GFP, noted that Antoinette Brown "had no gifts as a public speaker and has mistaken her calling most decidedly." Charlotte Forten agreed, writing in her diary: "Her manner is too passive" (*Journal of Charlotte Forten*, 65). Cmiel, in *Democratic Eloquence*, 71, highlights Abby Kelley's abusiveness.

89. *Liberator*, July 14, 1848, in reference to Lucy Stone; ibid., January 12, 1855, in reference to Antoinette Brown; ibid., February 4, 1853, in reference to Sallie Holley. Notices for Sallie Holley's lectures include ibid., October 8, 22, 1852, April 25, 1856. Chadwick, ed., *Life for Liberty*, 87; letter from Sallie Holley to Abby Kelley Foster, July 19, 1856, Kelley-Foster Papers, AmAS; Herbig, "Friends for Freedom," 98.

90. *Liberator*, October 17, 1856, May 6, 1853, October 22, 1852, March 21, 1856; Herbig, "Friends for Freedom," 10, 98, 178–79, 182; letter from Sallie Holley to Abby Kelley Foster, July 19, 1856, Kelley-Foster Papers, AmAS.

91. *Liberator*, August 20, 1858; Herbig, "Friends for Freedom," 182; letter from Sallie Holley to Abby Kelley Foster, October 8, 1858, Kelley-Foster Papers, AmAS.

92. Herbig, "Friends for Freedom," 191; *Liberator*, February 4, 1853; David Turley, in *Culture of English Antislavery*, 63, points out: "The [antislavery] agents or lectures became not only dramatic figures in the theater of the public meeting but combatants." A letter about another lecturer refers to this question and answer format: "She is especially ready in any little debate wh. she frequently calls out at the close of her lecture" (letter from Caroline M. Severance to Wendell Phillips, June 21, 1859, Blagden-Phillips Papers, HL).

93. Chadwick, ed., *Life for Liberty*, 135; letter from Sallie Holley to Abby Kelley Foster, April 5, 1854, Kelley-Foster Papers, AmAS.

94. Letter from Sallie Holley to Abby Kelley Foster, April 29, 1852, Kelley-Foster Papers, AmAS; Herbig, "Friends for Freedom," 140–43.

95. *Liberator*, March 19, 1858; Chadwick, *Life for Liberty*, 126, 95, 99.

96. Quote from Sterling, *Ahead of Her Time*, 300. For discussions of the relationship between the two women, see Chambers-Schiller, *Liberty, a Better Husband*, 150–51, and Herbig, "Friends for Freedom," 58–61, 135–39, 169–72. A letter from Abby Kelley to Samuel May, August 19, 1852, Antislavery Papers, BPL, suggests that Sallie was also expected to make calls during the day.

97. Herbig, "Friends for Freedom," 85, 87; Chambers-Schiller, *Liberty, a Better Husband*, 168–69. For references to stage fright, see letter from Sallie Holley to Abby Kelley Foster, February 17, 1852, Kelley-Foster Papers, AmAS, and Chadwick, *Life for Liberty*, 134.

98. Herbig, "Friends for Freedom," 114, 127–28; *Liberator*, September 16, 1858; Chadwick, *Life for Liberty*, 78.

99. Herbig, "Friends for Freedom," 201.

100. Ripley, ed., *Black Abolitionist Papers*, 3:27.

101. Bacon, " 'One Great Bundle of Humanity,' " 22–23.

102. Ibid.; Hine, ed., *Black Women in America*, 5, 454.

103. Hine, ed., *Black Women in America*, 23–24; Melba Joyce Boyd, *Discarded Legacy*, 38; Sterling, *We Are Your Sisters*, 159.

104. Sterling, *We Are Your Sisters*, 160.

105. Ibid., 160–61.

106. Melba Joyce Boyd, *Discarded Legacy*, 39; Bacon, " 'One Great Bundle of Humanity,' " 24–25; Still, *Underground Rail Road*, 757, 763.

107. Black Abolitionist Papers, reel 10, no. 570, LOC. The point about audience identification with Watkin Harper's subjects because of her color is my own reading of the meaning of comments about her eloquence and pathos "calling forth the tears from many eyes." See *Liberator*, January 11, 1856; Hine, ed., *Black Women in America*, 533; and Melba Joyce Boyd, *Discarded Legacy*, 45.

108. Still, *Underground Rail Road*, 758–59. In her description of African American writers, Elizabeth Fox-Genovese notes their "double-consciousness, this sense of always looking at one's self through the eyes of others" ("Between Individualism and Fragmentation," 11). Such a consciousness certainly was shared by black lecturers.

109. Still, *Underground Rail Road*, 759–61, 763. Of course, white women also denied themselves for the cause. See Lucy Colman's account in *Reminiscences*, 23.

110. Yee, *Black Women Abolitionists*, 113; Colman, *Reminiscences*, 32–35.

111. Sterling, *We Are Your Sisters*, 162; Black Abolitionist Papers, reel 11, no. 139, LOC.

112. Stevens, " 'From Generation to Generation,' " 100; Black Abolitionist Papers, reel 12, no. 597, LOC.

CHAPTER SIX

1. Eaklor, ed., *American Antislavery Songs*, 305. A song composed for the Abington, Massachusetts, August 1, 1862, celebration.

2. Dover Anti-Slavery Sewing Circle Records, Constitution, 1840; August 30, 1842, February 5, November 19, 1845, January 25, March 4, 1846, June 2, 1847, January 31, 1849, April 13, 1850, November 1, 1855, September 3, 1856, January 29, April 9, 1857, May 1, June 5, November 21, 1861, NHHS. The name change took place in April or May 1862.

3. Quoted in McPherson, *Struggle for Equality*, 89–90.

4. Coffin, *Reminiscences*, 596; Gallman, *North Fights the Civil War*, 10; letter from Susan B. Anthony to Wendell Phillips, April 3, 1861, Bladgen-Phillips Papers, HL; Venet, *Neither Ballots nor Bullets*, 28.

5. Quotes from McFeely, *Frederick Douglass*, 211, 208–11.

6. Venet, *Neither Ballots nor Bullets*, 115, 46–48; McPherson, *Struggle for Equality*, 129–31.

7. Hewitt, *Women's Activism*, 193–94.

8. Ginzberg, in *Women and the Work of Benevolence*, ch. 5, suggests that during the war the language of efficiency replaced the gender-laden language of female benevolence. The Civil War represented a "critical" divide when the concept of benevolence was masculinized. Although she does point out that "there was no universal rush to embrace the new emphasis on efficiency and

nationalism" (173), she perhaps overemphasizes the sharpness of the change. This book makes the point that efficiency was a central value for many women abolitionists, along with their powerful sense of their moral duty as women, long before the war. Certainly, traditional understandings of benevolence persisted after it, as any consideration of the foreign and domestic missionary movement or temperance activities make clear. For a study pointing out the resistance of many benevolent women to new concepts and styles of operation, see Attie, " 'Swindling Concern.' "

9. For the difference between abolitionist women's response and that of the larger female public, see Attie, " 'Swindling Concern,' " 27.

10. Hallowell, ed., *James and Lucretia Mott*, 401; *Liberator*, June 7, 1861.

11. Quoted in Karcher, *First Woman in the Republic*, 447, 448, and in Clifford, *Crusader for Freedom*, 260. Venet, *Neither Ballots nor Bullets*, 96–97. For her account of the creation of her famous song, see Julia Ward Howe, *Reminiscences*, 273–76.

12. Venet, *Neither Ballots nor Bullets*, 27–43, 98–99; McPherson, *Struggle for Equality*, 128–29.

13. Quoted in Stevens, " 'From Generation to Generation,' " 136–37.

14. *Liberator*, February 21, 1862, July 26, 1861; Venet, *Neither Ballots nor Bullets*, 102.

15. The point about masculine ideals comes from Ginzberg, *Women and the Work of Benevolence*, 134. Venet, *Neither Ballots nor Bullets*, 106–10, quote on 108.

16. Venet, *Neither Ballots nor Bullets*, 109, 111, 116–17.

17. Stanton and Blatch, eds., *Elizabeth Cady Stanton*, 95.

18. Quoted in ibid., 120; see also chart on 121. McPherson, *Struggle for Equality*, 111, 125–27; Venet, *Neither Ballots nor Bullets*, 148.

19. Minutes of PFAS, November 12, 1862, PFAS Records, HSP. Carolyn Luverne Williams, "Religion, Race, and Gender," 621–22. The PFAS also initiated its own petition in 1863. Ripley, ed., *Black Abolitionist Papers*, 5:286; Venet, *Neither Ballots nor Bullets*, 110. For brief mention of black women's efforts in Ohio to secure black civil rights, suffrage, and emancipation, see Cheek and Cheek, *John Mercer Langston*, 248–49.

20. Sterling, *We Are Your Sisters*, 245; Colman, *Reminiscences*, 39–40; Richardson, *Christian Reconstruction*, 97. The first organization was in Geneva, New York, while the second was obviously located in Syracuse.

21. Ripley, ed. *Black Abolitionist Papers*, 4:78–79, 5:167–68, 285–86.

22. Ibid., 5:248–52.

23. Ibid., 167–68, 261, 212–13; Sterling, *We Are Your Sisters*, 257–58. The difficulties of recruiting blacks is clear in Cheek and Cheek, *John Mercer Langston*, 402–6. The Cheeks note that "Ohio's first black regiment had been slighted for political gain by the government it was sworn to defend and gotten up on the cheap to save white Ohioans from the draft" (405).

24. *Liberator*, November 18, 1864.

25. Hallowell, ed., *James and Lucretia Mott*, 411. Although neither focuses on abolitionist groups, the dissertations already cited by Attie, " 'Swindling Concern,' " and Anne C. Rose, *Victorian America and the Civil War*, show a stub-

born localism among many women's organizations and a desire to control their own affairs and aid.

26. De Boer, *Be Jubilant My Feet*, 11, 81; Richardson, *Christian Reconstruction*, 92.

27. Richardson, *Christian Reconstruction*, 92–96.

28. Ibid., 96–97.

29. Lucy Chase, working with contrabands in Virginia, gave these statistics for the Orthodox Friends and noted major support from Hicksites in Philadelphia and groups in New York and Boston (Swint, ed., *Dear Ones at Home*, 136; Hewitt, *Women's Activism*, 193–94).

30. Carolyn Luverne Williams, "Religion, Race, and Gender," 645, 647; Hewitt, *Women's Activism*, 193–94; Swint, *Dear Ones at Home*, 103.

31. McPherson, *Struggle for Equality*, 170, 389; *Liberator*, April 10, 1863. The *Liberator* gives ample information on fund-raising. The major vehicle for women connected with the AAS was the national antislavery anniversary, a yearly event that raised thousands of dollars. See *Liberator*, February 15, 1861, February 14, 1862, for some examples.

32. Haviland, *Woman's Life-Work*, 360, 265.

33. Ibid., 242, 251–53, 265, 266, 346, 354, 360.

34. Butchart, *Northern Schools, Southern Blacks*, 4; Black Abolitionist Papers, reel 12, no. 1021, LOC; McPherson, *Struggle for Equality*, 158, 140, quote on 162. Butchart draws distinctions between conservative religious organizations that harbored conservative aims for education and secular and Friends organizations that viewed education as liberating (see *Northern Schools, Southern Blacks*, 16–22, 37–38, 65–66).

35. Clark Robenstine, "Sarah Ann Dickey," in Seller, *Women Educators*, 193–94.

36. Butchart, "Perspectives on Gender," 5, 13–15. I wish to thank Professor Butchart for his generosity in making his essay available to me before the publication date.

37. McPherson, *Struggle for Equality*, 171, 389; Ripley, ed., *Black Abolitionist Papers*, 5:284; Swint, *Dear Ones at Home*, 4–6; Butchart, "Perspectives on Gender," 7.

38. Quoted in McPherson, *Struggle for Equality*, 163. Botume, *First Days amongst the Contrabands*, 48. Mary Still, a black teacher from Philadelphia, remarked from her post in South Carolina that "children and adults both seem famishing for knowledge" (Black Abolitionist Papers, reel 15, no. 859, LOC).

39. Swint, *Dear Ones at Home*, 21, 23, 24. Compare Lucy's reaction to slave religion to Charlotte Forten's comment that former slaves "are a truly religious people. They speak to God with a loving familiarity" (Sterling, *We Are Your Sisters*, 280).

40. Swint, *Dear Ones at Home*, 47, 48, 61. 29, 62, 103, 132, 134, 135. The Chases used their Quaker connections to get assistance from both Hicksite and Orthodox Friends but also were cooperating with Lewis Tappan's wife, who served as a link with a New York women's group. The two sisters also drew upon their Worcester relatives and friends.

41. Ibid., 105, 117–18.

42. Ibid., 26, 103, 165–69. McPherson, *Struggle for Equality*, 172, 3.

43. McPherson, *Struggle for Equality*, 171, 395; Richardson, *Christian Reconstruction*, 28–29.

44. Ripley, ed., *Black Abolitionist Papers*, 5:176. Quote from Linda M. Perkins, "The Black Female American Missionary Association Teacher in the South, 1861–1870," in Hine, ed., *Black Women in United States History*, 3:1054. Sterling, *We Are Your Sisters*, 264. Butchart's study of New York teachers found that 15.6 percent of the teachers were black, although African Americans made up less than 2 percent of the state's population in 1860 ("Perspectives on Gender," 6).

45. Perkins, "Black Female Teacher," in Hine, ed., *Black Women in United States History*, 3:1052–53. Other organizations also supported black teachers in Washington, Maryland, Virginia, Georgia, Kentucky, Louisiana, Mississippi, and North and South Carolina, and the experience of these teachers may have differed from those hired by the AMA. Hine, ed., *Black Women in America*, 462. Billington, ed., *Journal of Charlotte L. Forten*, 126, 136.

46. Perkins, "Black Female Teacher," in Hine, ed., *Black Women in United States History*, 3:1053–54; Sterling, *We Are Your Sisters*, 265–66.

47. Swint, *Dear Ones at Home*, 16; Butchart, "Perspectives on Gender," 7–8; Holland, ed., *Letters and Diary of Laura M. Towne*, 88, 165–66.

48. Perkins, "Black Female Teacher," in Hine, ed., *Black Women in United States History*, 3:1059; Sterling, *We Are Your Sisters*, 273–74.

49. Sterling, *We Are Your Sisters*, 265, 272–73; Billington, ed., *Journal of Charlotte L. Forten*, 136.

50. Butchart, "Perspectives on Gender," 6–7; Lawson and Merrill, *Three Sarahs*, 234–35, 223–27.

51. Quote from Willie Lee Rose, *Rehearsal for Reconstruction*, 172–73; Constitution of the LASD, February 9, 1835, LASD Records, NHHS.

52. As Lawrence J. Friedman points out in *Gregarious Saints*, 269–70, abolitionists who favored dissolving antislavery societies were not suggesting that freedmen did not require further assistance. McPherson, *Struggle for Equality*, 302–3, 305; Black Abolitionist Papers, reel 14, no. 341, LOC; AAS, *Proceedings of the American Anti-Slavery Society at Its Third Decade*, 83.

53. Merrill and Ruchames, eds., *Letters of William Lloyd Garrison*, 5:282; letter from Lizzie Gay to Sarah Pugh, April 3, no year, GFP. For an account of the efforts to desegregate Philadelphia's transportation system, see Foner, ed., "Battle to End Discrimination," July, 261–92, October, 255–380.

54. Chadwick, ed., *Life for Liberty*, 209–10.

55. *Liberator*, July 10, 1863.

56. Stevens, " 'From Generation to Generation,' " 147, 150; quote from Ginzberg, *Women and the Work of Benevolence*, 179.

57. Friedman, *Gregarious Saints*, 277–80; Chadwick, *Life for Liberty*, 209–10; Ripley, ed., *Black Abolitionist Papers*, 4:59.

58. Minutes of the Ashtabula County Female Anti-Slavery Society, January 4, 1837, Ashtabula County Female Anti-Slavery Society Records, WRHS; quote from Ginzberg, *Women and the Work of Benevolence*, 15. See also Ginzberg's

interpretation of the changing nature of reform after the Civil War. For an interpretation of the Civil War as a crisis in gender, see Anne C. Rose, *Victorian America and the Civil War*.

59. *Liberator*, November 3, 1837.
60. Ibid., and August 27, 1836.

Bibliography

ARCHIVES AND MANUSCRIPT COLLECTIONS
Ann Arbor, Michigan
    Bentley Library, University of Michigan
        Elizabeth Chandler Papers
        Treadwell Family Papers
Bangor, Maine
    Bangor Public Library
        Bangor Gazette
Boston, Massachusetts
    Boston Athenæum
        Prints and Photograph Collection
            Anti-Slavery Cathechism
    Boston Public Library
        Antislavery Papers
        Chapman-Weston Papers
        Garrison Papers
        Phelps Papers
    Massachusetts Historical Society
        Boston Female Anti-Slavery Society Records
        James Freeman Clarke Papers
        Daniel Foster Papers
        Jacob M. Manning Papers
        John Parkman Papers
        Robie-Sewall Papers
        Caleb Stetson Papers
        Swan Family Papers
        Wentworth-Merrill Family Papers
Brunswick, Maine
    Bowdoin College Library
        Advocate of Freedom
        Liberty Standard
Cambridge, Massachusetts
    Houghton Library, Harvard University
        Blagden-Phillips Papers
    Schlesinger Library, Radcliffe College
        Follen Papers
        Maria Theresa Hollander Papers
        Hooker Collection
        Loring Papers
Cleveland, Ohio
    Western Reserve Historical Society
        Ashtabula County Female Anti-Slavery Society Records
        Canton Ladies Anti-Slavery Society Records

Lukens-Gilbert Papers
Marius Robinson Papers
Concord, New Hampshire
New Hampshire Historical Society
Ladies Anti-Slavery Society of Dover (reconstituted in 1840 as Dover
Anti-Slavery Sewing Circle) Records
Loudon Village Anti-Slavery Sewing Circle Records
Hartford, Connecticut
Connecticut State Library
Brooklyn Female Anti-Slavery Society Records
Kent, Ohio
Kent State University Library
Cowles Papers
Lynn, Massachusetts
Lynn Historical Society
Lynn Female Anti-Slavery Society Records
Montpelier, Vermont
Vermont Historical Society
"Appeal to Females of [the] North" (by a Vermont female)
Clement Papers
Austin Johnson Papers
Achsa Sprague Papers
Thorp Papers
Wheeler Family Papers
New York, New York
Butler Library, Columbia University
Gay Family Papers
New York Public Library
Gay Family Papers
Langworthy Family Papers
Storrs Papers
Northampton, Massachusetts
Smith College Library
Hudson Collection
Sophia Smith Collection
Philadelphia, Pennsylvania
Historical Society of Pennsylvania
Philadelphia Female Anti-Slavery Society Records
Portland, Maine
Maine Historical Society
Mountfort Papers
Portland Anti-Slavery Society Records
Portland Inquirer
Salem, Massachusetts
Essex-Peabody Library, Essex-Peabody Institute
Martha Barrett Diary

Bowditch Family Papers
March Family Papers
Northey Family Papers
Salem Female Anti-Slavery Society Records
Washington, D.C.
  Library of Congress
    Black Abolitionist Papers (microfilm)
    Papers of the Western Anti-Slavery Society (microfilm)
Worcester, Massachusetts
  American Antiquarian Society
    Chase Family Papers
    Dorchester Female Anti-Slavery Society, miscellaneous papers
    Kelley-Foster Papers
    Lambdin Family Papers
    Lucretia Cargill Sibley Papers
    Records of Boothbay Lyceum
    Elizabeth Reed Papers
    Wesleyan Methodist Church Records, Leicester, Massachusetts, 1844-59
    Mary Avery White Diary (typescript)

NEWSPAPERS
Advocate of Freedom, 1838-40
Bangor Gazette, 1841-43
Liberator, 1831-65
Liberty Standard, 1841-47
Portland Inquirer, 1851, 1852, 1855, 1856
True Wesleyan, 1843-52

BOOKS AND ARTICLES

Allen, Robert L., and Pamela P. Allen. *Reluctant Reformers: Racism and Social Reform Movements in the United States.* Washington, D.C.: Howard University Press, 1974.

Altman, Janet Gurkin. *Epistolarity: Approaches to a Form.* Columbus: Ohio State University Press, 1982.

Altschuler, Glenn C., and Jan M. Saltzgaber. *Revivalism, Social Conscience, and Community in the Burned-Over District.* Ithaca: Cornell University Press, 1983.

American and Foreign Anti-Slavery Society. *The Annual Report of the American and Foreign Anti-Slavery Society.* New York: AFAS, 1848-53.

American Anti-Slavery Society. *Proceedings of the American Anti-Slavery Society at Its Second Decade.* New York: American Anti-Slavery Society, 1854.

———. *Proceedings of the American Anti-Slavery Society at Its Third Decade.* New York: American Anti-Slavery Society, 1864.

Ames, Mary Lesley. *Life and Letters of Peter and Susan Lesley.* New York: G. P. Putnam's Sons, 1909.

Anderson, Benedict, *Imagined Communities: Reflections on the Origin and Spread of Nationalism,* rev. ed. New York: Routledge, 1991.

The Anti-Slavery Almanac for 1836. Boston: Webster and Southard, 1836.

An Appeal to Females of the North on the Subject of Slavery, by a Female of Vermont. Brandon, [Vt.?]: Telegraph Press, 1838.

Aptheker, Herbert. *Abolitionism: A Revolutionary Movement.* Boston: Twayne Publishers, 1989.

Ashworth, John. "The Relationship between Capitalism and Humanitarianism." *American Historical Review* 92 (October 1987): 813–28.

Bacon, Margaret H. " 'One Great Bundle of Humanity': Frances Ellen Watkins Harper (1825–1911)." *Pennsylvania Magazine of History and Biography* 113 (January 1989): 21–44.

————. *The Quiet Rebels: The Story of Quakers in America.* New York: Basic Books, Inc., 1969.

Baker, Paula. "The Domestication of Politics: Women and American Political Society, 1780–1920." *American Historical Review* 89 (June 1984): 620–47.

Barnes, Gilbert H., and Dwight L. Dumond., eds. *Letters of Theodore Dwight Weld, Angelina Grimké Weld and Sarah Grimké, 1822–1844.* Vol. 1. New York: D. Appleton-Century Co., c. 1934.

Bearden, Jim, and Linda Jean Butler. *Shadd: The Life and Times of Mary Shadd Cary.* Toronto: New Canada Press Ltd., 1977.

Beedy, Helen Coffin. *Mothers of Maine.* Portland, Maine: Thurston Print, 1895.

Bernard, Joel. "Authority, Autonomy, and Radical Commitment: Stephen and Abby Kelley Foster." *American Antiquarian Society Proceedings* 9 (1980): 347–86.

Billington, Louis. " 'Female Laborers in the Church': Women Preachers in the Northeastern United States, 1790–1840." *Journal of American Studies* 19 (December 1985): 369–94.

Billington, Ray Allen, ed. *The Journal of Charlotte Forten.* New York: The Dryden Press, Inc., 1953.

Blackett, R. J. M. *Building an Antislavery Wall: Black Americans in the Atlantic Abolitionist Movement, 1830–1860.* Baton Rouge: Louisiana University Press, 1983.

Blassingame, John W., and Mae G. Henderson. *Antislavery Newspapers and Periodicals.* Boston: G. K. Hall & Co., 1980.

Blockson, Charles. *African Americans in Pennsylvania: A History and Guide.* Baltimore: Black Classics Press, 1994.

————. *The Underground Railroad.* New York: Prentice Hall Press, 1987.

Blumin, Stuart M. *The Emergence of the Middle Class: Social Experience in the American City, 1760–1900.* New York: Cambridge University Press, 1989.

Bogin, Ruth. "Sarah Parker Remond: Black Abolitionist from Salem." *Essex Institute Historical Collections* 110 (April 1974): 120–50.

Bolt, Christine, and Seymour Drescher, eds. *Anti-Slavery, Religion, and Reform: Essays in Memory of Roger Anstey.* Folkestone, U.K.: William Dawson & Sons Ltd., 1980.

Bonfield, Lynn A., and Mary C. Morrison. *Roxana's Children: The Biography of a Nineteenth-Century Vermont Family.* Amherst: University of Massachusetts Press, 1995.

Bonomi, Patricia U. *Under the Cope of Heaven: Religion, Society, and Politics in Colonial America*. New York: Oxford University Press, 1986.

Borome, Joseph A. "The Vigilant Committee of Philadelphia." *Pennsylvania Magazine of History and Biography* 92 (July 1968): 320–51.

Botume, Elizabeth Hyde. *First Days Amongst the Contrabands*. New York: Arno Press, 1968.

Boyd, Lois A., and R. Douglas Brackenridge. *Presbyterian Women in America: Two Centuries of a Quest for Status*. Westport, Conn.: Greenwood Press, 1983.

Boyd, Melba Joyce. *Discarded Legacy: Politics and Poetics in the Life of Frances E. W. Harper, 1825–1911*. Detroit: Wayne State University Press, 1994.

Boylan, Anne M. *Sunday School: The Formation of an American Institution, 1790–1880*. New Haven: Yale University Press, 1988.

———. "Timid Girls, Venerable Widows, and Dignified Matrons: Life Cycle Patterns among Organized Women in New York and Boston, 1797–1840." *American Quarterly* 38 (Winter 1986): 779–97.

———. "Women and Politics in the Era before Seneca Falls." *Journal of the Early Republic* 10 (Fall 1990): 363–82.

———. "Women in Groups: An Analysis of Women's Benevolent Organizations in New York and Boston, 1797–1840." *Journal of American History* 71 (December 1984): 497–523.

Bradley, A. Day. "Progressive Friends in Michigan and New York." *Quaker History* 52 (Fall 1963): 95–103.

Brooke, John L. *The Heart of the Commonwealth: Social and Political Culture in Worcester County, Massachusetts, 1713–1861*. New York: Cambridge University Press, 1989.

Brown, Eliza Potts, and Susan Mosher Stuard, eds. *Witnesses for Change: Quaker Women over Three Centuries*. New Brunswick: Rutgers University Press, 1989.

Brown, Hallie Q. *Homespun Heroines and Other Women of Distinction*. New York: Oxford University Press, 1988.

Brown, Ira V. *Mary Grew: Abolitionist and Feminist (1813–1896)*. Selinsgrove, Pa.: Susquehanna University Press, 1991.

Brown, Richard D. *Knowledge Is Power: The Diffusion of Information in Early America, 1700–1865*. New York: Oxford University Press, 1989.

Butchart, Ronald E. *Northern Schools, Southern Blacks, and Reconstruction*. Westport, Conn.: Greenwood Press, 1980.

———. "Perspectives on Gender, Race, Calling, and Commitment in Nineteenth-Century Americans: A Collective Biography of the Teachers of the Freedpeople, 1862–1875," mss. copy. *Vitae Scholastica*, forthcoming 1997.

Butler, Jon. "The Future of American Religious History: Prospectus, Agenda, Transatlantic Problematique." *William and Mary Quarterly* 42 (April 1985): 167–83.

Campbell, Karlyn Kohrs, ed. *Women Public Speakers in the United States, 1800–1925: A Biographical-Critical Sourcebook*. Westport, Conn.: Greenwood Press, 1993.

Campbell, Stanley W. *The Slave Catchers: Enforcement of the Fugitive Slave Law, 1850–1860*. Chapel Hill: University of North Carolina Press, 1970.

Carwardine, Richard J. *Evangelicals and Politics in Antebellum America.* New Haven: Yale University Press, 1993.

———. *Trans-Atlantic Revivalism: Popular Evangelicalism in Britain and America, 1790–1865.* Westport, Conn.: Greenwood Press, 1978.

Cashin, Joan E. "Black Families in the Old Northwest." *Journal of the Early Republic* 15 (Fall 1995): 449–76.

Chadwick, John White, ed. *A Life for Liberty: Anti-Slavery and Other Letters of Sallie Holley.* New York: Negro Universities Press, 1969.

Chambers-Schiller, Lee Virginia. *Liberty, a Better Husband: Single Women in America; The Generation of 1780–1840.* New Haven: Yale University Press, 1984.

Cheek, William, and Aimee Lee Cheek. *John Mercer Langston and the Fight for Black Freedom, 1829–1865.* Urbana: University of Illinois Press, 1989.

Clark, Calvin Montague. *American Slavery and Maine Congregationalists.* Bangor: privately printed, 1940.

Clark, Christopher. *The Roots of Rural Capitalism: Western Massachusetts, 1780–1860.* Ithaca: Cornell University Press, 1990.

Clifford, Deborah Pickman. *Crusader for Freedom: A Life of Lydia Maria Child.* Boston: Beacon Press, 1992.

Clinton, Catherine. "Maria Weston Chapman," in *Portraits of American Women,* Vol. 1. Edited by G. J. Barker-Benfield and Catherine Clinton, 147–67. New York: St. Martin's Press, 1991.

Clinton, Catherine, and Nina Silber. *Divided Houses: Gender and the Civil War.* New York: Oxford University Press, 1992.

Cmiel, Kenneth. *Democratic Eloquence: The Fight over Popular Speech in Nineteenth-Century America.* Berkeley: University of California Press, 1990.

Cockrum, William. *History of the Underground Railroad As It Was Conducted by the Anti-Slavery League.* New York: Negro Universities Press, 1969.

Coffin, Levi. *Reminiscences.* Cincinnati: Robert Clarke & Co., 1880.

Collison, Gary. "Antislavery, Blacks, and the Boston Elite: Notes on the Reverend Charles Lowell and the West Church." *New England Quarterly* 61 (September 1988): 419–29.

Colman, Lucy. *Reminiscences.* Buffalo, N.Y.: H. L. Green, Publisher, 1891.

Cox, John, Jr., and Percy E. Clapp. "Quakers in Rochester and Monroe County." *Rochester Historical Society Publication Fund Series* 14 (1936): 97–111.

Davidson, Carlisle G. "A Profile of Hicksite Quakerism in Michigan, 1830–1860." *Quaker History* 59 (Fall 1970): 106–12.

Davis, David Brion. "Reflections on Abolitionism and Ideological Hegemony." *American Historical Review* 92 (October 1987): 797–812.

Davis, Hugh. *Joshua Leavitt: Evangelical Abolitionist.* Baton Rouge: Louisiana State University Press, 1990.

De Boer, Clara Merritt. *Be Jubilant My Feet: African American Abolitionists in the American Missionary Association, 1839–1861.* New York: Garland Publishing, Inc., 1994.

Eaklors, Vicki L., ed. *American Antislavery Songs: A Collection and Analysis.* Westport, Conn.: Greenwood Press, 1988.

Eggert, Gerald G. "The Impact of the Fugitive Slave Law on Harrisburg: A Case Study." *Pennsylvania Magazine of History and Biography* 109 (October 1985): 537-70.

Ellis, Richard J. *American Political Cultures*. New York: Oxford University Press, 1993.

Ellis, Richard, and Aaron Wildavsky. "A Cultural Analysis of the Role of Abolitionists in the Coming of the Civil War." *Comparative Studies in Society and History* 32 (January 1990): 89-116.

Emerson, Sarah Hopper. *The Life of Abby Hopper Gibbons Told Chiefly through Her Correspondence*. Vol. 1. New York: G. P. Putnams, 1887.

Fairchild, James H. "The Underground Railroad." *Western Reserve Historical Society* 4 (1895): 91-121.

Farmer, Rod. "Maine Abolitionists View the South: Images in Maine Antislavery Newspapers, 1838-1855." *Maine Historical Society Quarterly* 25 (Summer 1985): 2-21.

Ferrero, Pat, Elaine Hedges, and Julie Silber. *Hearts and Hands: The Influence of Women and Quilts on American Society*. San Francisco: The Quilt Digest Press, 1987.

Finkelman, Paul, ed. *Articles on American Slavery*. New York: Garland Pub. Inc., 1989.

———. *Articles on American Slavery: Fugitive Slaves*. New York: Garland Pub. Inc, 1989.

Fladeland, Betty. *Men and Brothers: Anglo-American Antislavery Cooperation*. Urbana: University of Illinois Press, 1972.

Flusche, Michael. "Antislavery and Spiritualism: Myrtilla Miner and Her School." *New York Historical Society Quarterly* 59 (April 1975): 149-72.

Foner, Philip S., ed. "The Battle to End Discrimination against Negroes on the Philadelphia Streetcars." *Pennsylvania History* 40 (July and October 1973): 261-92, 355-80.

———. *The Life and Writings of Frederick Douglass*. Vols. 1 and 2. New York: International Pubs., 1950.

Formisano, Ronald P. "The Role of Women in the Dorr Rebellion." *Rhode Island History* 54 (August 1993): 88-104.

Fox-Genovese, Elizabeth. "Between Individuals and Fragmentation: American Culture and the New Literary Studies of Race and Gender." *American Quarterly* 42 (March 1990): 7-34.

Frederickson, George M. *The Arrogance of Race: Historical Perspectives on Slavery, Racism, and Social Inequality*. Middletown, Conn.: Wesleyan University Press, 1988.

Friedman, Lawrence J. *Gregarious Saints: Self and Community in American Abolitionism, 1830-1870*. New York: Cambridge University Press, 1982.

———. " 'Historical Topics Sometimes Run Dry': The State of Abolitionist Studies." *The Historian* 42 (February 1981): 177-94.

Gallman, J. Matthew. *The North Fights the Civil War: The Home Front*. Chicago: Ivan R. Dee, 1994.

Gara, Larry. "Friends and the Underground Railroad." *Quaker History* 51 (Spring 1962): 3–19.

———. *The Liberty Line: The Legend of the Underground Railroad*. Lexington: University of Kentucky Press, 1967.

Geary, Linda L. *Balanced in the Wind: A Biography of Betsey Mix Cowles*. Lewisburg, Pa.: Bucknell University Press, 1989.

Gerteis, Louis. *Morality and Utility in American Antislavery Reform*. Chapel Hill: University of North Carolina Press, 1987.

Giddings, Paula. *When and Where I Enter: The Impact of Black Women on Race and Sex in America*. New York: William Morrow & Co., Inc., 1984.

Gienapp, William E. *The Origins of the Republican Party, 1852–1856*. New York: Oxford University Press, 1987.

Gilkeson, John S., Jr. *Middle-Class Providence, 1820–1940*. Princeton: Princeton University Press, 1986.

Ginzberg, Lori D. *Women and the Work of Benevolence: Morality, Politics, and Class in the Nineteenth-Century United States*. New Haven: Yale University Press, 1990.

Goen, C. C. *Broken Churches, Broken Nation: Denominational Schisms and the Coming of the American Civil War*. Macon: Mercer University Press, 1985.

Goffman, Erving. *Forms of Talk*. Philadelphia: University of Pennsylvania Press, 1981.

Goodman, Paul. "The Manual Labor Movement and the Origins of Abolitionism." *Journal of the Early Republic* 13 (Fall 1993): 355–88.

Gougeon, Len. "Abolition, the Emersons, and 1837." *New England Quarterly* 54 (September 1981): 345–64.

Greene, Dana. "Quaker Feminism: The Case of Lucretia Mott." *Pennsylvania History* 45 (April 1981): 143–54.

Griffen, Clifford S. "The Abolitionists and the Benevolent Societies, 1831–1861." *Journal of Negro History* 44 (July 1959): 195–216.

Hallowell, Anna Davis, ed. *James and Lucretia Mott: Life and Letters*. Boston: Houghton, Mifflin and Co., 1894.

Hamm, Thomas D. *The Transformation of American Quakerism: Orthodox Friends, 1800–1907*. Bloomington: Indiana University Press, 1988.

Hanmer-Croughton, Amy. "Anti-Slavery Days in Rochester." *Rochester Historical Society Publication Fund Series* 14 (1936): 113–55.

Hansen, Debra Gold. *Strained Sisterhood: Gender and Class in the Boston Female Anti-Slavery Society*. Amherst: University of Massachusetts Press, 1993.

Hansen, Karen V. " 'Helped Put in a Quilt': Men's Work and Male Integration in Nineteenth-Century New England." *Gender and Society* 3 (September 1989): 334–54.

———. *A Very Social Time: Crafting Community in Antebellum New England*. Berkeley: University of California Press, 1994.

Harrold, Stanley. *Gamaliel Bailey and Antislavery Union*. Kent, Ohio: Kent State University Press, 1986.

Hatch, Nathan O. *The Democratization of American Christianity*. New Haven: Yale University Press, 1989.

Haviland, Laura S. *A Woman's Life-Work: Labors and Experiences of Laura S. Haviland*. Chicago: Publishing Association of Friends, 1889.

Hembree, Michael F. "The Question of 'Begging': Fugitive Slave Relief in Canada, 1830–1865." *Civil War History* 37 (December 1991): 314–27.

Hersh, Blanche Glassman. *The Slavery of Sex: Feminist Abolitionists in America*. Urbana: University of Illinois Press, 1978.

Hewitt, Nancy A. "Feminist Friends: Agrarian Quakers and the Emergence of Woman's Rights in America." *Feminist Studies* 12 (Spring 1986): 27–49.

———. *Women's Activism and Social Change: Rochester, New York, 1822–1872*. Ithaca: Cornell University Press, 1987.

Hine, Darlene Clark, ed. *Black Women in America: An Historical Encyclopedia*. Brooklyn, N.Y.: Carlson Pub. Inc., 1993.

———. *Black Women in United States History*. Vols. 3 and 4. Brooklyn, N.Y.: Carlson Pub. Inc., 1990.

Hodges, Graham Russell. *Slavery and Freedom in the Rural North: African Americans in Monmouth County, New Jersey, 1665–1865*. Madison, Wisc.: Madison House Pubs., 1997.

Hoganson, Kristin. "Garrisonian Abolitionists and the Rhetoric of Gender." *American Quarterly* 45 (December 1993): 558–95.

Holland, Rupert Sargent, ed. *Letters and Diary of Laura M. Towne Written from the Sea Islands of South Carolina, 1862–1884*. New York: Negro Universities Press, 1969.

Horton, James Oliver. *Free People of Color: Inside the African American Community*. Washington, D.C.: Smithsonian Institution Press, 1993.

Horton, Lois. "Community Organization and Social Activism: Black Boston and the Antislavery Movement." *Sociological Inquiry* 55 (Spring 1985): 182–99.

Howard, Victor B. *Conscience and Slavery: The Evangelistic Calvinist Domestic Missions, 1837–1861*. Kent, Ohio: Kent State University Press, 1990.

Howe, Daniel Walker. "The Evangelical Movement and Political Culture in the North during the Second Party System." *Journal of American History* 77 (March 1991): 1216–39.

Howe, Julia Ward. *Reminiscences, 1819–1899*. Boston: Houghton Mifflin Co., c. 1910.

Huston, James L. "The Experiential Basis of the Northern Antislavery Impulse." *Journal of Southern History* 56 (November 1990): 609–40.

Jacobs, Donald M., ed. *Courage and Conscience: Black and White Abolitionists in Boston*. Bloomington: University of Indiana Press, 1993.

Jarvis, Edward. *Traditions and Reminiscences of Concord, Massachusetts, 1779–1878*. Amherst: University of Massachusetts Press, 1993.

Jeffrey, Julie Roy, *Converting the West: A Biography of Narcissa Whitman*. Norman: University of Oklahoma Press, 1991.

Jentz, John B. "The Anti-Slavery Constituency in Jacksonian New York City." *Civil War History* 27 (June 1981): 101–22.

Johnson, Reinhard O. "The Liberty Party in Maine, 1840–1848: The Politics of Antislavery Reform." *Maine Historical Society Quarterly* 19 (Winter 1980): 135–76.

—. "The Liberty Party in Massachusetts, 1840–1848: Antislavery Third Party Politics in the Bay State." *Civil War History* 28 (September 1982): 237–65.

—. "The Liberty Party in New Hampshire, 1840–1848: Antislavery Politics in the Granite State." *New Hampshire Historical Quarterly* 33 (Summer 1978): 123–65.

Joseph, Paul. "Direct and Indirect Effects of the Movement against the Vietnam War." In *The Vietnam War: Vietnamese and American Perspectives*, edited by Jayne S. Werner and Lun Doan Huynh, 165–84. New York: M. E. Sharpe, 1993.

Karcher, Carolyn L. *The First Woman in the Republic: A Cultural Biography of Lydia Maria Child*. Durham: Duke University Press, 1994.

—. "Rape, Murder and Revenge in 'Slavery's Pleasant Homes': Lydia Maria Child's Antislavery Fiction and the Limits of Genre." *Women's Studies International Forum* 9, no. 4 (1986): 323–32.

Kasson, John. *Rudeness and Civility: Manners in Nineteenth-Century Urban America*. New York: Hill & Wang, 1990.

Keller, Patricia J. "Methodology and Meaning: Strategies for Quilt Study." *The Quilt Journal* 2, no. 1 (1993): 1–4.

Keller, Ralph A. "Methodist Newspapers and the Fugitive Slave Law: A New Perspective for the Slavery Crisis in the North." *Church History* 43 (September 1974): 319–39.

Kelley, Mary, ed. *The Power of Sympathy: The Autobiography and Journal of Catharine Maria Sedgwick*. Boston: Massachusetts Historical Society, 1993.

Knights, Peter R. *Yankee Destinies: The Lives of Ordinary Nineteenth-Century Bostonians*. Chapel Hill: University of North Carolina Press, 1991.

Kraut, Alan M., ed. *Crusaders and Compromisers: Essays on the Relationship of the Antislavery Struggle to the Antebellum Party System*. Westport, Conn.: Greenwood Press, 1993.

Kusmer, Kenneth L., ed. *Antebellum America*. Vol. 2. New York: Garland Press, 1991.

Lacy, Edmund Emmett. "Protestant Newspaper Reaction to the Kansas-Nebraska Bill of 1854." *The Rocky Mountain Social Science Journal* 7 (October 1970): 61–72.

Lapansky, Emma Jones. "Feminists, Freedom, and Community: Charlotte Forten and Women Activists in Nineteenth-Century Philadelphia." *Pennsylvania Magazine of History and Biography* 113 (January 1989): 3–20.

—. "Friends, Wives, and Strivings: Networks and Community Values among Nineteenth-Century Philadelphia Afroamerican Elites." *Pennsylvania Magazine of History and Biography* 108 (January 1984): 3–24.

Lasser, Carol. "Gender, Ideology, and Class in the Early Republic." *Journal of the Early Republic* 10 (Fall 1990): 331–37.

Lasser, Carol, and Marlene Deahl, eds. *Friends and Sisters: Letters Between Lucy Stone and Antoinette Brown Blackwell, 1846–1893*. Urbana: University of Illinois Press, 1987.

Lawson, Ellen MicKenzie, and Marlene D. Merrill. *The Three Sarahs: Documents of Antebellum Black College Women*. New York: The Edwin Mellen Press, 1984.

Leonard, Elizabeth D. *Yankee Women: Gender Battles in the Civil War*. New York: W. W. Norton & Co., 1994.

Lerner, Gerda. *The Majority Finds Its Past: Placing Women in History*. New York: Oxford University Press, 1979.

Lovell, Malcolm, ed. *Two Quaker Sisters: From the Original Diaries of Elizabeth Buffum Chace and Lucy Buffum Lovell*. New York: Liveright Publishing Co., 1937.

Lutz, Alma. *Crusade for Freedom: Women of the Antislavery Movement*. Boston: Beacon Press, 1968.

Mabee, Carlton. *Black Freedom: The Nonviolent Abolitionists from 1830 through the Civil War*. Toronto: Macmillan Co., 1970.

McCarthy, Kathleen D., ed. *Lady Bountiful Revisited: Women, Philanthropy, and Power*. New Brunswick: Rutgers University Press, 1990.

McCurry, Stephanie. "The Two Faces of Republicanism: Gender and Proslavery Politics in Antebellum South Carolina." *Journal of American History* 78 (March 1992): 1245–64.

McElroy, James. "Social Control and Romantic Reform in Antebellum America: The Case of Rochester, New York." *New York History* 58 (January 1977): 17–46.

McElroy's Philadelphia Directory. Philadelphia: Edward C. and John Biddle, 1859 and 1860.

McFeely, William S. *Frederick Douglass*. New York: W. W. Norton & Co., 1991.

McGerr, Michael. "Political Style and Women's Power, 1830–1930." *Journal of American History* 76 (December 1990): 864–85.

McInerney, Daniel J. *The Fortunate Heirs of Freedom: Abolition and Republican Thought*. Lincoln: University of Nebraska Press, 1994.

McKivigan, John R. *The War against Proslavery Religion: Abolitionism and the Northern Churches, 1830–1865*. Ithaca: Cornell University Press, 1984.

McPherson, James M. *Ordeal by Fire: The Civil War and Reconstruction*. 2nd ed. New York: McGraw Hill, 1992.

———. *The Struggle for Equality: Abolitionists and the Negro in the Civil War and Reconstruction*. Princeton: Princeton University Press, 1964.

McTighe, Michael J. *A Measure of Success: Protestants and Public Culture in Antebellum Cleveland*. Albany: State University of New York Press, 1994.

Magdol, Edward. *The Antislavery Rank and File: A Social Profile of the Abolitionists' Constituency*. Westport, Conn.: Greenwood Press, 1986.

Mandel, Bernard. *Labor: Free and Slave; Workingmen and the Anti-Slavery Movement in the United States*. New York: Associated Authors, 1955.

May, Samuel J. *A Sermon Preached at Hingham, March 19, 1837; Being the Sunday after the Death of Mrs. Cecilia Brooks*. Hingham, Mass.: J. Farmer, 1837.

———. *Some Recollections of Our Antislavery Conflict*. Miami: Mnemosyne Publishing Company, Inc., 1969.

Meltzer, Milton, and Patricia G. Holland, eds. *Lydia Maria Child: Selected Letters, 1817–1880*. Amherst: University of Massachusetts Press, 1982.

Merrill, Walter M., and Louis Ruchames, eds. *The Letters of William Lloyd Garrison*. 5 vols. Cambridge: Belknapp Press, 1971–79.

Mersh, Lori. " 'The Hand of Refined Taste' in the Frontier Landscape: Caroline Kirkland's *A New Home, Who'll Follow?* and the Feminization of American Consumerism." *American Quarterly* 45 (December 1993): 485–523.

Middleton, Stephen. "The Fugitive Slave Crisis in Cincinnati, 1850–1860: Resistance, Enforcement, and Black Refugees." *Journal of Negro History* 72 (Winter/Spring 1987): 20–32.

Midgley, Clare. *Women against Slavery: The British Campaigns, 1780–1870.* New York: Routledge, 1992.

Mills, Bruce. *Cultural Reformations: Lydia Maria Child and the Literature of Reform.* Athens: University of Georgia Press, 1994.

Mintz, Steven. *Moralists and Modernizers: America's Pre–Civil War Reformers.* Baltimore: Johns Hopkins University Press, 1995.

Moore, John M., ed. *Friends in the Delaware Valley: Philadelphia Yearly Meeting, 1681–1981.* Haverford, Pa.: Friends Historical Association, 1981.

Moynihan, Ruth B. "Coming of Age: Four Centuries of Connecticut Women and Their Choices." *Connecticut Historical Society Bulletin* 53 (Winter/Spring 1988): 5–112.

Muelder, Hermann R. *Fighters for Freedom: The History of Anti-Slavery Activities of Men and Women Associated with Knox College.* New York: Columbia University Press, 1959.

———. "Galesburg: Hot-Bed of Abolitionism." *Illinois State Historical* Society *Journal* 35 (September 1942): 216–35.

Myers, John L. "The Antislavery Agency System in Maine, 1836–1838." *Maine Historical Society Quarterly* 23 (Fall 1983): 57–84.

Nord, David Paul. "Religious Reading and Readers in Antebellum America." *Journal of the Early Republic* 15 (Summer 1995): 241–72.

Norton, Anne. *Alternative Americas: A Reading of Antebellum Political Culture.* Chicago: University of Chicago Press, 1986.

Nuermberger, Ruth Ketring. *The Free Produce Movement: A Quaker Protest against Slavery.* Durham: Duke University Press, 1942.

O'Connor, Lillian. *Pioneer Women Orators: Rhetoric in the Ante-Bellum Reform Movement.* New York: Columbia University Press, 1954.

Old Anti-Slavery Days: Proceedings of the Commemorative Meeting Held by the Danvers Historical Society, April 26, 1893. Danvers, Mass.: Danvers Historical Society, 1893.

Padgett, Chris. "Hearing the Antislavery Rank-and-File: The Wesleyan Methodists Schism of 1843." *Journal of the Early Republic* 12 (Spring 1992): 63–84.

Pease, Jane H., and William H. Pease. *Bound with Them in Chains: A Biographical History of the Antislavery Movement.* Westport, Conn.: Greenwood Press, 1972.

———. "Confrontation and Abolition in the 1850s." *Journal of American History* 58 (March 1972): 923–37.

———. *Ladies, Women, and Wenches: Choice and Constraint in Antebellum Charleston and Boston.* Chapel Hill: University of North Carolina Press, 1990.

Peck, William F. *Semi-Centennial History of the City of Rochester.* Syracuse: D. Mason & Co., Pubs., 1884.

Perrin, William H., ed. *History of Stark County with an Outline Sketch of Ohio.* Chicago: Baskin & Battey, 1881.

Perry, Lewis, and Michael Fellman, eds. *Antislavery Reconsidered: New Perspectives on the Abolitionists.* Baton Rouge: Louisiana State University Press, 1979.

Porter, Dorothy Burnett. "The Remonds of Salem, Massachusetts: A Nineteenth-Century Family Revisited." Part 2. *Proceedings of the American Antiquarian Society* 95 (1985): 259–95.

Porter, Mary H. *Elizabeth Chappell Porter: A Memoir.* Chicago: Flemming H. Revell Co., 1892.

Quarles, Benjamin. *Black Abolitionists.* New York: Oxford University Press, 1969.

———. "Sources of Abolitionist Income." *Mississippi Valley Historical Review* 32 (June 1945): 63–76.

Quist, John W. " 'The Great Majority of Our Subscribers Are Farmers': The Michigan Abolitionist Constituency of the 1840s." *Journal of the Early Republic* 14 (Fall 1994): 325–58.

Richards, Leonard L. *"Gentlemen of Property and Standing": Anti-Abolitionist Mobs in Jacksonian America.* New York: Oxford University Press, 1970.

Richardson, Joe M. *Christian Reconstruction: The American Missionary Association and Southern Blacks, 1861–1890.* Athens: University of Georgia Press, 1986.

Ripley, C. Peter, ed. *The Black Abolitionist Papers.* Vols. 2, 4, 5. Chapel Hill: University of North Carolina Press, 1991.

Rose, Anne C. *Victorian America and the Civil War.* New York: Cambridge University Press, 1992.

Rose, Willie Lee. *Rehearsal for Reconstruction: The Port Royal Experiment.* New York: Oxford University Press, 1964.

Roth, Randolph A. *The Democratic Dilemma: Religion, Reform, and the Social Order in the Connecticut River Valley of Vermont, 1791–1850.* New York: Cambridge University Press, 1987.

Ruchames, Louis. "Race, Marriage and Abolition in Massachusetts." *Journal of Negro History* 40 (July 1955): 250–73.

Ruchkin, Judith Polgar. "The Abolition of 'Colored Schools' in Rochester, New York: 1832–1856." *New York History* 51 (July 1970): 377–91.

Ryan, Mary P. *Women in Public: Between Banners and Ballots, 1825–1880.* Baltimore: Johns Hopkins University Press, 1990.

Sanchez-Eppler, Karen. *Touching Liberty: Abolition, Feminism, and the Politics of the Body.* Berkeley: University of California Press, 1993.

Saum, Lewis. *The Popular Mood of Pre-Civil War America.* Westport, Conn.: Greenwood Press, 1980.

Schmidt, Leigh Eric. *Consumer Rites: The Buying and Selling of American Holidays.* Princeton: Princeton University Press, 1995.

Schriver, Edward O. *Go Free: The Antislavery Impulse in Maine, 1833–1855.* Orono: University of Maine Press, 1971.

Scott, Anne Firor. *Natural Allies: Women's Associations in American History.* Urbana: University of Illinois Press, 1991.

Scott, Donald M. *From Office to Profession: The New England Ministry, 1750-1850.* Philadelphia: University of Pennsylvania Press, 1978.

Seller, Maxine Schwartz. *Women Educators in the United States, 1820-1993.* Westport, Conn.: Greenwood Press, 1994.

Siebert, Wilbur H. *The Underground Railroad from Slavery to Freedom.* New York: Macmillan Co., 1898.

————. "Underground Railroad in Massachusetts." *Proceedings of the American Antiquarian Society* 45 (April 1935): 25-100.

————. *Vermont's Anti-Slavery and the Underground Railroad Record.* Columbus, Ohio: The Spahr and Glenn Co., 1937.

Simmons, Nancy Craig, ed. *The Selected Letters of Mary Moody Emerson.* Athens: University of Georgia Press, 1993.

Sklar, Kathryn Kish. " 'Women Who Speak for an Entire Nation': American and British Women Compared at the World Anti-Slavery Convention, London, 1840." *Pacific Historical Review* 59 (November 1990): 453-99.

Smedley, R. C. *History of the Underground Railroad in Chester and the Neighboring Counties of Pennsylvania.* Lancaster, Pa.: Office of the Journal, 1883.

Southwick, Sarah H. *Reminiscences of Early Anti-Slavery Days.* Cambridge: Riverside Press, 1893.

Sillen, Samuel. *Women against Slavery.* New York: Masses & Mainstream, 1955.

Spacks, Patricia Meyer. *Gossip.* Chicago: University of Chicago Press, 1986.

Stampp, Kenneth M. *America in 1857: A Nation on the Brink.* New York: Oxford University Press, 1990.

Stange, Douglas C. *Patterns of Antislavery among American Unitarians, 1831-1860.* Cranbury, N.J.: Associated University Presses, 1977.

Stanton, Theodore, and Harriot Stanton Blatch, eds. *Elizabeth Cady Stanton as Revealed in Her Letters, Diary, and Reminiscences.* Vol. 2. New York: Harper and Brothers, Pubs., c. 1922.

Sterling, Dorothy. *Ahead of Her Time: Abby Kelley and the Politics of Antislavery.* New York: W. W. Norton & Co., 1991.

————. *We Are Your Sisters: Black Women in the Nineteenth Century.* New York: W. W. Norton & Co., 1984.

Stewart, James Brewer. "The Aims and Impact of Garrisonian Abolitionism, 1840-1860." *Civil War History* 15 (September 1969): 197-209.

————. *Holy Warriors: The Abolitionists and American Slavery.* New York: Hill and Wang, 1976.

————. *Wendell Phillips: Liberty's Hero.* Baton Rouge: Louisiana State University Press, 1986.

————. *William Lloyd Garrison and the Challenge of Emancipation.* Arlington Heights: Harlan Davidson, Inc., 1992.

Still, William. *The Underground Rail Road.* Philadelphia: Porter & Coates, 1872.

Stone, Thomas T. *An Address before the Salem Female Anti-Slavery Society at its Annual Meeting, December 7, 1851.* Salem, Mass.: William Ives and Co., 1852.

Stouffer, Allen P. *The Light of Nature and the Law of God: Antislavery in Ontario, 1833-1877.* Baton Rouge: Louisiana State University Press, 1992.

Strother, Horatio T. *The Underground Railroad in Connecticut*. Middletown: Wesleyan University Press, 1962.

Sumler-Lewis, Janice. "The Forten-Purvis Women of Philadelphia and the American Anti-Slavery Crusade." *Journal of Negro History* 66 (Winter 1981–82): 281–88.

Swint, Henry L., ed. *Dear Ones at Home: Letters from Contraband Camps*. Nashville: Vanderbilt University Press, 1966.

Swisshelm, Jane Grey. *Crusader and Feminist: Letters of Jane Grey Swisshelm, 1858–1865*. St. Paul: Minnesota Historical Society, 1934.

Taylor, Clare. *Women of the Anti-Slavery Movement: The Weston Sisters*. New York: St. Martin's Press, 1995.

Taylor, Henry Louis, Jr., ed. *Race and the City: Work, Community, and Protest in Cincinnati, 1820–1970*. Urbana: University of Illinois Press, 1993.

Thomas, George M. *Revivalism and Cultural Change: Christianity, Nation Building, and the Market in the Nineteenth-Century United States*. Chicago: University of Chicago Press, 1989.

Turley, David. *The Culture of English Antislavery, 1780–1860*. London: Routledge, 1991.

Van Broeckhoven, Deborah Bingham. *Abolitionists Were Female: Rhode Island Women Working against Slavery*. Ithaca: Cornell University Press, forthcoming.

Venet, Wendy Hamand. *Neither Ballots nor Bullets: Women Abolitionists and the Civil War*. Charlottesville: University of Virginia Press, 1991.

Volpe, Vernon L. *Forlorn Hope of Freedom: The Liberty Party in the Old Northwest, 1838–1848*. Kent, Ohio: Kent State University Press, 1990.

Voss-Hubbard, Mark. "The Political Culture of Emancipation: Morality, Politics, and the State in Garrisonian Abolitionism, 1854–1863." *Journal of American Studies* 29 (August 1995): 159–84.

Wahl, Albert J. "The Pennsylvania Yearly Meeting of Progressive Friends." *Pennsylvania History* 25 (April 1958): 122–36.

Walker, Cam. "Corinth: The Story of a Contraband Camp." *Civil War History* 20 (March 1974): 5–22.

Walker, Robert H. *Reform in America: The Continuing Frontier*. Lexington: University Press of Kentucky, 1985.

Walters, Ronald G. *The Antislavery Appeal: American Abolitionism after 1830*. Baltimore: Johns Hopkins University Press, 1976.

Wellman, Judith. "Women and Radical Reform in Antebellum Upstate New York: A Profile of Grassroots Female Abolitionists." In *Studies in the History of American Women*, edited by Mabel E. Deutrich and Virginia C. Purdy. Washington: Howard University Press, 1980.

Wheeler, Leslie, ed. *Loving Warriors: Selected Letters of Lucy Stone and Henry B. Blackwell, 1853–1893*. New York: The Dial Press, 1981.

Willey, Austin. *The History of the Anti-Slavery Cause in State and Nation*. Portland, Maine: Brown, Thurston and Hoyt, Fogg & Donham, 1886.

Williams, Peter W. *Popular Religion in America: Symbolic Change and the Modernization Process in Historical Perspective*. Urbana: University of Illinois Press, 1989.

Winch, Julie. "Philadelphia and the Other Underground Railroad." *Pennsylvania Magazine of History and Biography* iii (January 1987): 3–26.

———. *Philadelphia's Black Elite: Activism, Accommodation, and the Struggle for Autonomy, 1787–1848*. Philadelphia: Temple University Press, 1988.

Wyatt-Brown, Bertram. *Lewis Tappan and the Evangelical War against Slavery*. Cleveland: Case Western Reserve University Press, 1969.

Wyman, Lillie Buffum Chace. *American Chivalry*. Boston: W. B. Clarke Co., 1913.

Yacovone, Donald. *Samuel Joseph May and the Dilemma of the Liberal Persuasion, 1797–1871*. Philadelphia: Temple University Press, 1991.

Yee, Shirley J. *Black Women Abolitionists: A Study in Activism, 1828–1860*. Knoxville: University of Tennessee Press, 1992.

Yellin, Jean Fagan. *Women and Sisters: The Antislavery Feminists in American Culture*. New Haven: Yale University Press, 1989.

Yellin, Jean Fagan, and John C. Van Horne, eds. *The Abolitionist Sisterhood: Women's Political Culture in Antebellum America*. Ithaca: Cornell University Press, 1994.

Young, R. J. *Antebellum Black Activists: Race, Gender, and Self*. New York: Garland Publishing, Inc., 1996.

DISSERTATIONS AND THESES

Attie, Rejean. " 'A Swindling Concern': The United States Sanitary Commission and the Northern Female Public, 1861–1865." Ph.D. diss., Columbia University, 1987.

Augur, Susan B. "To Bring Forth Freedom." Honors paper, Fordham College, 1992.

Bass, Dorothy Courtnay. " 'The Best Hope of the Sexes': The Woman Question in Garrisonian Abolitionism." Ph.D. diss., Brown University, 1980.

Coleman, Willie Mae. "Keeping the Faith and Disturbing the Peace. Black Women: From Anti-Slavery to Women's Suffrage." Ph.D. diss., University of California at Irvine, 1982.

De Azevedo, Celia Maria M. "On Hell and Paradise: Abolitionism in the United States and Brazil, A Comparative Perspective." Ph.D. diss., Columbia University, 1993.

Dillon, Martin. "The Antislavery Movement in Illinois: 1809–1844." Ph.D. diss., University of Michigan, 1951.

Evans, Linda Jeanne. "Abolitionism in the Illinois Churches, 1830–1865." Ph.D. diss., Northwestern University, 1981.

Gray, Joanne. "The Diaries of Caroline Barrett White." M.A. thesis, Clark University, 1990.

Gruner, Mark Randall. "Letters of Blood: Antislavery Fiction and the Problem of Unjust Law." Ph.D. diss., University of California at Los Angeles, 1993.

Hansen, Debra Gold. "Bluestockings and Bluenoses: Gender, Class, and Conflict in the Boston Female Anti-Slavery Society, 1833–1840." Ph.D. diss., University of California at Irvine, 1988.

Herbig, Katherine Lydigsen. "Friends for Freedom: The Lives and Careers of

Sallie Holley and Caroline Putnam." Ph.D. diss., Claremont Graduate School, 1977.

Hochreiter, Robert Stephen. "The *Pennsylvania Freeman*, 1836–1854." Ph.D. diss., Pennsylvania State University, 1980.

Lang, William Louis. "Black Bootstraps: The Abolitionist Educators' Ideology and the Education of the Northern Free Negro, 1828–1860." Ph.D. diss., University of Delaware, 1974.

Myers, John Lytle. "The Agency System of the Anti-Slavery Movement, 1832–1837, and Its Antecedents in Other Benevolent and Reform Societies." Ph.D. diss., University of Michigan, 1961.

Ndukwu, Maurice Dickson. "Antislavery in Michigan: A Study of Its Origin, Development, and Expansion from Territorial Period to 1860." Ph.D. diss., Michigan State University, 1979.

Pierson, Michael Douglas. " 'Free Hearts and Free Homes': Representations of Family in the American Antislavery Movement." Ph.D. diss., State University of New York at Binghamton, 1993.

Stevens, Elizabeth Cooke. " 'From Generation to Generation': The Mother and Daughter Activism of Elizabeth Buffum Chace and Lillie Chace Wyman." Ph.D. diss., Brown University, 1993.

Swerdlow, Amy. "An Examination of the New York City Female Anti-Slavery Societies, 1834–1840: Organization, Leadership, Ideology, and Tactics." M.A. thesis, Sarah Lawrence College, 1974.

Wellman, Judith M. "The Burned-Over District Revisited: Benevolent Reform and Abolitionism in Mexico, Paris, and Ithaca, New York, 1825–1842." Ph.D. diss., University of Virginia, 1974.

Williams, Carolyn Luverne. "Religion, Race, and Gender in Antebellum American Radicalism: The Philadelphia Female Anti-Slavery Society, 1833–1877." Ph.D. diss., University of California at Los Angeles, 1991.

Baptists, 138, 262 (n. 58)

Barrett, Martha, 146, 194

Bartlett, Caroline, 113

Beal, Louisa, 100

Bell, D. W., 60

Bement, Rhoda, 145–46, 149–50

Benevolence, concept of, 273 (n. 8)

Benevolent societies, 25–26, 59

Benson, Helen, 243 (n. 12)

Bentley, Diana, 156–57

Berrien, Sarah, 32

Billings, Experience, 34, 47, 81

Black abolitionists: black women and male, 192 (*see also* Black women); on division in antislavery movement, 98; on free blacks, 4, 36–37, 65; Fugitive Slave Law and, 181; goals of, 45, 191, 234 (n. 11), 240 (n. 78); membership in all-black organization, 241 (n. 91); prejudice and, 241 (n. 90)

Black male military enlistment, 219, 274 (n. 23)

Blackmer, Phebe, 147

Black women: black education and, 129, 226–28; on black male enlistment, 219; contrabands and, 217–18; fairs of, 123–24, 253 (n. 32); formation of antislavery societies by, 35, 41; free produce associations of, 20; fund-raising by (*see* Fund-raising: black women and); identification with slaves, 196; movement against intellectual inferiority stereotyping, 240 (n. 79); occupations of, 270 (n. 62); petition drives of, 88; stereotyping of, 192, 206, 240 (n. 82); two groups of, 267 (n. 27); underground railroad and, 181–83; white women identification with, 39–41, 127. *See also* Cary, Mary Ann Shadd; Watkins Harper, Frances Ellen

Boardinghouses, 267 (n. 35)

Bogue, Horace, 145

Boston Emancipation League, 214

Boston Female Anti-Slavery Society (BFAS), 43–44, 62, 79; on anti-abolitionism violence, 51–52; circulation of *Liberator* and, 83; fund-raising by, 85, 108; petition drives and, 86

Boycotts. *See* Free produce movement

Boyd, Eliza, 100

Boylston Female Anti-Slavery Society, 62

Bradley, Harriet, 156

Bradley, Stephen, 156

British female antislavery groups: antislavery fair goods from, 111, 122–23; as example for American women, 24–25

Brooklyn (Connecticut) Female Anti-Slavery Society: creation of, 49; decline of, 71; education and, 69; "female influence" and, 38; meeting frequency of, 61; minutes of, 77; projects of, 81

Brown, Antoinette, 158, 272 (n. 88)

Brown, John, 174, 190, 209

Buckman, Ann, 59

Buffum, Arnold, 29, 30

Buffum, Elizabeth, 44. *See also* Chace, Elizabeth Buffum

Buffum, Lucy, 44

Burleigh, Charles, 56

Burrage, Mary T., 147

Butchart, Ronald E., 275 (n. 34), 276 (n. 44)

Cadiz (Ohio) Female Anti-Slavery Society, 83

Calvinists, 142

Campbell, Karlyn Kohrs, 271 (n. 81)

Canada: former slaves in, 114, 161, 229

Canton Ladies Anti-Slavery Society, 37, 67

Carwardine, Richard J., 259 (n. 20)

Cary, Mary Ann Shadd, 191–92, 218, 219

"Caste" schools, 204

Cent-a-week societies, 85

Chace, Elizabeth Buffum: abolitionism and family of, 194–95; antislavery society recruitment activities of, 55; association with blacks, 46; Civil War activities of, 215; on clothing for fugitives, 185; on "coming out" of church, 154; on hostility toward abolitionists, 3; on public speaking, 151; reaction to John Brown's death, 209; writings of, 187

Chace, Lillie, 194, 230

Chambers-Schiller, Lee Virginia, 239 (n. 65), 250 (n. 105), 254 (n. 38)

Chandler, Elizabeth: antislavery work of, 21–22, 32, 33; on free produce, 48; Sarah Douglass letter to, 42

Channing, William Ellery, 33

Chapman, Maria, 62, 116, 125, 229, 254 (n. 34)

Chase, Aroline, 95, 100

Chase, Lucy: on lectures, 261 (n. 42); on petition drives, 91; on political involvement, 164; Quakers and, 275 (n. 40); rhyming alphabet and, 258 (n. 95); teaching career of, 224–26; on women's supportive work, 165

Chase, Sarah, 224, 275 (n. 40)

Cheek, Aimee Lee, 274 (n. 23)

Cheek, William, 274 (n. 23)

Cheyney, Martin, 149

Chicago Colored Ladies Freedmen's Aid Society, 218

Child, Lydia Maria, 239 (n. 65); abolitionist argument of, 33–34; on alienation from antislavery organizations, 126; on antislavery societies membership, 66; on blacks, 127; on commitment to abolitionism, 36, 78; on division in antislavery movement, 97; fund-raising and, 85, 117, 219; on involvement with fugitives, 187–88; on ministers, 260 (n. 28); motto use by, 116;

on petition drives, 90; on politics, 137; on possibility of civil war, 177; reaction to John Brown's raid, 190; Republican Party and, 168–69; return to abolitionism, 174, 193; writings of, 130, 187, 214–15

Churches, 134–70; abolitionism and black, 141; antislavery society criticisms of, 102, 138; "coming out" of, 152–58; consequences of "coming out" of, 154; criticism of, 102, 138; effect of abolitionism on, 137–38, 148–49; formation of antislavery, 154–55; interdenominational meetings and, 144; proslavery spirit in, 147, 151–52; as public and private sphere, 234 (n. 18); revivalism in, 137–39, 141; role in abolitionism, 135, 144–45; role in antislavery lectures, 29; segregation in northern, 261 (n. 45); women's confrontations with, 137, 144–46; women's influence on, 141–42, 144, 260 (n. 20). See also Ministers; specific denominations

Civil War: abolitionists' wartime projects during, 214–15, 219, 220; gender and, 232; intolerance for abolitionism and, 211; petition drives during, 215–17; relief work by single women during, 223–25; relief work during, 221–22; unification of abolitionists by, 212–13; violence against abolitionists during, 211–12

Clark, Anna, 92–93

Clark, Mary: on class and abolitionism, 47; on female networks, 60; on petition drives, 86, 89; role in antislavery society, 62, 250 (n. 104); on women and abolitionism, 52; writings of, 133

Clark, Mr., 106

Class formation, 8. See also Middle class

Clergy. See Churches; Ministers

37–38, 56–57, 66, 67–68, 130,
144, 246 (n. 49), 256 (n. 70)

Earle, Eliza, 46
Earle, Elizabeth, 171–72, 173
Education: of blacks by abolitionists,
128–29, 130, 222–28, 275 (nn. 34,
40), 276 (nn. 44, 45); of blacks by
antislavery societies, 84–85, 161;
"caste" schools and, 204; of members by antislavery societies, 69,
76–77, 236–37 (n. 29); politics
and, 166; of women by *Liberator*,
22–24, 33
Efficiency: as motive for joining anti-
slavery societies, 39–40, 68,
273–74 (n. 8)
Elam, Ellen, 158–59
Emancipation. *See* Gradual emancipation; Immediate emancipation
Emancipator, 49
Envoy, 132
Ernst, Andrew, 10
Ernst, Sarah Otis: on abolitionists,
134–35, 159; background of,
10–11; on fairs, 110–11; on religious abolitionists, 139; sewing for
fugitives, 185–86
Estes, Gulielma, 152
Evangelists: abolitionism and, 54,
102, 127, 147–48, 236 (n. 12); Lib-
erty Party and, 259 (n. 3). *See also*
American Missionary Association;
Churches
Evans, Linda Jeanne, 234 (n. 11), 240
(n. 78), 262 (n. 58)
Evans, Ruth, 76

Fairbanks, Mrs., 70
Fairs, antislavery, 108–26; abolitionist
leaders and, 124–25; blacks at,
123; of black women, 123–24, 253
(n. 32); fugitive needs and, 186–87,
188; functions of, 122, 124; goods
sold at, 109, 111, 115, 122–23,
254 (n. 38), 255 (n. 59), 256

(n. 61), 257 (n. 76); large versus
small, 254 (n. 34); market sense
and, 118–20, 121–22; merchant
donations to, 115; obstacles to,
112–14; opposition to, 120–21;
organization of, 110, 115; politics
and, 165; pricing issues in, 118–19,
120; propriety and, 109–10, 118,
121, 256 (n. 67); role of, 5, 85,
104; stress and, 110–11; symbolism
in, 125–26; volunteers and,
112–16
Fairs, sanitary, 212
Fellows, Anna, 161–62
Female Association of Chatham Street
Chapel, 159
Female Literary Association, 41
Feminism: abolitionists and, 26
Finances: of abolitionists. *See* Aboli-
tionists: finances of; Fund-raising
Finney, Charles Grandison, 43,
137–38
*First Annual Report of the Dorchester
Female Anti-Slavery Society*, 76
Fitchburg Female Anti-Slavery Soci-
ety, 60
Ford Douglas, H., 218
Ford Douglas, Sattira, 217–18, 219
Forten, Charlotte: on Antoinette
Brown, 272 (n. 88); on fairs, 124–
25, 195–96; on former slaves, 227,
275 (n. 39); writings of, 226
Fossett, Sarah Walker, 128
Foster, Abby Kelley. *See* Kelley,
Abby
Foster, Daniel, 261 (n. 35)
Foster, N. A., 253 (n. 29)
Fox-Genovese, Elizabeth, 273
(n. 108)
Frederick Douglass's Paper (formerly
North Star), 187, 190, 192, 198
Free blacks: black abolitionists on, 4,
36–37, 65; connection to southern
blacks, 240 (n. 80); numbers in
South, 15; prejudice against (*see*
Prejudice: against free blacks); reac-

Manumission: numbers of free blacks and, 15
March, Alice, 149
Marsh, Sarah, 185
Martineau, Harriet, 196
Mason, Eliza, 66
Mason, Sarah, 190
Massachusetts Anti-Slavery Society, 86, 97
Massachusetts Female Emancipation Society, 162–63
Matthews, Mary, 78
Matthews, Phebe, 128
May, Samuel J., 108, 211; as agent of AAS, 27; on anti-abolitionism violence, 237 (n. 39); finances of, 85, 86; lectures for women only, 29; on Sallie Holley, 204
Methodist Episcopal Church South, 140
Methodists, 138, 139, 140, 144, 155–57
Meyer, Mary, 182
Middle class: impact of abolitionism on, 6–7, 59; reform approaches of, 4; women and impact of, 141
Military enlistment, black male, 219, 274 (n. 23)
Millerite movement, 100
Ministers: changing roles of, 138; reaction to female abolitionists, 149–50; role in abolitionism, 144–46; role in abolition lectures, 29; role in organization of antislavery societies, 31–32; women's lack of confidence in, 144, 145, 146–47, 260 (n. 28). See also Churches
Minot, Harriot, 246 (n. 64)
Mintz, Steven, 234 (n. 10), 235 (n. 4)
Missouri Compromise, 15
Mobilization: of communities, 267 (n. 31)
Montague, Lydia, 226
Montfort, Elizabeth, 108

Moore, Esther, 99, 188
Mott, Abigail, 179
Mott, Lucretia: association with black women, 65; on emancipation, 214; on financing of fugitives versus antislavery goals, 179–80, 188; on freedmen's association, 219; on inactive antislavery society members, 66; as lecturer, 272 (n. 88); on Native Americans, 231; on young leaders of antislavery societies, 173
Mott, Lydia, 179
Mottoes, 116–17, 122
Mrs. Pro-slavery, 56

Names, first: use of, to identify women, 235 (n. 19)
Nantucket Weekly Mirror, 201
National Anti-Slavery Standard, 108, 135
National Convention of Anti-Slavery Women, 98
Native Americans: Mott on, 231
Nell, William, 229
Networking: by antislavery societies. *See* Antislavery societies: networking by
New England Anti-Slavery Society, 35
Newport Young Ladies' Juvenile Anti-Slavery Society, 248 (n. 90)
Newspapers, antislavery: circulation of, 27, 34–35, 81, 83; on ladies and propriety, 42; printing of constitutions by, 30–31, 60; reporting on lectures, 30–31. See also *names of specific newspapers*
Newton, Betsy, 35
Newton, Patsy, 146–47
New York Evangelist, 128
Nile, Elizabeth, 110
North Star, 124
Nursing duties: white women and, 184

Orthodox Friends, 220, 243 (n. 3), 275 (n. 40)
Osgood sisters, 186
Oxford County Anti-Slavery Society, 164

Palmer, Deborah, 111, 116
Parker, Mary S., 43, 64, 162–63
Paul, Susan, 44–45, 46, 85
Pease, William H., 252 (n. 10)
Pen names, 130–31
Pennsylvania Abolition Society, 17
Pennsylvania Freeman, 94, 187
Pennsylvania Yearly Meeting of Progressive Friends, 268 (n. 43)
Perkins, Linda M., 240 (n. 79)
Personal liberty laws, 174. *See also* Fugitive Slave Law; Gag Law (1836)
Petition drives, 86–93, 108; badges of, 216; children and, 250–51 (n. 115); during Civil War, 215–17; effects of, 100; goals of, 250 (n. 112)
Phelps, Amos: as agent of AAS, 27; assistance to women abolitionists, 132; criticism of, 106; lecture format of, 29, 39; violent opposition to, 50, 197
Phelps, Charlotte, 43
Philadelphia Female Anti-Slavery Society (PFAS), 20, 60, 180; black members of, 44, 64–65, 217, 252 (n. 18); Civil War petition drives and, 217; education of blacks by, 84–85; fairs of, 193; Hicksite Quakers dominance of, 43; member attrition from, 164–65; Third Annual Report of, 69
Philanthropist, 49, 83
Phillips, Louisa, 27, 33; antislavery activities of, 35, 55; on members of antislavery societies, 47; on petition drives, 91, 92
Phillips, Wendell, 108, 124, 195
Pierson, Michael Douglas, 265 (n. 99)

Pillsbury, E. D., 254 (n. 34)
Plummer, Sarah: on circulation of antislavery newspapers, 35, 81, 83; correspondence of, 239 (n. 62), 244 (n. 27); on impact of domestic duties, 74
Poetry: abolitionism and, 14, 21
Politics, 162–70; abolitionists and, 5, 163–64, 252 (n. 7); education and, 166; fairs and, 165; influence of women in, 167–68, 259–60 (n. 20), 263 (n. 77); marginalization of women in, 259 (n. 5), 265 (n. 99); symbolism in, 165–66; voting and, 263 (n. 78); women and antislavery, 137, 164; women and banners in, 165–66. See also *names of specific political parties*
Pope, Eliza, 74
Portage Female Anti-Slavery Society, 69
Portland Anti-Slavery Association, 37
Portland Anti-Slavery Sewing Society, 3
Portland Female Anti-Slavery Society, 69, 84
Portland Inquirer, 167
Portland (Maine) Anti-Slavery Society, 102, 107–8, 147
Portland Sewing Circle, 248 (n. 90)
Post, Amy, 229, 256 (n. 70)
Prayer concerts, 106
Prejudice: antislavery society annual reports on, 127; against blacks, 64, 126–28, 129, 204, 228, 241 (n. 90), 257 (n. 75); Douglass on, 123; against free blacks, 41, 103–4, 196; against *Liberator*, 34–35
Presbyterians, 138, 140
Prince, Mr., 195
Private sphere: women in, 8, 240 (n. 75)
Propriety, female: abolitionist writings and, 130–33, 237 (n. 35); Anne Weston on, 48–49; antislav-

ery newspapers on, 42; antislavery
society constitutions and, 69;
fairs and, 109–10, 118, 121, 256
(n. 67); Garrison on, 26; lectures
and, 28–29; *Liberator* on, 25;
membership in antislavery societies
and, 57, 60; temperance petitions
and, 160
Protestantism: abolitionism and. *See*
Churches
Providence Female Anti-Slavery
Circle, 232
Providence Press, 215
Provincial Freeman, 191, 218
Public sphere: women in, 7–8, 25,
72–73, 200–201, 234 (nn. 16, 18),
240 (n. 75)
Pugh, Sarah, 120, 230, 272 (n. 88)
Putnam, Caroline, 203–4, 231, 271
(n. 85)
Putnam, Mary, 223

Quakers, 275 (n. 40); abolitionism
and, 140–41, 151; division among,
18; on gradual emancipation
and colonization, 15, 17; moral
assumptions of, 236 (n. 12); opposition to fairs, 120–21; underground railroad and, 182, 183–84,
268 (n. 43); women as lecturers
and, 271 (n. 81). *See also* Hicksite
Quakers; Orthodox Friends
Quilts: abolitionist designs in, 117

Racial equality: abolitionists on,
4, 64–65. *See also* Interracial
cooperation
Racism: of abolitionists, 45, 65, 189.
See also Prejudice
Radicalism, abolitionism as, 6–7,
25–26
Rakeshaw, Amy, 37–38
Reading (Massachusetts) Female Anti-
Slavery Society, 60
Reid, Jared, 46
Reid, Sarah, 46

Remond, Charles, 108, 248–49 (n. 90)
Remond family, 126, 195
Republican Party, 163–64, 168–69,
212
Reynolds, Betsy, 67
Rhoads, Sarah, 113
Rice, Maria, 107, 146
Robbins, L. M., 150
Robie, Hannah, 48, 177
Robinson, Marius, 51, 83
Rochester Female Anti-Slavery Soci-
ety, 3, 43
Rochester Ladies' Anti-Slavery Soci-
ety, 166–67, 212
Rogers, Mary P., 59, 110
Roote sisters, 33
Rugg, Sarah, 72–73, 77–78, 90, 91,
245 (n. 46)
Russell, Ellen, 118
Ryan, Mary, 7

Salem Female Anti-Slavery Society,
103–5; on American church, 138;
as female-only society, 102, 103;
first, 41–42; fund-raising by, 104;
on leadership, 70–71; meeting noti-
fications of, 73; organization of,
103; record keeping by, 104–5; on
women's role in abolitionism, 3
Sanbourn, Sarah, 263 (n. 77)
Sands, Ellen, 48
Sanford, Mrs., 32, 57–58
Sangerville (Maine) Female Anti-
Slavery Society, 75
Savage, Olivia, 146
Schriver, Edward O., 265 (n. 90)
Second Annual Meeting of the
New England Anti-Slavery Society,
35
Second Anti-Slavery Convention of
American Women, 88
Second Great Awakening, 17, 137,
178
Sewing societies, 72; impact of, 6,
165, 246 (n. 57); records of, 3–4;
underground railroad and, 186

Seymour, Almira, 133
Shaw, Sarah, 130
Signal of Liberty, 164
Single women: in antislavery societies, 43, 46, 47; Civil War relief work by, 223–25
Slave Power, 176–77, 178, 191
Slavery: Constitutional Convention on, 15; debate on end of, 229–30; female influence and opposition to, 38–39; Garrison on, 16–17; as sin, 4, 15–17, 56, 65–66, 234 (n. 11), 240 (n. 78); women's writings on (*see* Abolitionists: writings of female). *See also* Underground railroad
Slaves: religion of, 225, 275 (n. 39)
Slave trade: end of, 15, 174
Sloane, Caroline, 139, 142
Slogans: "immediate emancipation" and, 16
Smith, Ellen, 198
Smith, Evelina, 59, 111, 118, 148–49, 244 (n. 19)
Smith, Hannah, 47
Smith, Mary, 152
Smith, Miss, 91
Smith, R., 264 (n. 88)
Sociability: role in antislavery societies, 79
Society of Colored Ladies of Syracuse, 217
Society of Friends. *See* Quakers
South Reading Female Anti-Slavery Society, 247 (n. 68)
Spencer, Mary, 71
Stanford, Mary, 157
Stanley, Sarah, 226, 227, 228
Stanton, Elizabeth Cady, 216
Star of Emancipation, 125
Stearns, Phoebe, 132
Stearns, Rachel W., 93, 153
Stearns, Sarah, 96, 111
Stereotypes: of blacks, 192, 206, 240 (n. 79), 240 (n. 82)
Stewart, James Brewer, 263 (n. 79)

Stewart, Maria W., 35, 197–98
Still, Mary, 11, 231, 275 (n. 38)
Still, William: on Esther Moore, 188; hiding of fugitives and, 182; as primary underground railroad activist, 181; supplies for fugitives and, 185, 186; on white women in underground railroad, 183–84
Stilson, Ansel, 269 (n. 48)
Stilson, Lucia, 269 (n. 48)
Stone, Lucy, 204, 229, 272 (n. 88)
Storrs, Lucinda, 31
Stove, Thomas, 153
Stowe, Harriet Beecher, 168, 187
Stress: abolitionists and, 11, 75, 83, 89–90, 100, 130, 202–3
Sumner, Charles, 174, 195, 216
Swetland, Sybil, 33, 38
Swett, Elmira, 146, 260 (n. 29)
Symbolism: in antislavery fairs, 125–26; in political party rites, 165–66

Taber, Susan, 32
Tableaux, symbolic political, 165–66
Talbot, Abby, 30, 75
Tappan, Julianna, 89, 90, 116, 187
Tappan, Lewis: annual report of New York antislavery society and, 160; defection from AAS, 106, 220; Julianna Tappan and, 187; support for, 105; Weld's advice to, 53
Tappan, Sarah, 187, 221, 275 (n. 40)
Teachers. *See* Education: of blacks by abolitionists
Tea Meeting, 159
Temperance movement, 55, 56, 231
Third-party propaganda, 7
Thomas, J. W., 96, 115
Thomas, Mary, 187
Thomas, Mrs., 184
Thomas, S. W., 74
Thome, James, 56, 58
Thompson, Charles, 184
Thompson, George: as lecturer, 28,

Women's rights, 164, 230–31
Wood, Harriet, 162
Woodward, Mrs., 113
Wright, Elizabeth, 47, 75
Wright, Elizur, 26

Wright, Lucy, 56, 61, 68, 69–70
Wright, Paulina, 126, 257 (n. 75)

Young, R. J., 241 (n. 90), 267 (n. 27)
Young Ladies of Maine, 48